DAILY MEDITATIONS.

BY THE

REV. GEORGE BOWEN,

AMERICAN MISSIONARY, BOMBAY, INDIA.

SECOND EDITION, WITH AN INDEX TO THE TEXTS.

"SANCTIFY THEM THROUGH THY TRUTH; THY WORD IS TRUTH."

PHILADELPHIA:

PRESBYTERIAN BOARD OF PUBLICATION,

1334 CHESTNUT STREET.

WESTCOTT & THOMSON,
Stereotypers, Philada.

EDITOR'S PREFACE.

GREATLY though the Church of this day, amid all its activities, lacks deep heart experience of religion, yet there are many who hunger and thirst after righteousness, who desire a fuller work of the Spirit in their souls. Conscious of poverty of soul, they long for manna from heaven. To such, this volume will prove a grateful gift. It is not without good reason added to the number of the books that claim the attention and the time of the Christian. The reader will here find deep, precious and suggestive thoughts made vivid by a glowing imagination and striking inferences. If desiring a higher Christian life, and willing to meditate and pray, he will be edified by the fruits of a profound ly of God's word and of a rich experience of the kings of the Spirit. His faith will be strengthened contact with the Author's faith, and his zeal be kin- l by his passionate jealousy for the glory of God.

Of the work, an eminent New York pastor* says, "It is a book of rare merit, marked by deep piety, insight into the Scriptures, original genius and uncompromising directness. I know of no book of its class equal to it."

The Author, the Rev. George Bowen, formerly of New York, has been for eighteen years a missionary in India. He issued a Volume of Meditations at Bombay, where there is a considerable English community. This volume was brought to the notice of the Committee by the Rev. William Wallace Atterbury, and by him, at the request of the Committee, revised, new papers by Mr. Bowen being inserted in the place of some that seemed of less merit. The volume has been stereotyped, and is now given to the Christian public. Let the reader, as he reads, pause to meditate, and ask the blessing of the Spirit upon the truth.

J. W. D.

* Rev. William R. Williams, D. D.; and in this judgment the Rev. Thomas H. Skinner, D. D., than whom no one is more competent to judge of a spiritual work, concurs.

Missing Page

Missing
Page

)AILY MEDITATIONS.

JANUARY 1.—"And as thy days, so shall thy strength be.—Deuteronomy xxxiii. 25.

This probably means that time, instead of diminishing the strength and crippling the energies of the people of God, shall be commissioned to convey unto them increase of spiritual strength, and to render them day by day, month by month, year by year, more vigorous and more victorious in the conflict with sin, more energetic in faith, more sublime in patience and fortitude, more meek and lowly of heart, more fervent in admiration of Christ, more self-denying and devoted in his service, more generous, more pitiful, more useful.

In this view they are delightful words to greet us on the threshold of a new year; and we accept them as a sweet and blessed omen. Bring us strength, ye coming days, strength to glorify our Master, to resist evil, to accomplish good, to hasten heavenward; and ye shall be most welcome.

NOTE.—We aim in these remarks rather to indicate the lines of thought, and to make ready the materials of meditation, than to explore the galleries of wealth that underlie our texts. The :eader will, we trust, bear in mind his share of responsibility.

JANUARY 2.—"I am the Lord thy God which teacheth thee to profit."—Isaiah xlviii. 17.

Sometimes the soul gets angry with the instruction and says, "I will not believe that this is from the Lord my God. The Lord my God is one that loveth me and taketh pleasure in granting the desires of my heart. But this providence is rude and withering; my hopes are blasted, my expectations mocked, my trust belied. What could mine enemy do to me, more severe, more crushing, than this that has come upon me? And shall I be told that it is the Lord my God teaching me to profit?"

"Yes, it is the Lord thy God. As many as I love, I rebuke and chasten. Thine enemy would never have done to thee what I am doing. Thine enemy might indeed afflict; but not for thy profit. It might be difficult to distinguish between a wound inflicted by an assassin, and an incision made by a surgeon; but the results would soon show the world-wide difference between the two acts. It was needful that I should bring upon thee the very thing most intensely deprecated by thee. There was no need of sending trials for which thou wert prepared, and which had no power to disguise me from thee at all. Thou wouldest have greeted them laughingly, and said, I know that the Lord my God is coming to me in these. Therefore I have taken a thicker shroud; but still, if thou wilt hearken, the well-known voice will come to thee out of the midst thereof, saying, 'I am the Lord thy God that teacheth thee to profit.'"

"But do I need to be still taught my dependence, my sinfulness, my misery; the sole righteousness of Christ; the sovereignty of God; the vanity of the world? Have I failed to profit by past instructions? Is all my past experience in vain?"

"Not in vain. It is because of the evidence of a good work in thee, that I am led to discipline thee thus and to seek thy perfection. Thy words show that thou hast yet some lessons to learn. Thou art not yet altogether willing that I should be in all things sovereign, and thy will be made everywhere to succumb to mine."

"But, gracious Lord, how can one who has tasted of thy loving-kindness and been enraptured by thy smile, receive without deep anguish of heart the strokes of thy displeasure? Thou hast given me the very sensibility by virtue of which I now suffer. Is it better to be callous? Better to be without expectations, aspirations?"

"The trial of your faith is more precious than of gold that perisheth. Thoughts arise in your mind because the furnace is seven times heated; but will you not consider that I am seven fold more gloriously manifest to you, and eventually by you?"

January 3.—"My strength is made perfect in weakness."—2 Corinthians xii. 9.

The Christian must be weak that he may be strong; weak in the deprivation of those things which the world connects with the idea of strength; deficient in the strength that men seek and extol; emptied of all thoughts of his own independent and personal power; stripped of his own righteousness and wisdom; sensible of the mighty power of the enemy; a mere ruin and a wreck, apart from Christ. Then there is indeed a preparation for strength. A foundation is laid upon which Christ will build. Room is made for the wisdom and power and sufficiency of Christ. The Christian decreases, that he may, in another and blessed sense, increase. He is made perfect in weakness that he may be made perfect in true strength. Look at Peter with his miserable sword in the garden of Gethsemane; look at him again on the day of Pentecost.

JANUARY 4.—"Lord, increase our faith."—Luke xvii. 5.

This was one of the wisest apostolic utterances. The world is unconscious of its unbelief. It thinks that the reason why it has not more faith, is that there is no more evidence given to it. But no accumulation of evidence would remove the difficulty. A change within, a couching of the moral vision; this is that which is necessary.

The Lord answers this prayer, not in general by giving new evidence, but by inclining us to view and appreciate the evidence before our minds. By leading us to weigh his promises in the scales of faith against the proffers of the world. By making us to see that faith is the essential condition of blessedness. By showing us that we get no good by unbelief, but mere confusion and wretchedness:—that faith is the perception of truth, and leads us, not to a castle upon the earth, (which might be burnt up,) not to a castle in the air, (which vanisheth away,) but to a glorious mansion which hath foundations unremovable, battlements insurmountable, amplitude immeasurable, light inextinguishable, glory inconceivable, and happiness inviolable.

JANUARY 5.—"If thou canst believe, all things are possible to him that believeth."—Mark ix. 23.

"If thou canst do any thing," said the man, "have mercy upon us and help us." The question is not, says Christ, *what I can do;* but what *thou* canst *believe.* All things are possible to me; but this will help thee little. Have faith, and then all things will be possible to thee. My power is given to faith; and fills every channel that faith provides.

Christ has all power in heaven and in earth; and he is with his servants, even unto the end of the world: but something beside these facts is necessary that Christ's mighty power may be manifested among men. It is still true that faith determines the exhibitions of his power; he could not do many mighty works in Nazareth because of their unbelief; and it is doubtless because of the Church's unbelief that he doeth so few mighty works in this our day.

Compare the power that accompanied the Christian Church in her first evangelistic steps with what we behold now. See how she clothed herself with thousands in the city of the crucifiers, day by day; how these thousands had all things in common and were filled with love and joy; how a Saul was converted; an Ananias and Sapphira hurled lifeless back from the church they wished to desecrate; how Peter came to Lydda and Saron, and straightway all that dwelt in Lydda and Saron turned to the Lord; how he came to Joppa, and immediately many believed; how Philip went to Samaria and the people with one accord gave heed unto his preaching. Ask the world if it sees any such unequivocal displays of Christ's power in these days; it will reply to you thus:—We see nothing like it; we see that the Church is moving forwards with the general impulse of the age; participating in and profiting by the many facilities of these latter times; the press aids her, but it aids infidelity and everything else. So too with the providential movements of the day; what they do for her they do for her in common with numberless other systems; and she has so far accommodated herself to the spirit of the times we live in, that men can join her communion without sustaining any particular worldly loss or inconvenience. If we may believe what is written, from the days of Abraham to the days of the apostles, divine power was exerted in behalf of the Church in ways that were quite distinctive, and so as to give testimony concerning the people of God apart from other people: and this would seem to be the only kind of testimony available for the object in view.

Well, the Lord's arm is not shortened that it cannot save. He is the same yesterday, to-day, and forever. But our faith is feeble. We cannot suppose that he is any more loth to answer the prayer of faith, any more loth to be revealed in connection with his people than he was in former times. The spirit of Egypt was not drowned in the Red Sea, but appeared afterwards in the camp of the Israelites to the grievous detriment of the chosen people: and the Church is by no means emancipated from the spirit of the dark ages.

JANUARY 6.—"The Lord God is a sun."—Psalm lxxxiv. 11.

The sun is a glorious emblem of God, in his relation to all who know him and trust in him. It seems to exist only to dispense. Its beams know no intermission. They are intercepted but never withheld. We need only that we should be turned towards them, and that there should be no veil before our eyes, no clouds in our atmosphere. They enlighten, they warm, they vivify, they gladden. Their profusion is amazing One hundred millions of square miles of these beams descend each moment on the earth and vanish in the same moment to make way for another similar supply. The sun opens to us the door of the universe, so to speak, and reveals creation. Without it we could neither have the knowledge or the benefit of anything that is.

All this is gloriously suggestive of the God of all grace. Through the Lord Jesus Christ, we are brought into the path of his beams. Our understandings are enlightened, our hearts are warmed, our spirits are gladdened. We begin to get the good of God's creation. We are in 'marvellous light.' And as the natural sun visits all things, yet gives itself wholly to each, makes the whole earth prolific for the benefit of each, the heavens and earth beautiful for the joy of each, so does God grant to each of his children an infinite fulness of love, and gives himself with all his perfections, in wondrous union to each beloved one.

JANUARY 7.—"In all thy ways acknowledge him, and he shall direct thy paths."—Proverbs iii. 6.

Acknowledge him as thy guide, thine only, thy necessary guide. Refuse to stir a step without him, as the blind man that stops the moment he misses his guide. Without him thou art in utter darkness, and thy next step may be into a pit. He has made thee thus dependent. It is not enough that the sun shines for thee, the earth upholds thee, and all God's works wait upon thee; all these finite ministers cannot guarantee thee one safe step. God has ordained it. He created thee to be guided by himself, and unless thou canst call into existence another God like him for thyself, thou hast, without him, no guarantee in any of thy paths. Therefore acknowledge him as thy guide.

In all thy ways. In thy worship. In thy study of his word. In thy intercourse with his people. In thy traffic with the world. In thy business and in thy recreation. At thy meals. In thy correspondence. In thy reading. In thy dress. What! in these petty matters? Yes! in all thy ways. Thinkest thou that God will have no word for thee on such topics? Be undeceived. Thou shalt find a revelation of the will of God for every one of thy paths. There is no need for thee ever to let go his hand. Not a single hair in thy head receives its aliment without him. Why then should a single step be taken without him? Think, and you shall see that the fate of millions may be involved in the least step that you may be called to take.

JANUARY 8.—"I give unto them eternal life."—John x. 28.

Consider *the speaker*, the giver. Who is this shepherd? It is the Lord of Glory. All things were made not only by him, but for him. It is for all to yield the tribute of all they possess to him, and ever to ascribe unto him all glory and honor and wisdom and power. But lo! this Lord of all quits his throne, takes a shepherd's crook, and comes forth with a gift.

Consider then *on whom the gift is bestowed.* As you ascended high to learn the dignity of the giver, so must you descend beyond expression deep to know the unworthiness of the beneficiaries. They are distinguished in creation by this mark, that they resolved, whatever angels in heaven or saints on earth might do, they would yield no tribute to the Lord of Hosts, no, not so much as a shoe latchet, and would arrogate to themselves glory, honor, wisdom and power. Hell yawned for them, exulting. But the injured Prince came nigh to them, veiling his glory that he might not irritate, donning the habiliments of a humble and a friendly shepherd.

Consider *the gift*—eternal life. Not common life. Even common life is better than all material things. But a celestial life. Nay, a divine life. His own life. He breathed into them his own infinite spirit, and immediately they began to walk heavenward, in faith, love, joy, humility, peace, hope, dignity, and unspeakable blessedness. This life permeated all their being, reached their eyes, their lips, their hands, their feet, and made them what the seraphim in heaven are, servants of the most high God. Eternal life! Mighty mountains shall crumble beneath their feet,—they will ascend to higher; earth shall dissolve beneath them,—they will step into the heavens; the heavens shall pass away with a great noise,—they will mount up to the heaven of heavens; the stupendous cycles of the universe will revolve,—they will live on, crowned with garlands of never-fading youth, purity, wisdom, and delight.

JANUARY 9.—"My God shall supply all your need."—Philippians iv. 19.

He knows your need. It seems to you that no one can know it, it is so vast. He knows it better than you do yourself. He does not confound you with others, saying, I know what man needs; but he knows you, *yourself*, and is acquainted with all the necessities of your individual being, as though every thought, every desire, that had ever trembled in your heart had spent itself in his own infinite mind. It has done so! The multitude of your own aspirations are not present to you, are lost to you, but he has caught them all in his own vessel, and will see to it that all are duly fulfilled. He know your need; your bodily and your social need, your intellectual need, your spiritual need. Your need to-day, your need yesterday, and your need to-morrow.

And he knows it that he may supply it. Ask and receive. Your most urgent need he satisfies at once. Your most pressing need is to be free from vain desires, and to know how to prefer the best gifts. He does not make your need less, but he refines it from its grossness, and then he satisfies it.

"*My God*," the God of Paul, will do it. Think how he supplied the need of Paul on earth;—how he has supplied it since in heaven;—how he will ever supply it; and let all unbelief and anxiety vanish from your minds.

JANUARY 10.—"**All that the Father giveth me shall come to me.**"—John vi. 37.

Note—The gift:—the vilest thing in the universe,—a sinner's soul.

The Giver:—God the Father.

To whom given?—to his equal Son.

Why such a gift? First, because all else belonged to Christ. Second, its very vileness afforded the largest scope for divine love to manifest itself. Third, it shall be fashioned into incomparable excellence.

In coming to Christ, there need be no trembling. We are not the principals in the matter. We are but a third party.

The Lord of Hosts is bestowing upon the Prince of Peace a birth-day present. Woe unto us, if we start aside and seek to interfere with that divine bounty. Let Christ have what the Father has selected for him. The Spirit that leads you to Jesus, cries out to Jesus, "the Father gives you this." Then is there joy in heaven.

JANUARY 11.—"In time of trouble, he shall hide me in his pavilion."—Psalm xxvii. 5.

There is a time of trouble. It comes once and again. Murmur not against it. Say not, let mercy appear in the exemption from trouble. Mercy requires that there should be tribulation. There are some gems in your breastplate that only give forth their lustre when trouble comes nigh to you.

Your heart is agitated at its approach. It comes perhaps in such an unexpected guise. It appears so irresistible; you seem so helpless. You have what has long been thought by you a trusty blade, but it is now shivered in your hand. If there be faith as a grain of mustard seed, let it now manifest itself. Your enemies are now ready to swallow you up. You are in the centre of a plain; they are between you and the mountains. Remember God. Make mention of his promise. Behold! a curtain descends from heaven, and becomes around you a royal tent. Instead of danger you have safety; and trouble is succeeded by surpassing peace. You are in the pavilion of God, and your enemies go round and round; they cannot find you; you are hidden. Faith, submission, long-suffering, humility, these gems sparkled in your breastplate; wherefore now peace, triumph, joy and love light up the pavilion for you.

JANUARY 12.—"Wait on the Lord: be of good courage."—Ps. xxvii. 14.

Tell him your story; unfold to him your case; expect deliverance through him alone; be satisfied to receive it as it shall please him to give it and in the time that seems best to him. By prayer and faith on your part and promise on his, there is an alliance signed, sealed, and ratified. Your enemies see you alone, and dream not that the Almighty is your ally, and that they are rushing upon the thick bosses of his shield. See him that is to them invisible, and be of good courage.

Wait on him with an explicit statement.

Wait on him in continuous prayer.

Wait on him in the study of his word.

Wait on him in trust; in penitence; and in obedience.

Wait on him in the society of his people.

And be of good courage. He only has properly anything to do with courage, who waits on the Lord. To be bold without the favor of God, to be brave where we have no warrant for intrepidity, to be fearless where there is nothing but our own prowess, wisdom or luck to aid us, is simply to play the fool. A man must either have Omnipotence with him or against him. What matters it if he is able to cut his way through an army, if he wait not on God? A tile from a roof may crush him. The wrath of God abideth on him. His deeds are done on the border of a precipice which he sees not. His foot shall slide in due time.

JANUARY 13.—**"He that shall endure unto the end, the same shall be saved."—Matthew xxiv. 13.**

These words were evidently intended to produce the impression (1) that there are difficulties in the way of salvation, besides those at the entrance of that way; (2) that these difficulties may be overcome; but only (3) by him who contemplates them, appreciates them, prepares for them, and confronts them. The doctrine of "the perseverance of the saints" teaches that every one who is united to Christ by a living faith, will, by virtue of that faith, endure unto the end—will resist and vanquish the various assaults that shall be made upon him.

When the fierce struggle that sometimes precedes the first act of true faith in Christ is over, and the new disciple rejoices in the discovery of God's wondrous grace, it is difficult for him to apprehend, in its full extent, the necessity of future strife. When, by divine aid, the soul has climbed to some elevated region of which it had never before dreamed, and finds itself amidst flowers and fruits that had no existence in its former world, it rejoices at the translation, and is disposed to look upon that as the place in which to pitch its tabernacle and abide all its days. It is given it there to sojourn for a while; but soon a voice bids it come up higher. It starts to obey the summons; but finds, perhaps, the same formidable enemies that had been encountered below, arrayed to hinder its further ascension. It shrinks and says, There is no need; it is good to be here; God's grace and a true faith brought me hither, and here it is certainly safe to abide. But, presently, the rainbow of peace, joy and hope, the symbol of God's covenant with the soul, lifts itself from that region and removes to the higher and fairer place whither the soul is summoned. The soul of the true believer then rouses itself to battle with its foes, and takes no rest until it finds it in the higher region. This is still more heaven-like; but it is not heaven; and soon it is necessary to ascend to a higher plateau. "I am saved," says the soul, a thousand times; but the voice from heaven says, "*He that endureth to the end* shall be saved."

He that endureth shall be saved; and he that findeth salvation shall endure.

Endurance is salvation; salvation is endurance.

While faith endures, the soul endures.

The end here spoken of is that limit beyond which the enemies of the soul are not allowed to pass. Within that limit they may sometimes hide themselves, but it is only that they may surprise the more by their next assault. Even though we should see the prince of those enemies buried and sealed in the bottomless pit for a thousand years, it is not good to break up our camp. Blessed are you when you hear a voice saying unto you, "It is finished; come to the marriage supper of the Lamb."

JANUARY 14.—"**Whatsoever ye shall ask in my name, that will I do.**"—John xiv. 13.

This promise is introduced by a declaration that there is nothing but the want of faith to hinder Christ's disciples from doing works as great as those that Christ himself performed when on the earth; greater works even.

"Whatsoever ye shall ask in my name, that will I do. Ye shall do those works nominally, but I really. Understand that I do not deprive the earth of any of my power by my departure. I go to sit upon my Father's throne, that I may do greater works on earth than I have done. The leper that did not find me, when I was on the earth, need not despond; the blind and the lame that are just beginning to hear of me, need not despair, when they hear of my crucifixion; the unclean spirits have no occasion to rejoice, nor the god of this world to exult. The vine is present where its branches are present. I formerly stretched out one hand and blessed one locality, one company; but henceforth, on my Father's throne seated, I will hear the prayer of faith ascending from a thousand places, and by the hands of my disciples in all those places, I will do mighty works. They ask and I do. The mightiest religions that the world has ever seen, shall thus be overthrown. Pilate, the petty servant of the Emperor of Rome, may give me to an ignominious death; but my pierced hand shall only be clothed with the greater might, and shall bring the Pagan Emperor himself from his throne to my feet. My servants will ask it and I will do it."

JANUARY 15.—"There is, therefore, now no condemnation to them which are in Christ Jesus."—Romans viii. 1.

To them which are in Christ Jesus. Think it not a strange expression. It is well chosen. Faith in Christ, union to Christ, and similar expressions, mean much more than can easily be comprehended. The expression "them which are in Christ" is added, that we may not too soon think we understand the others. In Christ, as Noah was in the ark. Without, the besom of condemnation swept the universal face of things; but there was no condemnation to him who had fled for refuge to that sanctuary. In the ark with Noah was all that had life, and all that could nourish life. Abundance of blessing within, desolation without. How terrible a venture would it have been to go forth of that ark. There is now no deluge to them that are in the ark; no condemnation to them that are in Christ Jesus.

Estimate then these words:—*Condemnation.—In Christ.—No condemnation.*

Think not that "no condemnation" is a merely negative thing. The revoking of a sentence of condemnation, even in the case of an earthly prisoner, gives him to enjoy the blessings that descend in such profusion in the beams of the sun, spring up in the abundant crops and the manifold fruits, blow in the breeze, and murmur in the stream; restores him to the society of many loved ones, and affords him the opportunity of rising to wealth and distinction. And the words "no condemnation," in the case of the spiritual captive, removes the veil that hindered him from meeting the reconciled face of Him whose name is Love. The words not only liberate him, but liberate ten thousand ministers of God, celestial and terrestrial, who spring forth to wait upon him, and will never leave him till they have brought him, victorious, radiant, pure and blessed, to the company of Gabriel, and of Michael, and of all the saints in light.

JANUARY 16.—"There remaineth, therefore, a rest to the people of God."—Hebrews iv. 9.

This portion of Scripture is an exposition of the ninety-fifth Psalm. The word rendered "rest" in this verse, is different from the word so rendered in many other verses of the context. It does not, however, signify anything different: it is intended to elucidate. There is in it a reference to the Sabbath, and it indicates a Sabbatic rest—a great and glorious rest of which the Sabbath is an emblem. And Paul exhorts the Hebrew Christians to labor to enter into that rest. To labor now, that they may rest hereafter.

The following are elements in that future rest:—Deliverance from our own vain, unhallowed imaginations; from self-confidence and the spirit of self-aggrandizement; from unworthy conceptions of God; from the vacillations of our love to Christ; from worldly desires; from liability to fall; from misunderstandings with our brethren; in a word, from all the remnants of a carnal mind:—deliverance from indisposition to the service of God, and incompetency for the same; from the assaults of Satan; from the companionship of sinners; from a sin-injured body.

Take not your rest too soon, else you will never enter into your real rest. It is not here, on this plank, amid the billows; but yonder on that shore.

JANUARY 17.—"We have not a high-priest which cannot be touched with the feeling of our infirmities."—Hebrews iv. 15.

"We have not a high-priest incapable of sympathizing with our weaknesses," would be more literal, but would not be more beautiful. The statement is in the negative, and seems to summon us for a moment to consider what our condition would be, if we had a high-priest incapable of sympathizing with us. We may also view it as conveying a reproach to those who act towards Christ as though he were such a high-priest. They do so when the keen sense of their infirmities hinders their confidence in him, and their joy in his promises.

God hath suffered you to discover your weakness for the very reason that you might be drawn to Christ, the source of strength; and to discover your own unloveliness, that you might know the loveliness of Christ. God is teaching you your need of sympathy and aid; and yet in that very hour you hide yourself from the fountain-head of sympathy and succor. Is it not enough that you should lose the notion of your own goodness,—but must you strip Christ of his goodness and glory? For what would Christ be without sympathy, without compassion for the erring? If he were what you would make him out to be, would the ten thousand times ten thousand say with a loud voice, "Worthy is the Lamb that was slain to receive power, and riches, and wisdom, and strength, and honor, and glory, and blessing?" Do you wish to extinguish this chorus?

January 18.—" They that know thy name will put their trust in thee." —Psalm ix. 10.

Christ, in the prayer recorded in the seventeenth chapter of John, says: "I have manifested thy name unto the men that thou gavest me." And again: "I have declared unto them thy name, and will declare it." The manifestation of God's name is the manifestation of God. They that know his name know him, and they put their trust in him. Knowledge and faith are in inseparable alliance. Unbelief and ignorance go together.

Do you grieve over your want of faith? Grieve over your want of knowledge. Look unto Emmanuel, God manifest in the flesh. Remember his kindness towards the sons of men, his sacrifices of glory, felicity, power, rest, reputation, liberty, health and life; remember what he has been to you individually; look at him through his promises, invitation and predictions, and *trust in him.*

When any one withholds his confidence from you, you say, "He does not know me." The implication of the text is, that there is everything attractive about the character of God. It is impossible to know him without being drawn to repose all confidence in him, and to commit all our interests to him. To know him is to know in him one who is willing to employ infinite wisdom, knowledge, power, and wealth in the utmost possible promotion of our interests. To know him is to know that without him we are nothing—as dead men in respect to all true excellence.

JANUARY 19.—"If any man sin, we have an advocate with the Father, Jesus Christ, the righteous."—1 John ii. 1.

"I write unto you," says John, "that ye sin not." Such was his aim in writing this epistle, and such was his aim in writing the words of our text. The statement that we have an advocate with the Father, is intended to keep us from sinning. Any man that uses it merely as an opiate to his conscience, and to procure him peace in sinning, diverts it from its legitimate use.

But when a Christian has been overtaken in a fault, what shall he do? Let him remember that for him, the unrighteous one, there is an advocate, Jesus Christ the righteous. Fear not the javelin of divine wrath. It must come through Christ before it can reach you. Nay, it has already reached him. The marks of the wounds appear in his glorified body. Your sin, mounting up to the throne of God, does not get there before Christ, your advocate. It is a great thing when an advocate can get up in court and say, The trespass of my client has been already atoned for; the full penalty has been inflicted; and nothing now can be imputed to him. Christ's advocacy not only obtains for us justification, but also the

Spirit of God, who, with the blood of Christ, cleanseth us from all sin.

We are richer in heaven than we are on earth. We have Christ the righteous, our advocate,—mine,—yours,—in heaven; on the earth we have nothing that we can justly call our own. We are here in a wayfaring place; what we see is but the furniture of an inn; it does not belong to us, save for a momentary use. But we have unsearchable riches in the country to which we go. When any one says, "What have you?" May you be able to answer, "I have an advocate with the Father—the richest of friends in the most important of all places."

JANUARY 20.—"Ask, and it shall be given you."—Luke xi. 9.

This is a very defective world. Every body says so. We have here only the rudiments of things. There is beauty and there is blessing; but only in fragments. A great deal has been done to make man's condition agreeable; and a great deal left undone. There is health; but it does not endure. Strength; but it is evanescent. Rain in its season; but not invariable. Fruits; but they sometimes fail. Friends; but they are called away. Comforts; but we are liable to lose them. Wealth; but it takes wings. Objects of interest; but they lose their novelty. *Incompleteness* is the great characteristic of this world. There is no hope without disappointments; no acquisition without loss; no joy without interruption; no day without night. The consequence is, that we hear endless murmuring and complaining; much of it referring to God, who has given such scintillations of his goodness, only to make the general darkness more oppressive; such specimens of his power to bless, while he has left the world in such an unfinished condition, left such large unblest gaps in life.

"Ask, and it shall be given you," is the reply of God. "I have given you half; the other half is in my hand. You build a house, and one stone is wanting to complete it; you search everywhere, and are angry because you find it not. It is with me; I have kept it purposely, that your house may not be built without me. You build a ship; but the rudder is not forthcoming. I have kept it, that you may ask and receive, and discover that the whole is my gift. You find a book, but there is a chapter wanting, without which all is unintelligible. One blessing I have kept back, that you might know who gave the rest, and seek him." But man prefers to blame God for the privation, rather than to seek God for its removal. Let man know, then, that he is responsible for what is defective in his condition.

Ask in the right quarter, and it shall be given you. There is much asking. Men will ask of those, even, whom they despise. They spend their lives in asking; even the proudest, even an emperor, does so. But they are intensely loth to ask of God.

Ask in the right way. If you were asking a man to give you a cup of water, you would ask in the way that would please him. Let God prescribe how we shall ask him.

Ask for the most essential gifts first. Men on a wreck should ask for a sail, not for an embroidered garment.

Ask for regulated tastes and desires. This one gift will cut off at once a thousand occasions of murmuring.

Ask with importunity. Ask in faith.

JANUARY 21.—"Grieve not the Holy Spirit of God."—Eph. iv. 30.

I will suppose that you have travelled in a strange country with a congenial companion. You were careful to do and say nothing that would mar the pleasure of your intercourse. There were many pleasant objects to look at, but your experience taught you that any unpleasantness between your companion and yourself would quite do away with the attractions of the things around you. So you were careful not to grieve him.

The Spirit of God is your companion. Most exalted of all beings, he abides with you on the footing of a friend, to teach, persuade, purify, and bless. He is particular indeed; but it is for your good. He interferes with you at times;—not to make a display of his authority, but for your preservation. He restrains you at the entrance of some dark pit; it is because a wolf has made its lair there. He stops you as you are stepping into a boat; it is because a whirlwind is rushing to meet it. He hurries you away from some elevated spot; it is because the mountain is heaving, and a volcano is about to burst forth. Dispute not with him; grieve him not. He does nothing to grieve you.

Grieve him not by forgetting his presence; by forgetting the sufferings of Christ; by neglecting prayer; by slighting the word; by going into temptation; by reading irreligious or idle books; by waste of time; by disregarding the miseries of your fellow-men; by apologies for sin; by leaning to your own understanding.

You know how difficult it is to put things exactly on their former basis, when you have had some misunderstanding with your friend. If you have insulted him, and he has forgiven you, it is not easy to look him in the face just as you formerly did. It is sad to have brought to light the possibility of a falling out. If the thing has occurred repeatedly, the memory of it will sadden and straiten your intercourse. Then grieve not the Spirit of God. Sooner let the sick passenger insult the generous oarsman who is struggling to save him from the breakers. Sooner let the captive quarrel with the benevolent stranger who is laying down a fortune for his ransom. Sooner let Hagar revile the angel who points her to a fountain where she and her son may drink and live. Oh, grieve not the Holy Spirit of God!

JANUARY 22.—"Thou wilt keep him in perfect peace, whose mind is stayed on thee."—Isaiah xxvi. 3.

Bring your mind to God; bring it to him daily and hourly, and daily and hourly he will fill it with its true treasure.

All nature exists in vain where there is no peace in the mind. Wherefore are the skies blue, and the earth green, and the mountains sublime, and the rivers joyful, if there be not peace at heart? The flowers have no perfume, the birds no song, the voice of man no charm, where the mind which they were created to please is without susceptibility to their benefits. Bring me not the fruits of the earth, nor precious stones, nor thousands of gold and silver, nor the votive offerings of a nation. Bring me peace, restore my disorganized mind. Till then, I have ears, but they hear no music; eyes, but they see no beauty; an understanding, but it grasps not truth; feet, but they move with no alacrity.

Ah! it is only he that made your mind, that can restore it. He has the only bow that can draw music from this violin. He has made the mind for peace; and he has made peace for the mind, *perfect peace.* Perfect, as contrasted with any peace that the world can give. Perfect, because it is a holy peace; sin has nothing to do with it. Perfect, because enduring. Perfect, as being Christ's own peace. "My peace I give unto you,"—*the peace of God.*

The mind of man must be stayed on something greater than itself. It must be stayed upon the great mind of God. A house can better do without a foundation; a monument without a pedestal; an infant without the parents' arm.

"Thou wilt keep him." These words express the covenant of God; and faith in that covenant.

JANUARY 23.—"I will heal their backsliding."—Hosea xiv. 4.

God does this (1) by letting them taste some of the bitter

fruits of their backsliding. Dreadful shadows gather round their path. Anguish invades their souls. They discover the frightful desolation of a path where God is not. (2) He brings to their recollection the happy state from whence they fell; the blessedness of having the Good Shepherd to lead them, and to keep them. (3) He directs them to the promises, and so to the open arms of Christ. (4) He fills them with an intense abhorrence of their backsliding, by the cross of Christ. (5) He puts it into their heart to cleave unto him; to be wary and watchful; to renounce all self-dependance, and evermore to press forward in the divine life, hungering and thirsting.

To express it briefly, he heals them now as he healed them first, by the cross of Christ, by the unspeakable love of the crucified One. Mere conviction does not heal. Mere attention to religion does not. Mere promises of amendment do not. Neither does forgetfulness of declension. No palliatives are of avail here.

JANUARY 24.—"Sin shall not have dominion over you."—Rom. vi. 14.

A most important declaration to him who has fled over the borders, and taken refuge in the kingdom of God. For sin is now hateful to him, and the idea of being made again to bow under its sceptre, intolerable. He is now in a novel region. Before, even all his days, sin had dominion over him, an undivided sway. He found out the cruelty of that dominion, and, trusting in a divine promise, dared to flee. He is now made aware that all the powers of darkness are irritated greatly, and are fierce in pursuit. They cry in his ear, that his flight has been in vain, and that he will soon be brought again under the dominion of sin And at times also, it seems as though he were being dragged again to the dread dark region; that he will not be able to continue in God's marvellous light. Then he hears the delightful declaration that sin shall not have dominion over him; an assurance that gives him amazing strength, and enables him to slay more enemies than Samson did. Made partaker of the divine nature by this exceeding great and precious promise, he bids his foes observe that he is no longer the weak and helpless captive whom they once knew. They are amazed to see how their once-deadly darts are now turned aside by his shield; how their weapons are shivered against his breast-plate; and how the sword in his hand compels them to flee. "What! this slave a warrior? this captive a free man? this creature of our will, a defier of our sovereignty?—a scorner of us and our millions?" Even so. The prince of this world is cast out from a region where Christ and the followers of Christ have found a footing; a region whose limits must expand, till the god of this world has fought his last battle and sunk to his appropriate locality.

JANUARY 25.—"And he that overcometh and keepeth my works unto the end, to him will I give power over the nations."—Revelation ii. 26.

One of the resolutions made by that eminently devoted and successful combatant for Christ, President Edwards, was to the following effect: "Resolved, so to live and strive as I would do if I knew that only one man of this generation were to be saved, and I were fully determined to be that man."

This seems to be much the same spirit that breathed in the words of Paul: "Know ye not that they which run in a race run all, but one receiveth the prize? So RUN, that ye may obtain. I therefore so run; so fight I." The principle of emulation is abundantly appealed to in the Bible; but there is no selfishness in the emulation that is evoked by its magnificent promises. The Christian is assured that his gain, so far from being the loss of others, will be their gain also; and the greater his gain, the more will his path be strown with blessings for others. What he is called to overcome is self; he is to wage war with this hydra-headed monster, this protean enemy who is no sooner defeated under one form than he appears under another; and the promises of God are all that they need to be in order that the soldier of Christ may have the utmost possible incitements and encouragements in the prosecution of this strife.

The prize that animates the conquering Christian to undertake new conquests, is in kind like that which animated our Lord himself, namely, the power to bless a sin-cursed world. The highest attainments to be made by any servant of Christ here below, are to be made under the constraining influence of an intense desire to glorify Christ in the salvation of men. It is as we have this spirit, that we have the spirit of Christ. We are to be stimulated in our hungering and thirsting after righteousness, not only by the weariness of our own unrighteousness, but by the thought of the unrighteousness of others; not only by the desire for peace and joy and conscious purity, but by an ardent and sustained aspiration to do our utmost (Christ's utmost in us) for the recovery of a fallen world.

There are two errors that follow even the few Christians that go furthest in the divine life. One is this:—They are very eager to bring men to Christ, but neglect to obtain for themselves experience of a higher and more thorough work of sanctification. That love of Christ which they know, they abundantly proclaim, and are rewarded in so doing; but there are depths in Christ's love which they are neglecting to explore. In exploring these it would not follow that some of their usefulness would be sacrificed. The contrary would be the result

The second error is that of those who give themselves too exclusively to the cultivation of the interior life. They ardently desire personal holiness. Their soul is a watered garden; and they propose, when all the plants shall be fruitful and beauteous, to open the gates that others may come in and participate in their treasures; but in the meantime they almost forget the world without. They are in danger of falling under the power of an insidious form of spiritual selfishness. In the Lord Jesus, see the most uninterrupted communion with God, and the most unrestrained communion with men. He was holy, harmless, undefiled and separate from sinners, at the same time that he was going about doing good. To be like him, is the highest of all prizes. We seek to be holy as he is holy, that we may be useful as he was.

JANUARY 26.—Being confident of this very thing, that he which hath begun a good work in you, will perform it until the day of Jesus Christ."—Philippians i. 6.

He is not as one who begins to build without having counted the cost. Not as a sculptor who begins to execute a work without having ascertained the impracticable nature of his material. These are the shameful mistakes of men. God is not a workman that will need to be ashamed. He has called together a goodly company of the nobility of heaven to look on, while he brings a holy creature out of your unholy nature. Will he lay down his implements and say, "I miscalculated?"

They that know that a good work has been begun in them, are entitled to entertain an unwavering confidence that it will proceed until the day of Christ, when the believer shall be presented unblemished, spotless, perfect, before the throne. It proceeds until that day. It is not begun, relinquished, begun again, and again relinquished, but is performed until the day of Christ. So you have not to go to the past to know if a good work has been begun; it exists within you now. The work goes on. God is busied with you, and in you, while you live. From your first perception of Christ crucified, to your presentation before the Lord of glory, you are wrought upon by the creative power of God.

JANUARY 27.—"Let him that thinketh he standeth take heed lest he fall."—1 Corinthians x. 12.

By standing is here meant standing in the favor of God. This is the position of the believer. It is right for a man to think that he stands, if there be sufficient reasons for him so to think. It is not in itself a fault to entertain the idea that we stand. We are not told to renounce that opinion. We may entertain it even with the greatest confidence, the most unwavering assurance. The words of the text suppose indeed that the party spoken of does stand; for it is only one that standeth that needs an admonition to beware of falling. He that is down needs fear no fall. He has not recovered from the great lapse; and he need not fear to lose that which he has never gained. The admonition *he* needs is, "to stand." "Awake thou that sleepest, and arise from the dead." There are very many who regard themselves as standing, without any evidence whatever, to authorize this opinion. The words of the apostle do not seem to relate to them. This idea seeems rather to be, "Let him that thinketh he standeth, make manifest that his opinion is well-founded, by taking heed lest he fall." The true believer, one that truly standeth, is one that takes such heed. The mere pretender to faith is one that thinks it quite unnecessary to take heed; for he says, "I stand."

The true believer takes heed, by considering, and ever remembering, the number and strength of the powers that are bent on making him fall. He understands that a hostile force is out against him; and is bringing incredible craft, industry, and might to bear upon one point—his overthrow. He is aware that his enemy can assume all sorts of disguises; and can approach him as a minstrel, playing seraphic airs upon the harp, and singing the Psalms of David. He knows, too, that these foes have the enormous power that resides in invisibility, and can launch their fiery darts at him with hands unseen.

He has not merely learnt this from God's word; but also from experience.

He takes heed, by remembering his own weakness. He knows that the most feeble missile in the world, the most contemptible temptation, can make him totter.

He takes heed, by availing himself of the strength of God in Christ Jesus. Daily and hourly he seeks wisdom, strength, and holiness from the Captain of his salvation. He takes heed, by following this Captain, whithersoever he leads, even though it were into the most dangerous-looking places, for the path traced by his Leader and Commander is the only path of salvation.

JANUARY 28.—"When Christ, who is our life, shall appear, then shall ye also appear with him in glory."—Colossians iii. 4.

"In thy favor is life." When Adam sinned, he lost the favor of God, and thus *he died.* This is the worst of all deaths; for all other deaths are just the expression of God's disfavor. Ask one of the lost in hell when he died, and he will rightly tell you that it was when he lost the divine favor. When a man comes to Christ, he finds what Adam lost and what Adam doubtless regained,—the favor of God, life in the highest sense; for all the other things called life are but the expressions of this favor.

Christ is our life. He has brought us into the region of life, the region of God's everlasting smiles. He has put life within us—namely, the hatred of sin, the love of the Holy One, the knowledge of self. He has given us the Spirit that dwells in himself, and in the angels. He has reconciled us to the will of God. This is the beginning. But in himself exists an infinite remainder yet uncommunicated. He is called our life, not merely because he became to us the source of life, but because we live only by virtue of our union to him. Apart from him we have no existence; we are in the abyss.

We read much of the future manifestation of the Son of God; we also read of the manifestation of the sons of God. Our text declares that these two are identical. His and our manifestation in glory shall be consentaneous. And believers are taught to look forward to both these events or to this two-fold event. This is the special scope of their aspirations. And not of theirs only, but the whole creation groaneth and travaileth, waiting for this, which will be its redemption from the indignities and burden of sin.

JANUARY 29.—"Behold, the eye of the Lord is upon them that fear him, upon them that hope in his mercy."—Psalm xxxiii. 18.

There is a hope that cannot exist without fear, and a fear that should not be dissevered from hope. There is a fear that is obnoxious to perfect love; that is, a fear that has torment in it; it must be cast out, and sent to its own place—the bosom of the evil one. But the fear we speak of, angels would not be without for worlds; and saints cannot be without it. You may call it a loving solicitude to have Christ abiding in the heart by faith; to do our heavenly Father's will, without deviation or diminution. This fear is its own guarantee, that the things feared will not come to pass. Like one that possesses some potent spell by which every conceivable danger may be obviated, he has just so much fear of evil as hinders him from forgetting the spell; while the conscious possession of the spell fills him with joy in the sense of all-sufficient strength, and with a hopeful, confident anticipation of final everlasting victory.

The eye of the Lord is upon such. They hope in his mercy because they are already, and are hourly, the recipients of his mercy. They know that his eye beams with loving-kindness, and it is a foretaste of heaven to know that his eye is upon them. Their works are done for his eye. Their conduct appears strange to men; and men ask, "Who is the spectator for whom these strange actions are performed?" They go boldly forth, lambs among wolves, because the Good Shepherd has his eye upon them. He guides them with his eye. When they discover that they are quitting the path of his approving glance, they hasten back.

They meet the eye of the Lord in prayer, and in praise.

They meet it in the study of his word.

They meet it in the exercise of faith.

They meet it in their labors for the good of men.

They meet it when men frown and rage.

In the calm and in the storm; at noon day and in the dead of night; in sickness and bereavements; in health and deliverances. The eye of the Lord was upon the disciples when they were toiling in rowing; when they were sad, dispirited, bewildered on the lake of Gennesareth. They should have known that it was, but did not discover it till afterwards. Let us beware lest our little faith hinder us from seeing the eye of the Lord, when things seem contrary and wearisome.

JANUARY 30.—"Ye shall be my sons and daughters, saith the Lord Almighty."—2 Corinthians vi. 18.

This is the portion of those that come out from the world and are separated. Adam was called the son of God; for God breathed his own Spirit into him, and created him in his own image. The sons of God shouted for joy at the dawn of mundane things, and most of all, when they saw their new brother, the inhabitant of Eden. In order that we might recover the knowledge of what is meant by the expression, "Son of God," Jesus Christ came into the world. The Father speaking from heaven, bade us look on him and recogn.ze the type of what we were called to be.

The great things in sonship are identity of nature and identity of interests. Along with the identity of nature there is subordination; which is for the purpose of giving scope to the Father's love and capacity to bless. The Father recognizes the interests of the son as his, and looks upon all his property, his treasures of wisdom and knowledge, his resources created and uncreated, with reference to the blessing and glorifying of his sons and daughters. To acknowledge a son is to acknowledge an heir. The Father's house is the house of the son and of the daughter: they may go in without knocking; the mansions are prepared for them.

The world does not know you, sons and daughters of God. That which is born of the flesh is flesh, and the world knows of no other birth than this: but ye are born of God. Unknown and invisible to others, your Father is the Lord of the universe. Daily you ask and receive; you are in constant intercourse with him; you sleep not without his blessing; you act not without his counsel; you suffer not without his consolation.

We know not what we shall be, for we know not yet what Christ is. We know in part. Christ came to teach one half of the lesson; he will come again to teach the other half. We shall see him as he is, and not as he was, when on the earth in a state of humiliation. Then will our exile be ended; the righteous shall shine forth in the kingdom of their Father.

JANUARY 31.—"**Cast thy burden upon the Lord, and he shall sustain thee.**"—Psalm lv. 22.

Who is there that hath not a burden?—who that stands in no need of relief?

The burden of ignorance weighs heavy on one man. He

finds himself so lamentably in the dark with regard to many most important things. The burden of responsibility weighs heavy on another. The burden of some secret frailty, some unconquerable weakness oppresses another. The burden of doubt is crushing to this sin-tormented soul. The burden of mortality, the fear of death, is more than another can bear. The burden of levity and thoughtlessness is heavier to some than is generally supposed. To one and all the command is, "Cast thy burden upon the Lord."

Many go staggering under the burdens of life, cursing God as they stagger along. What do they wish? That God should give Satan authority to remove their burdens? or, make Satan's yoke easy and his burden light? No; God reserves it as his own distinctive privilege to lighten the burdens of mortals. "Come unto me," says Christ, "and ye shall find rest."

How is a man to cast his burden upon the Lord? By faith in the Lord's promise. He must stop groaning, and *believe.* He must go to his task in prayer, expecting that an unseen hand will take hold of the wheel simultaneously with his own, and lift it out of the mire. If he has to speak, he must lay hold of the promise and look for a mouth and wisdom that none shall be able to gainsay or resist. We are not to suppose any burden too small to take to God. If we think it small, and seek no help, it will grow in bulk till we are crushed beneath it.

He will not remove your burden so that you shall have nothing to do, no more need of him; but he will sustain you—he will administer support, so that men shall wonder to see you walking with such alacrity, to hear you singing so blithely with a great burden upon you. Then will you tell them of the sustaining hand.

Cast, then, thy burden on the Lord, and he shall sustain thee.

FEBRUARY 1.—"What time I am afraid, I will trust in thee."—Psalm lvi. 3.

David was not a man unsusceptible of fear; nor was he ashamed to confess that he could fear. Often he makes the confession. In this he was braver than many. But David stood firm, when a thousand brave men would have fled. Few shepherds would have stood by their sheep, on the approach of a bear; fewer, on the approach of a lion; but David, the stripling, did this: he met the bear and conquered it; he fought the lion and destroyed it. Afterward he met him before whom the whole Israelitish army cowered and quailed. There were doubtless in that army the usual proportion of brave and gallant captains, and dauntless soldiers. David was a timid youth, in comparison with them. He had no self-confidence, no contempt of danger. He knew his own weakness. But he had one glorious resource. He had a mighty friend in God, and God was with him; with him when he met the bear and the lion; with him when he met Goliath.

Faith is true courage. It is the courage of discretion; the courage of man rather than that of the beast. Some go to battle like the war-horse, crying, "Aha, aha;" and with no other courage than that of the war-horse. They glory in their shame. Their courage is contempt of God. They disclaim his aid. Their own right arm is their divinity, a divinity that may be brought into dust by a few grains of powder. Thousands of the world's heroes have taken hell by storm; carved their way through mighty obstacles and amid acclamations, to a citadel where they found Satan enthroned, and a passage to the bottomless abyss. Courage, without God, is a defiance of the Omnipotent one, and an invocation of his wrath. Paul, like David, speaks of himself as often in fear and trembling. He discourses largely of his own weakness. But like David he strengthened himself in the strength of God, and came off more than conqueror.

The resolution expressed in the words of the text is equally a resolution to walk in the ways of God's appointment. They that seek forbidden paths will find nothing for their faith to take hold of

---

FEBRUARY 2.—"The Lord's portion is his people, Jacob is the lot of his inheritance."—Deuteronomy xxxii. 9.

Canaan was divided among the ancient people of God. Each tribe had its portion. The question might have been asked, What portion has the Lord reserved for himself? The answer would have been, "The people of God are his portion. They are his peculiar possession in the earth. They are his habitation. Not merely the first fruits, not merely the Sabbaths, not merely the firstling of the flock:—all is his. The people are his; their allegiance, their service belong to him."

So it was then, so it is now. God has never ceased to have a people in the world from the beginning to the present time. They stand in covenant relations to him. In vain will you give him anything else. Flocks, gold, silver, church-edifices—he takes them to the one side, and waits for thee to give *thyself*, thy heart, thine understanding, thy body; this give; this is the only portion he will accept. Give thyself to him, and he will give himself to thee. Give thy heart to him; he will purify it from all its defilements, and abide therein. Give thy understanding, and he will open all its windows and pour the true light of day into all its chambers. Give thy body, and he will make it like unto Christ's glorious body.

Satan is the god of this world. But the Lord has a portion in it. There is the beginning of his kingdom in it. Fear not, little flock! you are given to the Lord; and it is your Father's good pleasure to give you the Kingdom. A few feet of ground have been the beginning of more than one mighty empire.

February 3.—"Be watchful and strengthen the things which remain that are ready to die; for I have not found thy works perfect before God."—Revelation iii. 2.

The church of Sardis, as a whole, might be spoken of as dead. The ordinances of religion were indeed maintained and attended; the word read; prayer offered; the communion partaken. In the estimation of many of the members, the church was anything but dead; but their conception of a living church was different from Christ's; and he pronounced it dead: dead, as a church. Yet was not vital godliness altogether extinct; some believers there were; and their position was one of great responsibility and danger. The standard of practical piety in the mind of each one, is modified by the standard that prevails in the church. It is immensely difficult to hold fast to our conception of the piety that becomes a Christian, when very inferior conceptions are almost universal around us. So, too, when a higher standard than ours is prominently exhibited around us. But let every one that loves the Lord Jesus Christ consider that the failures of others, as well as the graces of others, powerfully urge us to redouble our zeal. If the ship is buffeted by some violent tempest, and many of the hands refuse to exert themselves for the salvation of the vessel, it is only the more incumbent upon the few faithful found to put forth their best energies. If few love the Saviour, there is more need that I should love him to the utmost of my capacity. The Spirit of God would certainly have me draw this argument from the supineness, the unfaithfulness, the worldliness of other Christians. It is bad enough that a dead Christianity should exert its baneful influence upon the world; why should the few earnest Christians allow it to plunder *them* of half of their earnestness? Christ must have his tribute. If others out and out refuse to pay it, or pay it in part only, let me the more zealously pay it in the full measure, pressed down and running over. Upon the countenance of one we love, we trace easily the slightest indication of weakness; and if we love the church which Christ has purchased with his blood, we shall not fail to notice every unfavorable symptom that appears. Without commissioning our thoughts to travel all the way to Sardis, we may enquire how it is with us and with the church to which we belong? Are there any indications of decay? Does the word of God take effect? Does the work of God advance? Are souls quickened? Is there joy in God? Is faith in Christ radiant in the countenances and beautiful in the conduct of our company? Or is there an air of languor, of indifference, of lifelessness visible? Are the prayer-meetings neglected? Sacrifices discontinued? Religious conversation omitted? Excuses welcomed? Burdens deprecated?

FEBRUARY 4.—'He will keep the feet of his saints."—1 Samuel ii. 9.

We have here the perseverance of the saints.

God will keep the foot of those who walk in his paths. They are saints, inasmuch as the Holy Spirit dwelleth in them, as they are born of God, walk by faith, renounce the idea of their natural holiness, and hunger and thirst after righteousness. Their feet he will keep. He will not keep the feet of those who simply seek to be kept from eternal perdition; but of those who wish to be kept from all steps that accord not with the glory of God. He will keep the feet of those who commit all their steps unto his keeping.

He will keep them from frequenting the society of the wicked. From approaching the precipice of temptation. From that prosperity which bringeth a snare. From circumstances that are likely to be adverse to their piety and usefulness. From the burden of care, and from the excessive pressure of responsibility. From erroneous doctrines. From vain speculations From supineness and a blind confidence. From the fear of death. From a serious misinterpretation of his providences.

He will not keep them from trials, privations, bereavements, worldly losses, perplexing combinations, inward conflicts, the tongue of slander and the misjudgment of friends. But he will keep them under these, and bring them off more than conquerors.

He will keep them by the promises. By the commandments. By the example of Christ. By that of other saints, departed or contemporary. By good words, printed or spoken. By the preaching of the gospel. By the Sabbath and by prayer-meetings. By giving them the love of private prayer. By leading them to self-examination.

Sometimes, when a broad sea stretches before them, they are ready to say, "We are safer where we are." But the enemy presses upon them, and they have to go forward. Then a path is opened for them through the depths of the sea, and their feet are kept. Sometimes a mighty ocean expands before them, and beyond that the howling wilderness of an unknown world; behind them fires are kindled; a side path invites them to ease, opulence and honor: but the promise to keep their feet is valid only in that path which crosses the billows of the ocean, and lands them on a savage coast; and they follow it, singing the song of Moses and the Lamb.

FEBRUARY 5.—**"If thou seek him he will be found of thee."—1 Chronicles xxviii. 9.**

Observe, there is an *if* in the case. The prize exhibited is obtainable on a condition. There is a glorious certainty; but it exists only in a particular path.

If *thou* seek him. The words stop with thee. It does not glance by thee to another. The question is not, "What shall this man do?"—"Are there many that be saved?" But, "Wilt *thou* seek him?" Unless thou canst distinctly prove that he has been found of thee, this word will not let thee go. Its errand from heaven is to thee, and it must take back a report from thee.

If thou *seek* him. Not enquire about him, read about him, hear about him, desire him; but seek him. Seek him in his word,—with expectation,—with faith,—with prayer,—with obedience,—with perseverance; in his providences; in his people; in the new operations of your own heart; in the monitions of the Spirit.

If you seek *Him*. The chiefest among ten thousands. The Rose of Sharon and the Lily of the valley. God manifest in the flesh. The fountain of life. Even Him whose commandments you have broken; whose curse you deserve; whom angels adore; who upholdeth all things; who is unsought, a consuming fire; but who is, when sought, a God of love.

He will be found of thee. He will not send his angel to console thee. He will not refer you to some created mediator; nor to his works, his benefits. He, the infinite One, in whom are all conceivable and inconceivable treasures of blessing, he will be found of thee.

He *will be found* of thee. He is willing to be found. If he is not in the fore-ground of your possessions, it is simply that your desire for him may be expressed in search. He will be found, certainly. The thing is beyond all doubt; for you seek him. Let this assurance sustain you under present disappointment and privation.

Of *thee*. Yes, even of thee. Why not? The greatest saints that ever lived were as mean in origin, as poor in resources, as obnoxious to wrath, as plagued with an evil heart, as unbelieving as thou art. All thy opprobrious characteristics do not equipoise this one new and blessed peculiarity that thou seekest him.

FEBRUARY 6.—"*Acquaint now thyself with him, and be at peace.*"—Job xxii. 21.

Scarcely with anything can man be properly said to be acquainted. He is painfully alive to the fact of his limited comprehension of even the least department of the works of God; yet has no trouble at heart on the score of his want of acquaintance with the Lord of the universe. "God, I know," says one; "leave me alone with regard to any account of him. See, I am very busy in the study of these caterpillars; your talk of God hinders me from getting some valuable knowledge." "Why is this Sabbath coming perpetually in," says another, "to hinder me from pursuing my experiments in Natural Philosophy? With God I am acquainted; but I have many discoveries to make in electro-magnetism."

We have here a *positive command.* We think it very kind of some great man, to encourage us to make his acquaintance. The greatest of all beings, the fountain of all excellence, encourages us, commands us even, to become acquainted with him. Shall we go to heaven to become acquainted with him? No, he comes to us. He stands at the door and knocks. He has hidden so much of his glory as would have awed and intimidated us. He has taken the form of a man that this acquaintanceship might be easily effected. He was acquainted with grief, that we might become acquainted with him and with peace. Acquaintance is not perfected in an instant. It may be carried, in some happy hour, to a wonderful extent. But it is essentially a thing of cultivation.

There is a false peace based on misconceptions of God. The beginning of a true acquaintance breaks up this and perhaps fills the soul with terrors. But shrink not; go on; acquaint thyself with him; press into his palace; take no heed of seraphic guards whose swords turn every way; seek the private apartments of the king, and hesitate not to sit down in his banquet-chamber. Converse with thy Maker; confide all things to him; make those guards your own; that palace your house; that majesty your defence; the blessedness of that divine atmosphere your portion; and from the sublime position to which the Prince of peace has brought you, look down with serene compassion on a world where the peace of God has been offered and rejected, daily, for thousands of years; and where strife, torment and confusion must reign till men are willing to acquaint themselves with God.

FEBRUARY 7.—"And round about the throne were four and twenty seats: and upon the seats were four and twenty elders sitting, clothed in white raiment; and they had on their heads crowns of gold."—Revelation iv. 4.

Our translators have shown an unnecessary timidity, in substituting the word "seats" for "thrones." The original is: "And round about the throne, *thrones* twenty and four." "I am glorified in them," said Christ. Their glory does not detract from his glory, any more than his from the Father's; but their glory is his glory. Christ is enthroned over again and crowned over again, in every redeemed one who is brought up out of the horrible pit and miry clay of sin, and advanced to a stupendous height of felicity and glory. "On his head were *many* crowns." How many? As many as there are sinners redeemed through his blood.

Who are these four and twenty presbyters whose thrones compass the throne of God and of the Lamb? They themselves tell us in their new song given in the next chapter: "Thou wast slain and hast redeemed us to God by thy blood, out of every kindred and tongue and people and nation." They represent the entire host of the redeemed as it shall be after the day of full evangelization. The redeemed were to be brought immediately to the throne of God; they were to sit upon the very thrones that constituted a part of God's throne; and further, the representation, while looking forward to the day of complete triumph, is intended to take in all the generations of believers ever living on the earth, and to be good for the days of incompleteness. Twenty-four are selected for the whole, perhaps, because there were twenty-four courses of priests; and under the present dispensation, all believers are priests and kings, (v. 10.) We are risen with Christ. We sit with him in heavenly places. We are come unto the city of the living God. In John's vision we are actually permitted to see ourselves in heaven. Looking at the throne of God and of the Lamb, we find ourselves there; the glory of the place would, it appears, be incomplete, without the redeemed and the glory which Christ has purchased for them. We ourselves become to ourselves objects of faith. Believe in God, believe also in me, said Christ; and we do so; we believe in him unseen, believe in him upon the throne; and we are to believe in ourselves now in heaven with Christ; as we believe in his glory, so we should believe in our own. Satan arrayed before the eyes of our Lord the kingdoms of this world and the glory of them, and said, All these will I give thee. But the Spirit of God gives us a vision of the throne of God, and of thrones prepared for the redeemed in the very midst of the inhabitants of heaven, and says, "All these the Lord giveth thee."

It must be that Christians are marvellously without faith, seeing that the honors and the dignities of this world have so much attraction in their eyes, so much power to sway their movements. What manner of men should we be in all holy conversation and godliness? He that is last of all and servant of all, the same shall be chief in the kingdom of heaven. If we die with him, we shall reign with him. Our life is to be a protest, the strongest we can make it, against that love of the world, that delight in the world's pleasures and treasures and dignities that stand between the souls of men and salvation.

"As thou, Father, art in me and I in thee, that they also may be one in us." The inconceivably intimate union of the believer with God, is set forth in two ways. Christ says, we shall come unto him and make our abode with him; *God dwelleth in us.* The other way is by a representation of God enthroned in heaven, and believers on thrones encompassing that throne. The question is, What is the heaven of your heart? Is self on the central throne, or, is God there?

FEBRUARY 8.—"God resisteth the proud."—1 Pet. v. 5.

Pride is robbery. It is the robbery of that which is most precious and sacred in the universe, namely, the glory of God. To the Maker of the universe belongs all the glory of the universe. Pride takes its stand over against God and defies him. It claims for itself the tribute that belongs to God; and would have all eyes directed to itself, all knees bent before itself. God must resist pride: resist it when angels sin; when men build a tower of Babel; when men say of the voice of Herod, "it is the voice of a God." He must resist it for the sake of truth; for the vindication of himself; for the safety of his Church; for the well-being of the universe; for the satisfaction of angels; for the chastisement of the wicked.

But do you know who are the proud? Do not err. You think of them as a particular class, of whom you occasionally meet one, and who are generally disliked by men. But these are simply those whose pride manifests itself offensively to mankind. Men are all proud, even the universal family of man; and those only are escaping from the stigma who have deeply repented of sin, renounced all confidence in their own goodness, avouched themselves bankrupts in the sight of God and man, received the whole testimony of the Scripture, believed in the Lord Jesus Christ, and through him approached the throne of grace.

God resists the proud, by awakening in their breast a monitor to remind them of their sin, weakness and ignorance; by letting them pursue the course they proudly chose for themselves, and taste the bitter fruits thereof; by the example of Christ's sublime humility; by the unhappiness and morbid sensitiveness that wait on pride; by his providences which leave them shorn of the things they glory in; sometimes even by the insults of men.

You are resisted in your prayers and know not the reason. The difficulty is that there are enormous pits of unworthiness within you, over which pride has cast its mantle. Seek to know these, to hate them, and to have them filled with regenerating grace, and you will no more be thwarted in your prayers.

You are resisted in your attempts to do good, and wonder greatly at this. But you have not a single eye. You are ready to take honor to yourself. Humble yourself and become a simple steward, a conveyancer of God's mercies.

FEBRUARY 9.—"I am the resurrection and the life."—John xi. 25.

The resurrection because the life. He is the life, in that by him our souls live before God, and draw from the everlasting fulness of divine grace, and are changed into the image of our heavenly Father. He is the life that came into the world by one gate, almost at the very moment when death entered it by another. When Adam tasted the forbidden fruit, Death entered in state and enthroned himself in the world, with his royal train of terrors and miseries; but Life also entered in the meek and quiet guise of the word concerning Christ; and has ever found some footing for itself from that time to the present.

Your brother is dead, you say, and buried. "Look upon me," says Christ, "and let your tears be dried; for I am the life. If your brother had life, that life is in me; my life is the pledge of his. Because I live, he shall live also. By faith perceive your brother clothed with the boundless wealth of the life that is in me. The life of your brother can only be reached through me."

"True, dear Lord, thou art the life; and he whom we mourn, as he believed on thee, must be in the realms of life and bask in the smiles of the Blessed. But his body anchored him among us; and we now have him not. All of him that was palpable and visible, all that the sun shone upon and the wind breathed upon, our breathing, speaking, hearing brother, our earthly companion, is a prey to death."

"I am the resurrection as well as the life. I am your companion; it is the privilege of believers to be present with me; your brother shall rise again. The incorruptible body of your Saviour is a pledge of the redemption of the believer's body from corruption. He that believeth on me is baptized unto the redemption of the body as well as of the soul. Faith brings to me a lost and corrupt soul; it brings me also a dead and corrupt body, and receives in exchange an imperishable, glorious body."

All that we have then to do with death, is to march through his dominions after the captain of our salvation, and issue, from the portal beyond, in body, soul, and spirit like him who is at the right hand of the majesty on high.

FEBRUARY 10.—"**Surely I know that it shall be well with them that fear God.**"—Ecclesiastes viii. 12.

Observe here the *character* of those that are spoken of: "they fear God."

Observe their *condition*, present and prospective: "it shall be well with them."

Notice the *certainty* of this: "surely I know."

God is love. This word embraces all his perfections. But let none suppose that he is therefore bound down to a single line of manifestation. Light is one; yet, says the prism, manifold. The sternest acts of Providence unfold, in their own particular way, the love of God. Again, all that God requires of us, is love. But this love will manifest itself diversely, according to the divine perfection contemplated. In view of his holiness, we stand in awe; of his sovereignty, we fear; of his faithfulness, we believe; and in view of his kindness, we rejoice.

It shall be well with them. A quiet, modest word; but full of significance. The fear of God took Abraham to Mount Moriah; but it was well with him there. It was *not* the fear of God that took Lot to Sodom; it went not well with him there. The fear of God took Daniel into the lion's den, and the three Hebrews into the seven-times heated furnace; they feared him who had power to cast both soul and body into hell; and it was well with them. The spirit of glory and of God resteth as a dove, upon them that fear God; invisible to the world; telling of the new Jerusalem that cometh down from God out of heaven! Who shall estimate the measure of this word "well?" Ask Lazarus to tell thee from the bosom of Abraham, what it means;—ask Paul;—ask the primeval angels;—ask God!

I know surely, says the Preacher. There is no item of knowledge based on more absolute certainty than this. If God be God, then whatever else be certain or uncertain, this one thing is imperatively true; it must be well with him that feareth God. This unquestionable axiom laughs all mere philosophy to scorn, and condemns all that disdain the paths of God. Are you willing to bid eternal farewell to this word which shuts up in itself as in a mystic casket all the riches, all the beauty, all the splendor, and all the bliss of God's vast universe? Oh! what a bankrupt is he that lets go this word!

FEBRUARY 11.—"Fruitful in every good work."—Colossians i. 10.

The Almighty Maker of all demands no more of anything he has made than he has made it capable of yielding. Enough when each tree yields its appropriate fruits. The plants of righteousness have pre-eminence above all the trees of the field; for on their boughs, they bear, wonderful to relate, many varieties of fruits. There is one Spirit; but his fruit is love, joy, peace, long-suffering, gentleness, goodness, faith, meekness, temperance. How beautiful when the trees planted in the courts of God, exhibit, each of them, all these varieties of celestial fruits. Does a man say, I am fruitful in *one* good work, I have fulfilled my legitimate function? I reply: You know not your calling, neither the grace of God; you are called to be one of those peculiar trees that are to be transplanted to paradise; be fruitful, therefore, in *every* good work.

Who is he that speaketh against good works? Such an one speaketh against God. Good works are the works that God approves. To disapprove of what God approves, is something that should be left to Satan and his angels. It is impossible to take a step in the path-way of life, but by a good work. A man must do what God would have him do, or he will make very little progress in that path to heaven. The first thing, of course, is to renounce all trust in one's own righteousness, and look to Christ as one's sole wisdom, righteousness, sanctification, and redemption. We are created anew in Christ Jesus unto good works.

Fruitful in every good work. Not but that a man may be specially fitted for a particular service. We are not bidden to fritter away our powers in vain efforts to do a multitude of things. But opportunities of diverse character come to every man. It is of great importance to be on the look out for these. The devotee of gain is wonderfully keen for the recognition of opportunities; and grasps with all his energies at each successive hope that darts across his path. The Christian is a merchant of a peculiar kind; his whole aim is to enrich others. Golden opportunities in his estimation are such as enable him to do good. He cultivates a habit of looking upon every man as one to whom good is to be done. The day is whitest in his calendar in which he has been enabled to communicate most. Let us look around us and see if we cannot be fruitful in some good works that our hands have not yet known. The glory of a tree is to be fruitful.

FEBRUARY 12.—"He that trusteth in his own heart is a fool."—Proverbs xxviii. 26.

Self-confidence, self-reliance, pride of character, sense of power, consciousness of strength, self-possession,—these make a man great in the eyes of the world, and a fool in the sight of God. For strength is in the consciousness of weakness, not in the consciousness of strength. Wisdom is in the consciousness of ignorance; and true confidence is in the utter mistrust of self. Man by himself is a fragment. He is the sport of circumstances,—the foot-ball of time. Yea, though he have imperial power and subdue the world, if his trust be in himself, it is in a reed shaken with the wind. Man is complete only in God, only in Christ. Let the tree laugh at the soil and glory in its bared roots; the folly were not so great as that of him who trusteth in his own heart.

Trust not in your own heart. For he that does so, trusts in the heart of a fool. You have been deceived by it a thousand times. You know it to be incorrigibly given to falsehood. It is in the pay of Satan, and would lure you in a flowery path going to destruction. Self-trust is the abandonment of God. To go forth in the consciousness of your own strength, wisdom, or virtue, is to go forth as Goliath; but what is your stupendous sword, what your brazen armor, in comparison with the stone of the brook in the hand of faith? "You have heard a great deal of faith, and cannot understand it." Know that it is just the opposite of your self-trust. It is the genuine source of strength and victory; you have but the counterfeit.

FEBRUARY 13.—"He shall redeem Israel from all his iniquities."—Psalm cxxx. 8.

So says the Psalmist. A thousand years after, the angel who appeared to Mary takes up the refrain, saying, "He shall save his people from their sins." Peter in due time learns this admirable song, and thus modulates it in the hearing of the Jews:—"Unto you first, God, having raised up his son Jesus, sent him to bless you, in turning away every one of you from his iniquities." Paul suffers not the strain to die, but gives it the following utterance:—"Christ gave himself for us that he might redeem us from all iniquity, and purify unto himself a peculiar people, zealous of good works."

By his death he reconciles the Godhead to us. By his Gospel he reconciles us to God. He redeems us from all iniquities, finally, by his Spirit and sanctifying word. This result is accomplished by inspiring enmity between our souls and our iniquities. We discover these to be so many folds of an anaconda about our soul. We are made to hate them with a perfect hatred,—also to know our own impotence,—then to know our strength in Him,—then to burst these successive chains, and walk emancipated in spirit. In general, we may understand that there is no actual deliverance from any sin, until the odiousness of that sin has been seen. The odiousness of it is often first seen when we come into actual conflict with it; but most seen when we contemplate the opposite perfection in the lovely character of Christ.

FEBRUARY 14.—"If it were not so, I would have told you."—John xiv. 2.

There is something exceedingly gracious and affecting about

this declaration. It is the language of pure friendship and open-hearted confidence. "If things had been darker than they are, if your difficulties greater, if your future less glorious, be sure that I would have told you. Did I ever seek to disguise the difficulties that would throng your path, if you became my followers? Did I speak in a whisper of the cross that you would have to bear? Did I keep you ignorant of an opposing world, oppressive governors, persecuting monarchs? Did I not speak emphatically of scourgings, stonings, imprisonings?"

"Again, did I ever keep back anything from you that was really needful for your encouragement and your guidance? I have told you all things that were calculated to contribute to your fortitude and to your joy. I know well that the idea will creep some time into your mind, (for what idea is so wild that it finds no access to the mind of man, even of the man whom God hath taught,) the idea will present itself to you that the revelation made by me is not all that it should be. Curiosity, for instance, may desire to know very much about the many mansions in my Father's house; but be assured, if that more detailed information had been truly desirable for you, I would have communicated it. Infinite wisdom and infinite love have not only prompted the words that I have given you, but my silence also. I might have expatiated much upon my Father's house of glory; but it would have hindered you from paying due attention to the way that leadeth to that house. Enough for you to know that I am there, with the glory which I had before the world was; that ten thousand times ten thousand sons of God walk there in purity and majesty; and that there are vacancies in their ranks which it is understood that you are to fill. What is of chief exigency is that you should know well the spot on which you are putting down your foot, and be perfectly instructed in the way of righteousness."

Reader, are you satisfied with the revelation that God has

been pleased to give you? Dare not to doubt this word of Christ, that *if it had been best for you he would have told you more.* Shall man hand God a table of contents, and ask the Almighty to make a revelation thereto accordant?

FEBRUARY 15.—"I glory in my infirmities."—2 Corinthians xii. 9.

With gladness and with exultation Paul contemplated the fact that God had made him what he was, a very dependent creature, in himself altogether incomplete, and in unceasing need of the presence and blessing of God.

Imagine a flower able to shine by phosphorescent rays, dim and dying at the best; and saying to the glorious sun in the heavens, "Depart from me, I have no need of thee; trouble not thyself to move through my skies; I am my own sun." What fatuity were this. It is the glory of the flower that it has so magnificent a bridegroom, rising day by day to run his course of love through the skies. Let the flower rejoice and be glad that it has no power of its own over the earth, over the air, over the least of its own internal vessels; and that without the sun it can do nothing. Let it be tenacious unto death of its dependence. And let Paul, enlightened by the Spirit of God, exult in a condition that keeps him in perpetual and heavenly alliance with the King of kings. Let him glory in his poverty that binds him to the treasury of heaven; in his isolation that procures him a legion of angels to camp about him; in his ignorance that demands the teachings of the Omniscient; and in his moral helplessness that requires Christ to abide in his heart by faith

---

FEBRUARY 16.—"Give us help from trouble, for vain is the help of man."—Psalm lx. 11.

There was a poor woman that spent all her living upon physicians. She went everywhere soliciting the help of man, and experimenting upon the capacities of earth. Finally she despaired. The shades of night were gathering around her; she cried unto God, saying, perhaps, "give us help from trouble, for vain is the help of man;" then speedily came the Prince of Life, and the mere sweep of his garment imparted what had been so long and vainly sought from man.

Altogether the bitterest element of trouble is the foolish expectation of man's help, of the world's consolation. Has man then no power to succor his fellow-man? Does the Bible wish to make us misanthropists? Is the voice of human friendship the voice of a syren? And shall we treat with suspicion and contempt the sympathizing ones who hasten to us at the report of our trouble? Not so. If God notices the cup of cold water, it cannot be that we should slight it. Christ would have the sweet odor of the act performed by Mary, in the house of Simon the leper, diffused through all the world. Far be it from us to repel the kindnesses of any.

Yet consider;—Christ was pleased with Mary's tribute; but the sorrows of his soul were not stanched by it. He knew what was in the heart of Judas; he knew what Peter was ready to become; he had troubles that human solaces were vain to remove. When Peter was in prison, there were thousands that loved him and would have made all sacrifices to liberate him; but all they could do was to go to God in his behalf. Where, in all the world, is the man that has not had experience of troubles that the help of man was powerless to remove? No one can remove them effectually and permanently, but that Divine being who bore our sins in his own human body on the tree; no one but he who is able to remove our unbelief, our selfishness, our wrong desires, our inordinate affections.

Lord, give thou us help from trouble, for vain is the help of man.

February 17.—"Thou hast a few names even in Sardis, which have not defiled their garments; and they shall walk with me in white; for they are worthy."—Revelation iii. 4.

"*Even* in Sardis." How full of reproach this little word "even." The wonder was that any good should live in such a sea of iniquity as that. Even in Sardis! It will be well for us to act as though our residence were in Sardis; as though there were the greatest possible danger of our soiling our robes. The robes that are polluted are robes that were given spotless. You cannot pollute that which is intrinsically vile. The garments which so many Sardians had defiled, were such as they had in connection with their Christian profession. When a man receives the truth, and embraces Christ, and identifies himself with the people of God, he is, in the eyes of rejoicing angels above and saints below, clothed with a new nature. His old nature is laid off as a garment; and his faith in Christ is a pledge to us that he will live under the influences of new principles, with new aims, habits, feelings.

"A few that have not defiled their robes." They have been distinguished by great reverence for the Master's words. They have diligently sought to know and do his whole will. They have mistrusted their own hearts. Have rightly estimated the power of the enemy. Have been unceasing in prayer. Have sought diligently to grow in grace. Sometimes, they have forgotten to watch, and have committed some trespass. Then Satan sought to take away their confidence, and rear the image of the sin formidably between them and God. Doubts and fears beset them; they began to question if they ever could be proof against temptation. Their garments were almost defiled. But no, the grace of God came to their rescue. Others were betrayed into wrong-doing, and then were assured by Christian friends that that was not wrong-doing; there was great danger that they would take up this lower view of what Christ demanded; great danger that their robes should be defiled; but the gracious Spirit enabled them to cling to their best convictions, their truer standard, and they were safe. There came once a period of coldness; cares of the world, pursuit of wealth, alliances with irreligious persons; these choked the word; this thing went on too long; their garments threatened to become defiled; but they happily awoke to a sense of their perilous state, and with great earnestness, they turned again to the animating beams of the Sun of Righteousness.

They who thus maintain their garments unspotted from the world, shall walk with Christ in white. Their white garments shall become in whiteness and lustre such as no fuller on earth could produce. They will walk in the very lustre of Christ; his glory shall be upon them; they shall be made like unto him.

"For they are worthy." They have identified themselves with the only true worth, even Christ. So long as we wrap ourselves in our own native worth, though it should be something resplendent in the eyes of all our fellows, we are not worthy to walk with Christ in white. Young and noble aspirant after an admirable and worth-revealing life, know that if your utmost dreams should come true, and earth's most distinguished chaplet of worth should become yours, yet would not that constitute you worthy of companionship with Christ on high Observe, the glorified ones all unite in the song of testimony, "Thou alone art worthy to receive glory, and honor, and power and blessing." They renounce the worth of which they once dreamed, and lose themselves in the contemplation of the infinite and all-absorbing worth of the Redeemer-God. And all his worth becomes theirs. All things become theirs; for his heart is theirs.

FEBRUARY 18.—" Bless the Lord, O my soul."—Psalm ciii. 22.

That is to say, " let thy vocation be that of the seraphim, O my soul, and enter on the life of heaven !"

Why should I praise him ? Can my praise be of any advantage to him ? No ; nor that of all the heavenly hosts. It is infinite condescension in him to hearken unto the praises of his most exalted creatures.

Let me bless the Lord, because no function will be more rich in blessings to my soul than this. The admiring contemplation of his excellence is in reality the appropriation thereof. The heart cannot delight in God, without becoming like God.

Let me do it, because it is the peculiar privilege of man on this earth to bless the Lord. When he would find any to join him in this, he has to ascend the skies.

Let me do it, because the earth is fully furnished with the materials of praise. The sands, the seas, the flowers, the insects; animals, birds, fields, mountains, rivers, trees, clouds, sun, moon, stars,—all wait for me to translate their attributes and distinctions into praise. But, above all, the new creation.

Let me do it, because of him, through him, and to him, are all the things that pertain to my existence, health, comfort, knowledge, dignity, safety, progress, power and usefulness. A thousand of his ministers in earth, sea, and sky, are concerned in the production and preparation of every mouthful that I eat. The breath that I am commanded and enabled to modulate in praise, neither comes nor goes without a most surprising exhibition of the condescension, kindness, wisdom, power, and presence of him whom I am to praise. Is it not dastardly to be receiving benefits, without even mentioning the name, or describing the goodness of the giver ?

Let candidates for heaven bless the Lord. There is no place there for such as have not learned this art.

How shall I praise him ? Not with fine words. No poetic

talent is here necessary. Any language that expresses heartfelt admiration will be accepted.

Praise him so far as you know him; and he will make known to you more of his glory.

FEBRUARY 19.—"Though he slay me, yet will I trust in him."—Job xiii. 15.

If we want a sublime utterance, here is one. Let us give glory to that Blessed Spirit of grace, who thus sometimes teaches the lips of man wondrous things.

Though he slay me,—not simply, though he take away my life. Job would have had no reluctance to part with his life. It would have been an inexpressible relief to him to escape from the load of misery laid upon him. The expression, "Though he slay me," is the strongest possible, and startles us with an exhibition of peculiar horrors. Though God should come against me, and destroy me with marks of signal wrath; though death should visit me as the king of terrors, and though my departure from this world should be in harmony with and as a mighty climax to my present agony; yet will I trust in him. I believe his word, rather than the aspect of his providences. The fire that fell from heaven and destroyed my flocks, is not able to destroy the promise on which I rest. A great wind from the wilderness smote the house where all my loved ones dwelt, and at one swoop removed all in which I delighted on earth; yet the word of God endureth forever. I have a ground of confidence that cannot be shaken by elemental wrath. Though the floods should lift themselves against me, and every billow proclaim that God is my enemy; though streams of liquid fire should advance, declaring that God's ancient love is extinguished; though the earth beneath should shake, and the heaven above be black; though all things should seem commissioned to preach unto me the unquenchable wrath of God; yet will I trust in his unalterable word.

The perfection of faith is to cling to the word of God, when all his works, and all his ways, seem to proclaim the very opposite of that word. Isaac no doubt had confidence in his father; and when he saw him with the knife in his uplifted hand, ready to slay him, still he trusted in him; nor would he have fled to any other earthly refuge. "He that believeth in me, though he were dead, yet shall he live." It was a terrible trial of the faith of Lazarus and his sisters, when they hearkened, hearkened, hearkened for footsteps of Jesus, and after all, those of death came first; but we may hope that the dying one passed away with something like the words of Job upon his lips.

FEBRUARY 20.—"Be patient, therefore, brethren, unto the coming of the Lord."—James v. 7.

Because, first, there is no doubt about that coming. His first coming was the most wonderful, the most staggering to faith. That the Son of God should have been found in fashion as a man, without form or comeliness, with but rare coruscations of his glory, enduring the contradiction of sinners, and dying on the cross; this is a marvel that swallows up all marvels, and frees from all embarrassment the question of his second advent.

Because he will come in glory such as no heart of man ever conceived, shedding an infinite lustre upon the least jot and tittle of his slighted Gospel, and embracing in his own matchless radiance and felicity, those who now accept the legacy of his promises, and walk in the path of his humiliation.

Because we shall be for ever with the Lord. The day of his coronation and of ours is a day on which the sun shall never go down.

Because he cometh; he cometh! The bell of his providence

is sounding ever and anon, telling that another prophecy is fullfilled, another hour of this our day of expectation elapsed, another footfall of his glorious approach accomplished.

Be patient, therefore. Yet think not that by this we are bidden to wait supinely, and with our attention given to other things. But rather as they that watch for the morning, let us hasten unto the day of the Lord.

FEBRUARY 21.—"The Lord is very pitiful."—James v. 11.

Few believe this. Men know what pitifulness is. They know how a very pitiful parent will act towards a suffering child; how he will show himself tenderly solicitous to staunch its wounds and alleviate its sorrows. They do not view God as characterized by this sympathizing tenderness and pitifulness. They regard him as a physician, who, by long familiarity with suffering, is able to look upon it without emotion, and coldly to calculate what remedies are best.

If we choose to see God thus, we shall perhaps find him thus; for according to our faith is he manifested. Nevertheless, he is what the prophets and apostles declare,—very pitiful. There is in him no indifference to human suffering. He does not willingly afflict, nor grieve the children of men; nay, "in all their affliction he was afflicted." The tears shed by Christ are a part of the manifestation of God to man.

Tell me, pray, *who taught the mother her pitifulness?* who introduced that wondrous feeling of kindness into her heart? Who constituted her in so admirable a way, that, though in all other relations she might be selfishness itself, yet in this she is compelled, as by the instinct of her own good, to hang in patience, in pity, and in love, over the cradle of her little one? Who hath made her maternal ear of such sensitiveness, that the faintest cry of her babe shall smite piercingly upon it? Behold her! she is wholly dedicated,—her ear, eye, tongue, her hands, her feet, her body and soul, her wealth, her all,—to a conflict with the sorrow of her infant, to the accomplishment of its utmost welfare. Through this glass, then, gaze upon the perfections of thy God. The pitifulness in the mother's heart bespeaks a greater pitifulness in the heart of him who made her thus. He that made her lips so that gentle and heart-affecting accents might fall from them, is one that knoweth exquisitely how to caress, to solace, and to bless Where however, is the infant whose sorrows are all overtaken by the solicitude of the parent? But the believer has no experience of suffering, great or slight, common or peculiar, for which there is not some special and some gentle word of God, with a medicinal virtue only limited by his want of faith.

FEBRUARY 22.—"The blood of Jesus Christ his Son cleanseth us from all sin."—1 John i. 7.

The sufferings and death of the Lord Jesus Christ, our willing substitute, were such a satisfaction for sin, such a reparation to the law of God, that it has become every way consisten with divine justice, wisdom, and truth, to accord mercy to sinners, and bless them without any other restriction than that which their own unwillingness and unbelief interpose. There is a fountain opened up for sin and for uncleanness; and whosoever will, may take of the water of life freely. "The well is deep, and thou hast nothing to draw with," said the Samaritan woman to Christ. One might be embarrassed at a well or fountain, to know how to avail himself of the waters; but if he saw another draw water and drink, he could profit by his example. On the cross, we see Christ dying, the just for the unjust; and perhaps may wonder how the unjust are to profit thereby. until we see the thief on the cross put out his hand and drink of that fountain, and obtain life for evermore.

Then our difficulty is removed; we see that we have just to believe, and be cleansed from all our iniquities.

We may plead the merits of this blood as an indemnification for all our sins; so that we may ask and receive from the same all-willing hand that blesses the angels. And this blood has not only the power to conciliate God; it has power over hearts. Not only in the way of inspiring us with faith in God's forgiving grace, but also with hatred of the sins that caused the death of Christ. And we never truly receive pardon for sin without receiving power over sin. He that has a true hope in Christ, purifieth himself even as Christ is pure. Faith in him is vital union to him; and as the branch cannot but partake of the qualities of the vine, so we must partake of his qualities, or confess ourselves unbelievers. The increase of faith is the increase of all the fruits of righteousness.

FEBRUARY 23.—"So shall we ever be with the Lord."—1 Thessalonians iv. 17.

One of the last desires to which Christ gave utterance before leaving this world, was expressed in these words: "Father, I will that they whom thou hast given me, be with me where I am." And these words "I am," have a meaning that is very vast, referring perhaps to his place in the affections of the Father, to his moral purity, and specially to the manifestation of his divine glory. "I will come again and receive you unto myself, that where I am, there ye may be also." When Peter saw his Lord transfigured, he wished the blissful hour to endure forever. But the time had not yet come for him to be forever with his glorified Redeemer. It was needful that he himself should fight the good fight of faith, and come off conqueror—be made like unto Christ spiritually, and at last in eternal glory.

"Lo, I am with you always," says Christ, "even to the end

of the world." Till then, he is with us the object of faith; afterwards the blessed object of sight. "Ye believe in God the Father, whom ye see not; believe also in me, spiritually present with you." They that are most affected by the glorious anticipation of perpetual residence with Christ in glory, are most assiduous in the endeavor to discern his presence here, and walk with him on the earth. He has promised to manifest himself to us in this our pilgrimage; and in vain we look for that future beatification with him, if we have not these promised manifestations. To be ever with the Lord, is to be never with our sins, never with the tempter, never with sorrow; ever with love, ever with wisdom, ever with power, ever with glory, and ever with rapture; ever with the Lord; ever with all that love the Lord.

FEBRUARY 24.—"The effectual fervent prayer of a righteous man availeth much."—James v. 16.

We are not to take the word righteous here in an impossible sense. "In many things we offend all," says James; and in the very verse we quote from, he says, "Confess your faults one to another." Otherwise understood, the promise would check prayer, instead of exciting it. The righteous man is the true Christian; one who hungers and thirsts after righteousness, and in whose life appears the fruit of the Spirit. But the expression is doubtless intended to discourage the man who, while he gives himself to prayer, regards iniquity in his heart.

The Greek consists of five words. One of these we translate "of a righteous man." Another, "the effectual fervent." The word so rendered, means literally "inwrought," and seems to refer to the energetic operation of the Spirit upon the heart. Our word "fervent" is a very expressive word, and does not much lag behind the original. "Fervent prayer of the righteous can much."

"We ask, and receive not." It is not surprising. The promise is not to prayer, but to true prayer, fervent prayer, prayer with the whole heart in it; with concentration of desire, singleness of aim, warmth of affection, strength of purpose, absolute grasp of the promise, and invincible perseverance. Consider Abraham, Jacob, Elijah. Your prayers are not fervent. You pray, and the response from a throne of grace is, "The fervent prayer of the righteous availeth much." The records of that throne will furnish a satisfactory account of the fortunes of every prayer.

"Can much." The Bible generally disparages human ability. It pours contempt upon the might of princes It sometimes laughs to scorn the great armies and proud navies of the nations. Yet it points out a way by which man may clothe himself with strength; with "much" strength How much? This modest word stretches into infinity, and discloses omnipotence within it. God giveth power to his witnesses, his fervent petitioners, to shut heaven, to smite the earth, to turn waters to blood.—(Rev. x. 6.) Through Christ strengthening me, I can do all things.

February 25.—"Happy is the man whom God correcteth."—Job v. 17.

Happy, because the correction is designed to bring him into paths of pleasantness and peace.

Because there is no unnecessary severity in it.

Because the disciplinary stroke is in the place of ten thousand strokes of divine vengeance for our sins.

Because the chastisement is not so much against us, as against our most cruel enemies—our sins.

Because we have abundant words of consolation.

Because the sacrifice of a broken heart, and of a contrite spirit, God despiseth not.

Because there is at such seasons an influx of most precious knowledge.

Because whom the Lord loveth he chasteneth.

Because all the good have had experience of this

Because Christ has said, "The cup which my Father hath given me, shall I not drink it?"

Because our light affliction is but for a moment.

FEBRUARY 26.—"Rejoice evermore."—1 Thessalonians v. 16.

We have here a command. He that spake from Sinai, saying, "Thou shalt not covet," speaketh now from the cross, saying, "Rejoice." He that finds Christ, finds this command. It is not a matter of choice with him whether he will be a rejoicing Christian, or a downcast Christian. He has no more right to neglect the fulfillment of this duty, than to forget his duty to his neighbor. In fact, this command is so inextricably interwoven with other obligations, that he who does not obey it, exposes at once his deficiency in the matter of faith towards Christ, gratitude towards God, love towards his fellow-men, and hope of future bliss.

But can tears be dried, the wounds of the heart healed, the face irradiated with smiles, by a simple command? Were it not more reasonable to bid the leopard change his spots, the Ethiopian his complexion? God has not been pleased to discover to us a tree whose leaves will blanch the skin; but he has been pleased to open up a fountain for the removal of human woes. To command a person to rejoice, without at the same time presenting a sufficient consolation for his sorrows, is but to mock his grief. But he that bids us rejoice, shows us what to do with our griefs. If we will let him, he will take up each several grief, and cast it into the crucible of his word.

The command to rejoice, is a command—to contemplate God and his affections; especially as manifested in Christ; in his relations to us individually—to feed upon the promises—to study God's will; and, paradoxical though it may seem, to be not much occupied with the matter of our personal happiness, but rather with that of others. "It is more blessed to give, than to receive." (Read Isaiah lviii.)

Rejoice evermore, because Christ is the same yesterday, to-day, and for ever. The word of God abideth for ever. All things work together for good to them that love God.

FEBRUARY 27.—"We are the clay, and thou our potter."—Isaiah lxiv. 8.

Happy are they who can use this language;—who have renounced the mad enterprise of fashioning themselves, and, ceasing to play presumptuously the part of potter, have come to the original author of their being, that he may create them anew in righteousness and true holiness. Even Christians are sometimes long in understanding what part they are to play in the divine laboratory. The idea of the divine agency in the transformation of their souls, is shadowy; that of their own obligation, painfully distinct. Let them learn to use the language of Israel of old. "Thou art the potter, and we are the clay." There is no more sublime function of the Godhead, none that more inapproachably exalts him above all created efficiency, than the metamorphosis of unholy souls. It were a less preposterous thing for us to undertake to create a globe like this, and find a planetary path for it, than to dream of substituting the similitude of angels for that of devils, in our characters. It is not merely the love of God, but also his power, that challenges the praises of the universe for the accomplished work of redemption (Rev. v. 13.)

"But, the clay has no volition of its own." True. But it is a fact, whether it be a doctrine or not, and a fact that we ought not to be so long in learning as we mostly are, that our own volitions utterly fail of themselves to effect the purification of our natures. It is God that worketh to will and to do, of his good pleasure.

"Thou art our potter." What words of tender confidence are these. What a representation of God. Our potter,—mine, yours. He has taken up this as his vocation,—namely, the redemption and glorification of your nature, and of mine. Between your soul and God there is a wonderful relation established. All nature looks on in admiration, to see the Creator at work upon the clay of your soul. The sculptor is not more enchained to the marble he is employed in chiseling, nor the gardener to the spot which he is converting into a garden.

February 28.—"There is forgiveness with thee, that thou mayest be feared."—Psalm cxxx. 4.

This is the gospel. Christ is with God; therefore, there is forgiveness with God. "It is expedient for you that I go away," that I go to heaven. The only question is, Is Christ there? Then we shall assuredly find forgiveness there.

A proper understanding of this word "forgiveness" would fill the soul with a bliss, the like of which was never yet experienced upon this earth. It designates two immensities,—that of our sins, and that of the love of God in Christ. To fathom it we must descend to the lowest depth of endless misery; to know its height we must ascend to the throne which the seraphim encompass.

This forgiveness, this smile of God, binds the soul to God with a beautiful fear. Fear to lose one glance of love. Fear to lose one word of kindness. Fear to be carried away from the heaven of his presence, by an insidious current of worldliness. Fear of slumber. Fear of error. Fear of not enough pleasing him.

Our duty, then, is to drink deep of God's forgiving love. To be filled with it, is to be filled with purity, fervency, and faith. Our sins have to hide their diminished heads, and slink away through crevices, when forgiveness,—when Christ enters the soul.

February 29.—" Behold, these three years I come seeking fruit on this fig-tree, and find none."—Luke xiii. 7.

And yet you profess to be a fruit-bearer. The position you occupy implies that you have separated yourself from the fruitless trees of the world. You are in the vineyard of the Lord. You are called by his name. In assuming the designation of Christian, you have invited the Lord to come and seek fruit on your branches.

All things have been duly organized, in order that you may bring forth fruit. What could have been done more to my vineyard, that I have not done in it? Has there been any lack of instruction as to the nature of the fruit required? There has been no lack. It has been shown you by precept, by example, poetically, historically, in parables, and in unadorned speech. Have inadequate motives been presented? The Son of God with arms outstretched upon the cross, pleading with God for you, and with you for God—what an infinitude of motives are comprehended in this spectacle! Fruitlessness is not merely wrong to others; it is self-injury, penury of the soul; and fruitfulness is the only true wealth we are capable of knowing. The absence of fruit is the presence of pride, vanity, selfishness, and all forms of unloveliness. Is there no adequacy of motive here? The whole earth is fruitful, in order that you may be fruitful. Far, far away there is a plantation, whose products are matured through many a day of patient shining of the sun, that they may, after the ministry of innumerable hands, by numerous channels, reach you, and furnish you with clothing. Other fields, beneath a more tropical sky, some in one continent, some in another, yield the ingredients of your morning beverage. In the unfrequented depths of vast forests, the powers of nature watch day and night over the plant that is commissioned to furnish an antidote for your fever. The whole world is put under daily contribution for you, and hardly is the least of your thousand wants unattended to, that every opportunity and every inducement may be furnished you for the producing of fruit. Why is that flower painted so exquisitely, and fashioned to be the momentary utterance of enduring love, and then thrown in your path by the Maker of it, but that you may render fruit? "Knowest thou not that the goodness of God leadeth thee to repentance," and to all the fruits of the Spirit that follow on repentance?

The Lord of glory himself has come to you, and come again, and again; by his servants, his Spirit, his providence; as a still small voice in your heart, and perhaps as a whirlwind among your possessions. Where found he you? In sloth, in revelry, in worldliness, in pride, in passion,—far, very far from fruitfulness. How wonderful that your probation was not then and there cut short. What reason is there to hope that a prolonged probation will witness any better results?

MARCH 1.—"My times are in thy hand."—Psalm xxxi. 15.

The time of my prosperity. In vain would I say unto my soul, "Soul, take thine ease, thou hast much goods laid up for many years." In vain I grasp the evidences of my wealth; look abroad upon my goodly mansions and large estates; reckon upon my wealth, and exult in the victory obtained over earthly vicissitudes. The victory is a mere cheat, a phantasm of my brain. The time of my prosperity is in the hand of God. He opens his hand, and all my possessions vanish into air.

The time of my health. It is God that determines its continuance, even to the very hour.

The time of my mental capacity. I boast of the powers of my mind; but they abide with me only while God commands them so to do.

The time of my adversity. Of sickness Of manifold sore trials. Of absence of loved ones. Of humiliation. Of conflict with sin.

The term of my mortal existence. Wherefore, let my eyes be unto the hand of the Lord, as the eyes of a servant are unto the hand of his master.

MARCH 2.—"**Thou Lord, hast not forsaken them that seek thee.**"—**Psalm ix. 10.**

The promise of the Lord never to forsake the soul that trusts in him, looks familiarly and kindly forth upon us, from many a page of Scripture, old and new. But we have here an historical statement to the effect that he has never forsaken them that seek him. This is a bold averment. History is a very large affair. Ten thousand volumes were but a small part of its library. It is startled by the challenge contained in our text; and takes down volume after volume, saying, "I will easily, with my voluminous records, levy an army of many thousand facts to confound this statement." Unbelief nods assent, saying, "The statement needs modification: We have often been forsaken of the Lord."

The promise is not that we shall always have a sensible manifestation of the Lord.—That we shall always have a soul-gladdening consciousness of his presence.—That we shall always be able to understand his dealings with us.—That we shall be kept from disappointments, and from anguish of spirit.

The promise is not that we shall never be cast into a den of lions;—never into a fiery furnace,—never be a fugitive by the brooks Cherith, or under the juniper tree—never be brought before Nero Look for the token that the Lord hath not forsaken you, in the right place. *Look for it in the den* of lions, and you will find it in the form of an angel. Look for it in the burning fiery furnace, and find it in the form of the Son of God. Look at Elijah under the juniper tree. He seems to have been surprised into a loss of faith, when he heard that the queen had sworn to take his life; to have imagined that the Lord had forsaken him; to have fled in dishonorable alarm; and to have cast himself, way-worn and anguish-stricken, under the juniper tree, with a feeling that it was about as well to die, seeing that no degree of intimacy with the Lord would secure a man from being forsaken of him. But it was not the Lord that had forsaken him; it was he that had forsaken himself; and this he now discovered. Afterwards the still small voice came, saying, "The Lord is in me, but thou canst not hear me nor discern him, if thou hearken to the voice of an angry queen; it is the privilege of faith to hear me even amid the thunders of God's most agitated providence."

March 3.—" The meek will he guide."—Psalm xxv. 9

Be content to lose the idea of thine own importance; cease to be wrapped up in the contemplation of thine own claims and rights. Be not counting on honors to be rendered thee, hour by hour, from this man and from that. Give up the vain idea that every hour owes thee an ample tribute of manifold benefits. Shrink into non-importance, and take the position of a simple servitor, whose business it is to do, to suffer, and to give thanks.

When you have become thus inconsiderable in your own regard, and have relinquished the honor which cometh from man, and are cordially willing that the gifts that adorn this present life should be withheld from you, and abundantly bestowed at your right hand and at your left; then will you become conscious that another hand is locked in yours, a friendly hand, a gracious hand, a tender, considerate, careful hand; a royal, a heavenly, nay, without disguise, a divine hand. In surrendering all self-importance you have become unspeakably important to the most exalted Being in the universe. You have entered the very path trodden by the Lord Jesus Christ. In that path you walk with God.

The secret of habitual meekness is the love of God habitually shed abroad in the heart. All pride, all avidity of worldly good, all insubmission, imply a grossly inadequate idea of the value of Christ's love. Thou canst disdain the riches that take wings, in the consciousness of unseen wealth—untold, imperishable.

MARCH 4.—"Except a man be born again, he cannot see the kingdom of God."—John iii. 3.

"Thou hast considered, Nicodemus, that except God were with him, no man could work such miracles as I have wrought. Thou hast considered, also, that one in whom such celestial power resides, must have a great deal of knowledge respecting the heavens, their marvels, their glories, their inhabitants. Thou wouldst fain hear me speak of these things, and have me enchant thy mind with a description of the amazing things that are found in the paradise of God. I am indeed a teacher come from God, nor is there besides me any one who, having dwelt in the heavens, has descended to the earth. But art thou truly in a condition to hear me tell of the characteristics of heaven? While I speak to thee of the purity of the angels wilt thou not be longing to hear of their stature? When I tell thee of their love, wilt thou not desire to hear of their ivory palaces? When I speak of the songs of the redeemed, will not thy thoughts be of golden rivers and gem-laden trees? When I tell thee of the absence of sin and of temptation, wilt thou not prefer to have the strain relieved by the description of a heavenly banquet? There is reason to believe that a description of the kingdom of God, or, if such be in thy thought, a description of the Messiah's kingdom, would convey no definite ideas to thy mind, and greatly fail to interest thee. *Except a man be born again*, he cannot see the kingdom of God. He cannot appreciate the nature of it, or be wrought upon by the descriptions of it. Before the eyes of the blind, the picture were in vain held up. Believe the earthly things I tell you; the things already revealed; the things which relate to your present duty; and then you will b enabled to see in their true glory and beauty, the heavenly things. You must be born again; get a new mind, new views, new affections, new tastes, new perceptions; and then you will speedily discover the kingdom of heaven. This kingdom cannot be seen from without. Men might lie all day beneath its crystal walls and pearly gates, without the slightest conception that there was anything near them of an extraordinary character."

MARCH 5.—"Blessed are they that mourn."—Matthew v. 4.

That mourn over their alienation from God.—Over their past years of ungodliness.—Over the evil that they have wrought in the world.—Over their neglected opportunities of usefulness.—Over their moral unloveliness.—Over their insensibility;—their irresolution;—their bad memory for sacred things.—Over the unsatisfactory condition of the church.—The sin and danger of those near and dear to them.—The oppression, unrighteousness and misery that desolate the whole earth.

They mourn over the fugitive loveliness that meets them in their path. They hear the whole creation groaning in pain. They mourn to see so many exquisite and magnificent works of God, defiled and dishonored by sin.

But their mourning has its limits. It is lost in a sea of blessing. Blessed are they that mourn. Happiness is linked to their mourning. This beatitude comes from the lips of the

Lord Jesus to kiss away their tears. They are blessed, because their mourning is an important preliminary of their deliverance from that which they mourn. Because they are in sympathy with Christ. Because a thousand consolatory expressions of God's word come trooping to the chamber of their sorrow. Because their heart is fructified thereby to yield the flowers and fruits of joy.

Sometimes there is not the consciousness of the blessing. At such times God puts our tears in his bottle. He does not wipe them away; but keeps them for future explanation, and future vindication of his tenderness. We may slight our own past sorrows; but God slights them not. After a long silence perhaps, he brings forth the vial of our former tears, and shows what a wonderful memory Love has. He then clears up the long mystery, and convinces us of the perfect kindness of a dispensation that seemed so strange.

MARCH 6.—"Except ye be converted and become as little children, ye shall not enter into the kingdom of heaven."—Matthew xviii. 3.

Many things are becoming in a child that are not in a man; and many things required in a man that are not looked for in a child. The idea here, or one aspect of it, is that we should be *made over again*, from the very beginning.

Simplicity, freedom from guile, candor, retiringness, affectionateness, trust; these things are not uncommon among children, and are important elements of a Christian's character. Especially is the Christian required to entertain towards God, the feelings that parents expect from their children; and to demean himself in the sight of God as children demean themselves in their intercourse with those over them.

Are you a little child in this sense, that you are willing to learn all things *de novo* from God? Are you willing to receive what counsel he gives? To have all your conduct determined by him? Your plans altered or dismissed by him? Your affections disposed of by him? Your property taken by him? Your sorrow cared for by him?

Are you willing to live with an open heart to him, and confidingly pour out all your experiences into his bosom? To have no secrets from him? To confess everything and to confess it at once?

MARCH 7.—"How sweet are thy words unto my taste!"—Psalm cxix. 103.

Even the words of a fellow-creature of earth, how inexpressibly sweet sometimes, how beyond all calculation precious! All gold and silver would be despised in comparison with them. They come freighted with something as dear as life, with love, and the heart is enriched with them as though the breath of God had come into it. But does not this rainbow of earthly joy die gradually out? Do not the enrapturing words sooner or later become exsiccated in the memory, and may they not meet with contemptuous treatment as remembrancers of a worthless illusion? Indeed they do; indeed they may.

Nevertheless the heart may find its happiness, its true and undying happiness, *in words.* At this moment there is nothing in the whole world so much to be desired as certain words. Words of love. Words expressive of infinite love. Treasures, pleasures, honors of earth, what are they? My unsatisfied soul cries out, Give me words. Words whereby I may know the love that God has towards me. Words declaring the unchangeable attachment of the Saviour. Words purifying my heart. Emboldening me in prayer. Exhibiting to me the blissful future. Words that shall give life to my dead powers, and change me from glory to glory, as by the Spirit of the Lord.

Nor does my soul cry out in vain. My palate hath a thousand appetencies; nay, if they were counted, has far more than a thousand capacities for distinct perceptions of flavor. He who thus wondrously endowed the human palate, has made to grow on ten thousand different trees, fruits with flavors exactly responsive to all these distinctions of taste. He who has so marvellously and lovingly shown his acquaintance with my physical tastes, will he overlook the deeper wants of my soul, and withhold those words of consolation and of blessing, without which the world, with all its profusion of fruit, were a mere wilderness? He will not. He has given words whose sweetness satisfies the soul.

What is necessary in order that we may find God's words sweet unto our taste?

A belief that they are in an absolute sense, God's words. A belief that they are God's words to us, as individuals,—to you, to me; that we have forfeited all title to his favor, deserve his everlasting wrath; that in his favor is life; and to hunger and thirst after righteousness.

March 8.—"Be ye kind one to another."—Ephesians iv. 32.

Not courteous merely; for courtesy is but one expression of kindness. Not kind to this or that choice one, with whom you have a facility of sympathy; but generally. Be ye kind; there are few words in our language more endowed with meaning than this. It has both a soul and a body. It signifies both a state of the heart, and the manifestations of that state, in acts, words, tones, looks. Some words look more to outward acts; others more to inward qualities. We cannot say to which this most looks. It has two hands so to spéak, and grasps both ideas refusing to let either go. This word claims also the whole heart. Kindness is not a quality of one's nature: but it is the aspect of one's nature. It is not something to be introduced into our character; but our character is to be baptized in it, penetrated with it.

How this command expresses the kindness of God! He is not satisfied with extending over you all the day long an azure canopy of love, with making his sun run for your pleasure his daily course through the skies; with causing the breath of his winds to visit you, his flowers to bloom for you, his fruits to ripen, and ten thousand other ministries of his to wait upon you; he is not satisfied with the proof of his kindness given in the knowledge of Christ communicated to you; but he gives a solemn charge concerning you to every human being that comes near the throne of grace,—a charge to be kind to you. And when they ask, how much is intended by this command, God refers them to the signal proof of his own kindness, as the example that may guide them in their kindness to you.

If you say, how can I be kind to those whose characters are unamiable, and the look of whose soul is not inviting? By looking at God over their shoulder. Remember that you are pleasing him in showing kindness to them. Your goodness extendeth not to the sovereign of the skies; you cannot be kind to him; but your love to him whom you have not seen may fitly express itself, it must do so, in kindness to your brother whom you have seen.

MARCH 9.—"Blessed are the pure in heart, for they shall see God."—Matthew v. 8.

Man is without God. He walks in the mansion of the King of kings, wondering who contrived it, and what has become of its royal owner; sometimes even doubting if it ever had a contriver, a proprietor. To his mind, God, if he is at all, is an absentee. He examines the treasures around him, studies them, weighs them, grasps them, and speculates of the

Creator as of one who may be or may not be. Generally, indeed, he speculates not at all. In his conception, God is so remote that it is idle to waste time in searching for him.

Yet God is nigh and wonderfully manifest. To see him we need not climb the empyrean, nor wing our way to a central sun. Even upon this earth it is possible to behold, by virtue of an uttered spell, one after one the successive walls of the mystery of God melt away and disappear, until the Almighty, unveiled and glorious, is seen where the seraphim saw him when they sang, "Holy, holy, holy, Lord God Almighty, the whole earth is full of thy glory." To them the whole earth was full of the glory of God, and they would have veiled their faces in love and adoration, even in the heart of Arabia Deserta; while, in the midst of the most beautiful and teeming landscapes of the earth, man, unsanctified man, condescends to occupy his mind with the baffling question, "Is there a God?"

Some who have been taught from above to desire greatly the manifestations of God, and who wrestle earnestly, perhaps passionately, in prayer, that their Lord would be pleased to draw nigh unto them, and give them visions of his excellence, would find it to their inexpressible advantage to cease from the pursuit of extraordinary manifestations, and by faith and purity of heart school themselves into the ability to discern a present God, and to abide in blissful intercourse with him in whom they live and move and have their being. Let them understand that what they need is not the accomplishment of some change out of themselves—the bringing near of something that is afar—but a purging of their mental vision, the removal of a film that yet too much beclouds the eye of their soul. There is a word with us, and it is as follows:—"Lo! I am with you always." To the unbeliever, a mere word, and no more; but to the initiated, a means of finding forever, and in every place, the brightness of the divine glory.

If any one be offering the petition of Moses, "I beseech thee, shew me thy glory," let him hear the Saviour reply, "Seek purity of heart, and thou wilt find me. Be like me, and thou shalt look upon me. Cease to regard thyself; be meek and lowly of heart; let no guile be found in thy mouth; delight thyself in the Lord; thus shall thy power of discerning and enjoying me be day by day augmented." This word "purity" invites us to linger. But when could one satisfy himself with discourse upon it?

MARCH 10.—"Blessed are the peace-makers."—Matthew v. 9.

Christ is the Prince of peace. Peace on earth is the object of the Messiah's mission, said the angels in their song. His followers are accordingly sons of peace. They have peace with God, and they are pacificators; they follow peace with all men. Their great object is to induce men to lay aside their hostilities, and renounce their resentments. This is their vocation in the world. They seek to extend the empire of their Master; but as that empire (and that alone) is peace, they seek no other victory than that which consists in bringing them one to another in holy concord.

Yet Christ said, I came not to bring peace, but a sword. His word, launched into a family, comes often like a thunderbolt, riving and shattering the harmonies that had before existed. It is like fire, and like a hammer.

The word of Christ is stern in its opposition to all that is incompatible with true peace. Peace with sin, is what it ever must make war upon. If we are peace-makers, it is by means of the gospel of peace. We seek to make men acquainted with the cruel facts of their present captivity to sin, and alienation from God; to tell them of the peace of God which passeth all understanding; to bring them into sweet accord with the great author of their being; to have them moulded by the

Holy Spirit into a peace-loving disposition; to enfranchise them from pride, selfishness, covetousness, unbelief, malice, uncharitableness, moral weakness, and the other natural enemies of peace. Some that are near and dear to them may turn against them, and the manifestation of bitterness on the part of these may seem to belie the claim of the gospel to be a pacificator; but that manifestation only affords scope for an exhibition of long-suffering, kindness, gentleness, and tender interest—in a word, for the exhibition of a heaven-born peace.

A sea of opposition has ever raged around the good—sometimes more, sometimes less fiercely. But, like the coral islands—whose serene unruffled lakes, stately palms, and quiet tenements present a wonderful contrast with the reef-broken angry ocean around—the elect of God, the friends of the gospel, have peace with God, follow peace with all men, and exhibit the fruits of righteousness, even when persecuted by the world.

Commune with yourself touching this thing, and ask, "Am I a peace-maker? Do I love well the things that make for peace? Does it grieve me to behold men unacquainted with the Prince of Peace? Do I make manifest in my own life that the kingdom of God is righteousness, peace and joy in the Holy Ghost? Do I understand and observe the precept to speak evil of no man? When I hear of strife between those who should be friends, does it grieve me as though I heard of the breaking out of the cholera in their families? And, as the physician feels that he has a mission among the sick, do I arise at the report of strife, and hasten on an embassy of peace to the conflicting parties? In a word, am I a merchant with much balm of Gilead, seeking to dispose of it among all, and to assuage the desolating enmities of the world? And is my constant prayer this, that God would teach me how I may most thoroughly subserve the cause of peace in the world?"

MARCH 11.—"Endure hardness as a good soldier of Jesus Christ."—2 Timothy ii. 3.

If you are a disciple of Christ, you are a soldier of Christ. If you are an expectant of salvation, you are a follower of the captain of salvation. When it was proposed to you to become his follower, it was distinctly intimated that you were to follow him to a field of conflict.

Endure hardness—that is, endure things hard to be endured. The army of Christ resembles not a Northern army rushing down from its inhospitable home into the fertile plains and genial climate of Italy, encountering a dispirited and enervated race, and grasping with a facile hand the wealth and honors of that region; but resembles rather the little company that gathered around David in the days of Saul's indignation, and followed him from glen to glen, from rock to rock, sleeping under the open skies or in caverns, snatching their scanty food where they found it, every moment on the alert for their numerous and powerful enemies, with the whole nation ready to fall upon and crush them, and with nothing to look to but the promise of God, the promise of a kingdom. We know that it is our Father's good pleasure to give us the kingdom; not that we should dream that we have it now. We say therefore with Elisha, "Is it a time to receive money, and to receive garments, and olive-yards, and vineyards, and sheep, and oxen, and man-servants, and maid-servants?" Rather is it a time to endure hardness. For the servant is not greater than his Lord; the soldier not greater than his general.

Therefore let us consecrate what we have to God; cease from seeking great things of earth for ourselves; receive in sweet submission the daily trials that will force their way into the presence of the Christian, in whatever retired apartment he may dwell; and give ourselves heartily to the conflict with our adversary, in whatsoever form he may approach us. What things to some are hard, to others are not; our Commander places us in such a corps as is most likely to furnish us with the probation that we need. You have to endure hardness, not to seek it; be sure, however, that the dread of it does not keep you out of any path in which God would have you walk.

MARCH 12.—"Light is sown for the righteous."—Psalm lxvii. 11.

Almost all our sorrow is connected with darkness, with misconceptions, with defective knowledge of the reasons that influence God in his dealings with us; and light is fitly used as a metaphor expressive of gladness and of a soul-satisfying manifestation of God.

The scattered seed disappears in the ground that receives it. He that is to eat its fruit does not see it fall, knows nothing of it in its prolonged incarceration. Perhaps he is far away, and millions stand between him and it. He is occupied with his cares, great or minute; yet all the while the unslumbering, unhastening providence of God watches over that ripening plant, and conducts it to a state of faultless fruitfulness; then gathers it, conveys it, and presents it to him for whom it was intended.

In like manner, does God hide long the blessing intended for his servant that trusts in him; and thus proves his servant whether indeed he trusts in him.

This servant perhaps passed through a season of strange and inexplicable experiences. A spirit of intense supplication was poured upon him, without a single response to his fervent petitions. His soul was consumed with desires, and those not unhallowed; yet the heaven of brass and the earth of iron seemed only to mock his longing. A strong and an enduring faith enabled him to grasp the mightiest promises of God, and vigorously to knock with them at heaven's gate; yet echo seemed only to say, "What is faith? what is a promise?" He was ready to conclude that all creation, even all earth, and all heaven, had received an inviolable command from the Deity to yield him no light—no, not a glimmer; and that he was given over a prisoner to everlasting night. He drank the cup his God had given him; got almost used to its daily bitterness; became familiar with the midnight of God's unanswering providence; wondered how God could reconcile it with his perfections to let prayer and sanctified desire go so long unanswered; but wondered without murmuring, and was willing that God should have his own way, and vindicate as it pleased him, his own reputation. Yet all the while that wondrous God, apparently cruel, yet in reality beyond expression faithful, was busied pouring out in superabundant fullness in some remote undreamt-of spot, the supplicated blessing. Yes, God took in his hand a seed the very day that servant cried to him; and as he continued in supplication, he continued enriching the selected object, freighting the chartered vessel; a thousand of his providential angels were commanded to wait upon it, and bring it every excellent ornament, load it with most beautiful fruit. Light was sown, light was reared, light was perfected. Then, with no little joy on the part of the heavenly ones, who had been in the secret, the unexpecting suppliant was brought into the presence of the light, and with equal confusion, admiration, and delight, saw that the Almighty had not despised his affliction, nor disregarded his impassioned supplication.

Captives in Egypt, the Israelites cried unto God. They cried vehemently, and long; yet, God came not. They had boasted of their God to the Egyptians as the hearer of prayer; and the Egyptians waited with them to see whether he would come; but at last taunted them with the fruitlessness of their prayers, and recommended them to call upon the idols of Egypt. But all the while God was listening eagerly to their cries, and daily heaping up a depository of blessing in answer to them. His selected seed was in the land of Midian. There dwelt and wandered Moses, the shepherd. Ten thousand prayers for deliverance, offered up by the far-off captives, were answered in ten thousand incidents and influences, all tending to make this Moses one of the meekest of men, God-fearing, nobly intellectual, sympathetic, believing. At length, we may suppose, the Israelites had almost begun to think that God had given no heed to their misery, and to their prayers. But Moses appears; the light that had been sown dawned upon them; and sounding the loud timbrel, they went forth celebrating the faithfulness of God.

Even the Sun of Righteousness was first a seed in the silence and solitude of Bethlehem, and remained long unmanifested in the obscurity of Nazareth. So Paul in Tarsus. It was not till many a year after God had sown this light for the church, that Barnabas went to Tarsus and brought him thence to Antioch, where he was commended to the grace of God and sent forth to be the means of dispelling much darkness in Asia Minor, Greece, and Italy.

And is there light now sown somewhere, growing unto Isaiah lx?

MARCH 13.—"Serve the Lord with gladness."—Psalm c. 2.

It is our privilege to serve the Lord in all things. It is ours to please the Lord in loosing the latchet of a shoe; and to enjoy the expression of this favor therein. The servant of God is not serving at the same time another master; he has not been hired for occasional service; he abides in the service of his God, and cannot be about anything but his Master's business; he eats, he drinks, he sleeps, he walks, he discourses, he findeth recreation, all by way of serving God. For the will of the Lord imposes at one time a task; commands at another time a recreation; bids him listen in this hour to music, and in that to speak the words of life; places in his hand a newspaper now, and after a while a pen; guides his feet to the bedside of the sick, and to the hovels of the degraded; leads him to the banqueting chamber of the rich, and gives him words for that place, and seats him at the humble board of the laboring man, and teaches him words for that occasion; bids him bow the knee in prayer, and bids him also come forth from prayer; compels him to exhibit gravity, and again bids him be all cheerfulness. The will of God concerning us is manifold. Let us pray to be filled with the knowledge of his will in all wisdom.

Serve the Lord *with gladness.* Can you bear to be waited upon by a servant who goes moping and dejected to his every task? You would rather have no servant at all, than one who evidently finds your service cheerless and irksome.

Serve him with gladness, for he is the best of beings.

For his commandments are not grievous.

For he is your Saviour, as well as Creator; your friend, as well as Lord.

The angels, so much greater than yourself, know no reason why they should not serve him with gladness.

In serving him, you serve yourself.

You make religion attractive.

You get a fitness for heaven.

MARCH 14.—**" He will regard the prayer of the destitute."—Psalm cii. 17.**

A man that is destitute knows how to pray. He needs not any instructor. His miseries indoctrinate him wonderfully in the art of offering prayer. Let us know ourselves destitute, that we may know how to pray; destitute of strength, of wisdom, of due influence, of true happiness, of proper faith, of thorough consecration, of the knowledge of the Scriptures, of righteousness.

These words introduce and stand in immediate connection with a prophecy of glorious things to be witnessed in the latter times. We profess to be eager for the accomplishment of those marvellous things; but are we offering the prayer of the destitute? On the contrary, is not the Church at large too much like the church of Laodicea? Will not a just interpretation of many of its acts and ways, bring forth the words, "I am rich and increased with goods, and have need of nothing?" And do not its prayers meet with this reproachful answer—"Thou art wretched, and miserable, and poor, and blind, and naked, and knowest it not. Thy temporal affluence implies not spiritual affluence. Thy spiritual condition is inversely as the worldly prosperity that has turned thy head. I counsel thee to buy of me gold tried in the fire. Give all thy trashy gold—trashy while it is with thee—give it to my poor; and I will give thee true gold—namely, a sense of thy misery and meanness; a longing for grace, purity, usefulness; a love of thy fellow-men; and my love shed abroad in thy heart."

MARCH 15.—"**Bless the Lord, O my soul.**"—Psalm ciii. 1.

Daily, habitually. Consider that thou hast every day an engagement with God to praise him. He has certainly a claim upon thee to consider and, in some measure, estimate his benefits bestowed on thee. A generous soul cannot bear to think that perhaps some one has bestowed on him some favor of which he is not aware. The thought of an unacknowledged kindness would keep him awake at night.

The command to bless the Lord is a command to take up, and not tread under foot, a shower of joys that have descended upon the place where you stand. Some fruit comes to you wrapped in many envelopes. You tear them off, throw them away, eat the fruit, and think of something else. But those envelopes were bank-notes of great value. God gives you something; you say this is to be eaten, and you eat it; but it was not merely given to be eaten; it was given to reveal unto you something of the wisdom, power, love, and condescension of God; to spread out before you an illuminated page of a book of heaven. I say again, the command to bless God is a command to take up many joys that you have let fall.

MARCH 16.—"The fear of the Lord is the beginning of wisdom."—Psalm cxi. 10.

It would be strange indeed if it were otherwise. If we believe in God the Creator of all, the Giver of every good gift, and if we believe it to be his wish that men should acknowledge his authority, and yield to his guidance, we cannot but believe that he will bestow his best gifts, especially such a gift as wisdom, on those only who defer to his authority, and aim to please him. The supposition that this gift is as fairly bestowed upon the ungodly as upon any implies that God disregards all moral distinctions, and has no tokens of his satisfaction to bestow on those whose great concern is to honor him. He undoubtedly bestows many gifts upon the wicked, for a season, that he may lead them to repentance by the experience of his goodness. But his best gifts are given after, not before, their repentance.

Can it then be said that the non-religious world is without wisdom? Has it no Aristotle, no Socrates, no Tacitus, no Goethe, no Gibbon? Let us understand what wisdom is. It is not any mere amount of knowledge that constitutes wisdom. Appropriate knowledge is essential to wisdom. A man who has not the knowledge appropriate to his position, who does not know himself in his relation to God and to his fellow-men, who is misinformed as to his duties, his dangers, his necessities, though he may have written innumerable works of a most exalted character, yet is he to be set down as a man without wisdom. What is it to you that your servant is acquainted with mathematics, if he is ignorant of your will, and of the way to do it? The genius of a Voltaire, a Spinoza, a

Carlyle, only makes their folly the more striking. As though a man floating rapidly onwards to the Falls of Niagara, should occupy himself in drawing a very admirable picture of the scenery. Men who are exceedingly great in the world's estimation have made the most signal blunders with regard to the most important things; and it is only because these things are not considered important by the world, that the reputation of these men remains.

If you have learned to estimate things in some measure as God estimates them, to desire what he offers, to relinquish what he forbids, and to recognize the duties that he has appointed you, you are in the path of wisdom, and the great men we have been speaking about are far behind you—far from the narrow gate which you have entered. He only is wise, who can call Christ the wisdom of God.

The fear of God is that deference to God which leads you to subordinate your will to his:—makes you intent on pleasing him; penitent in view of past wilfulness; happy in his smile; transported by his love; hopeful of his glory.

MARCH 17.—"Say ye to the righteous, that it shall be well with him."—Isaiah iii. 10.

Fear not, thou righteous man, thou lover of righteousness, who hast taken Christ as thy righteousness, and whose sincere desire is to walk even as he also walked, who hath made the Lord thy refuge, and hath put thy trust in the shadow of his wings, fear not; we bring thee a message from God; it shall be well with thee.

Thy sins alarm thee. They say; "We have possessed thee all thy days, and thy heart is our home. Thou hast always served us, and every day of habit has bound thee by a new chain to us. Of late thou hast been making fearful struggles; hast busied thyself day and night with God's word; thrown thyself into the society of the good; repented of sin; aspired to heaven; and hast even exercised faith in Christ. Yet here we are where we always were; swaying thee as of old; mocking thy new and frantic endeavors. We are a part of thy life; is it not evident? And the attempt to escape from us is as though thy arms should attempt to tear themselves from thy body. None can deliver thee from the body of this death."

Thy sins shall not have dominion over thee; it shall be well with thee. Thy present experience is good for thee. It is good for thee to know the extent of thy captivity, that thou mayest know how great a deliverance is required; and to know the true character of thy captors, that thou mayest love him who setteth thee free. It is because Christ is at the door that there is this agitation and conflict within. It shall be well with thee.

Unbelief says, "It might be well with thee, if thou hadst a stronger faith. But what can Christ do for one that has scarce any faith, and dares not grasp the promises? No, it can never be well with thee." We reply, It shall be well with thee. The mightiest faith has an insignificant beginning. Thy faith shall grow; it grows while we speak. Take this word God sends thee, and be strong in faith.

Timidity says, "Who knows what fierce antagonists may start up along this narrow path? Though thou triumph over the present evil, yet the future things may prove too much for thee." Who maketh thee to triumph over the present evil? And is he not a match for the future evil? The future difficulties shall only afford new occasions for the display of his faithfulness and all-sufficiency.

The world says, "It shall not be well with thee. We have traced the course of thousands who gave themselves up to the pursuit of righteousness. They fared not well, but ill. They were cut off by their ideas of duty from all our joys; and during all the journey of life they were haunted by a sense of unfulfilled obligation, were vexed by an inward conflict, and racked by fears of the future; and all men were against them; gloom, gloom, gloom, was the sum of their experience." But here the righteous man answers for himself, and says, "This representation is false; it is because a life of piety hath no attractions for thee that thou dost so describe it. Thy boasted joys are but blooming poisons, banquets spread by an enemy. It is not well with thee, but with him that leaveth thee."

Say ye to the righteous that it shall be well with him!

MARCH 18.—"I will trust."—Isaiah xii. 2

Not in uncertain riches, not in my own sagacity, not in my probity, not in my social position, not in the felicity of circumstances; not in the friendship of the world, not even in the favor of Christians; not in the sacraments, not in my prayers, nor in my repentance, nor in my obedience.

I will trust in Him that became man in order that he might bear my sins in his own body on the tree.

I will trust in him, for he is the most trustworthy being in the universe. Shall a child trust in its parent, a bride in the bridegroom, a soldier in his general, a captive in his deliverer, a patient in his physician,—shall men in all conditions abound in trust towards their fellow-men, and shall I not trust in the Almighty who hath shown himself all-gracious? Is there more than one being existent, of whom it can be said that heaven and earth shall pass away sooner than his least word? There is but one, and in him I will trust.

"*Take*," says Satan; "*trust*," says God.

"Almost nobody trusts," says my unbelieving neighbor. For that very reason I will trust. Is it not an infamy that the Lord of heaven and earth, the source of all blessedness, should be untrusted? You lie down to sleep trusting in your breath that it will continue to come and go all night, although a single interruption would be fatal; trusting in the beams over your head that they will not break; in the wind that it will not blow any inflammable thing into the vicinity of your lamp; in the atmosphere that it will not allow any pestilential influences to come nigh your couch; in ten thousand things without life or sense; and shall not I trust in him in whom I live, and move, and have my being?

I will trust, said Peter; and the sea became as rock beneath his feet. I will trust, said the Syro-Phœnician woman; though the disciples said, send her away; and her daughter was healed. I will take, said Balaam; and became rich for a day, accursed forever. Let me live, said Jonah, and was cast into the sea. I will trust, said he afterward, and all Nineveh bowed at his word. I will trust, said Daniel, and was delivered. I will save my life, said Peter, and denied his Lord. I will trust, said he afterward, and laid him down to sleep; then came the angel of the Lord, and brought him forth from prison. What mean ye to weep and to break my heart? said Paul; *I will trust.*

MARCH 19.—"A bruised reed shall he not break."—Matthew xii. 20.

In carrying out a great enterprise, individual suffering is very little regarded. Revolutions are not generally effected without the immolation of many lives. Thousands, how many thousands, of human reeds were first bruised, then broken, and thrown to the winds of the Crimea, that Sebastopol might be taken. And can it be that Christ, in going forth to the conquest of the whole world, will not suffer a bruised and bent reed, ready of itself to snap asunder, will not suffer one such to be broken? In a revolution that is to affect the destinies of so many millions to all eternity, is it possible that he will be tenderly solicitous for the meanest and weakest individual of his host? It is possible, it is true. He has but to let it alone, and it will break; but he will not let it alone. How then? Will he stay the march of the whole army out of consideration for a poor, frail, tempted creature? Will he forget the interests of the whole body in his strange concern for such a one? It is not necessary that he should do so. Were his wisdom and power a little less than infinite, this might be necessary. But the word infinite implies that he can at once make all things work together for the good of each, and for the good of all.

"He is all that you say," remarks some one; "but he is the Captain of our salvation, and must be obeyed. He is our Master, and he giveth to each of us a work. No one can ask that it should be otherwise. But I have a nature so detestable, so undone, so repugnant to everything good, that with ever so good a will to his service, the least commandment crushes me, the slightest task convulses me."

The *least* command crushes you? What is the *greatest* command? It is that you should love him with all your strength—not more than your strength—not more than your powers. His burden is adapted to your force. He asks from a sapling the strength of a sapling; from a bruised reed the strength of a bruised reed. "Say that I have no strength at all." That is best. Ask of him, and he will give thee.

He will give thee first sympathy. He will show his pierced hands and feet, tell of his sweat in the garden, and relate how he was once himself bruised for your iniquities. He will give you encouragement by showing you plants of righteousness flourishing in the courts of his God, who once were bruised reeds.—Peter, for instance, of whom Satan made sure once on a time. He will give you a shield of faith—will succor you in the time of temptation—will be your strength.

MARCH 20.—"Come unto me."—Matthew xi. 28.

Here is an invitation. Some one invites you. Some one

has thrown open his doors to you. The words convey a privilege—you have it now—the privilege of going to him. No difficulties exist with him. If you have a will to go, you may go. Ponder this fact,—whatever you do, wherever you go, you are nevertheless among the invited.

He that invites you has cast many angels out of his presence because they were not worthy. The seraphim, of such exceeding might and majesty, are overwhelmed at his glory. His face shineth as the sun in its strength. John, that holy evangelist, fell at his feet as one dead. Yet he invites you—has a place for you—spreads a feast for you.

He died upon the cross that you might have this invitation. And if you would know what that exceeding great cry was with which he gave up the ghost, know that it was this, "Come unto me! It is finished! thou mayest come!"

How many of his providences were simply echoes of this cry. He bereft thee of dear friends; deprived thee of health; stripped thee of wealth; baffled thee in thy schemes; destroyed the world's illusions; that thou mightest hear this invitation, and come unto him.

Come then at once. Come in earnest. Come in faith.

MARCH 21.—"Whosoever shall confess me before men, him will I confess also before my Father which is in heaven."—Matthew x. 32.

What an extraordinary world is this that such a sentence should ever have been uttered in it! Consider what is implied in these words. They manifestly imply that it is an opprobrious thing in the estimation of mankind to give honor to him who is the brightness of the Father's glory, and to acknowledge any connection with him. They imply that it is necessary to present the most powerful motives to the mind in order to subdue the feeling of shame that would naturally arise in the confession of Christ. Is not this a fallen world? Is not the race of mankind an utterly depraved race? Were it necessary to hold up powerful motives in order to induce a person to confess his alliance with some arch-villain, one could think better of man. But the most magnificent rewards are proposed, as an inducement to those who are acquainted with Christ, to acknowledge their acquaintance; to those who rely on him for salvation, to confess him as their Saviour.

The world that pursued Christ unrelentingly, until it had driven him forth, has ever since been doing its best to make his followers silent concerning him. "Thou shalt not confess the Lord Jesus Christ," is the first and great commandment of the world, and if it can only get this obeyed it will give a dispensation from all other duties. It has tried fire and the sword abundantly; but in these latter days its tactics are more subtle. It is all courtesy, and addressing the Christian, says:—"There is a great deal that is admirable about Christianity, and I blame myself very much that I have so neglected it. Allow me to be your scholar. I will sit at your feet, and learn of you. In return I will be happy to teach you what I know. We must go hand in hand along the journey of life." The Christian is charmed by this amicable proposal, and falls into the snare. The world learns something, just to lull the Church asleep; and the Church learns, alas! much of the world.

MARCH 22.—"Sin has reigned unto death."—Romans v. 21.

About the reign of sin there is no doubt. The tyrant, with an astonishing refinement of tyranny, forbade you to believe in his tyranny, and compelled you to go hither and thither chanting his praises as though he were one of the most loving of masters. How grossly you were deluded. A king is for the protection of his subjects; but this monarch reigned unto death. He was a deformed and revolting monster; you were cheated into the idea of his loveliness. He taught you to boast of liberty, while he loaded you more and more with chains. You staggered beneath great burdens which you bore to his treasury, while you were taught to believe that you were enriching yourself. He showed you pictures of superb banquets, and swore that you should sit down at such; and all the while he gave you but mouldy crusts to eat. He introduced his courtiers to you as a troop of friends; but gave them each a whip to lash you. He gave you a poisoner to be your cupbearer; a gaoler to be your guardian; a headsman to be your guide. An earthquake rocked your house; your bed was poised on the verge of an abyss; and a drawn sword was suspended over your table. You supposed that there was a sun there, but it was sackcloth; and a moon, but it was blood. In the garden was the upas tree, and in the field the hemlock. The streets of that city of death were streets of tombs. Ye shall not surely die, said all men, one to another; but they were all dead men while they spake. Sin reigned unto death, and cheated all his subjects into the idea that they owed life to him.

Happy for you that this is a thing of the past. Sin hath reigned, but has now no more dominion over you. You have been translated into another kingdom.

MARCH 23.—"Led by the Spirit of God."—Romans viii. 14.

Led by the Spirit of God. By the glorious being who led Christ. Without him was nothing made that was made. Without him the sceptre of the Godhead was never once extended. The highest archangel would not stir a step without him.

The children of God, all who inherit eternal life, have this infallible characteristic, they are led by the Spirit of God. They are led by him to a sense of their sinfulness and shortsightedness; to an open recognition of the same; to the throne of grace; to the use of the most prevailing arguments in prayer; to the society of Christians, the assemblies of the saints; away from temptation; through temptation; to the dwellings of the poor and needy; to the resorts of the ignorant and erring.

Let some of them be asked, why are you scattered abroad over the face of the earth, speaking diverse languages, addressing heathens and errorists? They may in their reply speak of ships and carriages, wind and steam, money and skill. But they must also say, "The Spirit of God led us hither."

There can be no safe guidance that is not perpetual. The advantage of a year may be lost in an hour. If we act independently of the Spirit in little things, we will look for him in vain in great things.

His leading is not violent. He acts by our own convictions and our own will. There is nothing degrading in this guidance, but the highest possible exaltation. God who has given us senses, understanding, free-will, memory, has given us something infinitely above them all, because they all by it enter into their highest perfection—namely, the guidance of the Spirit. Let the mariner say, "I need no wind, for I have a noble ship, with ample suits of sails, an excellent crew, with charts and compass." Let the commander of a steamer say, "I need no steam, no fuel, for the engine is everything that could be desired, and I have the most skillful engineers." But let the child of God say, "I am led by the Spirit of God."

March 24.—"Joint heirs with Christ Jesus."—Romans viii. 17.

We read of Christ that he has been made much better than the angels, as he hath by inheritance obtained a more excellent name than they. God hath highly exalted him, and given him a name that is above every name. God hath treated Christ as though he were the only heir. All the universe looks on amazed, as he ascendeth up above all principality and power, and might, and dominion, above every name that is named; and then learns with greatly more amazement that he is a representative heir; that there is a vast number in union with him, and that each of these is joint-heir with him, not for the diminution but for the enhancement of his glory.

An heir is one who passes from a state of privation to a state of affluence. Christ was the poorest of men on this earth, without where to lay his head, without reputation, with out a friend to speak for him when he was in the hands of sinners, without so much respect as would hinder servants from smiting him, and soldiers from blindfolding him in mockery. Soon see him however in the place of highest exaltation. And of his disciples he says, "the glory that thou hast given me I have given them." All power in heaven and in earth is given unto him; and even in this believers have a community with him; for "he that overcometh" (he says) "and keepeth my words unto the end, to him will I give power over the nations,—even as I received of my Father."

We are co-heirs with him of the Father's love; and of the various expressions of the Father's love. For instance, th peace of God, the Spirit of God, joy, strength, patience, usefulness, on the earth; a building of God, a house not made with hands, eternal, in the heavens; pleasures for evermore; crowns of righteousness; a body like unto his glorious body, spiritual and incorruptible; and the love of all the holy ones.

By virtue of the warrant given in this expression, wherever in the universe you find anything of Christ's, you can say, "this is mine."

MARCH 25.—"The glory which shall be revealed in us."—Rom. viii. 18.

In us; in me, in you. Sin, not satisfied with the manifestation given of itself in the angels that left their first estate, not satisfied with the degradation into which it has caused the devils to sink, came to you and me, that it might obtain a fuller exhibition. You and I dwelt in a world the soil of which had been moistened with Christ's sweat of agony, with the drops of Calvary, in a world where the Gospel of God's amazing grace is preached to every creature. Sin said, "It is one thing to make a creature ruin itself by sin; it is another thing to make a creature, so ruined, daily and hourly treat with contempt the proffered love, the Calvary-bought grace of the Lord of the universe." The very fabric of our minds tells frightful tales of what sin has wrought within us. Had our aim been to make ourselves so vile that the Spirit of God should be utterly and eternally repelled, we could not have gone further than we have done. Sin reveled in its victory over us; but this very victory only becomes the occasion of a greater triumph on the part of grace; and the glory of God is to be revealed in us more illustriously than it ever has been revealed in any order of beings. And we shall then be kept from self-glorification by the thought that it was our excessive sin which became the occasion of this excessive glory. "The glory which thou hast given me, I have given them," said Jesus. See Christ as Isaiah saw him, surrounded by the Seraphim; and as Peter and John, Moses and Elias saw him on the mount of transfiguration; and as the angels saw him when he ascended up on high, leading captivity captive; see him as John saw him when he fell at his feet as one dead; see him as all shall see him when he cometh in the clouds of heaven with great power and glory; and consider that we shall be like him. He is glorified in us.

No wonder that an angelic host encamps around the sleeping-place of the believer. The believer is an emigrant from the region of the shadow of death, bound to a country where he is to be clothed with glory like that of the King of kings. Christ is to be admired in us, honored in us, blessed in us, glorified in us. It is in gifts to us, in dignity, honor, and splendor, enjoyed by us, that God is to make manifest to the universe how beyond all estimation he appreciates the merit of the death of Christ.

Help me, O God, in the presence of my brother or sister, of thy son or daughter, to look with intense interest upon one who is to walk hereafter in the lustre, beauty, and excellency of Christ to receive dominion over kings, to be clad in glory that shall make the brightness of the firmament to pale. Let me make haste to love those whom thou so lovest, to honor those whom thou deignest so to honor.

MARCH 26.—"If we confess our sins, he is faithful and just to forgive us our sins, and to cleanse us from all unrighteousness."—1 John i. 9.

Confession implies compunction. The mere statement of one's fault is not confession. The fault may be aggravated by a heartless mention of it. Some men are very tenacious of their imaginary rectitude; but others think it a pretty accomplishment to be able to speak of themselves as graceless characters. Into the idea of true confession humiliation enters. Confession should be particular. Individual sins must be seen in their hatefulness before the word of forgiveness can come in between them and our conscience. And be not surprised If I add that forgiveness is particular. It is both general and particular. "Son, thy sins be forgiven thee" does not relieve the conscience from the necessity of afterwards looking at particular sins forgiven, appreciating their special features of ugliness, and finding relief in the details of divine forgiveness.

This shows us how much occasion there is for commerce with God. Confession, prayer, gratitude, these three duties give the soul an amount of business at the throne of grace which it can never overtake. God in his overflowing graciousness does not make us wait for a pretext to come to him; he does not suffer us to find any pretext for ever absenting ourselves from him.

There can be no true confession of sin without the contemplation of Christ crucified. For, an appreciation of sin is necessary to adequate confession, and this is not obtained save at the cross. If a man has taken from you a thousand pounds, and says, "Forgive me for having purloined a handful of silver from you;" or if he struck your child so that he died, and says, "Forgive me for the injury I did your child;" such confession will not suffice. He must first see his own deed aright. And it is utterly impossible that any sin should be seen in its proper flagrancy, until the Lamb of God is seen to have been slain for it.

Confession, forgiveness, purity, these three things stand in indubitable connection in the history of a saved soul.

It is a pity to quit this text, having only skimmed it. What does the apostle mean, dear reader, by the words "faithful and just?" Understand this, and you will be an Elijah, a Daniel, a Moses.

March 27.—"Beloved, if God so loved us, we ought also to love one another."—1 John iv. 11.

Two sublime arguments here present themselves. The first is this: God hath so loved *me;* therefore, beloved, I must love you. The second is: God hath so loved *you;* therefore, beloved, I must love you.

By virtue of the first argument, every expression of the love of God toward me that I have ever received, lays aside its smile, and assuming a beautiful air of authority, commands me to love you. All the promises that ever flocked in laughing troops or came singly and gently to my soul, though they seemed to have but one aim, namely to convey to me ottar of heaven's roses, vials of divine love, all now acknowledge that they have another commission even to bind me and not let me go unless I love whom they shall name. Far be it from me to make any difficulty. Did I so, this would be the same as sending contemptuously back to God those radiant messengers. To refuse to love is to reproach God with loving. It is to make all the promises of God shrink back as I open his word, and say to me, "Who is this?" It is to make Christ frown me from his cross. It is to make all the glorified ones say, "He will never walk with us beside the river of the water of life." But I must walk there; I must love you, beloved of Christ! and I must be diligent in accomplishing my apprenticeship in this matter.

Through the virtue of the second argument, I find myself sovereignly attracted to you by all the precious tokens of his love that God hath ever bestowed upon you. There is a voice of thunder, so authoritative, but of course not intimidating, a voice of gentle thunder in a single hair of your head, for it has a long story to tell to my attentive ear, (with proof-texts from the gospel) about the interest of God in you.

Leaving unwritten a long, long chapter, come we to the manifestations of God's amazing love to you in connection with the regeneration of your nature. His preparatory goodness in all the arrangements by which you were kept from being carried away in the whirlwind of sin, and were brought under various benign influences; his convincing you of sin; his revelation of himself to you in Christ; his minute attention to your education in holiness; his consolations in your time of trouble; his chidings in your day of error. Let me consider these and love you. He made you to shed tears and then carried them to heaven for his prize; nor is there an account wanting on high of your smiles; while your prayers are presented odoriferous from golden vials before his throne.

All these matchless indications of love speak to me and say, "Where is your love for the beloved of God?"

If God so loved us, we ought also to love one another.

MARCH 28.—"God is love, and he that dwelleth in love, dwelleth in God, and God in him."—1 John iv. 16.

Let us define. But who can define? For the interpretation of this word, *love*, is the interpretation of God. It is easy to say that love is a delight in the happiness of the loved. But the mind will not rest satisfied with this definition; it again and again replies, that the meaning includes more. Love cannot be defined, for it is itself a definition, the definition of God; but it may be described in its operations and effects.

The love that God has towards you, passes knowledge. The whole universe is intended to express it. When he reared the sublime mountains and clothed the plains in beauty, he said, this is for my beloved. The course of his providence is commissioned to express it. Your own form is a revelation of his love to you. Your endowments are other utterances of the same. His word and all the marvels of redemption are a token of love given to you over the head of angels. In its augmenting utterances, the divine love stops not with the cross of Christ. It comes to the believer and says, "Be thy heart emptied that I may dwell therein, and render thine eyes, thy tongue, thy hands, thy possessions, thy time, thy all, expressive of the love that God bears to thy fellow-believer." Every believer is thus made to become another multiple of that love that is enthroned on the throne of the universe.

There never was a door opened in heaven so wide as this word. We learn from it the mystery of heaven. We see what is the nature of its felicity.

Sin has armed all its host against love, and hath given a commandment that if any man know where it be, he may show it, that it may be taken. Fiery darts fall thick and fast about him that gives it a home. The ugliness of man's nature becomes gigantic, and, seizing a tremendous spear, says, "Love, if thou darest." But here, as elsewhere, there is a victory for faith.

To abide in love is to abide in the thoughts of God's love, in the memory and consciousness of Christ's love, in the sense of one's own unworthiness and in the renunciation of self, in the rejection of selfish pleasure and advantage, and the study of the true happiness of others, in intercession, in the Holy Spirit, in the faith that discerns a present God and knows how to discover the relations of every creature to God. Especially is it to abide in the great thought that Christ tasted death for every man, and that your life is to be an embodiment of the gospel for every creature. And if you set about this heartily, with entire consecration, it may please God to help you by a wonderful device of his own. But this is a secret.

MARCH 29.—"When I said, my foot slippeth; thy mercy, O Lord, held me up."—Psalm xciv. 18.

Man walks in slippery places, saying, there is no danger. Yet every rock has one declivity that descends, gently and imperceptibly at first, perhaps, but still descends to the lake of fire. And carefully examined, it reveals the names of thousands and thousands who perished there, all saying, there is no danger. And scarcely is there an hour of the day when, to one who listens attentively, there comes not the wail of a forlorn being whose feet have slipped, without any to hold him up.

One of these rocks is popularity. Another is an ardent love of literature. Another is a taste for art; be it music, painting, or some other art. Another is a taste for business. An enterprising spirit. A love of luxury. A passion for money. Fondness for society. Venturesome reading, whether of romances or of sceptical books. Love of excitement, fondness for stimulants. Evil associations. Talkativeness. Impulsiveness. Wit.

These are slippery rocks. Some of these have been crossed

in safety. But vast numbers have perished on them. Some have said, we will take heed to our steps that we slip not; yet did they slip; and not remembering the watchword, they perished.

Happy are they who ever remember that the best paths of this world are slippery enough, and keep near to God that he may recover them the moment their feet begin to slide. These persons are found breaking away now and again from their avocation or recreation, because they perceive their foot to be sliding, and crying to God are helped by his mercy. A child walking among slippery rocks cries out to his parent, my foot slippeth; there is but a moment in which a helping hand can reach him; yet it reaches his, for his father is just there. And so, if we walk carefully, our Father's helping hand will be stretched out in the opportune moment. Jesus was nigh, when Peter cried out, "Save, Lord, or I perish."

MARCH 30.—"**Hold that fast which thou hast, that no man take thy crown.**"—**Revelation iii. 11.**

Hold fast the gift which divine grace hath already bestowed on thee; the loss of it were the loss of thy crown.

This exhortation is made necessary by such facts as these:—There is a tendency in the mind to under-estimate the gifts already in possession, and to forget how absolute is the connection between present grace and eventual glory; and there is also a tendency to depreciate the power and subtlety of the adversaries.

Conceive of a crown that guarantees to him who possesses it life beyond the reach of interruption, health that can never be invaded, purity unsulliable, wealth universal, dignity archangelic, power unlimited, a vast dominion the inalienable affections and cordial services of millions of holy beings, joy unspeakable and endless, and an unrestricted liberty to communicate the most precious gifts. Conceive of such a crown, conceive of it in thy hand, thyself walking amidst the robbers of this world, and thou wilt understand the necessity of Argus-eyed watchfulness and unremitting endeavor in order to reach the gate of the celestial palace without loss of that which has been committed to thee. Perhaps the true glory of that crown is yet somewhat latent; its splendor in this atmosphere of sin is not so great as that of many a tinsel crown that men wear; and to the unanointed eye of sense there is nothing about it to tell of the amazing mysteries that are locked up in it. But has not thine eye been anointed? Dost thou not discern the sacred signature of God upon it? And has not a divine refiner and purifier of silver given thee demonstration that all the regalia of earth's kings and emperors could not purchase the tiniest jewel that sparkles in that crown which the Lord hath given thee to wear in the day of his Son's espousals and for ever more?

Hold fast that which thou hast of love, faith, patience, prayerfulness, humility, knowledge, courage, perseverance. It may seem a light thing to give way to an erring momentary impulse; but understand that in that moment a bold, unscrupulous hand was stretched out to snatch away thy crown.

MARCH 31.—"To him that overcometh will I give to eat of the tree of life, which is in the midst of the paradise of God."—Revelation ii. 7.

There is not only the one transcendent prize of everlasting life held up to the assured hope of every believer; but it would seem that the Lord Jesus Christ (out of his treasury bringing forth things new and old,) holds out particular and altogether wonderful rewards to those who throw themselves into the thick of the conflict of life, and overcome where there were peculiar difficulties in the way of their overcoming. The records of the past bear their not unwilling testimony to this

They speak of Enoch and Elijah; of Moses and Ezekiel; of Elisha and Daniel; of Paul and John; of Luther and Whitefield. But we know that this earth is to be the scene of things more glorious than have yet been witnessed; the kingdoms of this world are to become the kingdom of our Lord and of his Christ; and all his enemies, the last being death, are to be made the footstool of the King of glory. Nor does it please the Lord Jesus Christ to accomplish the sublime reduction of all things to himself, otherwise than by the instrumentality of his servants; for he says expressly, "The glory which thou hast given me I have given them." It is by the branches that the vine brings forth fruit and glorifies itself. And the universal kingdom which the Son of man in the presence of the Ancient of days is represented as receiving (Daniel vii. 14) is that kingdom which (in verses 18, 22, and 27) in language most explicit, the saints of the Most High are described as taking and possessing for ever, even for ever and ever.

The paradise of God vanishes from our view in the first chapter of the Bible, and returns to our astonished gaze in the last, where the description of it is subtly and beautifully interwoven with that of the descending Jerusalem. The tree of life was a tree of whose fruit had Adam eaten, he would have lived forever; and lest he should eat thereof he was expelled. What is the life that he was not allowed to appropriate? Not surely the life of the soul, for nothing but want of faith could separate him from this. No doubt it was corporeal immortality. Had he refrained from eating the fruit of the tree of knowledge of good and evil, he would thereby have retained the life of God in his soul; and the tree of life seems to have been appointed to supply an immortalizing aliment to his body, by which it should be nourished with a life that nothing could harm, a life corresponding in exaltedness with the life of the spotless soul. This tree was a type of Christ in one of his aspects. He has brought life and immortality to light. He that overcometh and entereth upon the full fruition of spiritual life. shall eat of the tree of life, and live forever. We shall not all die.

APRIL 1.—"That he might bring us to God."—1 Peter iii. 18.

Take this text as your interpreter, and join yourself to the Lord Jesus, as he sets his face steadfastly to go up to Jerusalem. With tears he gazes on the city. He endures the contradiction of many sinners;—Pharisees, Sadducees, and Herodians. He partakes of the passover with Judas. Washes the feet of his disciples. Gives the symbols of his broken body and shed blood to a little company the hope of the world, the elect of mankind, that were about to forsake him and flee. Look at these things under the surprising light of this explanation, that he might bring you to God.

See him in the garden of Gethsemane. Approach to within a stone's throw of that awful place, and by the light of the pallid moon, notice the agony, the sweat, as it were great drops of blood, the face in the dust, the frequent cry of anguish to the Father. Measure, if you can, the frightful depth of that abyss into which the Prince of life, the Lord of glory, has been willing to descend; and as you measure, remember why all this was—namely, that he might bring you to God. See this Lamb of God led to the slaughter; follow him step by step, from tribunal to tribunal, to the cross; ask why he opened not his mouth to transfix all his enemies with a word; the answer is, that he might bring you to God. Are there not ten thousand glorious things in the word of God, the true glory of which only comes out when the light of this text is turned upon them? You see how far you were from God. Omnipotence, not merely omnipotence, but self-immolating omnipotence, had to embark in the enterprise of recovering you to God; while all the angels of heaven looked on with wonder and semi-incredulity.

Why are you brought to God? That he may have a superlative opportunity of showing that God is love, by raising you to the sublimest heights of purity and perfection.

APRIL 2.—"He giveth power to the faint."—Isaiah xl. 29.

The Bible, first and last, insists that man shall give unto God, all power, honor and glory, and distinctly recognizes his own dependence, ingloriousness and insignificance. Some foolishly gather from this that God is against man, and is jealous lest he should attain to too much dignity. But the very word of God that makes such bitter warfare on the imagined strength and goodness of man, shows us the Lord of the universe ready to bestow his treasures of strength, wisdom and righteousness upon these very defeated and spoiled children of earth, with a bounty that knows no limit. Man imagines that unless he grasp with an unrelaxing hand his rags of righteousness and his bruised reed which he calls a sceptre, he will be utterly and forever a bankrupt. But he is now a bankrupt: his treasures are counterfeit; his power is that of a disordered machine, whose wheels revolve for nothing; the fragmentary thing must just be given back to God. Faint with his losses, man then exclaims, "What have I?" And the word of God makes answer, "Thou hast power, wisdom, knowledge, salvation, heaven." He giveth power to the faint. In him are hid for thee all the treasures of wisdom and knowledge. No, the Bible is not the mere spoiler of humanity. It takes from us the dream of things, that it may give angelic realities. It comes to give, believing what it preaches, that it is more blessed to give than to receive; and when it removes aught from man, it is simply that it may make room for its gifts.

Thou hast a friend therefore, thou fainting one. There is power for thee. Dost thou like Esther faint in thy approaches to the king? See, he stretches out the sceptre of his grace that thou mayest confidently draw nigh. Dost thou faint at the thought of appropriating the merits of the Crucified One? Hearken, he speaks to another atrocious felon, of the same deep dye with thyself, saying, "This day thou shalt be with me in paradise!" Dost thou faint under some vast responsibility? Thou hast no responsibility that is not also Christ's; for he is one with thee, and says, "Without me ye can do nothing." Dost thou faint under a multitude of petty responsibilities? He says, again, "Without me ye can do nothing." Dost thou faint under a sense of thy spiritual feebleness, and inaptitude of resolution? Thou dost well to faint, and to let Christ succor thee. Be faint, and take the power that belongs to the faint. Let faith wait upon fainting.

APRIL 3.—"He shall feed his flock like a shepherd."—Isaiah xl. 11.

Who is this that spends his time with a company of poor despised sheep, seeking for them appropriate pastures, leading them beside still waters, defending them from evil beasts with his crook, carrying the lame ones in his bosom, studying all the peculiarities in the condition of each; apparently wrapped up in them, with no wisdom, no power, no resources save such as are needed for their welfare? Why! this is He that measured the waters in the hollow of his hand, meted out heaven with his span, and weighed the mountains in scales; who taketh up the isles as a very little thing; to whom the nations are counted as less than nothing and vanity. This is the Omnipotent one at whose fiat the universe sprang into existence, before whose great white throne the heaven and the earth shall flee away, and find no place.

And who are the flock that so possess his regard?

These are they that formerly refused to have a divine shepherd, and boasting in their own wisdom and power, surrendered themselves to sin, that disguised wolf, and followed him to his lair. But they were remembered by him whom they had scorned and insulted, and snatched from a frightful fate by the good shepherd, who gave his life for them and took it again that he might lead them into ever-verdant pastures.

Like a shepherd. A shepherd and his flock constitute a unity; the one is not found without the other. The interests of the flock are those of the shepherd. Their wisdom is in him. They take no thought for the morrow; he taketh it They are not anxious about nourishment or protection; he watches for their welfare. He knows them; knows their need. their ignorance, their wandering: and they know him; know his faithfulness and his all-sufficiency.

April 4.—"Blessed is the people that know the joyful sound."—Psalm lxxxix. 15.

Blessed are they to whom the gospel is proclaimed; that is, a blessing is put within their reach. But especially, essentially blessed are they who know it as glad tidings of great joy.

One land is blessed with great fruitfulness; another with great mineralogical treasures; another by its geographical situation, favorable for commerce. One nation has a liberal gov ernment; another an admirable system of education. One country has numerous and exquisite remains of ancient art; another has carried the cultivation of modern art and science to a high pitch; while another has made the most marvellous strides in manufactures. One region is blessed with magnificent rivers; another glories in its sublime mountain ranges. But neither of these nor all in combination suffice to secure the happiness of a people, or to perpetuate the prosperity of a nation. Another chapter should be added to Volney's "Ruins of Empires," telling truly why those empires passed away. The gospel has never yet prevailed in any nation. Never yet has it been cordially received by more than a very small minority of the people of a country. But in proportion as it has been received has a blessing from on high rested on the nations.

They who truly know the joyful sound, will endeavor to communicate the knowledge of it to other hearts and lands. Can you imagine a kind of music produced by invisible choristers, inaudible to all save those who have been endowed with a special sense for the perception and enjoyment of it? These walk in ecstacy, ever and anon, hearing the wondrous strains, while the unperceiving multitude pursue the sordid tenor of their way. Such strains are those of the Gospel, and they that have faith are they who have received a faculty appropriate to the reception of them. The music of the words of the Son of God is borne to them from the golden harps of the invisible ones They open the word of God, and while their unadept companion sees a dull, ineloquent page, the eye of the believer pierces the cloud-like door of the letter and detects a vista reaching to the New Jerusalem, with angels moving to and fro; exquisite melodies are wafted to his ear, and he rejoices with joy unspeakable, tasting the powers of the world to come.

APRIL 5.—"They that wait upon the Lord shall renew their strength." —Isaiah xl. 31.

It is regarded as one of the saddest facts in our condition, that the objects which interest and attract us, have no power to perpetuate their own attractiveness; and the mind obtaining what it passionately sought, and by degrees getting accustomed to its particular features of beauty, loses day by day something of its own delight in them. Fascination can get no victory that is not stolen from it again by time. And this is said to be an *inevitable*, Nemesis-like fact in our finite condition. Transport must give way to an inferior sentiment. Well for us, it is said, if, by a judicious and well-timed moderation of our desires, we sink into contentment and are satisfied with that condition of the soul, while the extravagancy of our former admiration sails away, like a painted bubble, to the skies.

We do not believe that this is a divinely-appointed element in our condition. An enemy hath done this. He wishes us to be as gods, and to lead a life of independence, and this is the paradise into which he brought us out of Eden. While we are swayed by him, while sin mingles so largely with the fabric of our earthly condition, while we are without God in the world, and seek the things of the world without reference to their connection with God, it is undoubtedly so. Beauty vanishes, and excellence by familiarity loses its power to captivate. We are taken up by hope into some cloud heaven, and have the choice perhaps of descending abruptly and disastrously, or of gliding down to earth by an imperceptible declivity.

Is there no remedy? Must the imaginative, esthetic, aspiring portion of our nature hasten to shrivel up, and leave us to sober hopes, disciplined desires, and dwarfed expectations? Not so. What we need is an object whose excellence is ever fed, ever augmented by supplies from an infinite source; whose perfections seen are only introductory to other perfections to be seen; in the contemplation of whom our admiration can never overtake the limit of the admirable, for there is no limit. We need a divine object; and having this, we need not fear to cry, "*excelsior!*" Thou shalt love the Lord thy God with all thy heart, and soul, and mind, is the first and great commandment. Delight thyself in the Lord, and he shall grant thee the desires of thy heart. They that wait upon the Lord shall renew their strength; they shall mount up with wings as eagles.

APRIL 6.—"Fight the good fight of faith."—1 Timothy vi. 12.

There is a fight that is good; a warfare that is eminently laudable. It is lamentable to see how easily men err in deciding what is worthy, what is not worthy to enlist their noblest energies. A question of unspeakable importance;—for what boots it that you undergo hardships, surmount difficulties, make the most incredible sacrifices, exhibit the most brilliant valor, or the most consummate skill, if the cause in which you have embarked be one not worthy of your energies and sufferings? The same action is sublime when performed in its appropriate path, and insignificant when thrown away upon an inadequate cause. The tales of human heroism too often merely bid us come and see how wonderfully man is endowed, and how unworthily he throws away those endowments.

What is that conflict of which we can say that from whatever point of view it is contemplated, it manifests itself to be beyond impeachment, good? The annals of mankind reveal to us but one, the conflict of faith.

A life of faith is a life of victorious warfare. The unbelievers around us are all led captive. They have no weapons for this fight, and no heart for it; they wear the badges of servitude, without shame or reluctance. We hear them say, "Our business hath paramount claims upon us;" "There is time in the future for religion;" "Heaven cannot be understood on earth;" "We must enjoy ourselves while it is day, for the night cometh;" "What harm is there in going to scenes of festivity?" "It is enough that a man be sincere;" "There are strange things in the Bible;" "It was once perhaps suited to the condition of men."—These and a thousand corresponding expressions drop from their lips and tell us too plainly, alas! that these poor persons have been smitten down by the bludgeon of the adversary, carried off to be his helpless slaves, and taught the language of his realm.

As we look over the map of the world, innumerable places claim our notice as the scene of celebrated battles. And as we look over the pages of Scripture we find these thickly dotted with the indications of great spiritual battles fought there.

We light upon the word, "One thing is needful;" and to our mind's eye two hosts present themselves, one inferior in number to the other; one fighting the good fight of faith and coming off victorious; the other sustaining a shameful defeat. "They that fear the Lord shall not want any good thing," is a citadel into which few have succeeded in entering; the whole plain around is strewed with the unbelieving dead. "Ask, and it shall be given you," is surrounded by a trench, which tens of thousands have attempted to pass, but have not been able. But we see the flag of faith waving from its topmost battlement. "Ye shall not enter," said the world, deploying its legions; "but this (we reply) is the victory which overcometh the world, even our faith."

APRIL 7.—"When the enemy shall come in like a flood, the Spirit of the Lord shall lift up a standard against him."—Isaiah lix. 19.

The position of the church in the world is like that of the low countries. Its ground is all recovered ground; dykes compass it about; and against these the mighty ocean mutters, dashes, rages, as its mood may be. The law of all waters is opposed to its existence; Pacifics, Atlantics and Antarctics, seem ever to be uttering a protest against it. Anon, they, or their representative waters, arise in strength and precipitate themselves upon it. A flood is always ready for the Church; at every moment she is threatened with a deluge that shall sweep her away. Yet she unaccountably continues to exist. She has no visible strength; no appreciable resources; and the enemy is at a loss to understand how she is enabled to keep her footing thus from generation to generation.

When the enemies of Judea invaded and overran that land in the early days of its history, it pleased the Lord to raise up by the mighty operation of his Spirit some bold deliverer, around whose banner the people rallied, and by whose wisdom, courage and faith, the land was freed from the hostile flood. So also are great periods of jeopardy and deliverance found in the history of the Christian Church. In these latter times the enemy has come into the Church like a silent and peaceable flood, intending no harm; and has crept very gently into the valleys and stolen imperceptibly up the glens, and spread itself by amiable and conciliatory advances over the plains of the Church's territory; assuming to enrich and to bless, but really involving all in one dead glassy mantle of brine. The Church is led to believe that she has no enemies; it is announced that there are scarcely any assaults made upon the dykes; but the fact is that the enemy is within, and has undertaken to constitute itself the Church.

How many and how diversified have been, of late, the doctrines inculcated in hostility to the fundamental principles of Christianity, by persons holding positions in the Church, and using the most approved language of piety. How complete is the evidence that avarice, the idolatry of this age, is diffused through the length and breadth of the Church. How quietly have we settled down into the idea that the standard of conduct given to the primitive disciples, and in each gospel embalmed in the undying words of Christ, is not a standard with which we have anything practically to do. How much is it considered a matter of course that the unlimited promises of the New Testament should be treated as curiosities of literature, and not at all as the appropriate means designated by God for perpetuating in the Church, Elijahs, Daniels and Pauls.

And the greatest evil is that all our conceptions being cast in the mould of a vitiated standard, we remain without the power of perceiving how much our standard is vitiated. If the salt have lost its savor, wherewith shall it be salted? Our hope is with him who hath promised to lift up a standard in the critical hour, and who will lift up on some conspicuous and inviolable summit, whither the people may flee from the rising deluge of iniquity, and find themselves safe beneath the banner of God. If foremost men are needed, it is easy for the great Head of the Church to raise them up. If the hearts of princes are in his hand to turn them as he will, how much more the hearts of those who are avowedly his own. He will revive his work. In the midst of wrath he will remember mercy.

APRIL 8.—"Blessed is the man that trusteth in the Lord."—Jeremiah xvii. 7.

We should greatly err if we understood this word "blessed" as teaching that the man who trusteth in God will pursue a path of tranquil enjoyment and exemption from sorrow. He is blessed because he is enabled to pursue the path, the only path, that leadeth unto everlasting life. Because the favor of God is his. Because Christ forsaketh him never. Because the Spirit of God dwells in him. Because he has grace to seek the welfare of his fellow-men. And he is blessed because of the peculiar nature of his sufferings. His tears are not as others' tears. His agony is not the agony of impious men. His despair even has a dignity and sacredness about it.

Jeremiah was a man that trusted in God. But it is evident from the sublime bursts of misery occurring in his prophecies, that he was permitted to sound the depths of human woe. It was his faith in God that separated him from all his countrymen, deprived him of their sympathies, made him a stranger to their joys, and compelled him to drink the cup of sorrow which they should have drunk. He trusted in God, and therefore he could not hide from them that God was about to pour upon them the vials of destruction, and to surrender them into the hands of a heathen king. They listened with amazement to words that seemed to them nothing less than blasphemy, and denounced him as the enemy of his country, a traitor to the hallowed and God-defended interests of Judea. When, in the freshness of youth, he received his prophetical commission from the Lord, it was distinctly intimated to him that "all should fight against him," the kings, the priests, the people, the bad and the good, not excepting even the God-fearing and devout. He was a man ever spoken against; and those that could agree upon no other topic, cordially harmonized upon the one subject of the baseness and treachery of Jeremiah. Other reputed prophets might be true or might be false; but that Jeremiah was a false prophet was something not to be questioned. And it did not please the Lord to give unto his servant that stern indifference that would have lifted him above the reach of these cruel shafts. No, he left him to the native sensitiveness and keen susceptibility to injury that characterized him. His was a nature of exquisite poetic sensibility; and many a piercing cry of anguish escapes him as he meets, remembers and broods upon the opprobrious looks and words addressed to him. At times he loathes his very existence, and abhors the day that gave him birth. "Woe is me, my mother, that thou hast borne me a man of strife and a man of contention to the whole earth."

Is our faith in the goodness of God staggered by the discovery of what he permitted this his chosen servant to suffer? Are we at a loss how to reconcile this inexorable rigor, with the many declarations of the divine pitifulness? Or, on the other hand, do we decide that the prophet's faith must have failed him in those hours of bitterness, and that a deeper-reaching glance into the future would have saved his susceptible soul those fearful shocks? No, faith has no alliance with stoicism. It does not make us ignore present things. Faith goes beyond sense and shows us actualities that cannot otherwise be discerned; but it does not set aside sense, or separate our soul from the body that is in the world.—And what becomes of the divine compassion? Why, Jeremiah the sufferer, himself bears unequivocal testimony to the goodness of God. It is he that teaches us to say, "Blessed is the man that trusteth in thee."

At long intervals God calls a Job, a Jeremiah to the experience of their aggravated sorrows: but he supports them; and their triumphant faith animates the drooping faith of thousands who are called to tread inferior paths of sorrow. Honor to Jeremiah, who notwithstanding all his excruciation of soul, hath left us this testimony, "Blessed is the man that trusteth in thee!" What believer will refuse to take up the refrain?

APRIL 9.—"**Heal me, O Lord, and I shall be healed.**"—**Jeremiah xvii. 14.**

For the devices of man only increase my malady. The utmost they can do is to conceal a plague-spot here and a plague-spot there; but concealment is not abatement. What is my pride the better for all their prescriptions? What have they done for my self-will? For my unbelief, slothfulness, irritability, prayerlessness, impulsiveness? I come to thee, O Lord. He that created me, and whose creation I have spent my days in marring, can alone restore to me his image, and make me to walk in the health of heaven. Heal my heart, my understanding, my memory, my desires, my imagination, my hopes, my fears, my body, my speech, my looks, my acts. I am in a condition that renders me the prey of suffering in every form. All my faculties torment me. My words come back upon me, and pierce me like daggers. My memory is continually fetching some coal of fire to me. My desires carry me into paths where venomous serpents lie in wait. My imagination still beguiles me with the idea that it is my royal friend, and taking me by the hand to lead me to some canopied and luxurious seat, presently lets it go and with derision sees me sink into some black abyss. Hope sits enthroned as it were a delegated angel; but a life-long and frightful experience leaves me unable to doubt the fact that a legion of tormenting spirits are the ministers of this still-smiling enemy. Many endowments of my nature—which, were I not a moral wreck, a spiritual leper, would have each of them with its own particular key given me the freedom of a heaven all its own—in this my corrupt condition show themselves each provided with a key to a place of torment all its own. So that the properties which seemed to have most of glory and of paradise still hanging about them, and which therefore inspired me with the most undoubting reliance, are the very properties which have most excoriated my soul and aggravated my malady. But heal thou me and I shall be healed. Release me from my own perverted will, my rash desires, my reckless imagination. If thou wilt thou canst, and there is evidence of thy willingness.

April 10.—"Thou hast destroyed thyself; but in me is thy help."—Hosea xiii. 9.

God hath said, "Thou shalt not kill." But thou hast done more than this. Imagine thyself in the presence of some pure and spotless inhabitant of heaven, clad in perfections that enable him to smile at any difficulty however gigantic, and resplendent with the glory of God. Imagine thyself assailing him in his purity, wisdom, love, power, and glory; and stripping him of all his perfections one after another, and finally precipitating him to earth, a poor depraved sensual rebel. Cease now to imagine; and recognize the stern reality of this description. Thou hast done it; thou hast wrought this destruction; and upon whom? Upon thyself. Thou hast destroyed thyself. But for thy sin, thou wouldst have been that bright celestial being.

Raise thyself now anew to that pitch of purity and excellence. Regain paradise. Reinstate thyself among those who walk in the light of the enthroned Creator. Get thyself enveloped with an atmosphere that knows no taint of sin. Cast all thy sins into a bottomless abyss, and roll an everlasting stone upon them; and decorate thyself with the virtues of Gabriel, the seraphic energies of Raphael! Thou canst not do it; the very thought savors of madness. But it may be done. From heaven thou didst bring down in frightful ruin one of God's noblest works. The Son of God has come to earth for the purpose of redeeming this ruined humanity, and raising it to a higher, safer, more blessed pitch of dignity than that from which it fell. "In me is thy help," saith the Lord.

April 11.—"The Lord is good unto them that wait for him."—Lamentations iii. 25.

This modest text is supported by a bolder and more eloquent one in Isaiah. "Men have not heard, nor perceived by the ear, neither hath the eye seen, O God, beside thee, what he hath prepared for him that waiteth for him."* Those that waited for the Messiah, and at length beheld him, found the promise of these texts verified in their experience.

But we have not in this dispensation bid farewell to the attitude of waiting. The great and precious things bestowed upon us, do not hinder our aspirations after more transcending things to come. Faith wrestles. Faith also waits. Some have faith to wrestle; but not to wait.

This waiting implies an unconquerable conviction that the manifestations of goodness which we have asked of God, he will grant in some more fitting time than the present, and after full proof of our faith. It is immensely difficult for faith to endure, if the season be protracted. For day after day comes and goes, saying, as it goes, "You see the folly of your expectation. God has denied your request for some sufficient reason. Your expectation is vain." The providence of God

* Isaiah lxiv. 4.

seems to use similar language, declaring with a thousand voices, that your faith is erroneous and vain. By the law of your nature you pass through multitudinous moods whose differences of light and shade make things look very differently, and if faith pass serenely through them all, it is a wonder of wonders. But the exercise of faith tends also to perfect it; and the repeated, deliberate, prayerful, re-examination of the foundation laid for your future edifice, leaves at length the soul as firmly persuaded of the expected, as it is of the present. Nor while it seeks the future is it impatient with the present, but cheerfully intelligent of whatever there is of good around.

APRIL 12.—"The Lord is my portion, saith my soul."—Lam. iii. 24.

Poor man, says the world. But no, says the believer; he is to be pitied who boasts of any other portion than this. If the Lord be not thy portion, will any portion that thou hast continue? Let it be power like that of Napoleon, wisdom like that of Socrates; fame like that of Bacon, imagination like that of Scott, wealth like that of the Bourbons; let it be beauty, or valor, or wit, or industry; let it be troops of friends, or one most loving heart; let it be what it may, it is a contemptible portion, if it be thine all.

He that becomes a follower of Christ, declares that the Lord is his portion. He counts all but loss for the excellency of the knowledge of him. And not only does his soul say it; his life, his daily life, must say it; must testify that he has forsaken all for Christ. How singular that, after all the glimpses of his boundless wealth, and power, and majesty, granted by Christ to the sons of men when on the earth, he should find so few willing to take up with him for a portion. It was the merest trifle for him to spread a table for five thousand men, besides women and children; with but a word he loaded several boats full of large fishes; he raised the dead; all power in heaven and in earth was manifestly his. We see plainly that all other portions must at last revert to him, and he will give them to whom he will. But independently of all material gifts, there is that in his character which makes him, him alone, able to satisfy the soul throughout eternity.

APRIL 13.—"Then shall we know, if we follow on to know the Lord."—Hosea vi. 2.

Is it at all unreasonable to suppose that the contemplation of God will yield us greater, more precious results than the consideration of anything or of everything in this world that he has made? You are wrapt up in the study of mineralogy, or botany, or conchology; and have no time to spare for the cultivation of your acquaintance with God. The sight of a little shell has wonderful power to awaken all your faculties: and you have no rest till you have ascertained its characteristics, traced and counted the lines upon it, and determined its specific relations; but an invitation to come and contemplate God leaves you listless and apathetic. You delight in archæological researches, and with your whole soul embark in the study of certain antiquities, with a view to determine at what period, and by whom they were produced; yet are you never for a moment tormented by the desire to increase your knowledge of God. You, my friend, have a great dread of being found imperfectly acquainted with a certain literature, and think nothing of devoting whole nights to the acquisition of it; but your conscience is visited by no painful sense of your defective knowledge of him from whom is every good gift.

Once we too were thus. If a man had anything curious to tell us concerning the most distant star that twinkles in the firmament, we waited for his words with eagerness; but no solicitude to improve our acquaintance with the Divine Disposer of all, ever agitated our soul.

But now we grasp at this assurance: "Then shall we know;" and at the similar asseveration of Paul: "Then shall I know, even as also I am known." And the joy with which we hail this prospect is a clear evidence that we have passed out of the region of our former ignorance, and that we know God. Indifference and ignorance are here indissolubly linked, as also are knowledge and thirst for knowledge.

Then shall we know, if we follow on to know the Lord. The Lord has brought us into the pathway of the knowledge of him, and bids us pursue that path through all its strange meanderings until it opens out upon the plain where God's throne is. Our life is a following on to know the Lord. We marvel at some of the experiences through which we are called to pass: but afterwards we see that they afforded us some new knowledge of our Lord. Our path suddenly disappeared in some hideous cavern where we seemed to hear the roaring of wild beasts; and we could not at all conceive what benefit would result from our entering; but we entered; and when by a favoring passage we emerged from that obscurity and danger, we felt that we had obtained some new and valuable insight into the divine character. Again, our path shot right down into the impenetrable darkness of some deep pit; it was some time before our eyes got accustomed to that darkness; then we discovered a little door, and soon found ourselves in a gallery of hidden treasures, several of which we gathered and still retain. Pursuing thus the knowledge of God we found ourselves like Joseph in Egypt, alone in the midst of a nation that knew not God; and found that there was something here to be learned concerning the divine perfections that could not elsewhere be learned.* We have not then to wait for some future brighter opportunity; but by improvement of the present are to build for ourselves a bridge to that future.

* Referring to India, where these Meditations were written.—A.

APRIL 14.—"When I sit in darkness, the Lord shall be a light unto me."—Micah vii. 8.

He will, thou prophet of the living God! More happy art thou in this thy strong and well-warranted persuasion than if a tiara of the most effulgent diamonds were set upon thy brow, to light up the chamber of thy darkness. Didst thou always know this? Couldst thou from the beginning look thus serenely along the paths of life, conscious that betide whatever might, thou shouldst enjoy the manifested presence of thy God?

Perhaps not. Perhaps there was a period in thy life when thou hadst indeed a strong conviction of the incomparable desirableness of such an assurance, and hadst a belief in its attainableness, but couldst not possess thyself of the privilege. Withont this distinct perception of a present God, thy Saviour, Friend, and Guide, life seemed an odious blank. For this thou wert willing to sacrifice all things, and deem thyself an infinite gainer by the exchange. But how enter this hidden life? By faith, was the answer. But how believe? Oh how immense this difficulty seemed to one accustomed to the death-state of the soul, to unbelief, to the insane vision that perceives everything save Him by whom all things subsist. But he that had given thee so much faith as to perceive the all-surpassing blessedness of a life in which God is throughout consciously intermingled, forsook thee not; and soon enabled thee to open wide the eye of faith, and behold Him gloriously nigh, overpoweringly manifest; enabled thee to take into thy very soul his indestructible promise to abide with thee as thy Helper, Lover, and Satisfier, for ever.

When God gives faith, he gives the opportunity of proving it. He loves the sweet expression of it in confidential words; loves still better the exhibition of it in indubitable acts. "Thou shalt sit in darkness," he says to his trusting servant. But first he leads the believer along some flowery walk, and accustoms him to a high measure of spiritual prosperity. Then suddenly an unexpected tempest gathers about him, and he finds himself in deepest, strangest night. Darkness is come; but it is different in some of its elements from what the believer had contemplated in the day of his declared faith. Yes, designedly different. It was needful that his darkness should be something never anticipated, in order that his faith might have its full proof. The darkness seems to say, "God is not in me, I am sent in wrath. Thy faith is presumption. I am come to banish from thee the promises which thou hast hitherto delighted in—to dispel the delusive idea of God thy Comforter. Despair is the only thing that harmonizes with me." The shadow thus speaks and frowns. But faith comes nobly out of this conflict. It lets not go its talisman. It seizes the word of God with a compulsory grasp. Immediately the believer is compassed about with light, and looks with an air of complacent triumph at the baffled shadow.

April 15.—"Men ought always to pray and not to faint."—Luke xviii. 1.

The context informs us what that prayer is in which we ought not to allow ourselves to faint. The prayer is that God would be pleased to judge between his people and the world. The world denies the claim of the righteous to be considered the children of God. The one great need of the Church is, that God should bear testimony unto the word of his grace, and rebuke the nations with a voice they can but hear, saying, "Touch not my anointed, and do my prophets no harm." The Lord Jesus taught us what to ask for, when he said to the Father, "That the world may know that thou hast sent me and hast loved my disciples as thou hast loved me." The revelation of God in his relation to believers, by their sanctification, by the perfection of his image in them, by the gifts and graces of his Holy Spirit, by his providence, and by unprecedented methods reserved to be the special glory of the latter days—is what we ask. Is this a thing to stop asking? Does the sick man give over seeking for health, because his sickness is protracted? Or does the hungry man desist from his search for food, when it is not soon found? No, for he well knows that if he fail of obtaining food, he fails of all. This benefit withdrawn, all others are withdrawn. Well therefore may we continue in prayer, for what we ask is indispensable.

This continuing in prayer is a singularly profitable exercise. When we cry to God and receive no answer, and still continue in supplication, not wavering, we find our minds running with a surprising vigilance through the pages of Scripture, snatching up a word of help here and another there. We become most rapidly intelligent of its precious contents. Our views of God expand; his character, his government, his purposes, present themselves to us with a definiteness that they never had before in our perceptions. Our knowledge of ourselves in like manner advances in an equally accelerated ratio. And all this tends to the increase of faith. The very discovery of our own unworthiness tends, at such a time, to make us rest more confidently on the righteous Advocate. We get a hundred preparatory blessings, and then at last we get the blessing sought. Meantime our conceptions of that blessing have been greatly elevated. If at first it ranked in our estimation as a thousand, it now ranks as millions. We have looked at it in the future, and seen it undergo many transfigurations. We were consoled in the hour of our disappointed faith, by seeing the prize put on superior beauty, and show itself more worth pursuing than we had previously believed. Imagine a vase with your name upon it, fast by the throne of God. As you prayed, your heavenly Father dropped ever and anon a gift brighter than your best conception into that vessel. Meanwhile he sought among the hours of your future life for one in which the bestowal of this accumulating wealth would be largest in results; and marked that hour also on the vase. And while you thought yourself poor, angels looked with admiration on your treasure in heaven.

April 16.—" The beloved of the Lord."—Deuteronomy xxxiii. 12.

Who is this beloved of the Lord? It is one who believes n the love that God has toward him. We have not to bring about the love of God towards us; but to recognize that love. Peter had a great idea of his own love to Christ; " though all men forsake thee, yet will I not forsake thee;" but John was content to speak of himself as the beloved of the Lord. Herein is love, not that we loved God, but that he loved us. His love to us is as our faith in his love, and in our own unworthiness. " O Daniel, greatly beloved," said the angel to that man of God; and oftentimes a similar declaration runs down to us from the skies. Surely facts speak as loudly as words; how many facts can you at this moment point to, each and all declaring that you are the beloved of the Lord.

Do you still hesitate to class yourself as a third with Daniel and John? Tell me, is there any greater expression of the love of God, than was given in the surrender of his Son to Gethsemane, Gabbatha, and Calvary? Did Daniel or John ever receive any more affecting love-token than this? Be only bold enough to know the love that was expressed when Christ tasted death for you, and you may without hesitation sit down beneath the same tree with Daniel and John, and expect them to listen while you speak of the crucified one.

But ever remember that you cannot begin to estimate the love of Calvary, till you have given up all notions of your own goodness. It makes an immense difference in estimating God's love, whether that love was bestowed on an utterly vile and repulsive sinner, or upon an amiable being, adorned with many graces, and naturally attractive. If you judge yourself to be this last, then you can never know anything about the love set forth in the gospel; and you will do well to avoid the society of Daniel and John. Divine love *made* them amiable and attractive; not found them so.

April 17.—"Come now and let us reason together, saith the Lord."—Isaiah i. 18.

"Let there be an understanding between us. Let us talk over the points of difference between us, and see if we cannot come to a settlement. If you have any fault to find with me, state it. If I am not what you would have me be, put your objection into words. Be explicit. You alienate yourself from me, shun my paths, avoid all approaches to communion with me, shut up my word, look coldly on my people, and if you can possibly get anything else to think of, no matter how contemptible it be, you will not give a thought to me or to my solicitations. Again I say, be explicit, be honest. I will not object to any statement of your views, so that they be made in a spirit of frankness, and with a willingness to be enlightened. Come and let us reason together. Let us go by ourselves, where there may be no curiosity of man to interfere with the fullest intercommunication."

The Lord invites me to a conference with himself. Why should I not go? Why should I not state to God himself my difficulties. Is it right, is it honest, to be entertaining this lukewarmness, this aversion, and not be willing to have the grounds of it clearly defined? O my soul, come to an understanding with thy God. The main difficulty with thee is a consciousness that after all the guilt will be found with thee, and not a particle of blame attach to God. But observe, my soul, how admirably this difficulty is met by his generous proposal. My sins are as scarlet, but he hastens to say that they shall be as white as snow. He meets me with a robe of justification, and royally adorns me at the very threshold of his house; so that I need not to dread the humiliating contrast of my rags with that resplendent audience-chamber. And if he so hasten to justify me, the most unholy of beings, shall I not be willing to justify him, the holiest and best? Yes, Lord, let me reason with thee; for where thou mightest condemn, there thou dost vouchsafe the most surprising promises, the most transporting tokens of love.

APRIL 18.—"O God, thou art my God."—Psalm lxiii. 1.

Mine! All mine! All the revelation of thee in the Bible is the revelation of my God. Thy wisdom is all for me. So is thy power. So is thy goodness. So is thy truth, thy purity, thy justice; thy time is for me, thy eternity for me; thy works for me. Thou sittest on the throne of the universe for me; pervadest all space for me; arrangest all thy plans for me.

Many millions of millions of miles away, but a star to thine eyes, is a sun huge in mass, dazzling in splendor, weighty in attraction, beneficent in function. Around it, in orbit succeeding orbit, with velocities, densities, bulks, revolutions, times, beautifully harmonized, are numerous planets, each having its oceans and continents, its forests, its animals, its intelligent creation. Shall God take thought for thee, in that distant group of worlds? Can he not let go the thought of thee, as he enters that distant system and directs its sublime movements? No, he cannot let go the thought of thee. That sun is commissioned not only to give light to those revolving worlds, but ever, without a moment's intermission, to send down to thee a ray of light expressive of his unforgetting love. It hangs above thee by day, hindered by other light from reaching thee; but no sooner does night open a door for it, than it rushes to the spot where thou art. All the night long it is there; thou hast but to look, and it meets thy glance. What meets thy glance? Yon distant sun, thousands of times the size of this earth. The ray that meets thy eye is all for thee; it is thine own particular token that the omnipresent God, in whatsoever part of the universe he may be displaying his perfections, cannot for an instant be unmindful of the relation existing between him and thee.

This in nature. How much more in grace. And we learn these things first in grace.

APRIL 19.—"The Lord lifteth up the meek."—Psalm cxlvii. 6.

The meek are they who have consented to receive the knowledge of themselves. Self-detection has led to self-spoliation. Their wardrobe has turned out to be a pirate's chest. The more richly they went arrayed, the more they exposed their own dishonor. They gladly now sink down to their proper level, and find no place too low for them. Perhaps they occasionally shrink back from some deeper humiliation. But the Spirit of God and his providence convince them, and they take that step too. They lose at length their reluctance, and are content to be last of all and servant of all.

Oh! how few, how rare, are those meek ones! Am I one of them, O Lord? Am I quite content to be overlooked in the day when thou distributest honors on the earth? Am I willing to be despised by all, and made of no account? Is my chief ambition to be useful, eminently but not ostensibly useful? And if I get this spirit one day, does it abide with me? Do I not find myself coming into new circumstances where my mean estate troubles me? And through some insidious suggestion does there arise impatience of God's depressing providence? Thou that art meek and lowly of heart, teach me to be meek, give me a meekness that shall pass through every ordeal.

The meek shall be lifted up; they shall be exalted very high. But in their utmost exaltation they will lose nothing of their meekness. In the highest or in the lowest situation, they are at home, they are blessed. The idea of their own merit has been ground out of them by the wheel of God's government; and their whole being is pervaded and beatified by God's love.

April 20.—"He shall never suffer the righteous to be moved."—Psalm lv. 22.

Some one may say: "He will never allow *the righteous* to fall away; but what right have I to regard myself as righteous? Of what avail is this promise to me?"

Well, it is of none, if thou art not righteous. In that case, the wrath of God abideth on thee; there are no promises for thee. But are there no promises for such as hunger and thirst after righteousness? Yes, for they are righteous. The Publican went down to his house, justified rather than the Pharisee. To look unto the righteousness of Christ, is the righteousness of sinful man. The measure in which a man renounces the notion of his own righteousness, is generally the measure according to which God estimates him as righteous. Our text corresponds with the words: "My sheep shall never perish, neither shall any be able to pluck them out of my hand."

Others say: "We make no pretensions to piety, but we are righteous, and none the less so that we have the boldness to declare ourselves what we are."

Let us see. You daily receive at your board a poor creature who, without your bounty, would be a miserable beggar, tottering to an obscure grave. You spread for him an excellent banquet, and that as often as he has appetite. Yet he never takes the slightest notice of you, never joins in any laudations of your name, turns the subject of conversation when you are mentioned. You have authorized him to go daily to your treasurer, and receive whatever he needs for his daily expenses, and even for his prospective expenditure; yet he never admits that he is indebted to you for the money, and is just as ready to bestow it on your enemies as on your friends. He lives in your house; sleeps upon your couch; receives raiment from your wardrobe; is made glad by your wine; regaled by the perfume of your flowers; entertained by your music; conveyed in your carriages; instructed by your teachers; aided by your wisdom; and upheld by your strength. Yet never is he found rendering you any due respect, or troubling himself to know what is your will. In a thousand things he violates your commands. But in his transactions with his fellow-servants, he is particular not to defraud them. Shoul he indeed learn from thee what his duties to them are, he would discover that he comes exceedingly short even in these. But be it so. He is very careful to conduct himself in such a manner towards them as to be regarded as an honest man. Ten thousand mercies from thee leave him as indifferent to thy will and pleasure as ever he was; yet the least benefit from his fellow awakens in him gratitude and a desire to requite the favor.—Shall such a man be counted righteous? Does not the moral sense that reveals itself in his communications with his fellow-men, serve only the more signally to condemn him? He, and such as he, are unrighteous; and the unrighteous shall not inherit the kingdom of God.

APRIL 21.—"Let not your heart be troubled."—John xiv. 1.

If these words were appropriate at the time when they were spoken, then can we hardly conceive of a situation in which the people of God may be placed, in which these words would be inappropriate. If at that time the disciples were not to be troubled, then tell me, pray, what is the hour, what the emergency, when it is fitting that their hearts should be troubled?

Says one, "My child is dead; my beloved one. For years my predominant solicitude had been to make all things work together for the beautifying of her life. All my plans, my labors, my hopes, my prayers even, have had largely a reference to her happiness. My present joys were in some degree constituted by the thought of what she would be in days to come. And now she is suddenly gone—in a whirlwind of suffering—under circumstances the most heart-rending. The world is for me emptied, in a single hour."

But one of those who sat at table with Jesus might thus reply: "We were with the Messiah for whom we had left father and mother, wife and children. We had staked all our hopes upon him. By following him we had brought upon us the enmity of mankind; and by his departure we were to be exposed to the full blast of that enmity. We had made up our minds that he was the Lord of Life, and that all dignities of heaven or earth were in his gift, and that of the increase of his dominion there should be no end, and that he would presently prepare for us twelve thrones corresponding to the twelve tribes of the children of Israel. And now we were told, and that by himself, that he was to be taken away; taken violently away by the hands of sinners; subjected to all manner of outrages; be, as it were, denounced from heaven, God not interposing for his deliverance; and to die a most ignominious and barbarous death. And yet we were bidden not to let our hearts be troubled. The sun was to be as sackcloth, and the moon as blood; all the powers of heaven were to be shaken; yet we were to remain peaceful and serene."

One may say, "I could have met with equanimity all the common woes of life; but my good name, which has never been reproached, is now covered with opprobrium." The apostles may answer: "This was what was about to happen to us. We were to be universally regarded as the followers of a manifest impostor, preachers of blasphemy, enemies of all righteousness· yet we were told not to let our hearts be troubled."

Another speaks, and says: "These things may be endured by the grace of God. But where there is no manifestation of God to the soul, when spiritual darkness has set in upon us, can we be otherwise than troubled?" The apostles answer: "What darkness was comparable to ours? When Christ was crucified, it seemed that God was saying from heaven unto us, 'I know you not.' Depart from me, ye cursed, was what his providence appeared to say, in a language that all could understand. Yet the Lord Jesus, knowing all things that should happen, said unto us, *let not your hearts be troubled.*"

April 22.—"Bring forth, therefore, fruits meet for repentance."—Matthew iii. 8

A mighty angel stands in heaven upon a height at the foot of which you dwell unconsciously; and he bears aloft in his hands a stone, mountainous in size, which he is prepared to hurl upon you. But another mighty one says: Stay; for he repents, and will now bring forth fruits in evidence thereof. Then the company of the just made perfect, bend their eager gaze upon you to discern this evidence; and the stone descends not, though it hangs above you. Well may you therefore give heed to this admonition, and make haste to bring forth fruits.

A profession of religion is a solemn and open condemnation of and shrinking from our past life. It is a profession of repentance, of a changed mind relatively to sin and to unrighteousness. Christ is exalted to give repentance. He saves men from their sins by inspiring them with a hatred of their sins, and by giving them a heart to pursue an opposite path. For one that has made such a profession, to trifle with sin, to renew communications with his old sins, is a most dangerous thing. When he indulges in a forbidden thing, he calls back the ten thousand similar indulgences belonging to his past life.

Seeing him turn to Christ, these sins had begun to flee from him discomfited; but a single recommission arrests them, and they exclaim, "he yet belongs to us." The ten thousand talents had been forgiven the steward who professed repentance; but a single act that seemed to show his repentance unsound brought the whole of the huge debt back upon him.

Oh, my heart, is there not here instruction for thee? Is it not well for thee to entertain the idea that repentance is an indispensable barrier to keep thee from the tremendous claims of thy past sins? When a feeling of pride surges within thee, remember that the allowing of it will be like a standard lifted up for all thy old sins of pride, a fearful host, to rally round. Thy old sins, all of them, with all their power to alarm, to condemn, to destroy, are buried for thee, deep and safe; but the stone that covers them is sealed by the evidences of thy change of heart; and if at any time, something like the old heart is seen in thee, immediately the stone begins to heave, and the buried sins cry out, "We are unjustly here. He bringeth not forth fruits meet for repentance."

April 23.—"Lord, lift thou up upon us the light of thy countenance." —Psalm iv. 6.

Give us the tokens of thy favor, the expressions of thy grace, the revelation of thy glory. Acknowledge us as thy sons and daughters, privileged ones, having access to thine audience-chamber, and permitted to behold the majesty and kindness that to others are veiled. Let the light of thy loving glance descend into our soul. A day is coming when thy glory shall be flashed abroad through all the heavens, and when it shall fall like one immense sheet of lightning upon the nations. But what the world cannot now behold, let us behold. Though the rising of the Sun of Righteousness, in full-orbed glory, be not yet, let at least the day-star arise in our hearts.

It is not in the hour of worldly prosperity that we are best able to behold the light of God's countenance in its most transporting manifestations. The benefits that God bestows equally upon the just and upon the unjust, upon his children and his enemies, are not those that most favor our perception of the light of God's countenance. The Spirit of glory and of God resteth especially on those who are reproached for the name of Christ. Stephen, when encompassed by his numerous enemies, saw heaven opened, and the Son of Man standing at the right hand of the glory of God. Sometimes the revelation of the glory is vouchsafed in the midst of the trial; (call to mind several instances of this in the word of God;)—sometimes to prepare the believer for fiery trials; witness Isaiah, Ezekiel;—sometimes after the enduring of the trials; witness Job, Simeon, and others.

Is there not something held out to thee in this sentence, that looms far higher than any conception that thou hast ventured to form of the readiness of God to reveal himself to the friends of Jesus, and of his power to enrapture the soul by a glance that faith discerns? If there be anything soul-gladdening in the light of a created countenance, what exalted ideas may we not form of the incomparable delights that shall descend into the soul when God, the Creator, the Redeemer, the Sanctifier, fixes on us his unrestricted glance of love.

Let us utter this prayer with all intensity of desire and strength of expectation. Let our life utter it. Men go down into deep wells that they may see a star. a mere star; let us not shrink from any position to which the angels of divine providence may beckon us, and from which we are likely to behold more gloriously the revelation of the countenance of our God.

APRIL 24.—"From him cometh my salvation."—Psalm lxii. 1.

From *whom?* From him whose commandments I have so flagrantly violated, and whose authority I have set at nought.

From him whose countless benefits I have clutched without noticing the hand that bestowed them. From the thrice-holy One at whose reproof the pillars of heaven tremble and are astonished; and by whose command the fallen angels are kept under the chains of darkness. Perdition has overtaken myriads of beings who went not so far in the contempt of God, as I did; yet salvation cometh to me from him. All his perfections, the stability of his government, the interests of his holy universe, seem to require the outpouring of his fiercest wrath upon my head; yet from him cometh my salvation.

From him it *cometh.* Every day, every hour, it cometh to me; by one agency, and by another; now in this manner, now in that. It cometh to me in his word; in the answers to prayer; in the examples of good men; in reverses and humiliations; and in the various providences that help me to see the loathsomeness of sin. It comes to me in the Holy Spirit, and in new views of the all-worthiness of Christ. And what has not yet reached me is on its way to me. By faith I rejoice in experiences to come; in deliverance from all sin and from all corruption; in perfection, moral, intellectual, and physical.

My salvation. I know more evil of myself, than I can positively know of another. When I take some of the pictures of my past life, and thrust them into the purity of heaven, the whole creation seems to suffer violence, to groan and shudder at the unendurable contrast. Shall this bosom that has been the seat of affections so dishonorable, be interpenetrated with the very love of God, love to all that are the fitting objects of love, love ineffable and immaculate?

My *salvation.* The Lord Jesus Christ, my Saviour, came to earth to make an atonement, proclaim his gospel, establish his church, pour out his Spirit. This was the Alpha of my salvation. I look for him now from heaven, in glory, to complete in me his wondrous work, and present me faultless, transfigured, angelic, before his Father's throne. This will be the Omega.

APRIL 25.—"Forget not all his benefits."—Psalm ciii. 2.

The meaning is, forget not any, remember all. The right recollection of a benefit is all but equal to a new benefit. As God is the same, as the expressions of his goodness are expressions of eternal goodness, the recollection of a past benefit may well be cherished since it is in a certain sense not past but present. Each token of love let down by God into my life, projects itself forward indefinitely, and accompanies me on an undying mission, to declare that God and I are friends through the Lord Jesus Christ. The domain of faith extends not only over the present and the future, but over the past also. It is faith that keeps snatching the past kindnesses of God from the sea of oblivion.

The gifts of God are not bestowed upon believers merely to relieve a want, or to meet a capacity for enjoyment. They are not merely bestowed for the good that is in them but to reveal something in the disposition of the giver. They are epistles telling of his love, wisdom, and power. Now it is evident that a past benefit remembered, must be about as valid for this blessed purpose as a present benefit. God is bound over to goodness by his past charities, if faith remembers them.

How odious is it not to remember benefits. The rich man whose treasures are greater than he can compute, should not treat with disdain a trifling present, if it express the good will of a poor man. Nevertheless the rich do often exhibit such disdain, especially in the form of forgetfulness. Benefits from those whose kindness we value, we presume not to forget. But is God a being so low in the scale, that gifts from him are grasped only for their own sake, and the giver immediately forgotten? Do you like that your own presents to another should be forgotten? No, not the least of them. It galls you exceedingly if one out of ten benefits should pass from the recollection of your beneficiary.

But how remember all these benefits? Those of a single

day exceed in number the hairs of the head. Well, let there be a readiness to remember them. Let faith look into the past for them. Let them not be slighted.

We are not always able to see at the time the true meaning of the benefit. The length and breadth of the divine goodness does not come out, until some time has elapsed, and we are able to look back upon it from some vantage point in the future. These past benefits are like books in our library that we suppose we have read; but we take them down some day, and are astonished at the wonderful things, before unrecognized, that present themselves to our improved perception.

April 26.—" The riches of his grace."—Ephesians i. 7.

Your idea of riches, does it run most naturally in this direction? Perhaps you are blessed (as men say) with worldly goods. Your wealth enables you to surround yourself with many beautiful and tasteful articles that some people might call objects of luxury; to live in a certain style; to associate with a certain class to which you think you belong in a peculiar sense. But, these are not your only riches. You are enabled to approach God by faith in Christ the mediator, morning and evening, to cast your care on him, commit yourself to his guidance, rejoice in his goodness, meditate in his word, and occupy yourself with elevating thoughts of the inheritance incorruptible reserved in heaven for you. Of these two portions, the worldly and the heavenly, which is dearest to you? You answer: "The heavenly of course. The favor of God, that is life. The love of Christ, this is true wealth. It pleases God to adorn my earthly path, by the gift of so much wealth as surrounds me and mine with things that a refined taste must prize; but my heart, while it accepts them with thankfulness, cleaves not to them."

The answer appears unexceptionable; perhaps is so. But

is it not a conceivable thing that God has given you of the riches of earth, to test the force of your attachment to the heavenly treasure? Are you not looking at things rather from the modern point of view than from the apostolic and scriptural? Examine yourself. Would it be a very disastrous thing to you to have to come down and associate with Christians of a humble order, as one of them? Do you grasp your worldly substance with much less tenacity than the heavenly? Do losses of the inferior kind seem to you every way inferior? Does Christian affection, at all times and under all circumstances, seem to you of greater price than the friendship of the worldly members of that society to which you fancy you inherently belong? Oh, be honest!

APRIL 27.—"**Learn of me; for I am meek and lowly in heart.**"—Matthew xi. 29.

In telling us this of himself, our Lord does not profess to tell us anything new, but simply to refer to a well-known fact. Everything in his life declared that he was meek and lowly of heart. Power, wisdom, generosity, love—these things were not more largely revealed in his life, than were his meekness and lowliness of heart. For instance, in the choice of a position. He entered one of the lowest grades of society. He had intercourse indeed with men of all ranks; but he was always a man of the people. His intimate companions, his brethren, those among whom was his home, were fishermen, carpenters, tax-gatherers. The rich invited him to their tables sometimes, but it was either by way of condescension or curiosity. Observe the reception given him by Simon the Pharisee. Simon doubtless knew well the laws of courtesy, and punctually conformed to them in his intercourse with people of his own grade; but when Jesus the Nazarene was his guest, he set them aside; he gave him no water for his feet, embraced him not, and anointed not his head with oil; thinking it quite sufficient that this Galilean should have a place at his table. Christ voluntarily assumed a position in social life, where he would be looked down upon by men moving in the higher spheres. He was the friend of publicans and sinners.

He chose to be a Nazarene, though the prejudice agains Nazareth was so strong that men familiarly said, "Can any good thing come out of Nazareth?"

He was not merely lowly in life, but lowly in heart. Some rich men feel ill at ease in the society of men of inferior grades; they task themselves perhaps to be civil, kind, considerate; but they have a feeling that they are out of their element, and they shrink back with much comfort to themselves into their accustomed sphere. But Christ was consciously at home among his poor and illiterate companions. Their habits of thought, their mode of life, their topics of conversation, were not something strange to him. The utmost cordially characterized his manner, and stamped his lowliness as genuine.

Learn of me; that is, be my disciples. The believer is one who is learning of Christ to be meek and lowly of heart.

Does the notion of our own merit make it difficult for us to walk in "all meekness and lowliness?" Surely, our merit is hardly to be put in comparison with that of Christ. It may be, we are not so bad as some people; but Christ is the most meritorious being in the universe. Shall we rate ourselves above him? In the assemblies of men, let us beware how we take the higher place; for though we may think ourselves better than some that are there present, yet are we not better than Christ; and if we will but notice it, he takes the lower place. If reproaches are offered us, let us consider that greater reproaches are offered Christ, and he endures them.

Almost all men are complaining of the burden laid upon them: they think that too much is imposed; every man would have his own yoke lightened in some respect. Now what makes the burden heavy is simply the unwilling spirit Let us get from Christ a cheerfully submissive spirit; let us learn from him not to quarrel with our appointed lot; and, on the instant, by virtue of this inward change, our burden loses a vast deal of its weight. Christ had a burden that would have sunk him to a most speedy grave, if it had not been for his meekness and lowliness of heart. And if we are like him in these characteristics, it will make comparatively little difference what the burden laid upon us is; it will be found light.

Again, the oppressive thing to most men is that they have to meet the responsibilities of life, alone. But Christ reveals himself to believers as bearing the yoke of life with them; their true yoke-fellow.

APRIL 28.—"Draw nigh to God."—James iv. 8.

There are too many, even among those reputed Christians, who seem never to have drawn nigh to God. They have a certain reverence for him, and occupy themselves considerably with the doing of his will. But they do not seem to have ever entered into the holy of holies, and beheld the peculiar manifestations of God. They remain at a certain distance, and think it reverential perhaps so to do. But true reverence will not allow us to slight any means of becoming fitted to glorify God. By drawing nigh to God, we are brought under the power of his perfections, and become subject to his most potent influences. He that is least in the kingdom of heaven is greater than the greatest of the ancient prophets; and there is no reason why we should not draw nigh as Abraham did when he heard that Sodom was to be destroyed; as Moses did when he saw the burning bush; and when he went up into the mountain to be alone with the glory of God; as Isaiah did in the temple, and as Daniel and others did. The Son of God ever offers to accompany us into the presence of the divine majesty, and to sustain us in the interview; wherefore we need not fear to go.

But how shall we draw nigh to God? What is meant by this?

There is a great deal that is shadowy and dubious about the communion that many have with God. They have no such consciousness of having met and conversed with God, as they have of their communications with men. There has been no bright and animating manifestation of God to their souls. They have not felt the power of his present majesty; nor have his divine perfections taken hold upon them as by a special revelation. They know that God is revealed in his word as gracious and merciful towards the race of man; but they have not considered that it is the province of faith to single out the believer, and bring him by himself into the presence of his maker. He is to enter into peculiar and well-understood relations to God. God is his God; he is the child of God; and there must be a conscious acquaintance and intimacy quite distinct from the general goodness of God towards mankind. In order that we may draw nigh to God, we must become utterly dissatisfied with the vague sort of communion that so many are content with. We must resolve to be satisfied with nothing less than the bright shining of the divine presence upon our individual soul. We must believe it attainable, and resolve to attain it at whatsoever cost.

Having begun to seek it earnestly, we shall perhaps experience many disappointments. The word of God unfolds itself, it is true, more richly to our souls than once it did; and we get juster conceptions of him. But the bright and soul-elevating discovery of him himself, we do not obtain. The more we seek, however, the more we perceive the importance of what we seek; and feel that life without this conscious union of the soul with God, is insupportable. We take this conviction as an encouragement from on high, to go on. As we continue striving in prayer we are led to examine ourselves earnestly to see if there is anything in our way of life that is displeasing to God. We become very scrupulous; very severe with ourselves; we cut off an indulgence here, and an indulgence there; and wonder how we should have formerly been so careless. Duties that we had not formerly dreamed of, now discover themselves to us; we find that we were before very ill acquainted with the will of God. These discoveries perhaps only make us the more unhappy. For we feel that we need a strength such as we have not, in order to live the life we are called to. More and more we see the absolute necessity of drawing nigh to God and strengthening ourselves in the consciousness of our indissoluble union with him in Christ. Finally, in some hour long to be remembered, there falls down as it were a great vail, and with joy unspeakable we behold the light of God's countenance, are made glad by the assurance deeply buried in the soul, that an Almighty friend accompanies us along the journey of life.

APRIL 29.—"Mercy shall be built up forever."—Psalm lxxxix. 2.

"Forty centuries look upon you," said Bonaparte to his soldiers, pointing to the pyramids. Compared with the ordinary structures of man, these are immense, massive, enduring. Yet all the monuments of men are built upon leased ground, and with borrowed materials. They must vanish away. Another monument is to be reared; a monument to the mercy of God. Nothing less than the entire length and breadth of the earth will suffice for its foundation. Even the sea must be dried up to make room for it.

Of course the paltry monuments of man must disappear when the time comes for the completion of this magnificent structure. It is already begun. The foundations have been dug in some places. The chief corner-stone has been laid, and so have the first and the second tiers of stones connected with the foundation. The stakes have been set up that indicate its dimensions. Laborers are at work in many quarries. The mountains are heaving. The bowels of the earth prepare to surrender their stores. A fiat has gone forth, heeded by some, by many not heard, declaring that everything in heaven and on earth is to be held in readiness for any exigency connected with this building. It is to be the most glorious edifice that the universe ever beheld. The light of it is to flash upon the most distant worlds, and give them a glory that they never had before. The central sun will find itself eclipsed by the effulgence streaming from this monument. The boldest conceptions of those who began the Tower of Babel, were utterly childish in comparison with this structure that is to rear its head far aloft above the highest mountains, far above the highest clouds, up, up among the stars, indeed far above all stars; nor will any finite admeasurement ever determine its height. This monument contains the mansions of the elect. It is the Palace of the Lamb. Its stones are living stones. Its pillars bear the image of Christ in living, breathing characters. Around the gallery of its dome, is an inscription, whos every letter is a host of redeemed beings, all together spelling the sentence, " God so loved the world, that he gave his only begotten Son."

APRIL 30.—" All her paths are peace."—Proverbs iii. 17.

Can I trust thee, Wisdom? Dost thou tell the whole truth? If I embrace this bold guarantee of thine, and commit myself to thy paths, is it certain that my course shall be one of uninterrupted and elevated peace?

" Walk in my paths, and God will be at peace with thee! What an infinite gain is this! Where thou now art, the wrath of God, the hostility of the Omnipotent impends over thee. Were all the hosts of the universe arrayed against thee, they would do thee the merest trifle of harm in comparison with what the Almighty by a single sweep of his hand could do thee. Destruction from him is not temporal, but eternal; not partial, but total. Were all the hosts of heaven, earth, and hell against thee, they could not make one hair of thy head perish, if God were on thy side. Walk in my path, and he is on thy side."

It must be of course, O Wisdom, an infinite gain to have the Lord God on our side, and it seems to be certain that they who walk in thy path have him at peace with them. Nevertheless, I have heard, if I mistake not, that there are many afflictions to the righteous. Is it not thy path that is called a narrow path? Is it not said that men must take up their cross to walk therein? What is it that I have read about "persecutions, afflictions, reproaches, distresses?" Does not thy path go down sometimes into dungeons, and into dens of lions? Are not fires sometimes kindled to burn those that walk therein?

"Nevertheless, all my paths are peace. Were the things you have mentioned, expressive of the wrath of God, they would then militate against my declaration. But they who walk in my path are taught by me what peace truly is. They learn to find it in the sense of the favor of God, and in the assurance that all who love God, must love them, sooner or later. So with unvanquished peace, they bear their cross, pursue the narrow path, descend into dungeons, and meet death at the stake."

O Wisdom, pardon my tardy acquiescence. Some doubts yet linger. Tears ran down the cheeks of holy men of old, night and day, because of those who kept not God's law. Will not our hearts bleed in thy paths, over the miseries of the unregenerate multitude? Will not the consciousness of evil in ourselves, war with our peace?

"I say not that if you walk *imperfectly* in my ways, you

shall have perfect peace. I will not show you the evil of your own heart, without showing you a fountain opened up for sin and for uncleanness; and I will not show you the miseries of the world without pointing out the all-adequate grace of God. I promise no immunity from tears in my earthly path; but consolation from a sublime source, and revelations of a divine sympathy which the believer will feel that it was better to have had than not to have needed."

MAY 1.—" Save us, O God of our salvation."—1 Chronicles xvi. 35.

Thou art content to be known by this name, " God of our salvation." Viewed in one light, the thing seems an infinite wonder; in another light, no wonder. For in the accomplishment of our salvation, thy perfections come out in glorious relief, and the whole creation finds itself unspeakably aided in the work of making thee known. Let but one of the redeemed, clothed in his full salvation, stand forth in the universe; and it will matter little if the heaven and the earth flee away, and return no more. For this redeemed sinner is such a monument to the power, justice, wisdom, truth, and love of God, that no finite being could ever master the entire revelation.

Thou hast devoted thyself, O God of our salvation, thyself and all thy resources, to the work of delivering us from all sin, from all folly, from all reproach of ignorance, from all corruption, from all misery, and from all weakness. Thou hast so identified thyself with this work which thou hast taken in hand, that not to accomplish it would be the extinction of thy glory. From thy throne thou must save us who have fled to thee for refuge through thy Son; or thou must quit that throne. Thou art already known throughout all worlds as the God of our salvation; and invitations to the marriage supper of the Lamb, have been carried into all parts of thy dominions.

Save us, therefore, save us speedily, save us perfectly, save us from all relapse into unbelief, and from all remains of unbelief; save us from undue deference to the world; save us from errors of understanding, and from cheats of the imagination; save us from an inadequate conception of the Gospel standard; from resting contented with our attainments; save us each day and hour from the particular hindrances of each day and hour. Save us from letting go the hand that was pierced for us.

MAY 2.—"**The grass withereth, the flower faileth; but the word of our God shall stand forever.**"—**Isaiah xl. 8.**

The contrast really intended here is not between the word of God and the grass of the field; for there are many other things to share with Scripture the honor of out-living the flowers of earth. In one sense the Bible resembles the grass of the field; if by great efforts the latter be rooted up and cast into the fire, much time will not elapse before that same spot is seen verdant again with a new growth. And many rulers have sought to destroy the crop of Bibles sown in their dominions, but have spent their strength for nought. The contrast is really between man, his works and his glory, and the word of God. Like grass, man shall wither; like the flower, his glory shall pass away; but the word of our God endureth forever.

Even so, Isaiah! The word of God uttered by thee has come down to us through twenty-five troubled centuries, serenely riding out the storms of every generation, and beholding the wreck of many empires. Whilst thou wert writing thine unnoticed page, stupendous monuments were being erected here and there in the world; but ruin has long since overtaken these. During seventy generations the providence of God has steadily corroborated thy statements, and shown that the nations, before God, are nothing, less than nothing and vanity.

With what avidity would men drink in the intelligence that a plant had been discovered whose fruit conferred immortality. With what a frantic joy would they precipitate themselves toward that stray plant of heaven found upon the earth. But the word of God really possesses and really communicates immortality. It endures forever, and he who embraces it by faith, endures forever. It is the word of life; and nothing shall by any means harm them who have made it their own. In the last day, when there shall be a terrific overthrow of the pomp, pride, and strength of man, the word of God, so oft rejected, so much despised upon the earth, will be seen upon the throne of God, and all the friends of that word around about the throne. Ye neologians and rationalists, and all who have sought to draw the pen of unhallowed criticism through this or that text, how will you stand confounded when you see indestructible life and glory belonging to the word of God. You will feel as though you had been detected in an attempt to murder angels, beings possessing the life of heaven.

MAY 3.—"Be not dismayed, for I am thy God."—Isaiah xli. 10.

There are many things in this stage of existence that are calculated to fright the souls of men. They are surrounded by dangers. There is hardly anything, no matter how minute and to all appearance contemptible, but may in some hour put on strength enough to kill us. Many a little insect has taken away the life of proud man. We do not know but that the breath we are now breathing may convey some deadly disease to our lungs. Our foot may slip; a blood-vessel may burst; a stone may fall upon us; we may get up in our sleep and fall from a window; a bone may stick in our throat. Men are dying in all these ways. The people of God have other dangers. They are walking in a narrow path. The God of this world is bringing all his cunning and all his resources to bear upon them, in efforts for their overthrow. Terrible is the open wrath of their enemy; not less formidable the blandishments of his disguised agents. The consciousness of sinfulness is paralyzing; and the path of duty seems adapted only for one a hundred times our superior in constancy, wisdom and power.

And can it be that there is one consideration which of itself suffices to qualify a believer to look upon all the ills that cluster thick around his pathway, and enables him to go victoriously onward to the end? There is. *God is thy God.* Thine, if thou hast believed upon his Son. His strength is thine; his wisdom thine; his resources are thine; his vigilance is thine; his omniscience thine. Not that thou becomest omniscient or almighty, but these perfections of the Godhead are available for thee to the full extent of thy necessities. If, then, at any time thou art dismayed, this is the same as saying, God is not equal to the difficulties that environ me. I need more strength than he possesses, more wisdom, more knowledge. I need another God besides him. Oh, utter nothing so dishonoring to the majesty of heaven as this. Beware, and never be dismayed!

May 4.—" I, even I, am he that blotteth out thy transgressions, for my own sake."—Isaiah xliii. 25.

This language, whether addressed to the partial Israel of ancient times, or the universal Israel of our times, is appropriate only to one who has been awakened to a true perception of his transgressions, and to an earnest, engrossing solicitude for pardon. The eyes of such a one have been opened. In every page of the word of God he finds some chapter of his own past history coming up to view, and exhibiting itself to him in an aspect never before witnessed. The commandments seem to address him by name; the denunciations seem winged from the throne of God solely for him; the promises shrink back from him affrighted. There seem to be not one, but ten thousand condemnations out against him. Where in all the universe shall he find friends powerful enough and cordial enough to come forward and so plead that these dread writs shall be cancelled? Alas! what oratory will avail here? What cunning excuses will induce the Almighty to overlook the guilt of the sinner at the expense of his own infinite perfections? The sinner may have once imagined that it was the easiest thing to get clear; but he now utterly contemns the help of all created beings. No eloquence could lull the storm of self-accusation within; much less appease the righteous indignation of Him who is greater than his heart. Ah yes! there is an eloquence that here availeth; but it is that of no created being. God manifest in the flesh speaketh from the cross, in words of wondrous healing. "I, even I, whose commandments thou hast transgressed, whose benefits thou hast forgotten, who cast down the angels, sent the deluge, and overthrew Sodom, I, even I, am he that blotteth out thy transgressions."

For my own sake. The perfections of God which require our destruction, in the absence of an atonement, require, now that Christ has died and we have believed, our deliverance from sin and misery, our elevation to glory, our everlasting felicity. "The Father is glorified in the Son." Christ is glorified in us. For his own sake, therefore, he will grant all that we need. We ask him as it were to put on glory. We ask him to enrich himself. We ask him to extend his kingdom, perfect his dominion, put on new lustre in the eyes of the universe. This is what we ask of him when we ask that our sins may be blotted out. In bringing our vile selves to God, we bring something infinitely precious. Angels could never be able to make up any offering comparable to this in value. What is the offering? It is the opportunity of glorifying himself in his Son and his Son in us. But if we pray unbelievingly, we destroy the opportunity; we cast away a pearl intended for the diadem of God.

MAY 5.—"Thou art mine."—Isaiah xliii. 1.

Once thou hadst other proprietors. Sin, self, death, misery—these formerly boasted that thou wert theirs. But the price I have paid shuts their mouths forever.

Self is slowest of all to understand this. Thou hast distinctly and joyfully recognised the transfer of thyself to me; and yet again and again have I seen thee acting as though it were simply an agreeable fiction. Thou hast sometimes lavished thine affections on objects with which thou hadst nothing properly to do. Thou hast given thyself to enterprises which I had not commissioned thee to prosecute. Thou hast refused to go at my bidding, when the sick waited for thee, and the prisoner languished. Thou hast suffered the hungry to go unfed, and the mourner uncomforted from thy door, whither I had sent them, saying, "He is mine; he will help thee, out of the resources which I have placed at his disposal." In the day of tribulation, when it pleased thee to put forth my hand upon that which is my own, didst thou not murmur, didst thou not shrink offended from the rude encounter of my providence? What meaneth this? Must my pleasure, after all, give way to thy pleasure? The infinite price which I have paid for thee, is it merely that self may sit upon a more royal throne? Nay, thou art mine, and I will put thee in whatsoever chamber seems most expedient to me; the chamber of sickness, of poverty, of humiliation, of defamation, of bereavement, of death.

Thou art mine. Wherefore I give thee the Holy Spirit. I have appointed thyself as his habitation on the earth. I sanctify thee by the truth. I bestow upon thee mine own image. I draw thy affections to myself; and teach thee to love the saints. I make thee meek and lowly. I make thee meet for the inheritance of the saints in light. Why should I not? Since I have called thee mine, adopted thee, bestowed on thee the family name, recognised thee as one of my nearest relations, surely there is nothing inappropriate in the gift to thee of the most abundant influences of the Spirit. It would be strange, if I should acknowledge thee as my own, and yet leave thee to walk in thy rags, to drag on a weary life, in spiritual emaciation.

Thou art mine. Wherefore I cannot think of leaving thee forever among sinners. A place is prepared for thee by Him that died for thee. Thou must dwell in mansions that have never known the contamination of sin. Angels must be thine escort. Thou shalt go crowned with glory, honor and immortality; and shalt shine as the brightness of the firmament forever and ever. And if any one ask, "Who is this that walketh in so much state, and is radiant with so much gladness?—let this answer suffice, "That he is mine. It is to my glory that all that belongeth to me be glorious and blessed."

MAY 6.—"And beginning to sink he cried, Lord, save me."—Matthew xiv. 30.

I thought myself to be strong in faith, and rejoiced in thy command to evince that strength. I thought I would show how much stronger my faith than that of others; and while they abode quietly in their vessel, I would tread the waters beneath my feet and hasten unto Jesus. I would put away from me at least the reproach sometimes addressed to us disciples of being weak in faith. But it was simple presumption. Now that the waves lift up themselves around about me, saying, "Jesus we know, but who art thou?" and threaten me with the full force of that majesty with which God has invested them, I find my supposed faith vanishing. Death himself has seized me by my feet, and is dragging me down to a horrible abyss.

Lord, save me! Higher than these waves arise the thoughts of my past folly and sinfulness. A light seems to flash along the multitudinous pages of past history, bringing into strongest relief the instances of waywardness, passion, self-will, neglect of instruction, pride and unbelief. I see myself as I never saw myself; and I see that the light in which I now stand revealed, is the very light in which my Lord has long sought to exhibit me to myself. I only now am learning a lesson that has been held up before me a thousand times.

Lord, save me, for I sink! I acknowledge, I feel, my helplessness. Thou mightest, indeed, still keep thine eye fixed on my past exhibition of independence towards God; and instead of my present cry, thou mightest justly hear former exclamations, contemning salvation. Oh! hear them not, remember them not. In this tumult of the waves it seems as though they were clamorous, those former utterances of an unbelieving and ungodly heart; clamorous more than ever to be heard in this very moment; and as though my poor present cry out of the depth could not possibly make its way to thee. Nevertheless, save me. Save me from going down into the pit.

Thou wilt say unto me perhaps, "If I save thee in this hour, what assurance have I that thy former mind will not return to thee? If I pluck thee from this death, wilt thou not soon be rushing again, in thy presumptuous self-confidence, along the path of death?" Well, Lord, thou must find the assurance in thyself—in thy power not only to save me from this horrible abyss, but from future dereliction, from a vain heart, from unbelief and self-dependence. Save me from all.

MAY 7.—"Though he was rich, yet for your sakes, he became poor."—2 Corinthians viii. 9.

Worlds, as countless as the sands of the sea-shore, were his, and innumerable sovereignties lay low at his feet. Tell off the sum of what he renounced, world by world, host by host, and a life would not suffice. Suppose the renunciation gradual, and watch it from the throne of the universe. You would see the suns of least magnitude, the heavens of greatest distance vanishing one by one, very rapidly, from the face of the universe; worlds of greater magnitude following them into night; great spaces would begin to appear on the outskirts of creation; faster and faster the mighty dominions of God would flee away from the sceptre of the Son of God; at length he would be left alone with our system; finally, with our earth. He is yet King of kings, and Lord of lords. But now he leaves the throne of his glory; and infinitely descending, shines for an instant among the archangelic dignities; is presently seen among cherubim; then passes downward with an expiring glory, through powers and principalities. Vanishing from the heavens, he is seen on earth, not in the likeness of an angel, but as a man. He traverses the exalted ranks of humanity, and refuses to tarry in them; nor does renunciation begin to find its limits, until he has found for himself an abiding place as a Nazarene carpenter, the son of a carpenter. He enters on his ministry, and has not where to lay his head; receives with gratitude a cup of cold water; is made of so little reputation that he is accused of being in league with Satan, is denounced as a blasphemer, and an enemy of religion.

Thus poor did he become. Wherefore? For your sakes. That his example might take hold upon your consciences, and lead you to follow in this path of renunciation. He teaches you, like him, to lay aside glory, honor and power, wealth and comfort. But what glory have you, the very dregs of creation, to renounce? The thing is this. In departing from God you have made for yourselves a world of delusion, and constituted yourselves lord of that world. You have put yourselves in the place of God, as the lawgiver of yourselves; you have put your honor in the place of God's, and desired to have the whole creation enraptured with yourself, rather than God; yet were urgent to have all things declare your glory, rather than his. Renounce then, oh! renounce this usurped dignity, and the wealth that you have chosen to call yours. Follow the example of Christ, and become poor. This is needful in order that subsequently, through his poverty, you may be made rich. You must be changed into his image at the foot of the ladder, and then shall you ascend it with him, even the very ladder by whose multitudinous steps he came from his sublime throne to earth.

MAY 8.—"This poor man cried, and the Lord heard him."—Psalm xxxiv. 6.

Who was this poor man? Let us see if we can find out; if we can ascertain the characteristics of those poor people whom God so honorably mentions in his word.

Mere penury of worldly goods is not a sufficient title. He must be poor in spirit—poor contentedly. His must be a spirit cheerfully acquiescent in the allotments of God—with all that he is reputed to have, placed unreservedly at his disposal; sensible that he is not even his own, but bought with a price; his abilities and opportunities, his time and influence, his soul and body, his tongue and pen, solemnly deeded to God. This poor man has no strength of his own. He is poor even in virtue, very poor; poor in wisdom. And so if you listen at his window, you will find him in the still hours, earnestly laboring in prayer that he may have given him strength, virtue and wisdom.

This poor man cried, and the Lord heard him. So the cry of this poor man is in reality a key by which he can unlock treasury after treasury of things beyond all price.

MAY 9.—"In thy presence is fullness of joy."—Psalm xvi. 11.

In the place where there is nothing to hinder the full perception of the glory of God, there is fullness of joy. The most we can do in this world is to get a conception, faint at the best, of beatific joy. As we perceive the presence of him who once became manifest in our nature, loved us and washed us from our sins in his own blood, we experience joy unspeakable; but we cannot describe our experience as *fullness* of joy, with out declaring that the company of the ungodly is as blessed as that of angels; the sense of imperfection as sweet as that of perfection; ignorance as good as consummate knowledge; lia bility to temptation as enviable a state as that of inviolable security. If we have here the presence of God, we have here also the presence of a great deal that is inimical to the glory of God. Creation groans beneath this, and day and night crieth out, "How long, O Lord, how long?" It waits for the manifestation of the sons of God, which will be the manifestation of God; for the descent of the new Jerusalem, which will be the advent of our expected Lord; for the new heaven and the new earth, wherein dwelleth righteousness, even the Lord of righteousness with his righteous ones. Then all that now prohibits the full revelation of the Redeemer's glory, will have been burnt up.

In that world of perfection to which we aspire, our eyes shall not be able to light upon anything that is not filled with all the fullness of God. All beings, all objects there, will be, as it were, reservoirs charged with the perpetual fulfilling of our joy; and nothing can be withdrawn from the cistern of our experience without the eagerly proffered supplies of innumerable fountains. The desire of Christ, that his joy may be fullfilled in us, will there be realized. The bliss of God himself will be drunk in by the infinite one whose name is Love, through our experiences Having the image of God, we shall have his felicity.

MAY 10.—"Boast not thyself of to-morrow."—Proverbs xxvii. 1.

How surprising the infatuation of man, in that while he despises and abuses the gifts of God actually bestowed, he makes sure of gifts to come. He makes havoc of to-day, as a child makes havoc of some valuable book fallen within its reach, and confidently expects that there shall be given to him a morrow, and a long series of morrows. While he, on earth, is busy with the transgression of God's commands, and with casting contempt on the authority of God, God, in heaven, is to be busy in prolonging the comfort, and giving all success to the unsanctified purposes of this rebel. He calculates on the subserviency of the elements, and even of the Lord of the elements, to his paltry will.

Far be this from thee, O man of God! While God is giving one inestimable boon, even the present with all its inherent wealth, snatch not thou another from the throne of thy benefactor. The only preparation for the morrow, is the right use of to-day. The stone in the hands of the builder must be put in its place and fitted to receive another. The morrow comes for nought, if to-day is not heeded. Neglect not the call that comes to thee this day, the call to humble thyself on account of many sins and follies, to break away from unprofitable ties, to look upon the poor around thee, to speak unto thy impenitent neighbor, to hunger and thirst after righteousness, to set thy love purely upon God; for such neglect is nothing else than boasting thyself of to-morrow.

MAY 11.—"Lord, save us: we perish."—Matthew viii. 25.

The disciples, we may suppose, had embarked with the Lord Jesus in that vessel, with a feeling of great confidence, and with the anticipation of a delightful sail over the familiar waters of that lake. Upon that lake most of them had spent the chief part of their time from childhood; and under almost no circumstances would they be likely to experience a feeling of fear. Now all things conspired to tranquilize their spirits. Behold them, as the sun sinks over the hills beyond Capernaum, and a gentle breeze wafts them over the placid waters; they are grouped here and there upon the vessel, some communing with the Lord Jesus of the works and ways of God, others relating to the sailors and passengers the wonderful things that Christ had performed. The sun sets; night steals quietly on; the moon and the stars appear. The Lord Jesus, fatigued with special labors, lies down and sleeps; and perhaps the last words that visit his ear are expressions of confidence uttered by his disciples. His human soul sleeps, but not the Divine Spirit that dwelt in him; otherwise the orbs of heaven would have stood still, nay, the heaven and the earth would have fled away, and the sleep of death seized upon all created things. He that keepeth Israel sleepeth not. Presently clouds, black clouds, come rushing over the face of the sky, and a strange sound is heard coming over the waters. The sailors start up in surprise and anxiety. But the disciples are heard saying, "There is no danger; Christ is on board; he must live, and so we cannot die. He has power over the elements; they cannot hurt a hair of our head." The entire face of the sky is now shrouded in darkness; winds from various quarters rush in quick succession down upon the waters; these lift themselves up in mighty billows; the vessel becomes unmanageable; each wave, as it tosses her on high, seems to say, "What doest thou here, oh thou frail and paltry thing of man's handicraft, in the presence of God's sublime agencies and ministers? What is man but a rebel? his life but a vapor? his work but vanity? It is a fearful thing to fall into the hand of the living God; and that hand is everywhere." Desolation and anguish take possession of the souls of those on board. The mariners say, "Never did we behold anything like this; no boat can outlive this." "But Jesus is on board," timidly reply the disciples. "Be he who he may," say some, "destruction hath taken hold of us, and there is no possible deliverance." Others look at the disciples, saying to themselves, "If they fear not, then there is yet hope." But alas! they see them soon give way to consternation. As the waters descend more and more ponderously on the frail boat, their faith dies out. They feel it expiring and say, "We have no faith, and therefore we perish," and immediately their faith expires. Then they hasten to Jesus. "Carest thou not that we perish?"

Oh! strangely tempered disciples! Afraid of the winds and waves, and yet not afraid to address such a stigmatizing word as this to the Lord Jesus? And are all his past works and suffering in vain? Do you still doubt his care? Jesus awakes, and the only thing that he beholds is the unbelief of his disciples; his ear tells him not of the fury and rack of the elements, but of the guilty fears of his Galilean friends. And his first reproof is for them. He lets the storm rage on unrebuked, until he has rebuked the agitation of their souls. And now they perceive that a most precious opportunity of signalizing their faith in Christ had been given, and given in vain. The elements had been let loose that their faith might gain a victory, and go on to perfection. The progress of ordinary months might have been made in an hour, had they been watchful. When will they understand that this matter of the education of faith is the most important thing going on under the sun? The school of faith is a school in which we are advancing, lesson by lesson, to a condition where the glory of God shall be perpetually revealed to the soul.

MAY 12.—"Although the fig-tree shall not blossom, neither shall fruit be in the vines; the labor of the olive shall fail, and the fields shall yield no meat; the flock shall be cut off from the fold, and there shall be no herd in the stalls: yet I will rejoice in the Lord, I will joy in the God of my salvation."—Habakkuk iii. 17, 18.

This is a noble utterance, Habakkuk! Thou hast surely

read the book of Job, and art echoing that great word of his —"Though the Lord slay me, yet will I trust in him." Thou believest that the love which God has towards us, rests upon some more solid evidence than the temporal benefits which he bestows upon us; upon evidence so satisfactory, so unimpeachable, that even if the greatly-prospered servant of God saw his flocks and herds rapidly perish, his merchandize carried off by robbers or consumed by fire, his houses and lands confiscated by unjust power, his gold and silver fraudulently taken from him, his friends alienated, his name beclouded, his person imprisoned, his health impaired, his appetite vitiated, his sight extinguished, his utterance impeded, he would still have occasions of undying and fervent gratitude, motives for joy unspeakable, a foundation for peace which passeth all understanding.

Thanks be unto Him that sitteth upon the throne for the innumerable avenues by which the expressions of his goodness come to us; but oh, while we adore him for these, let us feel that he has placed the great truth of his love toward us sinners, once for all, upon an inviolable basis; so that though the day, as it passes, may or may not have particular tokens of his goodness to impart, that goodness can in no wise be questioned.

It is most likely, O Habakkuk, that God took thee at thy word; and in some surprising way gave thee an opportunity of evincing thy singleness of heart toward him; and that thou now wearest some peculiar crown of honor and felicity in consequence of that proof given.

MAY 13.—"I am the light of the world."—John viii. 12.

What a wonderful consciousness was this for one that saw his life gliding rapidly away in an obscure corner of the world, among a despised class of persons, and knew that a cross was prepared for him at the capital. Knowing that the light of life is to go forth from him, from him alone, to all nations, peoples, and languages, how admirable is the quiet, unhasting humility that enables him to sit down among the poorest and meanest of earth, occupy himself with all their cares and solicitudes, heal their diseases, correct their errors, embrace their infant children, partake of their humble meals, and listen in their synagogues! He knew that he was to be the sun of all the world, bathe the continents in light, and create new heavens and new earth for the more effectual manifestation of his unimagined glory. Yet he could converse in a strain of perfect tranquility with the Samaritan woman at the well, and could go about Jerusalem looking for the poor man whom the Pharisees had put out of the synagogue.

This is something that should never be forgotten when we read the Gospel; and the wonder is that it does not more attract the attention of men. The evidence of Christ's humility and contentedness of spirit, rests upon the surest foundation; all his actions and his mode of life declare that he was at home among the poor and needy of earth, and sought not great things for himself; but there drop from his lips at times, expressions that indicate the perfect and abiding consciousness that he is to sit down upon the throne of this world, and fill it with the effulgence beaming from his countenance. Before the high priest and Pilate he was as a lamb led to the slaughter, and as a sheep before her shearers is dumb so he opened not his mouth; and it was only with the greatest difficulty that they could force him once to speak and to disclose the sublime consciousness that was in him, by a reference to his future coming in the clouds of heaven and in the glory of God, to take complete possession of the world.

MAY 14.—"He hath not despised nor abhorred the affliction of the afflicted."—Psalm xxii. 24.

This is said with reference to the allegations of the men who stood around the cross of Christ. They affirmed that God evidently despised the sufferer, and so far from sympathizing with him in his affliction, abhorred him as a deceiver, and was glad to have men execute their indignation with unchastened severity. "It is beyond all question," said they, "that the Lord is against him. He has delivered him into our hands, notwithstanding all the reluctance of Pilate and the attachment of his disciples; and in every way is aiding us to fill the cup of his anguish and to pour contempt upon him. The Lord himself is smiting him; and we are simply falling in with the current of his providences."

Often, most often, the same language has been used by the persecutors of Christ's people. They have averred that God was delivering these into their hands to be tormented, imprisoned, defamed, and burnt. God brought forth in due time the evidence that he had not despised nor abhorred the affliction of that afflicted one. There was evidence abundant in the character, the words, and works of Christ that God could not be indifferent to his sufferings; but a carnal world could not see this evidence. By the resurrection of Jesus, the baptism of the Apostles, the love of the Church, and the spread of the Gospel, evidence of an imposing kind has been given The experience of every sinner that believes on Christ, from its beginning onward through eternity, teems with evidence that the Father sympathized with the sufferer of Calvary. Every instance of a fulfilled promise, repeats this evidence.

MAY 15.—"Who is a God like unto thee, that pardoneth iniquity?"—Micah vii. 18.

There is a little flock who are acquainted with God; are so

far acquainted with his essential perfections, and see so much of his glory in Christ, that God is not ashamed to be known as their God, and to have it understood among the angels of heaven that the members of this flock do know him. But viewing these as exceptional, innumerable conceptions of God possess the minds of men; to express it otherwise, innumerable gods of widely different characters exist in the conceptions of men, and frown upon the only true God. "O righteous Father, the world hath not known thee," said Christ; but the world angrily asserts that it knows him very well. Every natural man has his deity, whom he prefers to the God of the Bible; and conversion is just consenting that the true God shall be God, and the god of one's fancy be annihilated. Men have the highest idea of their own faculty of bodying forth the true God, and look with proud disdain upon what seem to them the bungling attempts of Scripture. One boasts that his God has made no decrees concerning the salvation of particular persons. Another that his God saves all that are baptized. Another that his God finds much merit in man. The God of another will actually save all.

But almost all these gods of men's devising, agree in one respect. They make light of man's iniquity. They entertain no sterner view of it than man himself, man the sinner, ordinarily entertains. Of course they are ready to forgive it; for it is a light thing.

When, however, men begin to come to the knowledge of the true God, then their iniquity rises from its tomb in all its dread proportions, and the dread spectre lifts its head to the skies, stretches out its hands to the East and to the West, blots out creation from their view, and bids them come with it to the lake that burneth with fire and brimstone. Their former God is fled into everlasting night; and all their former conceptions of divine grace, though multiplied a million times, would fall short of that grace which they now see to be required. What shall they do? Perish? No, says God; look unto the cross, know my grace, and live. Then from an amazed heart cometh the ejaculation, Who is a God like unto thee, that pardoneth iniquity?

MAY 16.—"Every good gift and every perfect gift is from above."—James i. 17.

Temptation is not of God. What constitutes a thing tempting is something in the man or woman that looks upon it, namely, a disposition more or less active to transgress, and take what is forbidden. The fruit is suspended on the tree for an admirable purpose; namely that men may have an opportunity of evincing their fidelity towards God, and thus may obtain a crown of life. The same thing is to one man a temptation, to another a good gift of God, by means of which his walk of righteousness is made more steadfast and honorable. Whatever cometh down from above is good, unexceptionably good; whatever evil thing exists, it has its origin elsewhere. Sin is the devourer of the gifts of God, and the uncompromising enemy of his beneficence.

It is not enough that God has created a thing. Has he given it to you, to me, is the question. His gifts are perfect—that is, all their tendencies are good. And if we find some of the tendencies of certain things are not good, we may conclude that this is not one of God's gifts to us.

But all gifts are useless, if we have not the gift of the Holy Ghost. By this we are enabled rightly to judge of other things called gifts, and to know which are really sent us from above. Without this we know not the proper use of anything, and are sure to appropriate heaven's bounties to inferior ends. We are to covet earnestly the best gifts. We are often permitted to make our choice among the collections of precious things on exhibition around us. Now, the wise man will say,

These are all very good, but the blessing connected with each one depends upon the character of the chooser and the circumstances in which it is to be used; I need to know which among all these will be of highest profit to me; and this by my own wisdom I cannot know; wherefore I ask God to tell me which is the perfect gift designed for me.

Innumerable objects of luxury attract the attention even of the Christian, in this day; and he is ready to say, "My Father hath bestowed these; let me take them in all gratitude." But first ask thy Father, if these be the best, the perfect gifts; if thy circumstances and thy profession make these most desirable.

MAY 17.—"As many as I love, I rebuke and chasten; be zealous therefore and repent. Behold, I stand at the door and knock: if any man hear my voice and open the door, I will come in to him and will sup with him and he with me."—Revelation iii. 19, 20.

As many as I love. Is this the voice which has just been giving expression to such intensity of holy disgust? Well may we marvel at the modulations of which it is susceptible. Ah, if there had not been love somewhere in thy heart, thou wouldst not have threatened the Laodiceans with ignominious ejection, but wouldst have cast them forth without any words of condescending reproach. Thou sawest how that confusion and alarm were being borne by thy words to their hearts, and how they began to exclaim, "Whither shall we flee from his presence? Who shall stand before him? For the day of his wrath is come." Thy words were mighty to tear down the palace of delight in which they had enshrined themselves; to tear it down for some at least. Even among these Laodiceans were some who had no idea of parting with Christ; and who, as soon as they saw that they had been building for themselves an edifice that Christ approved not, looked upon it with detestation, and loathed themselves for their inconsiderateness;

they were appalled at the thought that Christ had perhaps had enough of them and had cast them clean off forever. So powerfully indeed was this view impressed upon them by the discovery of their folly, that they were fast giving way to a conviction that hope and they had parted company eternally But the Saviour draws them from the brink of despair with the cords of love. "As many as I love, I rebuke and chasten; be zealous, therefore, and repent."

Knowing the terrors of the Lord, we persuade men: The love of Christ constraineth us. To those that are lukewarm, both the language of stern rebuke and the language of encouragement are necessary. Without experience of his indignation, they will derive no profit from the exhibition of his love. Too many churches, perhaps, derive no benefit from the preaching of Christ's love; from week to week, and from year to year, they only sink deeper in their spiritual apathy. They need to be brought acquainted with Christ's glance of fire, and to get their own indignation against themselves kindled by his indignation. There is nothing like the mingled indignation and love of the Saviour, for inspiring the soul with a genuine zeal to do his will. The indignation does not diminish the love, for it is the indignation of love, of wounded love. And when the heart has begun to burn with a steady zeal, then the indignation may withdraw into the past, and be looked at by memory, and the soul's uninterrupted experience be of love.

Well for us, if we allow ourselves to hear the chastening rebuke of Christ contained in his word, and do not constrain him to clothe it in afflictive providences. Let us beware how we hide our conscience from the light of any portion of God's truth. At the door of many how long does Jesus stand and knock, while they hear not. They read, from time to time, the very words which express his deep dissatisfaction with the iniquity which they are regarding in their hearts; read, hear, but never discern the voice of Christ addressed to themselves.

When in a rougher fashion he at length knocks at their door they become aware that such a forcible appeal has been made necessary by their strange and long-protracted spiritual deafness.

It is the office of conscience to rebuke. It does this, not as the enemy of the soul, but as the guardian of the soul's highest interests. It has, however, participated in the general ruin of our nature; and seldom speaks as the sincere servant of truth. But Christ is formed in us the hope of glory. Our conscience puts on Christ. The great need of the Christian is, that Christ and his conscience should be identified; that the rebuke of his conscience may ever be the rebuke of Christ. To this end let him give utmost heed to such rebukes; and by cords of love enchain his whole nature to the new Christ-conscience coming forth from the sepulchre of his dead nature.

MAY 18.—"He will subdue our iniquities."—Micah vii. 19.

Having had a taste of the power of these our enemies, we look disconsolately around, much desiring, but little hoping, that a deliverer may appear. We discover some, perhaps, who excel in virtue. But we see at once that they can never medicine us to that sweet peace which they themselves possess. They may instruct; but we need something more than instruction; there is that within us which laughs at instruction, human or divine. If some angels would only come and tarry with us for a season; but alas! they would stand for a moment aghast, and then spread their swiftest wings for the regions where God reigns. They may sustain the believer, so that he dash not his foot against a stone, but they have no power adequate for the creation of a believer out of an unbeliever. Creation!—this is the word—to be taken to pieces, as it were; reduced to nothingness, and then made to live, a new creature.

This is no mere speculation. The Creator consents to create us over again. He takes us to the cross, and lifting up his hand to heaven, swears that if we consent to die there, we shall surely live there, and our new life shall be the participated life of Him who knew no sin. We shall rise in the image of God. If we have boldness to be crucified with Christ, happy are we.

He subdues our iniquities, then, by making us despair of ever subduing them ourselves.—By pointing out to us some trophies of his power, some incorrigible Peters, some wrathfu Pauls, who have been emancipated by his act.—By convincing us of his willingness to take our foes in hand.—By giving us a conception of his marvelous love shown to sinners, in the surrender of his only-begotten.—By giving us, through faith, a heavenly experience of that love. We feast upon it, and our enemies are not. They are gone without a battle.

Why should there ever be anything more? The enemies flee far and fast: one, however, remains crouching in the dark, unseen—mutability; and in due time the others return, hoping that their friend may have an opportunity of re-admitting them. Then there are sad conflicts; and we wonder if, after all, our iniquities are to abide unsubdued. We learn eventually that before their absolute subjugation, it is in many respects necessary that we should have an accurate acquaintance with them, an utter detestation of them, a most watchful habit of faith with respect to them. We learn, in fact, that the perpetuity of salvation is connected with the perpetuity of faith. It is merely because of the imperfection and slumber of faith that they ever venture to re-appear. They know very well that we have no more of God than we have of faith.

MAY 19.—"The Lord is slow to anger and great in power, and will not at all acquit the wicked."—Nahum i. 3.

Because the Lord is slow to anger, men suppose that they have nothing to apprehend from his anger. But, indeed, his anger is only the more terrible, because it is slow. He is slow to anger; this shows that his anger is something different from what we call anger. It is not an impulse; but moves with the utmost possible deliberation.

It would be of the greatest advantage to men if they would just take knowledge that the goodness of God expressed in the innumerable gifts of Providence that strew their paths, is not complacency, but suspended wrath. They lie down and sleep; in the morning they awake, give a careless thought to the circumstance that God has watched over them, and go their way. They embark in many enterprises, and meet with success. Comforts, honors, advantages, pour in from many quarters. Why? The reason is, say they, that God is well pleased with us. The question then arises, "Who is this God that daily fetches out of his treasury things, new and old, to bestow on hoary-headed sinners, whose life is dedicated to iniquity? What are we to think of a God who pays the salaries of the servants of Satan, and affords them facilities for doing his infamous will?" You know not God. He bestows upon you providential kindnesses, because he would attract you to his kingdom against which you are now in revolt; because he would have you hear the word of his grace, and escape the uplifted bolt of his vengeance. He prolongs the day of mercy, because he knows there is for you a lake of unquenchable fire, an eternity of woe.

It would be a fearful impeachment of the power of God, if the sinner, abiding in transgression, should after all come off victorious. Transgression is the assumption of power greater than that of God. Weak and contemptible is that legislator whose laws may be broken with impunity. Better a thousand times that he should make no laws at all. The sinner now for a while cajoles himself with the idea that he is greater than God; that he can contemn the commandments of God. But God is as great in power as he is in long-suffering; and the imagined victory of man only prepares the way for the sublimer victory of God.

MAY 20.—"I am the good shepherd, and know my sheep."—John x. 14.

Thou art indeed the good shepherd; but we must acknowledge that there often appears in us something that looks very much like a denial of this truth. Believing thee to be the good shepherd, why are we sometimes so slow to follow thee? Why do we ever doubt that thy commandments are better than our own conceits? Why murmur at the ruggedness of thy path? Why look with wistful eyes at the pastures which thou forbiddest? We name thee the good shepherd; but is there not some hypocrisy in the joy with which we do it? The words are familiar to our lips; but our lives bear an ambiguous testimony.

If an enemy should overcome us, take away our armor in which we trusted, and command us to follow him; fear might constrain us to do so; but we should take every opportunity of lagging behind; we should follow afar off; we should be ever glancing to the right hand and to the left in search of some solace; we should go as far as we dared in by-paths; we should look wistfully to the sunny fields of liberty in the distance; we should go slowly when our enemy called; we should do sullenly what he commanded. Has Christ any such disciples? Will he trouble himself long with those who cleave to him chiefly through fear? These are the greatest reproach to him. They stigmatize him fearfully. Whatever their mouth may say, their conduct asserts him to be the bad shepherd.

Let me honor thee, O Lord, and in all my ways proclaim thee the good shepherd, by doing cheerfully all thy will, not setting aside those precepts of the Gospel that have fallen into disuse in the Church, but ever acting upon the conviction that each jot and tittle of what thou hast uttered has a relation to my well-being as intimate as the breath that visits my lungs Whatever others may do, let me not pretend to know myself better than thou knowest me; by supposing that thou hast overrated my capacity in the tasks thou hast assigned, or underrated my necessity in the good things thou hast bestowed, or ignored my urgency when the answer to prayer is long delayed.

MAY 21.—"**The earth shall be filled with the knowledge of the glory of the Lord, as the waters cover the sea.**"—*Habakkuk* ii. 14.

The world with all its wisdom has not yet reached the platform where this humble servant of God stood more than two thousand years ago. But indeed, others had stood there before him. Isaiah had stood there and heard the song of the seraphim. Moses had stood there nearly a thousand years before, and heard the asseveration of the divine majesty, "As I live, all the earth shall be filled with my glory." It is the fashion with many to despise the stand-point of the ancient Israelites; nevertheless, it was the stand-point from which a number of them were permitted to see more of the future condition of the nations of the earth than the most sagacious politician is yet able to see.

What an idea of fulness does the contemplation of the sea convey to us! The basin of the sea is full. A very little added would cause a multitude of isles to disappear. The earth is the Lord's, and the fulness thereof. All his works show forth his glory; and a long life might be spent in tracing a little leaf through all the ramifications of its eloquent history. But the Gospel is being published; and thousands of tongues are telling in many, many languages, the length and breadth, the depth and height of God's immeasurable love in Christ. Still the whole creation groaneth and travaileth in pain; and the ministers of the gospel perpetually exclaim, "How long, O Lord, how long?" The voices of the old prophets assure us that a race shall tread this earth in the latter days, whose eye shall have been anointed with eye salve to behold the full glory of God as it shines in the face of Jesus Christ, and to perceive the word "Bethel" written upon the face of universal nature. Every tree shall be to them a pillar in the temple of God; and every stone shall have written on it the ineffable name of God. The mountains shall bring peace, and the little hills shall yield joyously their contributions to the world-wide righteousness.

In this view a great interest attaches to this earth of ours, even to every particular locality of it. Concerning every place that we may visit, we have the assurance that a time will come when the redeemed shall walk there and hearken diligently to its song of emancipation, to its praises of God and the Lamb. We know, indeed, that sin and the works and memorials of sin are to be burnt out of the earth. We know, also, that our bodies shall sleep in dust and arise glorious. The resurrection of Christ is not only the guarantee of our resurrection, but of that of the material world which was made by him, and for him.

MAY 22.—"The Lord thy God in the midst of thee is mighty."—Zephaniah iii. 17.

Most pitiable was the condition of the Israelites in Egypt. Pharaoh seemed to delight in eliciting the most incredible proofs of their subjection to his rod. There is ordinarily a limit beyond which masters dare not go in trifling with the lives and feelings of even the most abject slaves; but there seemed to be no limit to Pharaoh's power to oppress. The sacred sentiment of paternity he trampled on; and seemed to feel that the Israelites were the very impersonation of helplessness. But soon it appeared that the Lord was in the midst of this despised people, mighty to save; and with such exhibitions of might and majesty as never had accompanied the movements of any other people, they went forth from the presence of their oppressors.

The Church of Christ is an habitation of God through the Spirit. Lo, I am with you always, said Jesus. We know how mighty he was in the midst of his disciples. After a lapse of many years he appeared to John, and told him to reveal him to the churches as walking in the midst of the golden candlesticks. He is in the midst of us, mighty to save. Nothing of his might has been lost to the Church. It was expedient for us that he should go from earth in body, and be present with us in spirit. We lost nothing by this arrangement. We may therefore calculate on a manifestation of glory and of power not by any means inferior to those that render lustrous the pages of sacred history. Let us only be careful to put far away all insignia of our own power and glory; and what may we not expect!

But alas! what do we expect? Do we expect some sublime revelations of might in the way of subduing our selfishness, worldliness, passion, pride? Are we looking for divine might to disclose itself in connection with our efforts for the good of men? Are we rivalling Elijah in faith, Moses in meekness and zeal, Job in patience, Paul in earnestness, John in spirituality? Are we seeking to be holy as God is holy? Why not, if the Lord be in the midst of us, mighty to save.

MAY 23.—"They shall look upon me whom they have pierced, and they shall mourn."—Zechariah xii. 10.

Think not that they who were personally concerned in the crucifixon of the Lord Jesus Christ, were sinners above all the sinners of the world. Christ on the cross, the righteous Advocate, was able to find something extenuating in their conduct. "They know not what they do." Afterwards, when they saw what they had done, when the Spirit of Pentecost made him known as the Prince of life, many of them repented of their sin, and made haste to believe upon him. The measure of knowledge is an important element in determining the measure of sin. The measure of the means of knowing, let us say rather. There are thousands who are every day guilty of conduct as odious in the sight of heaven as that of the parties who nailed Christ to the cross, and thrust a spear into his side. These indeed, were mere Roman soldiers, having no personal animosity to Christ, whose language even they did not understand; the guilty parties of that scene did not themselves lift a finger against Christ. And their guilt falls immeasurably short, as we have said, of many who now live, read the Gospel, speak about it, profess to look to Christ for salvation, and yet utterly falsify his religion in their practice. When men attributed his blessed works and words to satanic influence, the heart of Christ was pierced; but it is even more pierced when men profess to be his disciples, and by continuance in sin teach the world that Christ has no objection to sin. These are engaged in crucifying the Son of God afresh. They crucify his love with their contentions; his holiness with their profane conduct; his justice with their unrighteousness; his mercy with their unmercifulness; his truth with their deceit; his generosity with their selfishness. They crucify him by falsifying him. Some pierce him by denying his divinity; some by teaching that he will save all, whether they repent or not; some by withholding his Gospel from the multitude; some by exalting a mere ceremony to a glory above that of Christ; some by substituting a crucifix for him; some in one way, some in another. All whose life, teaching, conversation, go to misrepresent or degrade Christ be they as numerous as they may, as admired as you please, they are piercing Christ, and they shall mourn. The thing which will fill Christ's meek ones with ineffable joy, will fill the hearts of these professors with anguish that no tongue can describe.

MAY 24.—"His mercy is on them that fear him."—Luke i. 50.

Is there not reason to apprehend that we presume upon a great deal of mercy that is not really accorded? We know that the world takes for granted that God forgives it, and reserves all its anxiety for matters that seem to it invested with much more difficulty. But may it not be that we, who consider ourselves, on apparently good grounds, as God's real children, that we are daily presuming on God's forgiveness when that forgiveness is not really pronounced? We are not notified of forgiveness by some special messenger; but are taught by the Spirit of God to find it in the word of God by a process in which there is some scope for self to intermingle and vitiate the result. It requires no little wisdom, but especially much meekness, and self-mistrust, and love of the truth, and docility, to ascertain unerringly, that forgiveness has been pronounced.

God's mercy is on them that fear him. It is not intended to make men think lightly of transgression; but greatly to increase their estimate of God's authority, and their loathing for the sin forgiven. Is it impossible to find in our practice the evidence that we continue on good terms with the sin that we presume God is day by day forgiving? Are we aware that this is a foul mockery of God, a caricature of his mercy? There is no true fear of God before our eyes, if to-day's sin keeps ever following upon yesterday's forgiveness.

MAY 25.—"There shall be a fountain opened to the house of David and to the inhabitants of Jerusalem, for sin and for uncleanness."—Zechariah xiii. 1.

The Jews were accustomed to regard themselves as a fountain of righteousness, the only one in the earth; their country an oasis made glad by these beneficent and hallowed waters while all the rest of the world was a wilderness; and Jerusa lem as the blessed spot where heaven and earth met together and held one another in a fond embrace. At no time were they more tenacious of these views than when the Son of God dwelt among them, drinking his daily cup of ignominy. His credentials showed that he had come to earth for the salvation of all nations. A word spoken against him, a hand lifted in opposition to him, was therefore not only the most transcendent outrage offered to the Deity, but the fearfulest crime against all the dwellers upon the earth. Yet the Jews rejected him; this is saying little; they put him to the most shameful and most cruel death conceivable.

But that which filled up the measure of the iniquity of man was used by infinite grace as a means for the most surprising manifestation of itself. The disciples were commanded to begin at Jerusalem, in the proclamation of the Gospel. Then did the Jews discover that their pre-eminence over the nations was a pre-eminence of guilt; and having been brought, many of them at least, into a posture of deep self-condemnation and self-loathing, they discovered the fountain of divine grace, drank thereof, and washed their sins away in its purifying waters. It was then that Jerusalem attained to a pre-eminence above the nations immeasurably more honorable than any it had previously enjoyed; then, in that little season which intervened between the first successes of the Gospel and its publication in other places. Solomon with all the glory of his court could not so ennoble Jerusalem, as the little company of believers did, who were all of one heart and of one soul.

We faintly remember to have read in some book of imagination of a fountain having marvelous properties, and this among the rest—that a few drops taken from it to any distant place and there poured out, would immediately cause a similar fountain there to spring up. Christ told the woman of Samaria that the water that he would give her, would be in her a well of water, springing up to everlasting life. Whosoever comes to him and drinks, not only finds his own thirst assuaged, but discovers in himself a wealth of waters sufficient to slake the thirst of numbers. Thus the fountain opened up to the house of David and the people of Jerusalem in that little company of believers, has been repeated and repeated, until now there is hardly any place under the sun where this fountain of divine grace is not accessible. How tame and puerile the efforts of man's fancy in comparison with the actual products of God's beneficence! "Thou art a God that doeth wonders." In order to discourse of wonders, men suppose themselves driven from the actual world into the world of sheer imagination. But they forsake the world of wonders when they forsake the world of truth. Be it that they conceive a fountain most beautiful to behold; the eye is not satisfied with seeing; or, streaming with gold; there are a thousand ills of life that mock at gold; or, communicating health; health is merely a deliverance from one class of sufferings. But a fountain which sheds abroad the love of God in the heart; which gives the best of light to the understanding; elevates the affections; banishes sin; gives everlasting life; and reveals a world worthy of that everlasting life: this is surely beyond all comparison, The Wonderful Fountain.

May 26.—"If two of you shall agree on earth as touching anything that they shall ask, it shall be done for them."—Matthew xviii. 19.

Men are fully aware of many of the advantages of partnerships. They even form partnerships for the prosecution of some labors that would seem most likely to be well performed by a single individual; as for instance, the labors of authorship. But they are not aware that any gain would result from entering into partnership, with the promises of God as their capital, and the throne of grace as their place of business.

The encouragement of the text does not address itself merely to an association formed of two persons; the context shows that it does not. But our Lord teaches that association in prayer is so exceedingly profitable, that even if two only should embark in it, there would be grand results. Let three, four, or a hundred and twenty, of one accord, of one mind, seek to utilize the promises; commensurate fruits shall appear in some early day of Pentecost. The great thing is not the numbers, but the agreement. The prayer of two whose souls are attuned to exactly the same key, and who have learned to merge their separate interests in one common interest, shall prevail more than the prayer of tens of thousands, whose minds are occupied, more or less, with lingering considerations of purely personal good.

The Church in these latter times has grasped earnestly at the advantages connected with association; and the number of its societies is beyond estimate. But it is comparatively overlooked that association in prayer should take the lead of every other association. Upon the plateau in front of the mercy-seat, God, as it were, sees innumerable suppliants, each one, in some sense or other, standing by himself; and hears innumerable petitions which only accidentally coalesce, for the most part are quite different in sentiment and aim from one another, and sometimes are strangely opposed to one another. Now God would teach us that in prosecuting our associate enterprises, we must prosecute them with united prayer.

The prizes held out to believing prayer, are also prizes for Christian concord of the most intimate kind. Oh, who can tell what mighty, what magnificent freight of celestial treasure will reach the shores of this world, when Christians bind themselves together with the utmost stringency, before the mercy-seat? surrendering all divided interests, and constituting themselves one firm; feeling that all depends upon their absolute agreement. Cannot every parent understand this? Is it not his delight when a gift bestowed on one child is a gratification to all? Is it not a grief to him to observe that his children have divided interest? Ten thousand prayers are dismissed daily, with this one word, "Love one another with pure hearts fervently."

MAY 27.—"Behold I come quickly; hold that fast which thou hast, that no man take thy crown."—Revelation iii. 11.

Hold fast what thou hast, because it is only for a little while that thou must hold it under the pressure of adverse circumstances; and hold it fast because everlasting victory and dominion and blessedness shall reward thy fidelity. So might a captain speak to a little band assaulted by a mighty host, when in the distance a relieving force is seen approaching; a nation's destiny depends upon their holding their own.

It is only for a little while, because the day of our salvation is now nearer than we believed; and because we have learned to wait. Delays that once were agonizing now pass with much less severity over our disciplined natures. We have learned obedience by the things we have suffered.

He, the plunderer, who goeth about seeking to despoil men of the gifts that God has bestowed on them through Christ, obtains his success chiefly by persuading men that in relinquishing or neglecting this and that spiritual gift, they are doing nothing to jeopardize their crown. A man yields up something of his energy, his watchfulness, his prayerfulness, self-denial, humility or love, because he manages to persuade himself that his title to glory, honor, and immortality, is safe enough, independently of the vacillations of his spiritual life. It is therefore for the Christian to keep carefully in mind, that whatsoever a man soweth that shall he also reap. The example of Paul is admirable here. If any man might think that he had got beyond the reach of being a castaway, it was Paul.

Well, he had; he had assurance of his indestructible interest in Christ; but he never allowed himself to feel that he had got beyond the need of keeping his body under, of running not uncertainly, of fighting not as one that beateth the air, lest he himself should be a castaway. His assurance was connected with the witness of the Spirit within him, the Spirit that led him habitually to count all things but loss that he might win more and more of Christ, more and more of Christ's likeness.

Christ will keep that which we have committed unto him; and we must keep that which he has committed unto us. None shall pluck us out of his hand; we are kept by the power of God through faith unto salvation; we are kept by the good Shepherd, because we keep within the hearing of his voice and follow him.

The consciousness of sin often causes men to relax their hold of Christ's salvation. They have been overtaken by temptation, have fallen into some snare, have yielded their heart to some seductive vanity; and when they come to themselves, then confidence in Christ is fearfully shaken, and it will be well if they let him not go altogether. Let them then hear his voice saying, Hold fast what thou hast, that no man take thy crown. Thy sin starts up with assumed indignation, pretending to have a great zeal for God, and says, "Is it not enough that thy path was sin till thou enteredst the gates of the kingdom, but wilt thou within the very borders of the kingdom, sow the dragon's teeth of sin?" But fall not back; drag thy sin to Christ, and there accuse both it and thyself, and call upon Christ to avenge himself on thy recreant nature by sanctifying it and clothing it with the armor of righteousness.

We can only hold fast what we have, by constantly using it. If we have a measure of love, we must daily study the means of manifesting it. It is easily recovered from yesterday but not from the day before. If we have joy, we must persevere in rejoicing; every day must have its spiritual joy. Our peace too, we must daily see to it that it is with us. So with long-suffering, gentleness, goodness, faith, meekness, temperance. Each day is to be considered a stage, and we must ascertain regularly that none of our treasures have been left behind. Christians are ready to think, until they have learned the contrary, that their graces are safe when they are slumbering; but their slumber is fatal. Whatever we would retain we must keep it near our consciousness; our will, our memory, our understanding, all must be conversant with it.

Look into the diary of such a man as Jonathan Edwards, to know how he held fast to what he had, that no man should take his crown. Look at these admirable resolutions, and at the admirable obedience he rendered to them, and see how high his estimate of every gracious communication from his Lord, how strenuously he battled for the preservation of it.

MAY 28.—"Unto you that fear my name shall the Sun of righteousness arise."—Malachi iv. 2.

Unto them that stand in awe of God and are conversant with the divine perfections, the Sun of righteousness makes haste to arise. There has been a fulfilling of this truth ever since the day of Pentecost. To one individual here, to another there, it is given to behold his rising. Here is one that has been enabled to look upon Christ as the sacrifice for sin, to approach God through him, and to rejoice in the goodly prospects opening up before him. But soon he becomes conscious, of a great and growing need. He is not satisfied with what he has seen of Christ. The very word of God excites in him conceptions of a walk with Christ, glorious, elevating, soul-satisfying, beyond anything that he has experienced. It seems to him that the world grows darker every day. He once rejoiced in the day-star and in the dawn, and thought the light amazing; but now he is consumed with longings to behold the bright manifestation of Christ to his soul; and it seems as though midnight had come again. At length in some happy hour, the scales fall from his eyes; the word of God becomes luminous like the very vestments of Christ transfigured; and instead of finding himself alone in the world, he finds himself in intimate alliance with a Being whose glory fills the heavens. The whole world is now to him enlightened. His sun is arisen. All the works of nature are seen as they never were before. In a particular language that others cannot understand, the heavens declare to him the glory of God. The sun that pursues its course through the skies is commissioned to remind him that God is love, and that God is his.

He goes far in the strength of this joy. But at length he discovers that Christ has laid the foundations of his new nature very deep; and that it is impossible for him to be conclusively satisfied with any private joy. He is so made like unto Christ that he cannot but look with longings as intense as he ever knew, for that appearance of the Lord in his unlimited glory, which will be the signal of the complete redemption of the Church, as well as of the creation that now groaneth and travaileth in pain.

MAY 29.—"He that believeth on the Son of God, hath the witness in himself."—1 John v. 10.

There is much evidence given anterior to faith; abundant evidence; far more than men care to gather up, concerning anything of worldly interest. Yet the greatest and most surprising testimonies are reserved for the satisfaction of believers. If unbelief has its necessities, faith has its privileges. Some would like to have, without any figure, a white stone thrown down to them from heaven, with their name upon it, beside the name of God—something that they can clutch in their hand. But believers are content with a testimony more appropriate to faith.

Christ promised his Spirit; he promised himself; he promised the indwelling of the Father in the heart of the believer, who then has the witness in himself; even the faithful and true witness, him that cannot lie, him that guideth into all truth.

But how manifold is the testimony of this witness—even as many as are his operations. The fruits of the Spirit are so many expressions of this testimony. Consider the offices of the Spirit as set forth by Christ to his disciples (John xiv.–xvi.) The eighth chapter of Romans also describes this testimony. The seventh shows the misery of being without it. There is no witness in the world more worthy of all acceptation. For who will venture to say that the spirit of man, with the best aid of Satan, is able to counterfeit perfectly the sublimest and blessedest operations of the Godhead?

May 30.—"The Son of man shall come in the glory of his Father, with his angels."—Matthew xvi. 27.

It seems to have been an important part of the divine plan that the people of God, from Adam onward to the actual advent of the Messiah, should be momentarily expecting that Messiah; the times and the seasons he dimly revealed, reserving them mainly for his own contemplation. And scarcely had the Saviour at length alighted on this earth than he began to direct the minds of the new people whom he was forming for himself, to his ulterior advent in glory. To wait for the Son of God from heaven, is as much the proper attitude of the Church of this dispensation, as of that of former dispensations.

When he came on his errand of humiliation, there was no

element of humiliation wanting; and when he cometh for the exhibition of glory, we may be sure that there shall be no element of glory wanting. For consider that he cometh in the glory of his Father. The inconceivable glory of God in the material universe, in the angelic hierarchies, in the heaven of heavens, must all be placed upon the Redeemer, even as once our sins were all laid upon him. Yes, he must come clothed with the virtues of all beings, with all the righteousness that is, with all the wisdom that is, with all the beauty that is, all the power, all the excellence of all existences. The glory of the sun will be changed to sackcloth, the brightness of the heaven to darkness, not by any change in them, but by the superior glory then introduced. This glory is to burst upon the world in a day and in an hour, when men expect it not: hence the need that Christians should expect it in every day and hour. The gospel includes both advents. Christ as often spoke to his disciples of his future coming in glory, as of his dying in Jerusalem.

MAY 31.—"I count all things but loss for the excellency of the knowledge of Christ Jesus, my Lord."—Philippians iii. 8.

Excellency is to be estimated by adaptation. Viewed in himself, Christ is without a peer. With all beings before him, the Father chose Christ, saying, "This is my elect, in whom my soul delighteth." When God has pronounced, what need remains of deliberation? But happily for us, there is in Christ not only infinite excellency, but adaptation to our state and requirements.

As he is excellent, so is the knowledge of him excellent; for we possess him by knowing him. There is nothing in the world that may not cheerfully be sacrificed in the effort to know Christ. If there be reason to believe that we shall enjoy better opportunities of knowing Christ in an inferior position, it is most becoming to descend into it. If wealth blocks up the avenues of our spiritual apprehension of Christ, it must be removed.

We cannot know Christ, if we are without a will to obey him. Since the path of duty is the path of this golden knowledge, let us go forward in it with delight. The peasant has his few articles of furniture, some paltry pictures, a little patch of ground, plain apparel, and perhaps thinks much of these possessions; but make him master of a palace, with galleries and treasuries, and how lightly will he then esteem his former goods. Thus with the Christian.

JUNE 1.—"I am the bread of life."—John vi. 35.

Men have what they regard as life; and if you tell them that it is not life, they smile at your quaint way of viewing things, and at your figurative language. But, really, what men call life is but a momentary evasion of death. Death dogs you everywhere. He hath long since written his name upon you; and he suffers not a day to go by in which he does not extort a new confession from your mortal constitution, to the effect that you are his. All pain, all weariness, all loss, all decay, proclaims that you are a respited criminal.

Men insist on regarding the existence they now possess as natural, regular, and just what the universal system of things requires. They cannot patiently hearken to the doctrine that man is fallen, that his present estate is in consequence abnormal, out of joint. They call this life, deeming this to be God's great gift, even his best; and are bewildered at the statement that this is death, God's real gift of life having been cast away. It is a great approach to emancipation for a soul to discover that humanity is wrecked; at sea in an open and shattered boat; defending itself from death for a little moment by a drop of water and an ounce of bread; ready to perish whenever it shall please the mysterious monarch to step from some billow into the boat. But when we have found that what men call life is not life, a question of unspeakable interest arises. Is there life for man? Will God, indeed, let us re-enter Eden, and put forth our hand and eat of the fruit of the tree of life, and live forever? When Christ, taking his stand in the centre of the human family, proclaims, "I am the bread of life," then Eden is come again, Eden with opened doors, with no sword-waving cherubim, but with its tree of life in full view, and within easy reach. The door that will be closed against many in the last day, is no other than the door that has stood open for them many a long year; and the life from which they with anguish will be forever divorced, is just the life that is now offered to them day by day, and offered in vain.

If we would have a lively illustration of the meaning of these words, we should give our attention to the few barley loaves that were taken from the basket of that lad, multiplied and distributed to the apostles; which kept multiplying as they kept breaking and distributing it to the multitude; which kept on multiplying as the multitude kept breaking it and handing it every man to his neighbor; which abundantly met the wants of five thousand men, besides women and children, and would have met the wants of the whole world had it been there; which was so much greater for all its communications that it required twelve baskets to hold it, after the banquet was over.

JUNE 2.—"God was in Christ."—2 Corinthians v. 19.

You have false conceptions of some being, some one that has claims upon your cordial love and heartiest obedience; his claims you cannot recognize, his worth is utterly hidden from you, and your embittered mind will not allow you to behold him otherwise than as invested with dark and forbidding qualities. Knowing the force of your prejudice, he comes to you in the disguise of a mean man, and is hired by you as a servant. Gradually you marvel at the admirable characteristics of this servant. He removes every stone from your path, and does it without ostentation. He garlands your house about with beautiful flowers. He spreads your table with food that angels might eat. He entertains your children by endless devices, and enriches their minds with the best instruction. He is continually averting some danger, saving some life. In some hour of special magnanimity on his part, you shout aloud your admiration of his character, and call Heaven to witness that you will ever love him and ever serve him. At that moment, the disguise falls from him, and your injured lord stands before you. The master against whom you had revolted was in that matchless servant. Your prejudices left him no alternative but thus to approach you, thus to propitiate you. What now can you do but fall at his feet with a contrite heart, deploring your former folly and wickedness, and consecrating yourself unreservedly to the service of such a master.

Here is a province that professes to have a great attachment to the sovereign, yet breaks all his laws without the slightest compunction, affirming either that he had never made the laws, or was indifferent about their execution. When any legate landed on their shores, demanding tribute, they tore him in pieces, affirming that he had come in his own name, and that the sovereign required no tribute at their hands. Perhaps they put a few lame and diseased animals that they knew not what else to do with, on board the vessel, and sent it back to the capital, while they boasted of their munificent fealty and self-sacrificing devotedness. At length a stranger comes and takes up his abode among them. His conduct is very different from theirs, for it is blameless. He teaches and exemplifies neighborly love; refuses to visit the places of amusement which the sovereign had forbidden to be opened, to take anything, do anything, speak anything, contrary to the laws. He speaks of the king, and relates what he has seen at his court and what he has not seen there. He assures the people that if they will repent and unfeignedly submit to their monarch, they shall meet with not only lenity, but boundless kindness; but if they remain obdurate, he will come and overwhelm them with his wrath. The people, from the highest to the lowest, hear all this with shouts of derision, unbelief, and anger; from day to day their anger becomes less and less controllable; at length they seize the stranger, determined to put him to the most barbarous and shameful death. "At last," they then say, "we shall free the earth from the presence of this blasphemer, who can do nothing but asperse the honor of our sovereign." They bring their instruments of torture and proceed to inflict upon him the most fiendish torments. At that moment his imperial cohorts arrive and snatch him from their hands; his nobles re-invest him with the symbols of power, and bow the knee before him; and all the company of the regicides stand appalled and utterly confounded. Their sovereign was in that stranger; and it was the character, the words, the ways of their sovereign, that they had been so intensely hating. "God was in Christ."

JUNE 3.—"Where two or three are gathered together in my name, there am I in the midst of them."—Matthew xviii. 20.

We cross sea and land to visit the holy places. We exult to look upon the wretched city that bears the name of the place where Christ was condemned to death. We say, this stream he crossed, this mountain he stood upon, this valley he traversed, this shore he visited, in this town he was born, in this place he was brought up. Romanists, Greeks, Armenians, who know of no other holy places, jostle us and outstrip us. But the question, "Where is Christ to be found now?" is far more important than the question, where he once was. "The world seeth me no more and thinketh of me in the past, but ye see me. The hour cometh when ye shall neither in this mountain, nor yet at Jerusalem, worship the Father; but when true worshippers shall worship the Father in spirit and in truth." The little companies that come together in upper chambers and bye places, in the name of Christ, remembering his promises, seeking his presence, cherishing his spirit, honoring his word—in these little companies Christ is to be found.

Is it possible that any one should be a lover of Christ and not a lover of these assemblies? That they should be a weariness to the world, we can understand. But alas! there are thousands who profess to be his, who never dream of frequenting these meetings of believers, held in honor of Christ, for communion with Christ. These believers behold Christ in one another. They speak his words; entertain his desires; occupy themselves with his resolutions. He is present in their characters, modelled upon his. He is present in the word which they read, hearken to, believe. He is the subject of their conversation. They dwell upon his life, sufferings, and love. He is present by the Spirit, that takes of him and shows unto them. They are convinced of sin, confess it, and forsake it. They behold his glory, and rejoice greatly in him. Such effects of Christ's words and glances often take place in these meetings, as greatly surpass what took place when he was visibly present with those twelve disciples of old. He is present as a righteous advocate and intercessor. They are his plenipotentiaries. He gives them their instructions, and clothes them with power.

If Christ be in these assemblies, then are they the true centres from whence the mightiest influences flow abroad over the world. Divine wisdom, truth, power and love, must be added to the folly, weakness, ignorance, erringness, of the two or three that meet in his name, in order that we may form a just estimate of the moral value of these meetings. Some of the grandest revolutions in society, have their origin here.

JUNE 4.—"Christ Jesus came into the world to save sinners, of whom I am chief."—1 Timothy i. 15.

Every man looks upon himself as belonging to a small minority composed of the world's best men. If there were one enormous circle drawn, and another very small one, the former for the great transgressors and the latter for the comparatively innocent, all the world with one consent would seek to crowd into the smaller circle. And in this they would be acting quite conscientiously. They are accustomed in their self-estimates to overrate the good and underrate the evil. Again, they judge of themselves, not by their actual works, but by their imaginations, aspirations, and unrealized capabilities. Circumstances, they say to themselves, keep us down; but we feel that we are capable of rising to the loftiest heights of moral power. Their bad qualities again are treated as accidents, not properly belonging to them; as barnacles cleave to the bottom of a ship. Thus it was with Paul, till the law came, and he found himself compelled to apply God's standard of goodness to himself. Then he was filled with horror; sin revived and he died; the former Paul whom he had known and admired, and wanted all the world to admire, disappeared, and in his place came Sin, revealing itself in all his nature, all his habits, and, as it were, possessing him, from the crown of his head to the sole of his feet. He now finds it impossible to see so much sin in any other as he sees in himself; just as it is impossible for the eye to see so much of things at a distance, as of things at hand.

This mighty and, as it seems, incredible change must pass upon all men. Yes, all the proud, the boastful, the self-complacent, the moral; the souls that eulogize themselves for heaven-born impulses and heaven-high aspirations; these all must be brought to the condition into which the law brought Paul. I say not that they will not be brought out of it.

When the wrath of the Lamb shall be revealed, who shall be able to stand?

June 5.—"Blessed are those servants whom the Lord, when he cometh, shall find watching."—Luke xii. 37.

How everything in this world wears the appearance of a house the master of which is away, far, far away; as good as dead. Every one doeth that which is right in his own eyes, and goeth about as though he had himself inherited all authority. A few, indeed, proclaim in this chamber and in that, the remembered will of the master, and endeavor to turn back the tide of rebellion and of ungodliness. But the others listen not. They say, "Our Lord delayeth his coming, and there is not the slightest likelihood that he will come in our days. He hath stationed no guard to interfere with us; we have liberty; let us avail ourselves of it." Carried away by the force of their example, some from whom you would have expected more fidelity, give over watching. But there is a little band who keep watching, watching on, amid all the confusion and iniquity around them. To a reflecting observer, it is quite amazing to see how they go about all their appointed occupations, just as though the Lord were there, looking on; not sparing themselves, not seeking their own, putting up with insults and injuries, multiplying their labors; introducing improvements into their way of doing things, increasing in skill, in patience, in success, as months and years roll on. What is the secret spring of their conduct? It is twofold. By faith they know that their Lord sees them, even now, and is acquainted with all their ways; and they know also that he cometh, none can say how soon, to take unto him his great power and reign.

JUNE 6.—"Pray without ceasing. In everything give thanks."—1 Thessalonians v. 17, 18.

You are always receiving; you are always needing. There is no position that you are called to occupy in which you will not find some expressions of divine goodness. There is no cup so bitter given you by your heavenly Father that has not in it some commingled good. *In everything* give thanks. In the pit of Joseph. In his prosperity. In his prison. In the belly of the fish. Upon Job's dunghill. Let John the Bap tist in prison give thanks that he had received boldness to declare the truth. Let the scourged disciples rejoice that they are counted worthy to suffer for the name of Jesus. In every trial you have this at least to give thanks for, that you are tried; for you might have been cast away as reprobate. The very fact of trial shows a thought of goodness toward you on the part of God. Observe what you are receiving, and give thanks for it: be sensible also of what you need, and pray for it.

Pray without ceasing, for—

The adversary is unceasingly on the alert.

The manna of grace does not keep.

Your nature is most volatile and mutable.

Prayer is the recognition of an unceasing fact, namely your dependence on God.

JUNE 7.—"Walk in the Spirit."—Galatians v. 16.

Let the Spirit have the control of all your movements. Do this thing, let alone that, adopt this habit, forsake that, speak this word, dismiss that, go, stay, as the Spirit shall choose. It is certainly a marvellous invention of God that the Spirit should come down from heaven, enter into these satanized constitutions of ours, and undertake to exhibit a divine life upon the earth through the instrumentality of anything so utterly intractable as these members, these hearts, these darkened understandings. It seems like expecting that some mud-boat shall mount into the skies, and wheel itself in beauty along the clouds.

He that walketh in the Spirit, will be very shy of mere impulses. He will cultivate a calm collectedness of soul, will keep himself in a listening attitude, that he may ever hear the still small voice of the Spirit. How wonderful that this mighty subjugation of his nature, should be brought about by the agency of a faint whisper that the least commotion renders inaudible! What all the physical forces of the world would have failed to accomplish, is brought about by a gentle mysterious whisper in the depth of one's nature. The world sees the surprising result, and is all bewildered at the absence of a sensible motive power.

June 8.—"I will not leave you comfortless. I will come to you."—John xiv. 18.

More literally, I will not leave you orphans—bereaved of all that you hold most dear, most necessary—helpless in the presence of many foes—friendless in the presence of many trials— skilless in the presence of an immense task. The parents are the complement of the little child. It operates through their wisdom and power and resources, to keep its place in the world, and act its part. The Christian without Christ, if such a thing can be conceived, is the most deplorably helpless being in the world. For he has been awakened from the delusion that possesses mankind, that they are complete in themselves; he has seen the length and breadth of the law of God; has discovered the bitter hostility of the world to the righteous; and just in the measure that his sense of need has been increased, he has seen the ability to help him vanishing from the world and all created things, to concentrate itself in Christ.

The nearest approach to such an orphan state of the Church was in the period between Christ's death and the resurrection. To the disciples at that time Christ was really dead; his power, wisdom, grace, were all dead; the promises were dead and buried with him; all the advantages conferred by his teaching, all the blessings derived from his presence, were crucified and gone. These disciples had been taken up by the Saviour almost into heaven; and now by the unexpected death of their leader and commander, they were let drop to a point of helplessness far below that of the rest of men. They shut the doors for fear of the Jews who had crucified him, and who might come at any moment and crucify them; and they looked upon the swords which Christ had told them to take, instead of all the promises; and a full conception of their misery burst upon them. Hundreds of thousands of enemies on the one hand; and they, a few inexpert fishermen with two or three rusty swords on the other. Could anything be more absurd than the idea of a conflict? One little word of promise had once invested them with power over all the power of the enemy; but all the promises were now buried with Christ, and a great stone rolled upon them; and they were left alone with their wretched swords. But Christ fulfilled his word. He left them not a prey to the wrath of man and the malice of the adversary. He came unto them; and with him came all the promises. In fact, they themselves with him arose. They breathed, they lived, when they again saw him breathing, living.

If at any time a soul be brought into a state of orphanage, and seem to itself separated from all grace and power and hope; let it lay hold of this word. It may have been fitting that it should have a taste of the misery of being without Christ, under a sense of the need of Christ; but a taste suffices. "I will come unto you," says Jesus.

June 9.—"If a man love me he will keep my words; and my Father will love him, and we will come unto him and make our abode with him." —John xiv. 23.

Jude wanted to know how the manifestation of Christ unto his people exclusively, was to be effected. Christ in reply, says, that the believer has something and God something to do; it does not concern the believer to know how God will do his part; all that concerns him is to know how he is to do his part. Let him then keep the words of Christ, and the manifestation will be brought about; the Godhead shall take up its abode with him; let him keep the words of Christ, and he will keep Christ with him; let the words of God abide with him, and God will abide with him.

To know how to keep the words of Christ is the most important of all knowledge; to keep them is the most important of all works.

The best of all teachers in this thing is *love*. Love of Christ will not allow us to make light of any word of Christ. It views the memory as a consecrated room fitted up for the reception of the words of its object. The words of a man embody his character;—imperfectly however;—for who is without guile? The words of Christ give us Christ himself. They tell me what he loves; in other words, what he wishes me to be; and I must keep them perpetually that I may know what I should perpetually be. I cannot keep the words of Christ and remove out of the path of Christ; or if they then abide with me, it is to torture me, and I can have no peace, till I make my way, wounded and wearied, back to the king's highway. While I keep the words of Christ, I keep the tempter at a distance; I thwart his endeavors as Christ himself thwarted them. Let me keep the words of Christ, and the principles of this world shall find no place in me. In keeping the words of Christ, I keep the watchword by which I have access at all times to the throne of God's heavenly grace. Let me keep them then in affection, in memory, in faith, in obedience, in prayer.

JUNE 10.—"Peace I leave with you, my peace I give unto you."—John xiv. 27.

Christ makes his will, the hour of his departure having come. Silver and gold he has none. To the eye of the world it is a pauper going his way; and the wonder is that there should be any to attend him in his last hours. He has lived in the world and amassed nothing; not so much as to pay his funeral expenses. His life is a failure; he has had the usual advantages, yet, leaves the world as he entered it. You will find no parchments in his drawers; no stray pieces of gold in his coffers; it is a dead man dying; for what but a dead man is he that has no worldly property?

This expresses the feeling, if not the reasoning, of many. Yet why do men seek property? Is it not from the want of peace? Why do we behold the world rushing passionately along ten thousand paths? Because they find not peace. They seek peace by appropriation, not by renunciation. Would not even their own wisdom teach them to purchase peace, if an opportunity presented itself, by the surrender of a globe of gold?

The peace that Christ leaves, is his own peace. Consider his life. He endured the constant contradiction of sinners. He was numbered with the transgressors. He was stigmatized as devilish in origin, character, and purpose. Each returning day brought him new trials, new sufferings. So that the peace he leaves is consistent with many trials, many afflictions. These in fact serve for the proof of it.

The legatees of Christ have peace of conscience. Myriads of sins, each of which—in the day of the mind's awakening—has the tormenting faculty of many devils, are bound as to this power, and that forever. We have peace in the deliverance from inordinate desires:—in the consciousness of God's favor:—

in the assurance that all things concerning us will be ordered for the best:—in freedom from worldly cares:—in the certainty of Christ's victorious coming and everlasting reign.

June 11.—"Herein is my Father glorified, that ye bear much fruit."—John xv. 8.

This is a valid argument with those that are concerned for the glory of God. It is addressed to those who are acquainted with this spring of action. The heavens declare the glory of God, and the firmament showeth his handiwork; but in vain, till Christians in a far higher degree exhibit his glory by showing that Christ is the true vine, and that they who abide in him obtain the communications of a divine life, and produce heavenly fruits on earth. What the sun, moon, and stars, the hills and the floods, volcanoes and earthquakes, rainbows and flowers, what the works of God in nature and in providence have not succeeded in doing, it is yours under peculiar circumstances, and by the subordination of mightiest means, to attempt. Innumerable spectators from the worlds on high, watch with breathless interest the progress of this experiment. And can it be that what the magnificent and all-resplendent orbs of space have not accomplished, shall be brought about by the instrumentality of a little company of converted sinners? That you shall show forth the glory of God, and constrain the world to take knowledge of his perfections?

Christ is the vine, and you are the branches; wherefore your fruit is Christ's fruit. The world did not get rid of him by killing him. He lives in you and produces fruit in you. His meekness and lowliness are to find their exhibition through you. His self-denial and love; his zeal and faithfulness; his faith and prayerfulness; his wisdom and patience; his fortitude, his impartiality, his purity, all his admirable characteristics are to abide in the world, for you are in the world. Then will the world find itself baffled and confounded, when having crucified Christ in Jerusalem, it finds him springing up again not only in Jerusalem, but in Samaria, Joppa, Damascus, Antioch, Ephesus, Corinth, Rome, and in fact everywhere throughout the world.

JUNE 12.—"As the Father hath loved me, so have I you."—John xv. 9.

These disciples were the representatives of the universal church. They stood in the place of all believers. We were all there by proxy. It must never be supposed that the beautiful words and condescending acts of Christ were just for Peter, John, James, and their companions. John is not the only beloved disciple who is encouraged to lean upon the bosom of his Lord. His love for the family of Bethany is not a singular love, with which other families have nothing to do. It is a specimen of his love rather, intended to make glad ten thousand families. That loving, solicitous question, "Lovest thou me?" addressed to Peter, stops not with Peter, but makes its whispered way to innumerable other professors, preserving all its tenderness of intonation and fullness of expression.

The great thing is to have a persistent, unvanquishable faith with regard to this, so as to be able to take our place at the side of Christ, and accompany him through Galilee and Judea; or, if you choose to express it so, to have him by us, in our own place of residence, mingling his life with ours, questioning us, upbraiding us, educating us for his own heaven of love. And it is a happy thing for us that there is nothing about the character of those first disciples to make us diffident in appropriating the gracious words addressed to them. There is no halo of excellency about them to intimidate us. In fact, they are just ourselves. Those things which, we are well aware, constitute the most repugnant elements of our character,—pride, unbelief, selfishness, passion, carnality, envy, sloth, cowardice,—these very things are found in them. They afterwards put on, it is true, the armor of light, and shed lustre upon their sacred calling, but this was after Christ had given all his proofs of love.

I have loved you; and if you wish to know how much, why, let us take the highest possible expression, even the love of the infinite Father for his Son; *so have I loved you.* Nothing could exceed the preciousness of this statement; no statement was ever more corroborated by evidence. It is painful to think of such a heavenly declaration being made in vain in the ear of men; for the honor of Christ, see that you receive it, believe it, live upon it.

JUNE 13.—"If ye keep my commandments, ye shall abide in my love." —JOHN xv. 10.

Christ's love takes us as it finds us; but it does not leave us so. If it did not make us better, it would not be Christ's love, but just common earth-love. There are two mighty chapters in the history of Christ's love. One relates to the means by which he brings us to himself, the other to the means by which he keeps us with himself. After we have been brought to him, a sublime work expands itself before him. We are to be made like unto himself. He will not rest until he has communicated unto us his own perfections. These souls so loved are to be made lovely. Christ would not be worthy of our continued regard, if he left us to follow our own evil will; and the whole story of his love would turn out a mere legend, if he taught us not to honor the commandments of God. But this reproach cannot be brought against Christ. Keep my commandments, he says, and abide in my love.

This is a different language from that of Sinai. It is not the language of authority, so much as of love. The speaker and his friend are taking counsel together as to the best mode of perpetuating the hallowed sentiment by which they are bound. "I cannot support the idea," says the friend, "of any interruption to this love. Tell me how it may be made immortal, unchangeable." "I will tell you. Keep my commandments. They shall be to you like an amulet, or mystic ring; so long as it remains with you, I cannot leave you." "Oh! how delightful," exclaims the friend, "that there should be commandments, expressive of thy will, and indicative of the way of abiding in thy love. For it is the life of love, to have something to do for its object, to have commandments to keep. These commandments will keep us bound to one another. For thou hast said, "Without me ye can do nothing." So I am to do nothing alone. Thy commandments remove me from thee? No! not for an instant; they will but draw me more and more closely to thee!"

JUNE 14.—"Verily, verily, I say unto you, whatsoever ye shall ask the Father in my name, he will give it you."—John xvi. 23.

Christ says this for the purpose, as it were, of inducing us to consent to his departure. Having come into the world and constituted himself our good Shepherd, and accustomed us to lean on him for everything, we are rather confounded at the suggestion that he is to go away again. Seeing this, he gives us this reassuring promise. Whatsoever we ask of the Father, he will give it. Well, suppose we ask for Christ. He will be given. Not with the limitations of an earthly body. "If thou hadst been here, my brother had not died." These reproaches are painful to the heart of Christ. It is expedient that he go, that he may come again in spirit, in glorious omnipresence, and be the shepherd of a flock feeding on ten thousand hills.

Will the Father, indeed, give us everything that we ask? Is thy name so potent in influence at the throne of grace, that it is impossible for any gift to be withheld, if demanded in that name? It is not merely the half of his kingdom that the Father must yield to us, if we ask; *whatsoever* we ask we must receive. But in fact the gift has already been made. "The Father loveth the Son, and hath given all things into his hands." When, therefore, we ask anything in thy name, we ask for what has already been made over to thee.

But to whom is this promise made? To the apostles and to all who stand in the position that the apostles stood in. To those who have apostolic work to do, and apply themselves to it with apostolic consecration. With promises so vast, how vast should have been the performance of the Church, how rapid and signal her successes! Every generation of believers that has come into existence, read the Gospel of John, and gone its way, must stand condemned in the presence of these unapprehended promises. Are we grasping them? Or even looking them in the face? Or feeling our way towards them?

JUNE 15.—"In the world ye shall have tribulation."—John xvi. 33.

There was a new and wondrous trial of mankind, when Christ dwelt on the earth. The world is always saying, "If we had been in Eden, we would not have brought ruin on ourselves." By the coming of Christ the earth was, as it were, made into a new Eden for the occasion, and men were tried over again. It was no longer the question, "Will they sin?" But, "Will they receive God manifest in the form of man? How will they treat the most glorious and admirable being in existence, infinitely humbling himself for their salvation?" The trial was made as easy for them as it could be. The Jews were specially prepared for his coming. They were educated to feel their need of an almighty Saviour. He came in the most propitiating guise conceivable. Yet he was rejected, abhorred, killed. Let the world now forever be silent about its love of goodness, its noble aspirations, its heavenward tendencies. He that made the world, the fountain of all excellence, came into the world, into the elect and well-tutored part of it, yet encountered from first to last nothing but opposition; and it was only by special efforts of divine power that his life was prolonged sufficiently for him to make a complete manifestation of the divine nature, and accomplish all that was requisite for the salvation of men.

As it is settled that the world has no sympathy with true goodness, so there can be no question what kind of reception it will give to those who come in the name of Christ, bearing the image of Christ. The world passes through many phases, puts on many aspects; but it has its own particular orbit, from which it never breaks away. Its changes are always within certain well-defined limits. It is true to itself, true to its own rebellious will; and under no felicity of circumstances, does it ever find itself sitting quietly and humbly on the steps of God's throne.

Expect, therefore, that the lion and the tiger will give a gentle and amicable reception to the lamb; but do not expect that the world will provide accommodation for those who travel along the narrow path that leadeth unto everlasting life; or busy itself to take up the stones out of that path. The world, indeed, has a great deal of wisdom, and has manifested it in these latter days by carefully studying how to treat the Church so as to make the Church as little a source of discomfort as possible. Formerly it committed some blunders, by proceeding against it with fire and sword; the faith, the joy, the dying hymns of those whom it burnt at the stake kept irritating the memory and making the ears to tingle, for a long time. But now the world parries the testimony of the Church by force of courtesy. It professes to be occupying itself with the subject of religion, and to have almost made up its mind to embrace Christianity; begging meanwhile that it may not be disturbed in its meditations. And then again, alas! it has got many unsuspected victories over the Church, and its banner is flying from many a fortress where it should never have been planted. But he that will live godly in Christ Jesus, will find the world very decidedly opposed to him. It will seek at first to bind him perhaps with ribands, and not with iron chains; but bind him it will, if it can.

JUNE 16.—"Being justified by faith, we have peace with God."—Romans v. 1.

We receive tidings of a treaty of peace between two nations lately belligerent. Anon, we receive intimations of another war possible. Rumors of wars never fail to agitate profoundly the general bosom of mankind. But there is a rumor of another war infinitely more dire than any, between man and his Maker. It is long since this war has broken out; for thousands of years it has been raging; and we see no signs of its immediate cessation. Men perceive not that all their other miseries proceed from this feud; they seem not aware that the cruelty of all other wars, the agony of all other scourges, are just scintillations from the battle-field where they and their Creator are arrayed against one another. Let this feud be healed, and there will be no need to entertain terror of this despot or of that; to build barricades, or lavish treasures on forts and men of-war. Diplomacy is spending all its strength in vain, while it merely occupies itself with the differences between States. Holy alliances may exercise the spirit of war in one direction, but speedily it will reveal itself in another. There must be peace between man and his Creator; then, and then only, will the nations understand one another, and perceive that they have one common interest.

Blessed be God, we have a Peace-maker, who gave himself that man might be reconciled to God. His coming was the expression of God's amity. The flag of truce is held out to the world. The friends of peace are running to and fro in the earth, informing men that by simple faith in the Lord Jesus

Christ, their accumulated sins shall be done away; that they shall be held justified, and shall have the peace of God which passeth all understanding.

JUNE 17.—"To them who by patient continuance in well-doing seek for glory and honor and immortality, eternal life."—Romans ii. 7.

The path of faith and that of well-doing are not diverse from each other; they are one. A man that is in the path of well-doing, and for whose deeds there is ever and anon dropping from the lips of God the expression, "Well done!" is already saved in an important sense. He has regained the footing from whence the world by transgression fell. He has certainly a large instalment of salvation. But, it is faith that brought him into this heavenward path, and that enables him to continue therein. It is faith that led him to renounce all dependence upon his own miserable works, and to avail himself of the works of Christ to obtain acceptance with God, and the freedom of that sacred path. It is faith that enables him to see the incomparable superiority over everything that the world can offer, of those grand prizes held up before him by the Lord of all; to see glory, honor, and immortality where they really are, where they exclusively are for man, in the new Jerusalem.

There are many who are seeking for glory, honor, and immortality in very different paths from that of which we are speaking. By the path of well-doing, we mean, in one word, the path of God's will; and all doing that is not strictly modelled on this, we reject: though it might seem to be such doing as would regenerate a continent, reclaim a Sahara, or banish the deadliest plagues.

Nothing in all the success that has waited upon Satan in his management of the world's affairs, is so saddening to contemplate, as the false direction he has been enabled to give to the enthusiasm of men. Enthusiasm is a beautiful and sacred thing, implanted in us that we might launch forth on sublime enterprises of mercy to man and of glory to God. Enthusiasm would make of a holy man a seraph. Men hardly know what to do with this divine faculty. They thirst for glory, honor, immortality, but limit their conceptions of these things to what the world, the fallen, ruined, doomed world can give. As though a criminal on his way to the place of execution, should concern himself to obtain honor and glory from his fellow-criminals. A world that rose up in utmost ferocity against the only faultless, the only truly glorious being that ever trod its soil, is not a world competent to decide where glory should be sought, what deeds are truly honorable, what immortality is worthy of man's utmost endeavor. It having rejected the elect of heaven, the only man found heroic in the eyes of God, we can turn away from its heroes, and think lightly of its honorable ones.

JUNE 18.—"Believe on the Lord Jesus Christ, and thou shalt be saved."—Acts xvi. 31.

And is this so difficult? Does your heart find itself competent to everything, rather than this? Oh, what a reproach to you! In fact, it is impossible to conceive of any more severe condemnation than that which you pass upon yourself, and day by day reiterate, while you continue not to believe on the Lord Jesus Christ. You are asked to take his righteousness in preference to your own; his wisdom rather than your own; his influence at the throne of God rather than your own. You are asked to become the servant of Christ, rather than continue the servant of sin; to be the friend of Christ, rather than the friend of Satan; and to receive the gift of the Holy Spirit to free you from the control of unclean spirits. You are asked to choose him whom the good have chosen; him whom all the angels, the most exalted of finite beings; whom

God himself has chosen. You refuse; and choose rather to identify yourself with the multitude that crucified him. The blackest catalogue of crimes cannot more truly condemn a man, than the fact that you believe not on Jesus Christ condemns you. Your character comes out dark, base, odious, by this one fact. In vain you pretend to have love for your fellow-men, while you declare, as you emphatically do, "Not this man!" Were a vessel freighted with provisions to approach an island whose inhabitants were dying with starvation, what would you think of him who should refuse to co-operate in bringing her to shore? And what must be thought of him who cannot believe on the Lord Jesus Christ? You may for the present be deemed respectable; but a day is coming when Christ will be known as the touchstone of morality, and all who are without affinity with him, will be known as utterly reprobate.

JUNE 19.—"While we were yet sinners, Christ died for us."—Rom. v. 8.

Imagine a number of men whose hearts are filled with bitterness against their sovereign, and, in a certain chamber, are industriously laboring at the construction of an infernal machine, to be exploded on some approaching day when the sovereign is to pass that way. The heart of this sovereign, say, is kindness itself. He receives information of what these men are doing. Disguising himself he comes among them, and succeeds in convincing them that he is friendly, and will prove a valuable confederate. They receive him into their band, initiate him fully into their projects, and take his advice on many points. He soon obtains a great influence over them. They are struck with the superiority of his character, the generosity that beams in all his words and acts. He labors assiduously to do them good; relieves their wants; visits their families that he may confer benefits upon them. His resources appear boundless, but not greater than his beneficence. When injured or insulted, he exhibits an astonishing patience; and in fine, by a purity and magnanimity such as they have never witnessed, he succeeds in inspiring them with the utmost admiration. And day by day he labors with them in perfecting that machine that is to be levelled against himself. They unanimously agree that he shall be their sovereign, when they have killed the reigning one, and that he shall distribute among them the offices of the State just as may seem good to him. At length the day arrives; and as the hour approaches, when the king should pass that way, they wonder what has become of their generous friend. Suddenly he appears among them; throws off his disguise, and the sovereign stands revealed. "I come," he says, "to save you from a great crime, and from a fearful doom. You have already chosen me to be your sovereign, and sworn to submit with delight to all my commands. I command that you shall come and dwell with me in my palace. While you have been preparing this engine for my destruction, I have been preparing sumptuous apartments for your abode. I will associate with you as your friend, even as I have done, and will do my best to fit you to fill the highest offices of State."

Now, the thing that will most surprise these men, is the fact that while they were sinners, while they were laboring for the death of their sovereign, he in secret was earnestly laboring for their highest good. And this is the thing that should most surprise us when we come to Christ, namely, the fact that while we were rearing higher the mountains of our iniquity, he was engaged in carrying out a scheme of the most transcendant mercy and kindness toward us.

JUNE 20.—"Be of good courage, and he shall strengthen your heart."—Psalm xxxi. 24.

Before you are conscious of any strength in your heart, while you feel yourself exceedingly weak and utterly incompetent, even then you are to be of good courage. It requires very little true courage to be bold when there is the consciousness of strength. The courage that is well-pleasing in the sight of God, is the courage of faith; the courage of David, whose sling and stone were nothing, but who trusted simply in God.

Nothing is more essential to the Christian than good courage. He needs in the first place courage to go into the presence of his sovereign, nothing daunted, however much humbled, by the thought of his unworthiness, assured that all the virtue of Christ is available for him. He needs courage to cancel the various articles of the compact of sin between him and the world; to come out from it and be separate; to be peculiar; to confess that he has transferred his allegiance to the crucified and risen one. He needs courage to break with the god of this world, and adopt the badge of the revolutionists who are seeking his overthrow. He needs courage to speak to those whom he loves, of their great need. He needs courage to manifest the new and better nature that has been given him. He needs it to advance in a path of duty where there is no pioneer, with only a chart for the day, and no intimation of the morrow's perils.

JUNE 21.—"His anger endureth but a moment; in his favor is life."—Psalm xxx. 5.

The idea is, that his anger is fugitive, his favor perennial. The contrast is between the words moment and life. The contrast is sustained in what follows: "Weeping may endure for a night, but joy cometh in the morning," even in the morning of a day, whose sun shall never go down. Paul renews it in the words, "Our light affliction, which is but for a moment, worketh for us a far more exceeding and eternal weight of glory." As the ages of our prospective existence unfold to us, the misery of our mortal span will be reduced by an easy arithmetical progression, to something utterly infinitesimal. Seventy years of suffering are not very much in an existence that reaches to a thousand years; far from much, when proportioned to a period of ten thousand years; in a hundred thousand years they are but as a drop to the bucket; in millions of years as a drop to the ocean, a mere thought, a flash of lightning; in eternity, what?

You venture to observe, perhaps, that man is so constituted that the present is to him necessarily like a mountain bounding his vision, and that he cannot be greatly affected by the conception of unending plains stretching beyond.

To man's true constitution belongs faith, by means of which he soars aloft and looks down upon his past, present, and future. Observe, that the momentary anger bears a most important relation to the eternal favor. It is that you may be led to press more eagerly towards this, and battle more bravely with the enemies that would cut you off from it, that weeping is given to you for a night.

In all God's anger to his people there is mercy. It is an unspeakable condescension in him to be angry. He might just put forth his power and sweep you away into everlasting misery. But no! he deigns to express to you his displeasure. Thus did he even to the Ninevites; and they inferred that he might, after all, pardon them.

JUNE 22.—"Teach me thy way, O Lord."—Psalm xxvii. 11.

It will hardly be denied by any reflecting person that it is reasonable to suppose that there is for every human being a particular line of procedure which commends itself to God as the best, and every deviation from which is a deviation from that which is best. When we consider how admirably God has organized man, how richly he has endowed him, with what authority he has invested him, and with what appliances he has surrounded him; when we consider what an infinitude of wise and good thoughts God has bestowed in the preparation of man for life; can we believe that God has no particular will in regard to the way in which that life should be spent? We should be greatly surprised if a man should expend an immense sum of money in the building of a ship; employ the most skilful artificers in perfecting her with respect to a thousand anticipated necessities; render her strong, beautiful, swift, commodious; and then launch her and leave her to float at random over the waters, without any commander, without any instructions. Yet this appears to be the idea that many inconsiderate persons entertain of human existence. They suppose that man is left without a chart, without instructions; and leave it to be inferred that God is the most inconsistent of all beings. Ask them why they suppose so; if they have searched for the will of God, and found none; if they have sincerely asked God for instructions, and obtained no answer; if they have been cordially willing to leave unto God the full control of their earthly existence; and they will be obliged to reply that they have not. Not only have they not sought, they have not been willing to see.

We know, however, that God has a will with regard to every man, a will that takes note of every conceivable particular. We know that he is disposed to make known this will, and disposed also to teach us to do it.

He teaches us to do it by making us sensible of our incompetency to guide ourselves. One after another, signal mistakes occur, to show us how absolutely we need a guide more intelligent than ourselves. We get disgusted with our own ignorance and short-sightedness. We are like a man who finds himself in the midst of a vast factory, crowded with the most complicated and ponderous machinery, where mighty engines of death threaten him on the right hand and on the left, before and behind; he makes a step in one direction, and receives a frightful blow; in another, and gets dreadfully lacerated; then he cries out in agony for some one to take him by the hand and lead him.

He teaches us to do it by showing us the incompetency of others to guide us. Some persons are conscious of their inaptitude, and look to others to show them what to do with life. They turn to Plato or Socrates, to Seneca or Confucius, to Carlyle or to La Rochefoucauld, to this novelist or to that. In fact, there is hardly any one desirous of teaching but has some scholars. But, alas! they find no way that is in any degree irreproachable. Life is with them a succession of bruises and losses.

He teaches us to do his will, by letting us see it acted out in the beautiful life of Christ.—By giving us to understand that this will has reference, first and last, in great matters and small, to our own best estate and most assured happiness.—By unfolding to us the Scriptures.—By writing his word in our hearts.—By teaching us to abide in Christ.—By giving the Spirit to abide in us.

June 23.—"**Whosoever believeth on him, shall not be ashamed.**"—Romans ix. 33.

After all, there is nothing that men detest so much as a feeling of shame. We hear a great deal of calamities, bereavements, losses, sorrows, troubles, and numerous other synonyms; but all these are not near so odious to a man as a feeling of shame. There is not any calamity that men have not accepted in preference to a momentary feeling of shame. A feeling of shame in the mind of a man would make him insensible to the loss of his father, or of any other very dear friend;

to the loss of property; nay, to the loss of a kingdom. Thousands have come up to the door which opens on the path that goes to everlasting life, and have seen that they were in danger of everlasting burnings, and have yet accepted of this danger rather than encounter the brief shame of entering.

So potent a principle has not been implanted in us for nothing. It was designed to be of unspeakable advantage to us. And the Christian should seek that it may be as great an aid as it has been a hindrance to him. True shame creates in us a horror of everything that may bring upon us the reproach of an enlightened conscience, the scorn of the holy, the renunciation of God. The soul has no more blessed guarantee, under the grace of God, than the presence of true shame in the heart. This will never for a moment allow us to blush for what is not morally wrong, not a wilful transgression of the will of God. This will suffer us to pay no tribute to the mere conventionalities of life. This will keep us without guile; enable us to walk without any cloak over our conduct; and to regard with perfect equanimity the world's misapprehension of our conduct.

A day is coming when self-condemning shame, shame inextinguishable, intolerable, soul-pervading, will take possession of those who have not believed on the Lord Jesus Christ. And all the shame that they have ever shrunk from in the journey of life, will return multiplied ten thousand times, and establish itself in their souls to go no more out for ever. Think of this, ye proud ones, that daily avoid some path of duty from some feeling of shame. You hold your heads erect among ungodly men, but it is at a fearful cost. What you refuse to experience is now but seed; it will grow to a whirlwind.

JUNE 24.—"Much more, being reconciled, we shall be saved by his life."—Romans v. 10.

If we owe much to the death of Christ, we owe much more to his life. It were little to give us the freedom of the universe, if in that universe we could not find Christ. It were little to give us immortality, if there were no Sun of Righteousness to make that immortality glorious and beautiful. It would be like discovering some unknown friend in his dying hour; we have hardly time to acquaint ourself with his amazing love, and to see the flash of his kindness illuminating our life, before he is removed by death, and we are left to a desolation greater than we had ever known before, because of the moral beauty and the heart of love that had for a moment revealed themselves.

The death of Christ was one exhibition of the love of Christ; he lives that he may, forever and forever, give us newer, still newer, still newer expressions of his unfailing goodness. Being reconciled, there is no longer anything to hinder the forthflowing of the divine beneficence toward us. God is love; and we belong to the number of those whose whole business in life, in everlasting life, is to be making advances in the experience of God's love. But there will be ever something special in the manner by which we have become reconciled, to make us singularly dear to God and to Christ. He hath graven our names upon the palms of his hands. He was pierced for us. We were chosen in such a furnace of affliction as had never been kindled by Babylonian kings. He can never look upon us without the thought of what he suffered to bring us nigh unto God.

JUNE 25.—"If God be for us, who can be against us?"—Rom. viii. 31.

If God be for us, we are justified in making light of all our enemies. Any injury that they can do us is of little account, while we have this all-powerful ally. This seems a mere truism; but it is really the language of an uncommon faith. He goes on to enumerate tribulation, persecution, distress, famine, nakedness, peril, the sword. Now, these things involve tremendous losses; loss of honor, friends, domestic and social enjoyments, wealth, liberty, security, and even food and clothing. Before the thousandth part of these evils, the boldest hearts have recoiled, the strongest have turned and fled. The assurance that God would be with them had no more power to nerve and comfort them, than if a shield made of cobwebs had been presented to them. The language of Paul is the language then of one whose faith has taught him to find everything excellent, everything desirable in God. In vain the world arrays its forces, puts on its terrors; he knows the utter insignificance of these compared with the treasures of might that dwell with him, because God dwells with him.

When the Israelites came out of Egypt, the entire force of Egypt was against them. The sea was against them. The desert was against them. The Amalekites were against them. All nations were against them. Their own inexperience, their waywardness, their evil habits,—these were against them. But God was with them. And they came off more than conquerors. Thus it was with the apostles. The Jews were against them, and so were the Gentiles. Stripes, bonds, and imprisonment awaited them in every place. The power of the priesthood was against them. All the powers of an empire, the mightiest the world had ever seen, were against them. Yet they triumphed. God was with them, and none but God.

Had the church a faith more apostolic, there would not be seen, as there is, alas! too much, a disposition to snatch at worldly aid, and to avail ourselves of worldly wisdom. We need to know that he who is with us is mightier than they that are in the world. Knew we this better, we would enter many paths from which we now turn away; address ourselves to many tasks to which we now shut our eyes.

JUNE 26.—" Quench not the Spirit."—1 Thessalonians v. 19.

This is the utterance of the Spirit, and teaches, if language can teach anything, that the influences of the Spirit may be lost. His presence is as the existence of a heaven-born flame in the heart, which needs to be carefully watched and guarded, which, if its proper aliment be withheld, will die out. The language of Scripture from beginning to end, is perfectly consistent with itself, though the points that establish this consistency are not thrust conspicuously forward. Scripture is exceedingly bold, far more bold than our theological systems; and while it dwells on any truth, gives that truth all its appropriate magnitude, its fullness of honor, without fearing that some other truth may thus suffer loss. The sovereignty of God, the dependence of man, the safety of the elect, the perseverance of the saints,—these things are declared with the utmost positiveness; the obligation of men to believe, to walk by faith, to exercise all Christian affections, to grow in grace, to bring forth fruit, to resist temptation, to work out their own salvation,—these things also are stated in a most emphatic manner. To deny the one class of truths is just as fatal as to deny the other. The Spirit of God is omnipotent, the purposes of God are absolute; but if an individual obey not the guidance of the Spirit, he will quench the Spirit. The man that discards the word "if" from his theology, has no longer a Bible. If a man mock the word of God, by saying that the Spirit may not be quenched, there is reason to fear lest he have already quenched the Spirit.

In order that you may not quench the Spirit, you must make it a constant study to know what is the mind of the Spirit. You must discriminate with the utmost care between his suggestions and the suggestions of your own deceitful heart. You will keep in constant recollection what are the offices of the Spirit, as described by Christ in the gospel of John. You will be on your guard against impulsive movements, inconsiderate acts, rash words. You will abide in prayer. Search the word. Confess Christ on all possible occasions. Seek the society of his people. Shrink from conformity to the world, its vain fashions, unmeaning etiquette Be scrupulous in your reading. "What I say unto you, I say unto all, Watch!" "Have oil in your lamps." "Quench not the Spirit."

JUNE 27.—"**Much more they which receive abundance of grace and of the gift of righteousness, shall reign in life by one, Jesus Christ.**"—Romans v. 17.

The object is to show that Christ has much more than repaired the ruin wrought by Adam, in the case of all those who avail themselves of the salvation wrought out by him. Instead of the one throne where Death sat and swayed the destinies of man, there are now myriads, millions of thrones, on each of which a believer is to sit and give the universe a visible demonstration of what Christ can bestow upon the soul that comes to him.

First, he is to receive abundance of grace, and of the gift of righteousness. It is impossible for him to receive this without the renunciation of his own imagined goodness, strength, and glory. He must be emptied of self; impoverished with respect to all that he has called wealth; ruined with respect to all that he has called life, honor, and excellence. He dies. He lives again. The full tide of God's abounding grace finds itself now at liberty to flow into his soul. He follows the highway of holiness. He has a white stone with a strange inscription, in exchange for which he is to receive a crown of far more than imperial dignity, at the treasury of heaven. When asked if he is a king, he, like his Lord, replies, "Thou sayest it;" and if you choose, you may mock him as men did his Lord; he cannot, however, but bear witness to the truth.

Thus there are millions of kings, and each of them immeasurably more exalted than any king of earth ever was. Do you ask, over whom they are to reign? Know that it does not become the kings of Christ's appointment, to reign over any but kings. All their subjects are kings. For they are all subjects to each. This is one badge of their kingdom, that they in honor prefer one another, and that each finds his happiness in consecration to the good of others.

JUNE 28.—"I know thy works, and thy labor, and thy patience, and how thou canst not bear them that are evil."—Revelation ii. 2.

How many thousands are striving, by the sweat of their brow, by sleepless nights, by sacrifices of health and wealth, by bitter mental toil, by the unflagging consecration of all their powers, to win the attention of men, and are striving in vain. What disappointments pour daily upon them without inducing them to seek another goal for their hopes. "The spurns that patient merit of the unworthy takes," do not extinguish the hope of winning from this unworthy world, sooner or later, some slight acknowledgment of the powers now so unsuccessfully exerted. How many nobly-endowed spirits live and labor under the constraining influence of the hope, for the most part delusive, that the world will one day say to them, "I know your works." To die unknown, is the one lake of fire which they unresistingly seek to escape. Ask them if they will not avail themselves of the consolation so certainly obtained by those that seek it, the consolation of being known to Christ, and they will laugh you to scorn.

On the other hand, the true people of Christ are stirred to

their inmost depths by the belief that he, the Lord of glory, knows their works, their labor and their patience. Their works are not appreciated by men; they are spoken against as evil doers; they spend their strength for naught, so far as the applause of men is concerned; but they are rewarded abundantly in the thought that Jesus knows their works. The words "labor" and "patience" seem to qualify the word "works." What they do for Christ they do energetically, with heart and strength, and they persevere in the doing of it, no matter how many hinderances and chilling influences present themselves.

Christ is jealous when he sees any servant of his, making great account of the praise of others, happy or troubled as he obtains it or misses it, discontented when there is only the approbation of Christ, and allowing the applause of Christians to hide from him the dissatisfaction of Christ. Teach me, O Lord, cost what it may, to find the peace which passeth all understanding in the assurance of thy regard for the poor service thou enablest me to render. Let me not be willing that the incentives derived from prospects held out by this rebellious, sinful world, should succeed in animating others to deeds of greater devotion and consecration, than shall be elicited from me by the anticipation of that greeting which thou wilt extend to him that overcomes, keeping thy works unto the end

---

JUNE 29.—**"Thou shalt compass me about with songs of deliverance."—Psalm xxxii. 7.**

If one want poetry, there is a whole poem in these few words. Heaven, earth; time, eternity; saints, angels; the redeemed soul; its sins, passions, frailties, woes, miseries fleeing in the distance;—such, and more, are the characters and the scenery presented to our imagination, or to our faith, as we gaze into this verse. Perhaps some reminiscence of what he had himself experienced in his earthly career, visited the mind of David, and assisted him to form a bright conception of what God would do for him hereafter. He may have recalled the morning when his offer to go forth and meet Goliath, elicited only shouts of derision; and the evening of the same day, when he was compassed about with songs of deliverance uttered by the host of the Israelites, while the surviving Philistines were fleeing overwhelmed with confusion, to their own borders.

A person known to us once had a dream, which may help to illustrate the text. He had been very recently brought to the knowledge of Christ's saving truth. He dreamt that he found himself in an open plain; when suddenly a terrible being appeared, from whom he felt that he must escape, if he would not forever perish. The only object that his eye could discern was a small and rather mean-looking house. To this he fled; entered it; and feeling that he was pursued, passed through it, and through a yard that was attached to it. Presently he found himself at the foot of a mighty precipice that rose as perpendicularly as a wall, and towered above the skies. The enemy was upon him. He felt that he must go up this wall-like precipice, or be lost; so he attempted the ascent. His hands were here of no use; for there was nothing for them to seize; and he had to plant his feet, in defiance of all laws of gravitation, horizontally against the wall. Yet he was actually enabled to mount up in this way. A prodigious effort was needed at first; (yet, if there had been no invisible aid, what could even a prodigious effort have accomplished under such circumstances?) but as he held on his way, and mounted higher and higher, even into the skies, the task became less difficult; and though new heights, not anticipated, remained to be climbed, yet he found a heart to climb them cheerfully and hopefully. At length he reached the summit, and a vision, glorious beyond description, burst upon his view. A multitude of the heavenly host were there, scattered over the plain, and crowded upon gentle hills that overlooked the scene; their eyes were all on him; and they all burst forth with songs of deliverance on his account; while a being glorious enough to be the Lord of all this enraptured host, came to him who had there arrived, and received him, as he fainted through the force of unspeakable emotions, and bore him away not altogether insensible, for the songs of the jubilant host still sounded in his ears.

JUNE 30.—"All are yours, and ye are Christ's."—1 Corinthians iii. 23.

The way to possess unlimited treasure is to give yourself away. How little the philosophers who sought by alchemy to obtain the art of transmuting mean things to precious,—how little did they dream that the art of acquiring worlds of wealth had been long before divulged, and that it consisted simply in giving one's self away to Christ. Men are victims of the unhappy delusion that their own self is a nucleus, a beginning of wealth, around which they must wrap acquisition after acquisition, till they have greatly magnified themselves. In this way, however, they are only heaping up riches for the last day, only fattening themselves for the slaughter. Let a man give himself, and all belonging to himself, to Christ; feeling at the same time that he is only giving what he had never any right to withhold, what it were the most audacious usurpation to think for a moment of withholding; let him rejoice to know Christ as the Lord of all; and in that very hour he will find himself possessor of all. All things were made for Him, it is said; that is, for Christ; and if for Christ, then for the believer; for the two are joint-heirs.

All things are yours; therefore all the arrangements of God are yours. In none of the arrangements of God is your happiness overlooked. The gold and silver of this world are found abundantly in the hands of others, not at all in yours,—well, this is one of those arrangements that contemplate your good. Worldly wealth does not belong to those who seem to have it; but to those who get the good of it. There are a thousand little conveniences of life which you could not enjoy were not other men rich enough to embark in enterprises. They themselves perhaps receive great damage from the wealth that they hold during the brief term of life; but your profit from it all is guaranteed in heaven. All things are yours; the prosperity of others, your own adversity, sickness, humiliation, losses, the elements, earth, heaven, time, eternity.

Your chief joy is, that you are Christ's; and you rejoice that all things are yours, chiefly because they will serve to make you a less unworthy possession to Christ. Holiness is yours; the image of God; spiritual, moral, and physical perfection; a crown of glory that fadeth not away; magnificent and inconceivable destinies. Viewing yourself as the property of Christ, you rejoice for his sake that this wondrous wealth is to roll in upon you, and that the mean stone is to be converted into a pearl of great price.

JULY 1.—"Take heed, and beware of covetousness."—Luke xii. 15.

Our Lord calls special attention to the danger by a special admonition. Out of that little band that accompanied him, one made shipwreck on this rock. The whole life of Jesus was cast into a mould of uttermost hostility to it; and the effect was seen in the Pentecostal Church, where no man called anything his own. But we are fallen upon very different times; and neither the example nor the earnest warnings of Christ and his apostles, have power to keep down this spirit in the Church. If the token of a pure Church is its freedom from covetousness, then is the Church of our day corrupt indeed. The parable spoken in immediate connection wi h these words, shows that our Lord understands by covetousness, the laying up of much goods for many years, and rejoicing in that provision. The man described in the parable did not, that we are told, practise extortion or commit frauds in order to be rich; but being, in the providence of God, made rich beyond all his present wants, chose rather to consider his own future possible wants, and make provision for them, than to alleviate the actual wants of the poor around about him. He was unwilling to relinquish money that he did not now want, because a time might come when he would want it.

The Church has utterly discarded the idea that there is anything in the word of God to hinder her from seeking any amount of wealth. There are thousands and tens of thousands of Christians, whose consciences would take alarm at once, at the presence of sin in other forms, who are deterred by no manner of scruple from embarking with all their heart in the endeavor to accumulate wealth far beyond any actual and even probable wants. "They pull down their barns and build greater," without a single ominous reflection coming to remind them of the poor, in whose barns there is nothing.

How shall a man beware of covetousness? Let him learn to look upon the things of others, to occupy himself more with the greater wants of others than with his own lesser wants, to know himself as simply a steward of the goods of God, and to shrink far more from being written down in the estimation of heaven "a fool," than in the estimation of earth. Had the man in the parable pursued any other course than he did, men would have said unto him, "thou fool;" but how infinitely more dreadful to hear it from God. Let the Christian know where his true wealth is; and trust God with his future wants. Has faith nothing to do with temporal matters? Who can say it that ever read the word of God?

JULY 2.—"Hide not thy face far from me."—Psalm xxvii. 9.

There are those who never need to use these words, because they have no experience of that which is deprecated They know not what is meant by such language as this: "Cause thy face to shine upon me." This language implies a personal acquaintance with a personal God. It teaches that God is pleased to make communications of his grace to the soul of the believer, that are to him like the uplifting of a veil from the face of the one beloved and adored. We ought all of us to have far higher conceptions than we have, of the power of God to manifest himself by the agency of the Holy Spirit. It is not to be questioned that in this dispensation we are able to have more glorious and surprising revelations of the Deity than were enjoyed under the previous dispensation. Isaiah and Daniel, Abraham and Ezekiel, envied us, and longed to be in our place; and we greatly dishonor the Spirit, if we suppose that in this dispensation there is no provision made for the occasional glorious manifestation of God unto the soul of the believer. We are saved by hope, and our greatest blessedness is of course in the future; but the best preparation for this is in the recognition of the sublime privileges now bestowed. Let it not be thought that we honor Christ more by overlooking our present opportunities of knowing his glory, and waiting for his appearing in the clouds of heaven. If we truly love his appearing, we will seek now to sound the utmost depths of the meaning of the promises contained in the fourteenth chapter of the Gospel by John.

JULY 3.—"He will be our guide, even uuto death."—Psalm xlviii. 14.

The guide of whom? Of those who feel that this world is a labyrinth, and that the secret of its mazes is known only to God,—that it is the camp of an enemy; and that unless the cloud of the presence of God encompass us about, we have no security, not for a moment,—that it is a field thoroughly undermined and honey-combed, with subterranean trains of gunpowder in every direction, exploding every minute; and that unless He lead us, we perish. What is the proof of this? Is not this language mere rhapsody? "It certainly is," say men in general; "the world we live in, is on the whole a safe and comfortable world; peace and safety wait upon our paths." Not so, we reply; we have the best warrant for our language. The number of the dead and dying testifies to the danger. You spread your table on the green sward; you bring forth generous wines; you sit down with your companions, and pass the hour in great conviviality; the birds sing pleasantly in the neighboring grove; the face of nature seems gladsome enough. Nevertheless, the field where you are sitting, is the field of the dead and dying. Are there many that be saved? Not hitherto. The multitude still go in at the broad gate, and hasten to destruction; the few go in at the straight gate, and obtain life. The things that seem to you to smile so friendlily upon you are the mortal enemies of men; the splendid halls to which you hasten have vaults beneath them, and in these vaults myriads of lost souls wait in anguish the day of Judgment. Man is so mortal, that almost anything is deadly to him. Were you in a battle where nine men out of every ten sent against the enemy were swept rapidly away, you would not say, "Peace and safety."

He is the guide of those who feel their need of an all-wise, all-powerful, all-condescending guide, and who are willing to yield their own preferences to his, their own ideas to his, in traveling over the glaciers of life. This word is a lamp to their feet, a light unto their path. He will hold their hand till they reach the gate of death; and passing through it, they will see that it is the gate of paradise. Death confesses itself vanquished, when it sees them walking on the battlements clothed in white.

JULY 4.—"Many sorrows shall be to the wicked; but he that trusteth in the Lord, mercy shall compass him about."—Psalm xxxii. 10.

These parallelisms of Scripture seem sometimes very rude. This one, for instance, teaches us that the wicked are they who trust not in the Lord. Men know not what to make of this definition. As for the wicked, they say, we know well who they are; these men that are brought up at the sessions of the Civil Courts, and tried for felonies, murders, misdemeanors; and besides these, certain other persons who have given us annoyance without rendering themselves amenable to the law. Men that beat slaves to death, women that destroy their infants, children that expose their parents to the waves or to wild animals,—these, too, are wicked.

But do you trust in God? have you made the everlasting God your refuge? do you walk by faith? do you condemn yourself and recognize Christ as the source of all your goodness, wisdom, strength? If not, then you need not go out of yourself to find the wicked. "Thou art the man;" the very man the Bible talks so much about, as needing to be born again, being under condemnation, a child of wrath, led captive by the god of this world. How deplorable is it that in reading the descriptions of the wicked in the Bible, you should always be thinking of another, rather than of yourself. For what we are now pressing upon you, though it may seem rude, yet has in it a well-head of exquisite consolation. For observe, it is a very simple matter to pass out of the ranks of the wicked, to escape *their* many sorrows, and to find yourself compassed about by mercy, as by a legion of angels. You have only to trust in the Lord; to discover yourself ruined, and hasten to a throne of grace; to let faith rule in your heart; to receive and be governed by the Holy Spirit. The best of men that ever lived, were once wicked like yourself, and only by faith in God's goodness, through Christ, were they made to differ.

JULY 5.—"The Lord is nigh unto them that are of a broken heart, and saveth such as be of a contrite spirit."—Psalm xxxiv. 18.

Here again, the parallelism tells us something. He is nigh to save. His presence is salvation. Their misery is not nearer to them than their deliverer. To their broken heart, the whole universe seems broken; to their desolate spirit, all creation seems desolate. Crushed beneath a sense of unworthiness, forlornness, helplessness, they dare not lift up their eyes to heaven, and they know that it is useless to lift them to anything less than heaven. Irremediable sorrow seems their portion. But the Lord hasteneth to the place where they sit solitary. He does not announce his coming by angelic precursors; he does not descend on a bright cloud; no visible glory, no audible sound attests his presence. But the eye of the broken-hearted sinner falls upon the eighteenth verse of the thirty-fourth Psalm, and beholds there the intimation of God's presence. The earthquake of the heart has opened a way for faith; and faith has opened a way for God. Formerly this word would have seemed like an engaging falsehood, a poetical fiction; nothing less than a hand of flame tracing the announcement in letters of fire upon the wall would have induced the recognition of such a truth. But faith lets God be true; and places him also among those whose words are to be believed. And if the Lord is nigh, then is all good nigh. When the Lord was with the first disciples, lacked they anything? All our lost treasures are found again in him. All our bankrupt powers are found perfected in him. In his presence is fulness of joy.

JULY 6—"Is any among you afflicted? Let him pray."—James v. 13.

This word that we now encounter is moving with haste and earnestness among the haunts of men. Up one street, down another, knocking at this door and at that, stopping to address here a company of noble personages, there a gathering of the poor and mean, it wends its way with something angelic in its mien, on very much the same mission that engaged the thoughts and energies of our Lord when on the earth.

"Is any among you afflicted?" It speaks in a kindly accent, knowing that many of these afflicted ones are unwilling to disclose their inward grief. It speaks with earnestness, as though it were conscious of possessing some medicament for the woes of mankind. It does not merely say, "Art thou afflicted? But are there afflicted ones among you? Do you know of any in the circle of your friends?"

"I know of some," will be the natural response. "I have been myself afflicted, and shall probably be so again. Some of my friends are even now afflicted, and most welcome would my visit be to them, if I could banish their affliction. But how may this be?"

Go and tell them to pray.

"But all men pray."

On the contrary, scarce any pray. And here is the evil, that almost all suppose they know what prayer is. As Naaman heard the command to wash in the Jordan, so they hear the direction to pray. They are perfectly unable to under stand how prayer should be the means of delivering them from sorrow. Many came in contact with the garment of Jesus as they crowded around him, without receiving any benefit; others, touching in faith, found in a moment what they had sought for scores of years. Go to your afflicted friends and tell them to pray; to pray in faith; by the prayer of faith to draw near to God the fountain of all good; in the name of our sympathizing High-priest; and they shall receive the Holy Ghost, who will disclose unto them the riches of the grace of God imbedded in the promises; will convince them of their own unworthiness and take away pride, that inward cancer, that great enemy of peace; will remind them that whom God loveth he chasteneth; will make them aware that they have been strangely oblivious of an inheritance most magnificent and soul-satisfying, fading not away; will give them patience, submission, hope and love; and compensate them a hundred-fold for that of which they have been bereft.

JULY 7.—"Many are the afflictions of the righteous; but the Lord delivereth him out of them all."—Psalm xxxiv. 19.

The Bible does not mock the anguish-bitten soul by telling it that the Christian cannot experience unhappiness or disappointment; or by telling it that it has no business to be wretched. The followers of the righteous Jesus are told distinctly that there are afflictions for them; and that these afflictions are many. So in drawing up an inventory of what belongs to them, they may put down many afflictions. These are a part of their property.

We see that it is not a disreputable thing to suffer. We are in good company.

The righteous man is infinitely more blessed in his afflictions than the unrighteous man is in his exemption. The den of lions may be a better place than the royal couch.

The afflictions of the righteous are those that he encounters in the attempt to walk righteously. Some come upon him from his unsubmissive nature struggling against the new principle that seeks to control it. Many from the wickedness of men, who do their utmost that he may not continue in a path that they abhor. Many from the lukewarmness and want of sympathy of his brethren. Some from the suggestions of the adversary, seeking to undermine his faith. Others again from the strange procedure of God, very different from what he had erringly anticipated. He thought that God would never let him be cast into a pit or sold to Ishmaelites. He thought that God would move with the speed of lightning to his rescue.

He thought that God would call to him out of the clouds, "I have heard thy prayer." Some afflictions come upon him from wounded affections. Some from the disappearance of loved ones. Happy for us if we are able to feel in all our afflictions that they are the afflictions of the righteous. Not brought upon us by our own folly—by the neglect of divine guidance—by the contravention of providence.

All the afflictions of the righteous open out into something glorious. The prisoner is not merely delivered, but he finds an angel waiting for him at the door. And with every deliverance comes a specific blessing. One angel is named faith; another, love; another, joy; another, long-suffering; another, gentleness; another, goodness; another, meekness; another, temperance; another, peace. Each of these graces says, "We have come out of great tribulation."

July 8.—"The Lord redeemeth the soul of his servants, and none of them that trust in him shall be desolate."—Psalm xxxiv. 22.

The parallelism shows us that his servants are those that trust in him. How can a man enter upon this service without trusting in him? To acknowledge this master is rebellion to the world. Thousands are ready to spring to their arms when they see us put away from our forehead and from our hand the sign of our submission to the powers of this world. A man that would serve God, has no longer sword or spear to trust in; riches or luck or cunning; rank or favor; the multitude or the prince; a fortress or a cavern; learning or genius or eloquence; nothing in fact remains for him to trust in *but God.* The servant is not greater than his master; he partakes with his master the hostility of the world; and he has naught to look to but the promise of his master. Desolation seems to stare him in the face; but he is assured that none of them that trust in the Lord shall be desolate.

Desolation seemed to frown upon the Pilgrim fathers as they forsook the shores of the old world and went forth to a land which they knew to be not at all flowing with milk and honey,—rather indeed inhospitable, bleak and savage. Innumerable dangers beset those infant colonies; but they found the grace of the Lord corresponding with the word of the Lord. Instead of being outlaws they became lawgivers; instead of being vilified as opposers of the faith, they became celebrated as expounders of the faith; and the howling wilderness became as the garden of the Lord around them.

But sometimes the most bitter experience of desolation is in the crowded walks of men; sometimes in the bosom of a large family. Nothing is more desolating than to be closely surrounded on every side by those who are called friends, kinsfolk, but who have no manner of sympathy with the ruling sentiment of our heart. Often has one so situated longed for the most lonely spot, and deeply felt that the solitary place would be glad, beautiful, heavenlike, in comparison with his situation. But often again has such a soul turned to God and found it possible to obtain a triumph over its desolation. The life of God perfected in that soul, has sent forth streams into the uncongenial elements around, and so vindicated itself by celestial love and patience that they too have been led to drink and live. How blessed a thing was it that that soul could not escape in the day of its weariness.

But those that do not trust in him shall be desolate. Perhaps they came to the borders of Canaan, and it seemed to them an uninviting land; a sad and solitary existence seemed to expand before them; they hesitated for a while; then the persuasions of their worldly friends prevailed; they went back to the multitude. But will the multitude keep them from desolation? Alas! can anything be more desolate than the soul that is without God.

An hour is coming when men, as they have preferred to be

without God, so they shall be driven with everlasting destruction from the glory of his presence; thenceforth will everlasting and universal desolation encompass them about, such as eye hath not seen nor heart conceived.

JULY 9.—" God is faithful, by whom we were called unto the fellowship of his Son Jesus Christ our Lord."—1 Corinthians i. 9.

Called unto the fellowship of Christ, seems to mean, called unto a community of interest and of destiny with Christ. One Spirit is to be common to the believer and Christ; to each there is one life of humiliation, one eternity of glory; to each the hatred of the world. Christ's peace and joy are the believer's; the same love of the Father is given to each; there is to each a resurrection and ascension. But he that is called to a part is called to the whole. If we suffer with him, we shall reign with him; not otherwise. He is indeed the Captain of our salvation; and the Lamb of God that taketh away the sin of the world. Though crucified with him, yet there were sacrificial sorrows of his which we know not.

Of course it will be thought a sublime thing in the last day, to sit down with Jesus on his throne, and participate a glory that shall light up the universe. But only he shall sit there who is now cordially associated with Christ in the midst of a gainsaying and perverse generation. The marvel is that, with the certainty of such an exalted destiny in reserve, there should be so little readiness to pursue the path that leads to it. Is it thought that God is not faithful, and that after enduring countless humiliations for the name of Christ, the reward will be withheld? But God is not only faithful, he is faithfulness itself; he must cease to be himself before he can be unfaithful. Faithfulness in God is simply acting in accordance with his own character, simply having his own way. In order to induce a man to be faithful, we labor to make him go out of himself,

—control his own inclinations and tendencies; it is almost like asking a barque driven with the wind and tossed, to remain motionless on the bosom of the agitated waters. But God is a rock; and a strange spectacle it would indeed be, if he should vacillate and be thrown from his native steadfastness. He knew our nature perfectly before he took that nature in hand to redeem it. He cannot be taken by surprise at any developments in us. It was not because he believed us somewhat corrupt, that he undertook our redemption; he knew us to be what we are only gradually discovering ourselves to be, utterly corrupt. Heaven and earth then may pass away, but He will remain faithful to his own declared purpose, and present us to the scrutiny of the universe, holy, unblemished, unblameable.

JULY 10.—They shall be abundantly satisfied with the fatness of thy house, and thou shalt make them drink of thy pleasures."—Psalm xxxvi. 8.

The blessedness of God will be the blessedness of his people. Their purity shall be without stain, their love without limit; wherefore their happiness shall know no bound. Their character will correspond to the character of God; wherefore their felicity will be the same as his. Men, as they are generally, could find no satisfaction in God's house, in the place where his glory has its highest revelation; nor is there anything attractive to them in the river of his pleasures. Satan has so vitiated their palate with the caustic of sin, that they have no faculty of appreciating the banquet that is spread in heaven. Even the Israelites preferred the leeks and onions of Egypt to the manna from heaven.

Happy are they that hunger and thirst after righteousness. Give them the most exquisite viands that man can prepare, and their tears will fall as they eat; they long to arise and hie them to some humble chamber where believers bow the knee before their heavenly Father and ask for his reviving grace.

They have tasted of a particular food, and their whole nature has been brought under the enchantment of it; they disdain all that they formerly thought excellent; and never can they be satisfied till that heaven-born appetite brings them to the mansion of their Father, and to that garden where the saints walk in light and drink of the river of the pleasures of God.

The river of thy pleasures. "This is my beloved Son in whom I am well pleased." Thus saith the Eternal Father. What sayest thou? "In these things I delight," saith the Lord; "in loving-kindness, judgment, and righteousness." What sayest thou? "As a bridegroom rejoiceth over the bride, so shall thy God rejoice over thee." "The Lord taketh pleasure in them that fear him." Dost thou? We must be drinking even now of the river of the pleasures of God; then have we an assured hope that our thirst shall be fully slaked in the beatific future.

JULY 11.—"With thee is the fountain of life; in thy light shall we see light."—Psalm xxxvi. 9.

In a few verses of this psalm, we have the elysium of God divinely sketched, and how do all the elysian scenes of poets fade in comparison with it. There is poetry and there is wisdom in the abstinence that controls the delineation. They that minutely depict the home of the blessed and seek to present us with a finished drawing of it, forget that whatever can be thus photographed is of necessity fallen from the region to which faith, hope, and whatsoever is heavenly in us, aspires. Give us a minute description of heaven and it is no more heaven. For what we need to understand by heaven is a place or a condition such as eye hath not seen, ear hath not heard, heart not conceived; having so little in common with earth that earthly language is no medium for the expression of its marvels; and whose distinguishing elements must just be hinted; negations being more employed than affirmations. Oh, how much reason have we to admire and rejoice in the reticence of the sacred writers, or rather of the Spirit who dwelt in them!

Let us not fail also to admire the fact that everything which is uttered concerning the place of God's glory, has reference to us. We are told of a fountain of life, because we long to be fully possessed by the life of heaven, to be emancipated from the body of this death, to drink our full of the redemption that is in Christ Jesus. We are told of God's light, because in that marvellous light we shall see light, and never more be compelled to look on darkness. There is darkness within us; the light that we have is but light shining through the riven darkness; and there is darkness on our path; and darkness in the mind and in the speech of every man we walk with; and a mighty pall of darkness stretches over the whole world. There is darkness in the government of every land under the sun, whether it be absolute, constitutional, or republican; darkness in all literature; darkness in the daily press; darkness in all codes; darkness in the ministry. Almost everywhere, utter darkness; in the Church, mingled darkness and light, and the promise of unmixt light. We now believe in God's light; soon we shall see it.

JULY 12.—"He died for all, that they who live should not henceforth live unto themselves, but unto him who died for them and rose again."—2 Corinthians v. 15.

He died for all; a glorious truth repeated in every variety of language, and oftentimes with the utmost explicitness that language can admit of. By virtue of this unlimited atonement, salvation may be offered to all, the gospel to every creature, the water of life to whomsoever will; by virtue of this, men that believe not are condemned because they have not believed on the Son of God, and men are convinced of sin because of unbelief. It is this that gives its pathos to the language of Christ. "How often would I have gathered thee, and thou wouldest not. I would, thou wouldest not. Ye will not come unto me that ye may have life." And to the language of Paul: "Seeing that ye put away from yourselves everlasting life." And to the language of wisdom: "Because I have called and ye refused, therefore ye shall call and I will not answer."

But though there be an unlimited atonement there is a limited redemption. He died for all, and the result is not, that all live; he died for all that *they who* live should not live unto themselves. He died for all in the sense that all may live if they will; he died for the elect in the sense that they will actually will to live. Life is offered to all; but all are not allowed to reject it

And this is the life that they obtain, namely a willingness to live unto Christ; a purpose and a power to live according to the mind of Christ. There is nothing that seems so much like death to men as the subjugation of their own will to the will of another. They know not that their own will is their greatest enemy; enthroned within them for their present misery and future destruction. The believer's happiness it is to discover that the will of Christ indicates the only path in which he will find peace, purity, genuine liberty, dignity, immortality, felicity.

July 13.—"**If we suffer, we shall also reign with him.**"—**2 Timothy ii. 12.**

When he was on the earth, leading a life of sorrows and perfecting his acquaintance with grief, no man appeared to covet the privilege of suffering with him. John and James, indeed, before they had obtained a glimpse of the cross, were bold to say, "We are able to drink of thy cup, and to be baptized with thy baptism." Thomas also said, "Let us also go that we may die with him." Peter said, "I will lay down my life for thy sake." So likewise said they all. Yet when the hour of his enemies came, and the power of darkness, he was left to tread the wine-press alone. His disciples forsook him; or if they ventured to approach the place where he was a prisoner, it was only to increase his suffering by the exhibition of their unbelief and pusillanimity.

Imagine yourself there. You are in the secret. You know that this is indeed the very king of the Jews, though they mock him with a crown of thorns and with some faded and tattered robe of state. You know that legions of angels are waiting to receive his commands; though these servants of servants smite him and revile him. You know that there is buried within that suffering body, glory sufficient to bathe all the mountains of the earth in radiance, and suffuse the heavens with splendor in the absence of the sun; you know that there is a joy set before him unspeakable, inconceivable, and that it will be the sublimest of destinies to participate in that joy. Well, what is the course you adopt? It seems to you—does it not?—that you must hasten to his side; nay, cast yourself at his feet, and solicit the honor of suffering with him; confessing withal that, if you had the goodness of an archangel, you would still be most unworthy of such a privilege. Christ is not willing that you should be debarred this privilege. He did not take his cross away to heaven with him. Ages have not extinguished the opposition of the world to him. Are you sure that you are really willing to perceive, to enter, and to pursue the *via dolorosa?* There does indeed seem something most base in the refusal to join this king of glory in the hour of his humiliation; but is it very certain that you are not this very day demonstrating your spiritual affinity to those who cried out, "Not this man, but Barabbas?" Have you not turned aside from many a path, chiefly because you caught a glimpse of something like calamity, and concluded that duty did not call you to enter it? Does not the anticipated elements of loss, shame, or danger, assist you much toc readily in reaching your conclusions as to what is duty?

Formerly, in the days of the Church's simplicity, Christians ascertained their path by the plain sense of Scripture. But now the Church has become exceedingly wise and prudent, and discovers that the old paths are many of them quite unnecessary. One is ashamed to differ from so many wise and good men. And it is certainly a very foolish thing to run after suffering. Yet is it a far more foolish thing to disregard the monitions of the Spirit. It is the acme of folly to do anything that may jeopard our hope of reigning with Christ, in the day that the kings of the earth shall be crouching in dens and caves.

July 14.—"If we believe not, yet he abideth faithful; he cannot deny himself."—2 Timothy ii. 13.

He will not modify his purposes to suit our unbelief. What madness to suppose that he will imitate us; and seeing that we make light of his faithfulness, make light of it himself. Let God be true, though every man a liar. God once declared his purpose of bringing a deluge upon the earth. Men would not believe the terrific word. The whole human race combined to rear up a wall of unbelief under the protection of which they thought themselves safe. On the one hand were all mankind with their "no;" on the other, God with his "yes." Unbelievers thought themselves safe in their vast numbers and perfect concord; but the word of God must be fulfilled whether a single individual be the opposer, or a whole world.

The thought of the immense numbers that are without Christ in the world, leads many to conclude that God will modify his declared purpose. Where there are so many to be punished, it is unlikely that the penalty will be inflicted. According to this reasoning, man has saved himself by getting the whole human family to persevere in rebellion. God delighteth in mercy; but he cannot cease to be a just and faithful God. It is altogether too much to expect that he will follow the example of man, and give up the attributes of faithfulness, truthfulness, and holiness, after man has denied them to him. The question from the foundation of the world has been, shall man accommodate himself to God, or shall God accommodate himself to man? The Bible says, "He that believeth not is condemned; there is no saving name but that of Christ; no man cometh unto the Father but by him:" and it is not denied that the Bible says these things. But, it is said, God must accommodate himself to the stubbornness of man. Vain hope. He abideth faithful, though not a believer were found in the earth.

Dost thou, O Christian, render due honor to the inviolable faithfulness of God? I fear lest occasionally thou incline to some forbidden path, hoping that God will not visit you with the rod. How unkind in you to set up God's love to you against his love to his word! Would you actually introduce division and conflict among the very perfections of God? Christ has never promised that he will become a sinner to gratify you. He will remain faithful; truth driven from every threshold of man, finds an everlasting asylum with him.

Happy are they who have on their side the adamantine faithfulness of Christ, and build upon it all their hopes of happiness.

JULY 15.—"The foundation of God standeth sure, having this seal, The Lord knoweth them that are his."—2 Timothy ii. 19.

This is said with reference to some that appear unto men to be the children of God, and afterwards fall away. Christians have no promise that they shall be kept from misconceptions on this point; and they are sometimes greatly shocked to find the court of God's house strewn with columns. God is the architect of his temple, and is cognizant of his own plan; he allows stones and pillars to be placed in the edifice which he knows do not permanently belong to it; but for the places they temporarily occupy there are other materials known to him; and no chasms, no unlovely vacancies shall after all appear. Let this console us. The Lord knoweth them that are his. These pseudo-Christians that figure for a while upon the platform, and then pass away in the whirlwind of sin, amid the triumphs of a scoffing world, were never known to him for anything but what they really were.

The foundation laid by the Lord standeth sure, and amid the shock of ages remains the same. The prophets and the apostles are this foundation, the chief corner-stone being the Lord Jesus Christ. In other words, the Bible exhibits the religion that God requires of man. Every generation is made to look upon this foundation, and is invited to build upon it. It builds and builds; but its work is perhaps not accordant with the foundation laid; and God quietly removes the superstructure, and summons the next generation. It builds and builds; and its work, too, is swept away. Finally we are reached. We behold the foundation, and we apply ourselves to the work of completing the house of God. Will God be pleased with our performance? Only if we adopt the apostolic standard, and banish the futile thought of improving on the plans of God.

JULY 16.—"He is able also to save them to the uttermost that come unto God by him."—Hebrews vii. 25.

The reason is assigned and it is unanswerable:—"He ever liveth to make intercession for them." He lives forever, clothed with all the power derived from his propitiatory death, and animated by the same heart of love that led him to die; he lives in the very place where we most need him; he is there perpetually in our behalf. He was not more truly on the earth for us than he is in heaven for us, and we may confidently expect to be saved unto the uttermost.

Once we had no access to God. There were no invitations for us, no promises. He saved us from that fearful condition. He has endowed us with liberty to draw nigh to God. He has given us his Holy Spirit,—has shed abroad the love of God in our hearts,—has changed our hearts; overcome our sins; and bound us to himself by indissoluble bonds. But all this is scarcely more than a beginning. We have received but an instalment. He is able to do vastly more than he has done. He is able to save us from all moral weakness, so that we may look serenely and fearlessly on all temptations, on all dangers that beset us.

Is there some infirmity in yourself, some difficulty out of yourself, that seems like a barrier in the way of your progress? He is able to remove this. Have you been so often overcome by the adversary, that you are ready to despair? Take care, and do not disparage the ability of him that is with you to succor you. Does some duty seem tremendous and altogether beyond your force? He is able. Has he done so great things for you that you are ashamed to ask him for more? He requires you to ask until you be saved to the uttermost. Do you shrink from death? Shrink not from the remaining salvation. You must be saved from this present inglorious and inadequate life; from a Church sadly imperfect to a Church clothed in spotless purity; from a mortal and corruptible existence to an immortal incorruptible one. You must be brought to the angels; to the seraphim; to the glorified Son of God; to the throne where the river of the water of life takes its rise.

JULY 17.—"Be not weary in well-doing."—2 Thessalonians iii. 13.

This is said to the well-doer. To one even who is no novice

in well-doing; but has been some time engaged in deeds of beneficence. You have begun well; you have gone on well; but persevere. It may be that your kindness is not appreciated; that your self-denial for the sake of others is even ridiculed; that your motives are misrepresented; and that the more you love, the less you are loved. But your well-doing is not well-doing if it be gone about chiefly for the sake of man's appreciation. He doeth well whose labors of love are amply rewarded by the smile of God. There was a time when you were not weary in seeking your own ease, pleasure, or advantage. Should you labor longer or more cheerfully for that solitary sinner, than for a world of unhappy ones around you?

Consider that Christ was not weary in well-doing, though his love was exhibited under the most adverse circumstances imaginable. Perhaps you may find on reflection that he has been remarkably persevering in his efforts to do good to you. Did you ever go to the door of some poor miserable degraded being, and knock and knock; and when driven from the door by a shower of reproaches, return at the first opportunity and knock and knock; and being again thrust back with your undesired gifts, still return and endeavor to gain admission? Hardly. But has there not been some such persistency as this on the part of Christ, in his efforts to recover you from the degradation of sin and the darkness of unbelief? God makes his sun to rise and run his daily course through the skies that you may be lighted along the path of duty; but how often does that sun arise and pour his deluge of light around you, without any other thoughts arising in your own mind than such as relate to your own pleasure. The marvel is that God should not be weary of doing good to such a one. When you are ready to get weary of your paltry beneficences, think that you are suggesting to God that it is not worth while to continue blessing the race to which you belong.

JULY 18.—"If any man will come after me, let him deny himself and take up his cross and follow me."—Matthew xvi. 24.

One of the greatest triumphs ever obtained by Satan, was when he induced men, from motives utterly unscriptural, and in connection with a system not Christian, to institute religious orders consecrated to poverty and external humiliation. In recoiling from this error, Protestantism has, it is to be feared, recoiled from the truth of which it is a perversion. The doctrine illustrating the spirituality of Christianity, voluntary sacrifice of position, wealth or ease, in order that the sincerity and faith and contentedness and hope and love of the Christian may be appropriately exhibited, this doctrine, though it may claim as large and broad a foundation for itself in the word of Christ as any other one doctrine, is now treated as a foolish fantasy, if not indeed as a heresy; and he that maintains it and practises it must exhibit a good deal of wisdom in other matters in order to be tolerated. There is no more sacred obligation resting upon Christians, under the sun, than the obligation to show forth the divine origin of Christianity by the exhibition, in their lives, of those evidences that are most calculated to affect mankind generally. God loves his people; he is no enemy to their comfort here; but he loves his truth and the removal of stumbling-blocks from the paths that tend to Christ; nor is it from harshness or indifference that he says to any, "Sell all that thou hast, and give to the poor, and follow me;" for he well knoweth that he has power to bestow—with poverty and inferiority of position—peace, and gladness such as riches can never impart. "But," you say, "what can a solitary individual do? If he resolve to do just what his Lord says, his course will be at once eccentric and unprofitable. The example of one man is nothing." But the question already considered recurs: Do the words of Christ accommodate themselves to the unbelief of the Church and are all his requirements relaxed because Christians universally shut their eyes to them?

JULY 19.—"Fear not, little flock; for it is your Father's good pleasure to give you the kingdom."—Luke xii. 32.

In these words we read the future destinies of the world When an Alexander arises and hurries through the world, snatching crowns on the right hand and on the left, and threatening to take unto himself all sublunary power, the people of God are told to fear not; the kingdom is for them, not him. So too when a Julius Cæsar grasps at the sceptre of universal dominion. And when a Napoleon appears on the scene, they calmly wait to see him and his kingdom vanish. For they have looked with Daniel on the image that expressed beforehand the vicissitudes of the world from the Babylonian dominion down to the time when dominion is given unto the Son of man, and by him given to the people of the saints of the Most High. The meek shall inherit the earth. Not only is there for them an inheritance reserved in heaven; but thrones shall come down from heaven and be set upon the earth; and they shall sit thereon. "For we shall reign on the earth."

But who are these unmanifested kings and priests? They are now a little company of sheep; a little flock; mutely submissive when led to the slaughter; willing to be inglorious, poor, weak, despised, rejected; fitting themselves to be all that is great and excellent and powerful, by their willingness to be nothing.

JULY 20.—"He that believeth on the Son hath everlasting life."—John iii. 36.

And he only; for "he that believeth not the Son shall not see life; but the wrath of God abideth on him." Several important matters loom upon us in this little statement. One of the most unintelligible things, to the world, is the declaration so constantly made in the Scriptures, that man is without life. At the very beginning of human history, Satan introduced, as a substitute for God's doctrine that man would die in the day of his transgression, his own opposing doctrine that man would not die. Adam believed Satan rather than God and it has been the same with Adam's descendants until the present hour. Men refuse to believe that they are in any proper sense dead; that they need the breath of life to be breathed into their soul. And refusing to believe this, they give no heed to the offer of life made to them in the Gospel. "In the day thou eatest thereof thou shalt surely die." "He that believeth on the Son hath everlasting life—hath passed from death unto life." Not knowing themselves dead through transgression, they fail to live through faith. The death that passed upon Adam was not a visible death; and the life that comes to the believer is not a visible life; but the results of both are in due time sufficiently visible.

You look upon the believer and upon yourself, and you say, What has he that I have not? Wherein is he richer than I am? I have physical and mental powers equal, if not superior, to his. Is he eloquent? Not more than I. Can he reason? Not better than I. Is he well informed? So am I. Is he respected? I am more so. Has he wealth? I have more. Is he generous? Men speak far more of my generosity than of his. Is he moral? I claim to be as much so. He has a hope of heaven. And have I none?

I will tell you what he has that you have not. He has the knowledge that sin is death. He knows that, naturally, he, in common with all mankind, is under condemnation; is without the favor of God; is exposed to eternal wrath. While deeply sensible of the great goodness of God in bestowing upon him many admirable gifts, he knows that these gifts only increase the odiousness of his sins. He loathes his sins; his pride, selfishness, irreligion, insincerity. He is aware that no mere efforts of his own, with all the aid that he can obtain from man, are adequate to restore his diseased, his dead nature. It is life that he needs. And it is blasphemy to say that any finite power can bestow this. He believes on the Son of God; recognizing him to be morally and in respect to dignity, the express image of the Father. He beholds God manifest in the Son; and all the acts and words of Christ reveal to him the character of the omnipresent God. He sees his own sins expiated at the cross; and the broken body of Christ is the legacy of life to him. The ascension of Christ is the guarantee of his own entire emancipation from sin, sorrow, frailty, corruptibility. You have many things in common with him; but, unlike you, he glories only in the cross of Christ. You make many donations, and men praise you for them; but he performs actions that will be mentioned with approbation by Christ at the last day, in words like this: "You have done it unto me." In a word, he has faith in Christ; and you have not. Your faith is in yourself; and until you know yourself to be without life, Christ can be of no advantage to you.

JULY 21.—"God forbid that I should glory save in the cross of our Lord Jesus Christ."—Galatians vi. 14.

Whatever constitutes, in our opinion, our chief ground of distinction, that is the thing in which we glory. Like the fabled jewel in the toad, so there is in almost every man, if we may believe him, a very wonderful jewel. He finds it in himself; though with respect to others the whole thing is a fable. But even if there were this diamond in a man's nature, the presence of self-esteem would turn it to carbon again. To pride yourself on any good is to lose that good. Virtue comes to you, not that she may make you love yourself, but love Him that sent her to you.

There are those, indeed, who glory in something beside themselves. A man glories in his ancestors. A child in its father. Men are proud of their country. Soldiers glory in their commander. A successful general inspires his soldiers with the most intense enthusiasm, so that they are ready to throw away their lives at the slightest expression of his will.

This enthusiasm, however, must be aided by a measure of ignorance in order to endure. Passionate admiration has only to come very near its object, to discover some fatal flaw. No reputation of man is safe where there is abundant light. And the great art of men is to veil their heroes. Sometimes, however, the greatest enemies of the Bible find themselves speaking the language of the Bible.

> "Where shall the wearied eye repose
> When gazing on the great,
> Where neither guilty glory glows
> Nor despicable hate?"

Reading the history of humanity, Paul found but one page on which his eye could rest, ever rest, with unmingled satisfaction. It was not the page that records the conquests of Alexander; nor that which describes the eloquence of Demosthenes; nor that which treats of Thermopylæ. He passed dissatisfied from Homer to Eschylus, to Plato, to Socrates, to Pythagoras, to Cato. The page on which humanity came out faultlessly glorious, was that which told of the death of Him who had come down from the highest heavens and assumed humanity that he might expose the worthlessness of all that man had gloried in and make such an atonement for the sins of men as would heal the division then yawning like a great gulf between God and man. At the cross he had first obtained a correct view of himself and of all mankind; an acquaintance with God; a knowledge of time and of eternity. And that which taught him to renounce the idea of man's nobility, was that also which disclosed the means of rising to the highest conceivable degree of nobility. It poured contempt on princes; but it raised men from the dunghill to array them in robes of never-fading splendor, to crown them with everlasting joy.

JULY 22.—"Walk in love, as Christ also hath loved us, and hath given himself for us."—Ephesians v. 2.

That is to say, carry on the life which Christ lived. In him love made its advent to the earth; and the prayer recorded in the seventeenth chapter of John, shows plainly that the idea of the Saviour was not that that divine love should take its departure with him from the earth, but that it should abide and have an inextinguishable life in his disciples, from generation to generation, until he should come again. This, then, is your vocation. To walk by faith, and to walk in love, let these things be one in your experience.

What a sublime mission! God on his throne in heaven is love. Love is with him enthroned in heaven; love, in you, wanders over the earth. The whole universe is made for the manifestation of his love; and the universe, as much of it as you will, exists for the manifestation of your love. It is the law of all created essences; and let there only be in you divine love enthroned, and the whole creation will answer your glance, and say to you, "Here am I." It must wait upon you, for it must wait upon love. You are the follower of Christ; consequently you live to love.

You are, however, surrounded by a world of unloving and unlovely beings; and how can you walk in love here? Consider that formerly you found no difficulty in loving yourself; in spite of all the repulsive things you knew about yourself, you went on loving yourself, with an unwavering steadfastness. Consider, again, that Christ sets you the example. Does it become you to be more fastidious than he is? Is the servant greater than his Lord? Do you presume to despise what he regards? Did he bring too much love down from heaven, and must you send some of it back? Consider, again, does it appear wrong that you should be loved? Does a little satisfy you? Would you have your brethren make light of the command to love you? Again, is there any better way of bringing men to be lovely, than this very way of love? Finally, Is there any habit more enriching and gladdening to your own nature, than this sacred habit of love?

You may well say that you have not attained, neither are already perfect. Nothing less is solicited at your hands, than that you should give Christ's mighty love an unlimited range of your nature.

"I cannot tutor my affections," you say; "I cannot by any word of command constrain my heart to love." Well, then, try this way. Be filled with the knowledge of Christ's love to you. Feed upon this food; the table is spread, and there is no stinted supply. Love to him will follow without difficulty. Then, as he is in heaven and his people are on earth, love him in them. In them he is near.

July 23.—"This is his commandment, that we should believe on the name of his Son Jesus Christ, and love one another."—1 John iii. 23.

We have here not two commandments, but one. Faith is naught without love; and love without faith is not the love that is here commanded. "Love believeth all things;" and faith "worketh by love," exhibits itself in love. Selfishness is the grand impediment of love; but faith is that which gets the victory over selfishness, by showing a man his utter unworthiness and the perfect folly of living unto himself. Faith makes us acquainted with the love of Christ, and in fact introduces it into the soul; and this love begets love. Faith enables us to contemplate the truth that Christ and his people are one, and that in loving them we are responding to his love. Faith shows us what there is of Christ in them, and what they are to be hereafter. We have seen the crowns, the royal robes, the celestial dwelling-places now in course of preparation for them. The Holy Spirit in us is the author of faith; and he will not tarry with us unless we love. If they have sins, faith teaches us so to pray for them as to obtain their deliverance therefrom. And faith also teaches us how to do good—not to be always saying smooth things; not to leave their faults unheeded; not to aim that they may be always comfortable in mind. But as it teaches us that the leaving of God's will undone, or the doing of what he willeth not, is the greatest calamity for ourselves, so it teaches us that this is their greatest calamity; and it keeps us more intent upon their growth in grace than upon their momentary pleasure, though even this we cannot overlook unless there be a necessity. Christ did not take it as a kindness when Peter said, "Far be it from thee, Lord, to go up to Jerusalem, the city of thine enemies!"

Any one that attempts to love without faith will be sure to make wretched work of it. For there will be no tendency in his love to draw the object of it near to him who is the only fountain of happiness, but rather to draw it more and more away. A great deal that is called love is fatal and withering toward the loved one. Pour the light of God's truth on what are called romances, and what melancholy ghastly things do they become.

JULY 24.—"He that covereth his sins shall not prosper."—Proverbs xxviii. 13.

Almost all men are intent upon appearing better than they really are. If a man cannot be what he ought to be, he attempts at least to appear so. His days are spent in a fraudulent attempt to pass himself off as something better than he is. The same amount of energy devoted to the purification of his character, might result in something good. What watchfulness! What circumspection! What attention to circumstances! What study of men's characters! What perseverance! What self-command! Were these qualities and habits devoted to the legitimate end of appearing well in the sight of God, what magnificent results would be witnessed. These are the very things that God requires of us: watchfulness, carefulness, perseverance, self-control. Man shows that he is capable of these things; but he exercises them in seeking not the essence, but a fiction; not the favor of God, but that of man.

The habit is so inveterate that few are conscious of it. They suppose they are acting naturally, and have no conception of the measure of their insincerity. I speak not of the hypocrite, commonly so styled; but of all. The man who says, "I thank God, I make no profession to be better than others;" he, too, is playing a role, though he cheats himself with the contrary idea.

Insincerity in religion, the endeavor to obtain and perpetuate a reputation for piety, is something exceedingly offensive. There is something monstrous about the idea of offering prayer in such a way as to secure the commendation of man.

He that covereth his sins shall not prosper; for while he covers them he cannot possibly get rid of them; and their presence will vitiate all prosperity. Let us endure the shame of confessing them, that we may have the abiding glory of being delivered from them. Let us act out our true characters, and take our true place; then we may expect to make progress of the most desirable kind. If man deride, no matter; we have something that they have not. Our position is a more promising one than theirs; for truth is now on our side.

JULY 25.—"They have washed their robes, and made them white in the blood of the Lamb; therefore are they before the throne of God."—Revelation vii. 14, 15.

These robes are symbolical of their characters once defiled, now made pure by virtue of the faith which they have exercised in him who died on Calvary that he might redeem us from all iniquity, and purify us unto himself a peculiar people. Observe here that their agency is spoken of. It was, indeed, the blood of the Lamb that purged away the stains; but they had something to do; they saw and loathed the impurity of their garments, they approached the fountain, and washed them white. Christ gave them the heart to do it.

The saints in light have something to distinguish them from all angels, all other holy beings. They are not pure, but purified. They were once impure, once steeped in sin and meet only for the inheritance of the devil and his angels. That they have become the companions of those who are before the throne, will be a wonder ceaseless through all eternity. The distinction is of course not honorable to them; but it is eminently honorable to Christ; and they seek no honor but his. By reason of their intimate alliance with him, they feel at home in heaven as though they had never dwelt elsewhere.

They wash their robes on earth that they may stand before the throne of God. Do you belong to their number? Have you knowledge of the blood of Christ? Such knowledge as tends to the purification of your character, to your emancipation from sin? Not without your agency will this spiritual transformation take place. Delay not; for how soon may "the great day of his wrath" burst upon the world.

JULY 26.—"Ye are bought with a price; therefore glorify God in your body and in your spirit, which are God's."—1 Corinthians vi. 20.

Rights relating to property are carefully guarded by men.

They greatly resent any unwarranted use of what belongs to them. To touch their property is to touch them. The earth is the Lord's and the fulness thereof. Man sold himself to Satan and presumed to transfer the earth and the fulness thereof to the arch-apostate, and God so far allowed the bargain (for the punishment of man,) that Satan may be correctly styled the god of this world. "He that committeth sin is the servant of sin;" this word is the charter of Satan's kingdom upon earth. But into the slave-market of this world God hath gone in the person of his Son, and paid the tremendous price which authorizes him to take as many as he can find willing to go, and create them anew in the image of the Son. They that go, go willingly; fully and deliberately recognizing God's absolute property in them; and any subsequent alienation of their powers to the will of another, is most base and inexcusable.

It is not therefore a fragment of you that has been purchased; but the whole. You would hardly presume to say that the price was inadequate. Yet do you not seem to say so? How much of your time is the Lord's? Do you dress, feed, employ your body as unto the Lord? Is your tongue, your hand consecrated all to him? Your memory, imagination, hope? Your love and faith? Your houses and lands? Your influence?

JULY 27.—**"Therefore will not we fear, though the earth be removed, and though the mountains be carried into the midst of the sea."—Psalm xlvi. 2.**

The language of the highest faith is the language of the highest courage. Men that are bold enough to seek the bubble reputation even in the cannon's mouth, and who fear not that they shall ever know what fear is, may at any moment be reduced to a condition of the most abject timidity by the revelation of that God whom they have scorned to make their refuge and strength.

Fear is to be the everlasting portion of him who in this life refuses to fear. Men exclude from their attention those truths that are calculated to alarm them; and resolve to retain their self-confidence unbroken, at whatever cost. They wish to be without fear; and in many instances their wish is gratified; they pass through life, and pass away from it, without any painful apprehension. But they have only been accumulating an everlasting fund of terror and agony, and they inherit, on the other side of the grave, with incalculable interest, what they refused to receive on this side. They defended themselves against fear by the amulet of delusion; by some scheme of future things which their own vain minds had elaborated; but delusion is not allowed to cross the grave; and there they will find themselves bereft of their armor. "Fear hath torment." Who can express this torment? The terror-stricken soul experiences not only the inflicted sorrow of the moment, but by anticipation the dread interminable suffering of all time to come.

How shall our souls be strong in the day when Christ shall come in flaming fire, taking vengeance on them that know not God, and obey not the gospel of our Lord Jesus Christ? There is another question more important; and if it be rightly answered, we can dismiss the first. What am I now fearing? The displeasure of man, or that of God? The scorn of man or that of God? When the world says, "Enter not this path," and God says, "Enter it;" when the world says, "Be conformed to me," and God says, "Be not conformed;" when the world says, "Speak not of God, of Christ, of sin, of eternity;" and God says, "Speak of them;" whom do I obey? If I fear not in my daily, hourly walk, the wrath and derision of mankind, I shall be kept from fear in the great day of God's wrath, and shall dwell in safety where I now dwell in safety, beneath the shadow of his wings.

JULY 28.—"God is my salvation and my glory."—Psalm lxii. 7.

God is my Saviour; and inasmuch as he saves me by bringing me into blessed relations to himself, clothes me with the garment of his own unsullied righteousness, and makes me to bear his image, I may well speak of him as my salvation. This, like a thousand other passages of the Old Testament, teaches the divinity of Christ, and it is a marvel how any one can say that the evidences of this are chiefly confined to the New Testament. Every passage in the Old Testament that exhibits God as the Saviour of his people, is as true a testimony to the divinity of Christ as anything in his own works and words. The doctrine of Christ's divinity is dear to the believer, not only because of the honor that thereby redounds to Christ, but because all the honor of Christ thereby redounds to God. It is not merely the exaltation of Christ, but the condescension of God, that attracts him to the gospel. He does not merely add divinity to him who sat upon the margin of the well at Sychar, and who sailed upon the lake of Gennesareth; he adds humanity to the infinite God, in whom he lives, moves, and has his being.

It is one thing to hold the doctrine of Christ's divinity, and it is another to draw from the doctrine its fullness of blessing. Have I been so long time with you, and yet hast thou not known me? Many that are accustomed to read the gospel have no idea of the power with which its statements would come to their soul, if they would allow this doctrine to flash its light upon the words.

They read for instance, Oh, ye of little faith, how long shall I be with you, how long shall I suffer you? Let them consider these words as revealing the mind of him who is not far from any one of us, the omniscient and immutable God; and let them discover by means of them with what strong dissatisfaction he who compasseth their path and their lying-down regards their unbelief. How long shall he be with us unknown and unperceived; how long shall the boundless and ever-present riches of his grace be offered us in vain? "He that hath seen me hath seen the Father." Let us labor to connect the idea of the Almighty, the Ever-living, Ever-present one, with the words and acts of Christ.

JULY 29.—"Humble yourselves in the sight of the Lord, and he shall lift you up."—James iv. 19.

Humble yourselves in the sight of the Lord; that is, humble yourself truly; for his eye is as a flame of fire; and no mere pretence of humility will pass current with him. He does not ask you to conceal your pride from the observation of men, but to mortify it. He does not ask you to be humble merely in your addresses to him; for he is ever with you.

In order to humble yourself, know yourself. Pride grows in the atmosphere of falsehood. It is only by dint of lying that a soul maintains its pride. Let God reveal you to yourself. Perhaps the esteem in which you are held by man, interposes a difficulty. You have a position in society. Men look up to you. They treat you with no little deference. Receiving thus attention and respect all the day long, it becomes difficult for you to entertain those depreciatory views of yourself that God requires. But, do men honor you for what is really commendable in you; or, for things that are merely adventitious, and that are found in innumerable instances connected with ungodliness? If they honor you for wealth, influence, or even for talent, call to mind that there are thousands of worthless men in the world that surpass you in these respects. It is in direct violation of the command of God that men give their admiration to these things. What they have not learned, you should quickly learn, namely, to recognize God as the giver of all good gifts, and to ascribe unto him honor and glory. It is of more importance that you should be humble, than that you should be wealthy and looked up to. And you know what Christ hath told us to do, when cherished things hinder us from obtaining something better. It is with reference to the difficulties you now plead that Christ has said, "How hardly shall they that have riches enter into the kingdom of heaven." It is hard for them to humble themselves in the sight of God; and without humility there is no entering into the kingdom of heaven.

Perhaps you say, "No, I am not rich, but poor; mean in station; unknown to the men of the world; but God has bestowed his grace upon me and enabled me to walk in his paths; Christian brethren admire the work that God hath wrought in me, and their commendation hinders me from being clothed with humility." Hearken! your attainments are of a very superficial character, if humility, the knowledge of your own profound unworthiness, be not a constant tenant of your breast. Most imperfect and questionable is the fabric of your Christian character, if it be not founded broadly and solidly in humility. Just exactly therefore in the degree in which you are vain of your attainments, you condemn your attainments. Say unto pride, I have no need of thee until I have acquired self-knowledge and the deep conviction of my own utter unworthiness and weakness, and until my soul has got thoroughly imbued with the persuasion of its dependence on the grace of Christ for all things. Let me first obtain that humility without which every individual is but a loathsome leper in the universe of God. Then, if thou please, come to me; but thou shalt come in vain. Thou wilt find no footing on the landing-place of my soul. Thy proper place is with the wicked, the incorrigible, the base, the carnal, the devilish. The wickedest being in existence is the proudest. A man's pride is ever commensurate with his blindness and alienation from God.

Humble yourselves in the sight of the Lord, and he shall lift you up.

JULY 30.—"To this man will I look, even to him that is poor and of a contrite spirit."—Isaiah lxvi. 2.

What mighty efforts, and how many, to obtain the regard of men: how rare the effort to obtain the regard of God! The admiring glance of God passes by the great and noble, the wise and prudent, the wealthy, the powerful, all the illustrious that shine as stars in the firmament of this world, and singles out some obscure person who is distinguished by nothing but a poor and contrite spirit. God looks to him and God alone. The mere possession of humility leaves him without the slightest power to attract the attention of men. If he had but an arithmetical talent; or an uncommon memory; or an unusual degree of muscular power; could he but dance, run far, walk quickly, eat much, drink much, fast much; had he any kind of ability almost, men would look to him; but being merely a humble man, of a contrite spirit, singular only in his freedom from pride; they do not look to him. God looks to him.

God can do something with such a man as that. God is love, and delighteth in mercy, and he is ever seeking whom he can bless; and when he finds a man of a poor and contrite spirit, he has the opportunity of blessing. For such a one will receive the gifts of God without being lifted up by them; he knows that all comes to him in the way of unmerited grace; and his heart will glow the more with gratitude and self-forgetting affection, the more that God bestows upon him. He is of course docile, teachable; he will learn the ways of God and will walk therein. Do not imagine that he is a poor-spirited creature, trembling at the face of man. No, this contrite-hearted man, when he hath once tasted of the joy of God's salvation, and taken knowledge of the eye of his God and his Saviour fixed upon him, is thenceforth lion-hearted in the presence of men. He is at the disposition of God, and is whatever his heavenly Master wishes him to be. It is a light thing for the Spirit of God to make of such a one a Luther, a Knox, a Paul; to bestow upon him all human excellencies; and give him power to thresh mountains, to revolutionize kingdoms, to do any work soever that needeth to be done. He is in the school of God, to be educated by God. He has begun aright; and eye hath not yet seen, ear hath not yet heard, heart hath not yet conceived, what he will become in the plastic hand of his divine Fashioner.

JULY 31.—"And unto the angel of the church in Sardis write: These things saith he that hath the seven Spirits of God, and the seven stars; I know thy works, that thou hast a name that thou livest, and art dead."—Revelation iii. 1.

The seven spirits and the seven stars have a relation to each other. It is the divine Spirit that is spoken of thus; and the intention is not to lower our conception of his divinity, but to exalt it. The Spirit is wholly wheresoever he is; but his manifestations are modified and affected by the exigencies of those whom he blesses with his presence. The unity of the Spirit shall be witnessed in its perfection, only when the different denominations of Christians flow together. He that hath the seven stars and knows their divers conditions, wants, trials, infirmities, and characteristics, hath the seven Spirits, and is able to minister unto each church just what influence and operation of the Holy Spirit may be demanded. The number "seven" seems suggested by the candelabrum of the tabernacle with its seven lamps. In chapter iv. 5 we read of seven lamps before the throne which are the seven Spirits of God. In v. 6, the Lamb's seven eyes are said to be the seven Spirits of God sent forth into all the earth. As no one could attribute seven eyes to Christ in any natural sense, so it would be wildly absurd for any one to conceive of essential plurality in the Spirit. It is by his divine perfections that Christ is present in all the world; and it is thus the Spirit of God is present.

"I know thy works that thou hast a name that thou livest and art dead." The expression "I know thy works" has been hitherto used in a commendatory and encouraging sense It was a matter of congratulation to the four churches mentioned in the preceding chapter, that the Lord was acquainted with their works. But it was otherwise with the church of Sardis. The works were such as to proclaim this church dead. The gardener has no difficulty in discerning the evidences that a plant is dead. The persistent absence of fruit when fruit is due, is sufficient to condemn the tree.

It is bad enough to be dead, but, oh, how perilous to be dead with a name to live! The life-giving influences that would seek the merely dead, turn aside from that which professes to have life. Salvation is running to and fro in the earth, seeking the lost; but when it comes near that which professes to be in Christ, it is turned away by the declaration, "I have no need." The more there is of this semblance, (with no reality) the greater the danger. But this is not all. The dead thing that has a name to live, is deadly; it deals in death; it assimilates all around to itself; it testifies powerfully against vital religion by the exhibition of a lifeless religion. If the light *in you* be darkness, how great that darkness! How mightily grew Sardis! how large the place it occupies in the ecclesiastical history of the last eighteen centuries! how baleful its influence upon the other churches, so that they had almost to hide their diminished heads; and how largely is it represented at the present day upon the earth! Men know our name; Christ knows our works.

August 1.—"Look unto me and be ye saved, all the ends of the earth." --Isaiah xlv. 22.

Thus early and thus distinctly do we find the gospel emancipated, and the Spirit of God breaking away from his prison-house, from Judea, to utter a premonitory invitation in the ears of distant nations, occupied with their idols. We should never allow ourselves to suppose that when God was bestowing so much labor of love upon the Jewish nation, that he was then unmindful of the rest of mankind. God took nothing away from the other nations of the earth, when he made the Jewish people the object of peculiar care. Not one prophet was taken away from the other families of the earth; not one truth that had been bestowed upon mankind at large was suppressed; and not one promise that made known God as the hearer of all who call upon him in truth, was taken back.

The Jewish economy was an economy of special grace, with reference to a glorious end embracing the destinies of all nations. When God chose Abraham, he over and over declared that his thoughts were on something more than the seed of Abraham. "In you shall all the nations of the earth be blessed." And from first to last, all that God did to the Jewish nation had reference to the hour when the Lord Jesus should command his Gospel to be preached among all nations, and when the completed volume of the grace of God, the Old Testament and the New Testament should be tendered, with all their revelations and all their promises, to every creature. The very Jewish feasts had a world-wide significance. The passover told of the Lamb that should take away the sin of the world; the feast of weeks told of the pentecostal publication of the gospel in all tongues; the feast of tabernacles tells of the mighty ingathering that is to be.

AUGUST 2.—"Behold I come as a thief. Blessed is he that watcheth." —Revelation xvi. 15.

A thief comes only where he is not expected. His great interest is that people should be off their guard. Where there is watchfulness, there is no opening for him. Our Lord comes as a thief upon the world, because the world has no expectation of him. The world has no more thought of his coming than it has of the coming of Socrates or Alexander. This is not, be it understood, because Christ has done anything to keep the world unaware of his coming. He has sent the fullest information to every creature. He has given an open book to the world in which is an ample account of his future coming. The mode, the circumstances, and something too of the time, are published beforehand. What makes his coming to be that of the thief, is the blindness, the stupidity of men in all that relates to religious matters. He shows them even the key by which he will enter their house; but nothing produces an impression.

There are those who profess to be his servants, who also say, "Our Lord delayeth his coming." Their sense of responsibility loses its keenness, and they are in great danger of being found in an unprepared state. Blessed are they who say, The time is short. We know not what the morrow may bring forth. They sleep not without seeing that there is oil for their lamps.

AUGUST 3.—"*Jesus Christ, the same yesterday, to-day, and forever.*"—Hebrews xiii. 8.

Amidst the mutations of character, the fluctuations of time, and the vicissitudes of events, the soul longs for something that does not and that cannot change, to which it may attach itself and thus find compensation for all the mutabilities of which it is compelled to have experience in this world. There needs of course something else besides immutability in order to constitute an object worthy of our earnest attention and heart-felt confidence. We cannot desire immutability where there is anything less than perfection. But where the highest possible excellence resides, there unchangeableness becomes a thing greatly to be desired. Above all when we stand in a certain relation to this incomparable object; when the perfections of this unchangeable one are made available for us; when his power supplements our weakness; his wisdom our ignorance; when he in all his plenitude of perfection is our own particular treasury from whence we may draw everlasting supplies. Then, Oh, then, let change approach him not, but stand respectfully beyond the circle drawn by his divine nature.

How vain were it to go everywhere preaching the gospel of the grace of God, of God's grace incarnate in Christ, if Christ were not the same yesterday, to-day, and forever. Why should we go telling men of what Christ said and did to the leper, of his conversation with the woman of Samaria, of his instructions to his disciples, his rebukes addressed to the Pharisees, his demeanor in the presence of his enemies, his emotion at the grave of Lazarus, his kindness to sinners and publicans, his invitations to the laboring and heavy-laden, his affliction and agony in Gethsemane, his sufferance of indignities in the Prætorium, his prayer on the cross, and his words to the penitent thief; why should we go about telling men these things, if it were not that they occurred in the life of one who is the same yesterday, to-day, and forever?

Yes, this gospel is everlasting. It is not an ancient book; but the book of this generation. There is not the least trace of decrepitude about it. It blooms with immortal youth. By means of it Christ this very day approaches you, and reveals feelings that he entertains for you, entertains for you now, will ever entertain. An archangelic trump uttering in the skies the words, "Come unto me ALL ye that labor and are heavy-laden, and I will give you rest," would not be to us any more reliable evidence of the present disposition of Him who sits upon the throne, than these same words in the Gospel afford. And it becomes us to be well aware of this as we peruse the gospel history or dwell upon its statements. Would not some find in their hand a new and wondrous gospel, radiant with a glory hitherto unsuspected, if they would begin to read it with this great truth firmly enthroned in their convictions, that Jesus Christ is the same yesterday, to-day, and forever?

AUGUST 4.—"Behold, I stand at the door and knock."—Rev. iii. 20.

In manifold ways, Christ reveals unto men that he is willing and ready to enter into relations with them; and to those who have already some knowledge of him, he gives many a token that he is ready to enter into more intimate and hallowed relations with them. He does not wait, that men should seek him; he does not send word that he is waiting for them; he comes to them. He does not merely come: he stands and knocks.

The door is for the purpose of excluding enemies, and those whose visits are unwelcome; and you quickly rise when you hear the voice of a friend, and hasten to open the door that there may be no barrier between him and you. Another person might easily discover your feelings towards the one that knocks, by the response you make. Your countenance, your movements, all would show the feelings you entertain. Christ stands and knocks, and men are not aware of it. They are so busy hearkening to voices of earth, the world makes such a sound in their ears, or the slumber of unbelief is so heavy, that they hear not the Saviour's knock. Blessed are they who cultivate the faculty of quickly detecting the foot-fall of Christ, and start up as soon as they hear his knock.

He knocks by his providence, as when he takes away your property, or your health, or your bosom friend; when he places you in new and trying circumstances with many and wide-branching responsibilities; when he takes you away from loved scenes; when some mighty display of his power in the natural world, arrests your attention;—by his servants, moving them to address you in the language of exhortation or admonition;

—by his word, with its gracious promises or tender upbraidings;—by a manifest work of grace in the heart of another.

I say unto you, hearken; hearken diligently, turning away from the vain babbling of the world; and you shall hear the knock of Christ. You shall never be without an intimation from him, that he is nigh and ready to bless. Show hospitality to him in the world and he will receive you into everlasting habitations; receive him into your heart and he will give you an abundant entrance into the glorious mansions of his Father. How wise was it in that poor woman to share her supper with Elijah; famine was just then coming over the threshold to instal himself at her board; but was compelled to take an everlasting flight. "If any man hear my voice, and open unto me," says Christ, "I will come in and sup with him and he with me; I will come and make his earthly lot glad with my presence, and he shall come and participate with me the glory and felicity of the heavenly life."

August 5.—"**The Lord will perfect that which concerneth me.**"—**Psalm cxxxviii. 8.**

He will perfect my happiness. "My people shall be satisfied with my goodness." He will perfect his own image in me. He will make me perfect in wisdom; perfect to know and to do his will; perfect to glorify the Redeemer; perfect in beauty and in strength.

The thought of humanity being again clothed with perfection is something altogether wonderful. It was a light thing to call a world into existence out of nothing; but to take a nature that had become earthly, sensual, devilish, and so refashion it that it should be transparent to all the rays of the Godhead, is what a mere finite conception would never have shadowed forth

Man is engaged in perfecting himself. From the very beginning he has insisted upon it that all he wanted was room and time and liberty, and he would make of humanity something very admirable. He has had all the opportunities and advantages he could desire. Sometimes, in some little corner of the world, God has permitted him to clothe himself with literary and artistic glory; to surround himself with beautiful statues and paintings; and to rise to the heights of a sublime eloquence. But Greece and Rome in their palmiest days, only afforded new evidence of the depravity and spiritual blindness of man, and what he was, only came out the more opprobriously by the intimations of what he might have been, and all succeeding cycles have shown his expectation of self-wrought perfection to be utterly delusive. In this our boasted day the most frightful immorality in the most favored places under the sun, shows anew the utter vanity of this most baseless hope. And all this time there has been present with man a heaven-descended system, pledging him perfection in the truest and amplest sense of the word. What need we talk of the perfectibility of man? It is impossible with man; most possible with God. There are in the midst of us men and women whom God is engaged in carrying to perfection. Let us join ourselves to their number. They are despised by the world; so was Christ. The world sees in them indeed what it could not see in Christ; much imperfection; but it might see something else if it would; namely, a germinant perfection.

It was because Christ was made perfect in suffering, that we have this hope. In the day of sorrow and of calamity, do I bear well in mind that God is perfecting that which concerneth me?

August 6.—"He which soweth sparingly, shall reap also sparingly."—2 Corinthians ix. 6.

The farmer could not make a greater mistake, than to suppose he would gain by not scattering his seed in the field. To keep the seed is to deprive it of its value; to cut oneself off from the blessing that might have been expected; and to inflict the greatest wound upon the future. No, scatter it; throw it away and let it go to naught, apparently, and be long lost, if need be, and forgotten; in its appointed time it will come up loaded with treasures which it has gathered from the secret places of the earth. Then will it appear that your wealth is proportioned to your liberality.

There is to be a judgment according to works. By faith in Christ we succeed to heaven; but our works, evincing the measure of our faith, will determine the place we are to occupy in heaven, the degree of glory with which we are to be invested.

But what is meant by sowing? Using the gifts of God according to the will of God, and consequently in a way that will produce the greatest amount of good to our fellow-men. Much wisdom is needed in order to give aright; but we are responsible to have this wisdom. The man who receives gifts from God, receives an appointment from God; namely, that of donor; and the wisdom to discharge the functions connected with this appointment will surely not be withheld, if it be ingenuously asked. We are to look upon the world as God looks upon it, and then we shall know how to minister to our fellow-men.

You are a believer, are you not? You are expecting heaven through the grace of Christ which you appropriate by faith. But do not suppose, O friend, that the faith by which you shall be saved is one faith, and the faith that leads to generous acts is another faith. When I see you scattering seed, I look at the very faith which is to bring about your salvation. Your daily, hourly movements, call men to look upon that precious principle which is to open for you, if they be opened for you, the gates of heaven. You are to live by faith; to live now by it, if you would live hereafter by it.

AUGUST 7.—"We are his workmanship, created in Christ Jesus unto good works."—Ephesians ii. 10.

If we are created anew, we are created unto good works. The world ought not to be angry with God for creating men anew; for he is creating them for this among other things that they may tread in the footsteps of their Divine Master and abound in good works to their fellow-men. The world, however, is irritated at the proposition that men need a special creation in order to become competent to bestow good gifts. It professes to be able to point to men, who have spent fortune, time, health, in a whole-hearted endeavor to do good to their fellow-men.

But consider that it is one thing to give a poor creature on his way to the gallows, a cup of water, and another thing to save him from the gallows. One thing to make the cell of a criminal comfortable, and another thing to save him from crime and put within his reach the means of attaining to everlasting bliss. The world, obedient to the instincts that God has implanted, often looks around to see what oasis it can create in the desert of this world; but alas! the trees which it plants yield no immortal fruit.

Until a poor creature has been brought to God, all that you can do for him is of comparatively little moment. If your benefits tend to this, even indirectly, well and good. You may exercise your generosity in such a way as shall tend to keep the man ignorant that there is a gospel, and that he needs it absolutely.

AUGUST 8.—"Be thou faithful unto death and I will give thee a crown of life."—Revelation ii. 10.

The meaning is not, Be thou faithful all thy days; but, have thou that faithfulness which characterizes the martyr disciple, leads him to count not his life dear unto himself, and enables him at any moment to lay it down freely in the service of his Master. The expression does not refer to length of service, but to entireness of consecration. Be thou unrebukably faithful in all possible situations and circumstances.

Christ requires of every disciple that he should have the spirit of a martyr. At the very outset he informs those who come unto him that they are to take up their cross and follow him. And if at any time he should summon any number of his followers, and send them upon a service where death is certain, not one of them has any right to complain. It was so written in the bond. They gave him from the very first their early life, to receive from him a heavenly life.

We are to be faithful unto death, this day, and every day. We are to live a life of entire consecration; crucified unto the world and the world unto us. And if we have sufficient faith to let him day by day, and in all things dispose of us, take what he will, give what he will, send where he will, we need not envy those who literally suffered martyrdom for his name's sake. For us, too, there is laid up a crown of life. Not merely do we obtain a true life in exchange for the false life of this earth; but a glorious life; a life that shall be to us more ennobling and exalting than all the crowns of earth.

AUGUST 9.—"These things have I written unto you, that ye may know that ye have eternal life.' -1 John v. 13.

By life the Scripture means, true life, life in union to God, in the image of God; life with bliss and purity. An eternity under conditions like those that belong to the life of sinful man, were utterly undesirable. True life includes everything desirable, and the entire universe of God is just one of its perquisites. They that believe in Christ have Christ. They that have Christ have life. They that have life, have it eternally. They that have eternal life may know that they have it, and rejoice in the antepast even in this world. The Bible is given to furnish them with the means of knowing that they have it. If they find their names there, they shall certainly find them in the Lamb's book of life. As many as are the children of God, they are led by the Spirit of God, who is the Spirit of truth, and not only sanctifies them by the truth, but shows them their own new image in the mirror of the truth.

AUGUST 10.—"He that hath the Son hath life; and he that hath not the Son, hath not life."—1 John v. 12.

Hast thou considered well, O John the son of Zebedee, the beloved disciple, what is implied in these words of thine? These words fly in the face of all human philosophies, and give a picture of the world such as all the world is sure to abhor. They will laugh thee to scorn, with thy description of mankind as being without life save as they find it in Christ. For thy words, if they mean anything, declare that all the world have become obnoxious to the everlasting wrath of God, and are going down to perdition, no man having any goodness upon which he can rely for salvation; and that the favor of God, even life everlasting, is only to be obtained by renunciation of one's own wisdom and virtue and strength, or rather of the vain dream of these, and by a simple, whole-souled faith in Christ who died for sinners. These words of thine contain the very essence of the gospel, and exhibit it in stern, positive, uncompromising language, such as men can by no means brook. The gospel thus uttered irritates men beyond endurance; and makes them bring fagots and prepare the stake. At all events they will think thee a poor, bigoted, self-blinded creature, with thy horrid Calvinistic representation of mankind.

I know what I say—might John reply,—and what effect it is calculated to produce upon men. And yet I know that I speak with love and with wisdom; love and wisdom given from on high. A great many beautiful gifts of God still linger around fallen humanity, and testify of that height from which it has fallen; these gifts men look upon as a pledge of salvation; a fatal error and a strange one; for they only enhance the condemnation of those who, possessing them, nevertheless abide not in the love and communion of God, but obey their own vitiated will. I would fain have all men know of the grace of God; therefore I tell them of their utter gracelessness and absolute need of Christ. This despised word of mine shall live. From this time onward through all generations, it shall be without interruption precious to companies of believing men. Philosophies, religions, empires shall pass away, but this word shall not pass away. He that hath the Son hath life; he that hath not the Son hath not life.

August 11.—"Be watchful and strengthen the things which remain, that are ready to die."—Revelation iii. 2.

Unhappily, it is when men most need to be watchful, when the flame of heavenly grace is flickering in its socket, that they are least disposed to be watchful. We find that as men advance in holiness, make great attainments, ascend far up above the region in which ordinary believers walk, that they become watchful to an amazing degree. A habit of argus eyed watchfulness is in fact, itself, the evidence of a great victory over the enemy of the soul. When men have declined from grace, and when the adversary has all but riveted his chains again upon them, in the moment when, if ever, they need to be watchful, just then they are least of all disposed to fear, to strive, to watch. Happy for them if they hear in that critical moment the sovereign voice of Christ, saying, "Be watchful and strengthen the things which remain, that are ready to die. Arise, get oil for your lamps, before it be too late."

Imagine a great army, reduced through the heedlessness and effeminacy of their general, to a mere handful of men;

their tents are pitched in an exposed place; the enemy in great numbers look down from the cliffs above, and you fully expect that in the next minute these overwhelming forces will burst upon the poor, weak remnant and annihilate it. But just then it discovers its danger, and its leader remembers in that momentous juncture that he has with him a sword of divine temper, a breast-plate that will quench all fiery darts, an invisible legion of angels: he scales the heights, he calls upon his Lord, his heavenly auxiliaries fight for him, and soon he finds himself in a large place. Thenceforward, let him never forget the ominous experience of that hour past; and let him tremble at the thought of every step that would take him down into that valley of confusion, hard by the abyss of perdition.

AUGUST 12.—"In due season we shall reap if we faint not."—Gal. vi. 9.

When the sinner turns from the error of his way, submits to God and gives himself to the service of Christ, he thinks that he will never fail to enjoy the tokens of his Father's favor. The change in himself is immense. He is now day and night intent upon doing the will of God, whereas formerly he recked not of it; he checks within himself a hundred impulses that formerly had full sway. He naturally expects that perpetual successes shall wait upon him in his efforts to do good. And at first, for the maturing of his faith, God often vouchsafes to him prompt and glad results. But he is soon called to pursue a higher walk of faith, and find long intervals between the seed-time and the harvest.

We shall reap. Others scatter in vain. Of all mankind, only the people of God shall gather a harvest unto everlasting life. They sow the seed that God gives them in the way appointed by him. They deny themselves for the good of others, of property, ease, friends, health; and whatsoever they do, they do for the glory of Christ. From men they oftentimes reap ingratitude, enmity, defamation. But these things only augment the splendor of their reward.

If we faint not. This prepares us for a stern trial of faith, for a long long period (at least so seeming,) in which we shall be giving much and receiving naught. We spend our days, our golden days, the most precious of all our possessions; we throw them as it were into a gulf, with all our energies, our intellectual efforts, our physical strength, the glow of our aspirations, the enthusiasm of our nature, our property of various kinds; and so far as there is anything to show for it all, we may take up the refrain, "We have spent our strength for naught and our labor in vain." But if we endure unto the end, if we keep Christ's works unto the end, if we faint not, we shall reap, and that, too, with a fullness surpassing our utmost conceptions.

In due season. What is the due season God can judge, better than any other. It is not so distant that we should be discouraged. It is sufficiently distant to afford an opportunity for the full exhibition of our faith.

AUGUST 13.—" Blessed are the dead which die in the Lord."—Revelation xiv. 13.

The additional words "from henceforth," give this passage a specific and prophetical meaning. Neglecting these at present, we may consider the great unquestionable truth that there is for the Christian a blessedness in death. Not but that there is something better than death. Death is one of the enemies of Christ that must be put under his feet, and his saints shall one day get the victory over it, and, undergoing a change at his advent, live on eternally. In the meantime however, death is constrained with other agencies to work together for good to the people of God. Their faith deprives him of his terrors.

Three thousand souls an hour, fifty a minute, pass away from earth. How few of these die in the Lord! Think of this you that know the Lord, and whom he has commissioned to make him known. You are to meet these souls again; and happy will it be for you if you are able to show that you sought earnestly to obtain for your fellow-men this blessedness.

They are blessed, for they have great peace in the hour of their dissolution. Their cheerful exit confirms the faith of those that behold, and brings heaven near. It sometimes carries conviction to the impenitent, and leads them to seek that God who has such power to sustain and bless the souls of his people. They pass away from a world of sin and temptation and disappointment and vanity, to a world of light and purity. They depart to be with Christ,—to dwell in the mansions which he has prepared for them,—to associate with angels and with saints in light,—to drink of the rivers of pleasure that are forever at the right hand of God,—to obtain a crown of righteousness.

And if the king has summoned one of his own away from your side, can you greatly grieve? Does not the blessedness of that departure greatly overbear your individual brief loss, and flash down a glory upon your own desolation? Do you think much more of your own poor blessedness, thus interrupted, than of the perfect beatitude into which the other has entered? Would you make war upon this text? For the dead that die in the Lord are blessed for this among other reasons, that they leave behind them unspeakable consolations. Yes, it teaches that the survivor, who had a property in the one taken away, has not lost anything, but has seen his property taken upon high, that it may be rendered immeasurably more valuable and kept securely till the day of the restitution of all things. We do not want our wealth with us, but in the country to which we are going. "How great is thy goodness which thou hast laid up for them that fear thee." And the loved ones taken are a part of that treasured goodness. Let

Him then prepare a place for thee, in the way that seems best to Him. Too large an earnest of the inheritance that is to come, might check the vigor of our aspirations. The little paradises of earth, very little worthy of the name, yet clothe themselves with the superior power that belongs to present things, and disrobe from our view the only true paradise above.

AUGUST 14.—"Be not slothful, but followers of them who through faith and patience inherit the promises."—Hebrews vi. 12.

Does not this word "slothful" accurately characterize the habit of mind of most professors of religion? While we behold them diligently in the pursuit of worldly good, laboring untiringly on in the acquisition of wealth; while we see them exercising circumspection, vigilance, forethought, sagacity in their temporal vocation, and giving to it the best energies of their nature, we see them indolent and sluggish in all that relates to their heavenly calling. They read the newspapers with a closeness of observation that nothing can escape; but the Bible with a carelessness that leaves them just as ignorant afterwards as they were before. When topics of the day are discussed, their minds are easily kept on the stretch; but in religious meetings they are obliged to exert themselves not a little to keep awake. Any excuse is sufficient to make them dismiss or postpone a religious duty; while in the other engagements of life, they are sufficiently punctual. They are minutely attentive to the state of their body, and take good note of every ailment however insignificant; but they are not at all vigilant in the examination of their hearts and in the avoidance of whatever is likely to be prejudicial to their spiritual interests. On the whole they think it enough to give to religion the mere fragments of their time and attention and thought and energy.

Be not as they are. *Be not slothful.* Be slothful with respect to all other things, rather than this. Let your greatest energy be given to this. Not merely because it is becoming, but because it is necessary. There would be a very serious defect in the way of salvation, if it bestowed its priceless gifts on slothful men. If you would inherit the promised kingdom, you must model your life upon the lives of those whose faith and patience are honorably mentioned in the eleventh chapter of Hebrews. Be sure that nothing less is required of you han was demanded of them.

AUGUST 15—"That ye present your bodies a living sacrifice, holy, acceptable unto God."—Romans xii. 1.

You are exempt from the necessity of bringing lambs and heifers to the altar; but the aim of the gospel is to lead you to do what the law could not induce men to do, consecrate your own body to the Lord, bringing it daily to the altar, and devoting it to the execution as well as the enduring of his will. You are ever ready to yield it unto death as Abraham was his son; but the angel of the Lord ever interposes and says, God has some work for this body to do; see to the doing of that and come again.

It is of course only by the consecration of the soul that that of the body can be accomplished. God's will must be cordially embraced by the heart, before the feet or the hands or the tongue will move to execute it. So intimate is the union of soul and body that the consecration of the one involves that of the other. Let no man suppose that his heart is really given to the Lord, if the functions of his body be not employed in carrying out the revealed will of God. The Holy Ghost does not nestle in the heart, shrouded from sight. He is not living in us if he is not effluent from us. He is perpetually forth-flowing by the tongue, the eyes, the hand, the feet, the entire person. (John vii. 38.)

August 16.—"Return, ye backsliding children, and I will heal your backslidings."—Jeremiah iii. 22.

Abandon the idea that you must recover yourselves from your backslidings and then approach God. Perhaps you think that you could then approach him with some confidence. But does God forget? And will he look complacently upon your mended piety? He will look with just as much disgust upon the patched robe as upon the rent robe. But further you ought to know better than to entertain such an heretical notion as that you are able to recover yourself from your backsliding. Could you do that you would be the wonder of created beings. To recover you is in fact the work of God's power in its highest flight. Do not suppose that your sin, the stigma of your declension from grace, must get a little old, and then you will have a face to appear before God. This delusive idea will take you every day further and further away from God, and make your case more and more hopeless.

No, with all the guilt of your backsliding full and fresh in view, hasten to God. The only place in the universe where sin can be disposed of, is the throne of God's grace. If you throw it into any obscure pit and think you have done with it, you make a signal mistake. A legion of armed warriors will one day come up out of that pit and fall upon you with unappeasable ire. God alone is able to heal your backslidings, and he does it by leading you to dwell upon the character and work of our sympathizing High Priest, who does not break the bruised reed, nor quench the smoking flax, nor cast away as worthless what seems to men irrevocably gone.

August 17.—"Delight thyself in the Lord; and he shall give thee the desires of thine heart."—Psalm xxxvii. 4.

Turn not disdainfully away from these words of God, as though they had no claim upon your attention. These words come to you, so to speak, upon your own invitation. For, what have you done all your life long, but rush hither and thither, into this path and into that, crying unceasingly, "How shall I obtain the desires of my heart?" Behold here an answer to your life-long question. The explanation of all your disappointments, the remedy of all your sorrows, is here. Though there were on your table, waiting your perusal, numerous missives, some with the royal seal, others communicating news of enormous gains accruing to you, yet would it be wise in you to leave them all unnoticed rather than this text. If this be left to you, no matter though the wind carried them all away. Nay, if you should escape from a burning house with nothing but this word, you were richer than the richest of the sons of earth. For what all other things faintly and stammeringly promise to bestow, this positively promises. What is anything good for, if it yield you not the desires of your heart? Do you take this to be one of those kind lies with which a mother lulls her child to rest? Or a flight of fancy with more strength of expression than depth of meaning? Is every foolish promise of the world to be believed before the deliberate promise of the most high God?

In order that the desires of a man's heart should be gratified, it is needful that they should be rectified. He must let himself be led into the path that leads to felicity. He must delight himself in the Lord.

"But," you reply, "this is mere mysticism, pietism. The world is full of beautiful and attractive objects, made so by God, and placed opposite to us, that we may look upon them and rejoice in them. Why should not a man rejoice in his own marvellous faculties, bestowed by his Creator? Why should he not rejoice in human society and in all the amenities that strew the path of life? Why should he not rejoice in art, in poetry, music, painting, in nature and in the representations of nature, in the characteristics of his time, the onward sweep of humanity, in the immense variety of literature, in the food so abundantly provided him? What can there be better than to delight in these?"

Is thy heart satisfied with them? Is discontent a stranger to thy heart, and do murmurs remain far from thy lips? Canst thou say, I want no more?

Couldst thou answer these questions in the affirmative, there would still remain a difficulty. Thy beautiful things fade; the objects of thy delight vanish away. The more attractive a thing is, the more fatal will it prove to thy happiness. For all that is in the world is merely here on exhibition. It appears, is admired, and is then withdrawn.

No, it is no mysticism, but the truest philosophy, the only wisdom, to delight thyself in the Lord. Do this, not by despising his works, but by discerning the connection between them and him, and hearkening to the tale which they tell of him. All beautiful and excellent things are sent to show you the perfections of your God and to whisper to you of his love. Delight yourself in him who gave his Son to die for you; in other words love the things that he loves, shun what he disapproves; and it becomes as certain that your desires will be gratified as that the desires of God will be fulfilled.

AUGUST 18.—"Commit thy way unto the Lord; trust also in him; and he shall bring it to pass."—Psalm xxxvii. 5.

We shall find it impossible to commit our way unto the Lord, unless it be a way that he approves. For it is only by faith that a man can commit his way unto the Lord; and if there be the least suspicion in the heart, that the way be not a good one, faith will refuse to have anything to do with it. As well might you expect Achan to bring his wedge of gold and Babylonish garment to Joshua and ask him to take care of them; or a deserter to inquire of his general the way to the enemy's camp.

Having found reason to believe that your chosen way is approved of heaven, let heaven have the entire direction of whatever relates to it. Having resolved to go to Rome to preach the gospel there, be content that God should bring you there in chains, as a culprit, and keep you there as a prisoner.

And this committing must be a continuous, not a single act. You are to trust ever in His wisdom, goodness, and power—not only in generals but in particulars. And however extraordinary may seem to be his guidance, however near to the precipice he may take you, you are not to snatch the reins out of his hand. "Whatever is, is best," to him who, with an enlightened and genuine faith, has committed his way unto the Lord, and to him alone.

Are we really willing to have all our ways submitted to God for him to pronounce upon them? Are there not some of our ways which have become to us through long habit like a second nature, concerning which we have never really taken counsel of God? There is nothing about which a man needs to be more scrutinizing than about his oldest ways, his most confirmed habits and views. He is too apt to take for granted the divine approbation of them.

Why are some Christians so anxious and fearful, in view of some anticipated contingency? Evidently because they have not left the matter with him. They have taken it to him and brought it away with them.

It may seem a prodigious faith to regard God on his throne as studious of all that concerns us; but such faith is really no bolder than is the faith that God spared not his only begotten Son.

Commit thy way unto the Lord; trust also in him; and he shall bring it to pass.

AUGUST 13.—"We walk by faith, not by sight."—2 Corinthians v. 7.

Every man's world is what his heart makes it to be. When his heart changes, the world changes. When faith has come in and renewed his heart, he thenceforth walks in a new world. A new aspect comes over the face of all things. Faith reveals to him new and most important truths concerning everything, so that he can no longer take a step in just the mood that he formerly did, nor look upon a single individual as he once did.

Imagine a man on a beautiful island where there are a thousand objects to allure the senses and gratify the mind. He walks in groves, or reclines in bowers, or sits upon the grassy bank of a stream, or wanders through the halls of a palace; now with one gay company, now with another. Or if he list he embarks in some serious enterprise, and seeks to give his higher energies play. Until, one day, wandering alone to the extremity of the island, he discovers to his amazement that it is a floating island, and that a mighty current is bearing it on with all its palaces and battlements and hanging gardens and with all its companies of pleasure-loving people, bearing it away, bearing it whither? Ah, this now becomes the most important of all questions! As he returns, everything assumes in his eyes an unwonted look. As he reaches the summit of a hill, or passes along the verge of a precipice, or looks upon a waterfall, or sees a company of men, or hears music, or notices a tradesman counting his gains, one thought possesses his mind; these are all in motion, whither are they going? Music is no longer music, wine no longer wine, health no longer health to him. The discovery he has made puts an extinguisher upon all that he once called light, all that he once called pleasure. At length, after many fruitless inquiries, he meets with one who inhabits another little island connected for the present with the larger one, and who tells him that the island is sweeping on to a gulf of destruction and to an abyss of darkness; and that at the last moment the little isle tenanted by those who have known their danger and taken refuge there, will be detached and anchored forever in a blessed region. He believes. Henceforth how different will be all his perceptions and all his conduct from what they once were.

AUGUST 20.—"Trust in the Lord and do good; and verily shalt thou be fed."—Psalm xxxvii. 3.

In many ways faith leads to beneficence. Faith discovers to us the infinite mercy shown by God in providing a ransom for us; and the contemplation of this sacrifice prompts us to engage in enterprises for the good of our fellow-men. It shows us God delighting in the reciprocal love of his creatures one to another, and seeking to make them mutually exponents of his love. It reveals to us the Lord Jesus who pleased not himself, and went about doing good; and teaches us, that we are his disciples only while we follow him. It keeps fresh in our memory the promises; such as, "he that giveth to the poor, lendeth to the Lord;" "inasmuch as ye have done it unto one of the least of these my brethren, ye have done it unto me." It shows us that we have nothing which we can properly call our own, since we are one and all stewards of God, and must hereafter give an account of our stewardship. And it enables us to rest in full assurance upon the declarations of God and of Christ, that we shall be fed, that no good thing shall be withheld from us, that we are of more account than many sparrows.

We need faith in order to know how to do good. To be charitable, we have not merely to overcome our own reluctance to give, but we must learn from God how to relieve the wants of men. It is not enough to stretch forth the hand; it must be stretched forth in wisdom, wisdom obtained by faith. Again, if a man whose character is not what it should be, who does not honor God, or the word of God, if such an one engages from some motive or other in works of beneficence, there is reason to believe that he will indirectly do more evil than he will directly do good. For his kind acts will tend to propitiate men with his defective religion, and will go far to make them believe that the fear of God is not after all of very great importance.

AUGUST 21.—"To him that ordereth his conversation aright, will I show the salvation of God."—Psalm l. 23.

It is perhaps needless to remark that the word conversation is intended to include the entire conduct,—literally, the *way*. The ordering of one's conversation, implies meditation and study as to what one's conduct should be, in its various particulars; a definite and well-understood standard; a solemn and sustained resolution to live according to that standard, by the help of God.

Most men allow themselves to be wafted along by the current of events; their conduct is determined by circumstances and casual influences rather than by their own forethought and decision. And so, too, with Christians. Very many of these simply rejoice that they are acted on by better influences than once they were; and do not realize their obligation to labor, under the teaching of the Spirit of God, at the formation of a new and holy nature. Many seem to imagine that the responsibility rests with the Spirit of God, and that they are to be perfected in holiness by some mysterious process, that may just as well go on when they are asleep as at any other time. But the Spirit of God does what he does in us through our own agency and with our own consciousness. This is the principal drift of the direction, "Work out your own salvation with fear and trembling; for it is God who [thus] worketh in you to will and to do of his own good pleasure."

Perhaps no man that ever lived (if we except the apostles) engaged more earnestly than Jonathan Edwards in the work of ordering his conversation aright. His diary reveals him to us, a youth of nineteen or twenty, exercising the most intense watchfulness over himself, and laying hold with the utmost avidity of every flaw that appeared in his heart or life, in order to bring his energies to bear upon it, frame a resolution adapted to it, and cry to God for deliverance from it. All that forecast, and preparation, and study, and determination, and prayer could do to furnish him with armor in the hour of temptation, he compelled them to do. Other men when they have once fallen into temptation, succumb to it afterwards the more easily; but with him it was otherwise; he availed himself of the knowledge of sin once obtained, to defeat it on subsequent occasions. Any one who will carefully read his memoirs, will discover a striking illustration of the fact that God awakens the utmost energy of the soul when he would accomplish the deliverance of the soul. He fought the good fight of faith. Others who have not come so prominently before us, may perhaps have fought it still better. If so, we shall know them in the day of judgment.

God will give unto those who order their conversation aright, glorious and transporting views of the Saviour and of redemption through him.

August 22.—"Call upon me in the day of trouble; I will deliver thee, and thou shalt glorify me."—Psalm l. 15.

There are some whose cry in the day of trouble God will not hear; those, namely, who, in the day of their prosperity, heard not the cry of the poor and stretched forth no helping hand to the afflicted, and thus gave good evidence that they had no ear for the voice of God. For in the guise of a poor man Christ stood at their door, time and again, knocking and asking for admittance; but they would not hear. In the day of their calamity, he will not hear their cry. To whom then is this promise given? To him who hath made the Lord his refuge, and taken the divine will for his guide.

How naturally does friendship say, "Should you fall into any difficulty, don't hesitate to call upon me; I will do what I can for you." Ah, but these earthly friends, they are not always as good as their promises. A man does not seem so interesting to them when he is in trouble as when he is in prosperity; his defects come out more conspicuously. And even when their affection remains unchanged, how poor is their ability.

God does not say to us, "You shall not know trouble." But he says, "Trouble shall come upon you in order that I may have a peculiar opportunity of signalizing my love toward you, and of exhibiting my power to sustain. And in order that you may have a peculiar opportunity of showing your love to me, your trust, your patience, your steadfastness. And in order that the world may see the wonderful understanding between God's people and himself."

I will deliver thee. Who can doubt it when he calls to mind how this Deliverer endured, in Gethsemane and on Calvary, trouble such as never visited the soul of mere man, in order to pluck us as a brand from the burning. If he delivered when it cost his soul so much to deliver, how much more may we confidently expect that he will be with us in our lesser troubles, seeing that he is now rich in mercy.

AUGUST 23.—"**The steps of a good man are ordered by the Lord; and he delighteth in his way.**"—Psalm xxxvii. 23.

When his Son was on the earth, clothing humanity with a perfection it had not known since it had forfeited paradise, the beautiful spectacle attracted the regard of God, and nothing would do but that he should send his voice down into the ranks of men exclaiming, "This is my beloved Son in whom I am well pleased."

When Christ was about to depart out of the world, he took steps to have this pleased regard of the Father continue towards those whom he was to leave behind, even to his disciples of all future time. He offered up the prayer, "That the love wherewith thou hast loved me may be in them and I in them. For I am no more in the world, but they are in the world; and I am glorified in them." The Father could not resist these arguments. And so the Lord delighteth in the way of the good man, of him whose steps are ordered by him, and who follows in the footsteps of Christ. For he only is a good man in the estimation of heaven, whose steps are ordered by the Lord, who is led by the Spirit of God, to whom the word of God is a lamp.

AUGUST 24.—"Blessed be God who hath not turned away my prayer, nor his mercy from me."—Psalm lxvi. 20.

This language is appropriate to one who, having been led to supplicate God with respect to some matter that was very near his heart, has afterwards perhaps waited long and seen many things that appeared to be designed by Providence to extinguish faith and hope, but has persevered in expectation, and finally in some golden hour, never to be forgotten, has received the answer to his prayer, in most abundant measure, pressed down, shaken together, and running over.

Thus was it perhaps with the sisters of Lazarus, in the day of his sore sickness. His sickness had at first no power to affright them, for they knew the love of Jesus, and judged it sufficient to communicate to him their need. They felt that their prayer must be answered, their brother must be saved; the necessity for it lay very deep, even in the depths of Christ's own character, who could not but be true unto himself. But thenceforward everything seemed to frown upon their expectation. Their brother sank rapidly; Jesus came not; there came no message even. The hours as they vanished seemed to say in louder and still louder tones, "Prayer avails nothing; faith in Christ" is a delusion. And when Lazarus was buried, did it not seem as though all the promises were buried with him, the faithfulness of Christ shut up with him in the sepulchre? But, the stone is at length rolled away, and Lazarus comes forth; best of all, comes forth into the light of noonday the imperishable faithfulness of Christ. Then with overflowing hearts they blessed God, who had not turned away their prayer, nor his mercy from them.

Nothing is more important than that we should cherish a habit of pouring forth our hearts in gratitude to God, in view of his mercy shown in responses to our prayers. One end for which he grants us our desires, is that we may express gratitude to him; and it is therefore a piece of dishonesty in us to neglect this. Gratitude is a most important aid to faith. It serves to sink the memorials of benefits deep into the mind; and our faith, in the hour of prayer, takes great courage from the contemplation of these. And then again, a thing may be a good deal more than itself. In itself a mere trifle, yet as an expression of God's mercy, and as a token that we have a friend on the throne, it is of priceless value. If we take it without gratitude, a mere trifle; but if we consider well what it betokens, and set our gratitude to work to gather from it a treasure of divine love, this treasure shall not be wanting.

August 25.—"Be thou exalted, O God, above the heavens, and thy glory above all the earth."—Psalm cviii. 5.

Whether men honor him or not, God is forever infinitely honorable. His perfections remain the same. By virtue of his divine power and Godhead, he is exalted where no conception of a finite being can follow him, much less add anything to or take anything from his exaltedness. But when God condescended to call creation into existence, it was for the purpose of revealing himself unto his intelligent subjects, and setting up a throne in the heart of each of them.

In this world, men are in a state of revolt; they have cast down the throne of God in their heart, and denied their obligation to glorify him. They are bent upon their own exaltation, nd conceive that they have enough to do to accomplish their own glory, without attending to that of God. We have all heard of the Calendar published in France within a few years, in which all the days of the year were distributed among three hundred and sixty-five great men, who in their several days were to be worshipped by men, and this was to be the only worship. But those who thus proclaim man to be the only divine being known, are just a little more outspoken than their fellow-men. For he who sees without sorrow and solicitude how God is slighted and forgotten in the world; he who protests not against the ungodly ways of men; he who is not intent upon knowing the perfections of God; earnestly and assiduously studies not the word; knows not Christ as God manifest in the flesh; prays not, labors not, that God by his Spirit may be enthroned in his own heart; he is one of those who are engaged in the bold and absurd attempt to dismiss God and put man in his place.

Christians are a little company who say from the heart, as they address God, "Thine is the kingdom, and the power, and the glory," and who are consecrated to the great work of restoring to God, so far as in them lies, the glory that is due to him. Understand then, O Christian, thy vocation. Thou art to live in such a way, that all thy actions, all thy deportment shall give expression to the great truth that God is on the throne of the universe, that He alone is worthy to have his will done by all, that he is ineffably, incomparably glorious.

And the blasphemous extravagance of self-glorification to which man is carried at the present day, should only be an additional stimulus to the Christian to exalt God by humble obedience, by love to his brethren, by the prayer of faith, by self-denial and watchfulness, by simplicity of life and of speech, by communicating the knowledge of Christ, and by wise, loving, and faithful remonstrances with men, upon the greatness of their error.

AUGUST 26.—"They that sow in tears shall reap in joy."—Psalm cxxvi. 5.

The tears of those that sow, flow from various causes. Here is one who has greatly hungered and thirsted after the communications of God's love; who mourns over his own heart of unbelief; over his inaptitude for the things of God; who has been fascinated by the conception of a divine life to be led on the earth, a life of conscious union with God attended by peace flowing like a river, and revealing itself by ardent love, cheerful labor, and large success. But the very conception of the thing only makes his actual experience more inglorious and more insupportable. Tears are his meat night and day. In this state, how can it be expected that he should go forth and exhort men to believe on Jesus; or engage in the distribution of tracts setting forth the preciousness of Christ? Nevertheless, he does it. With a heart breaking for the longing it hath, he tells his fellow-man that religion is the one thing needful; and brushing away a tear, he assures them that the only true happiness to be found on earth is to be found in Christ. And in this there is no insincerity. For his deepest conviction is this: that there is no joy worthy of the name save that which Christ gives to his people. He does not speak from present experience, but from faith.

Here is another who trusted on the Lord that He would

bear testimony to the word of His grace; but many a long year fulfils the ministry of this word without any such testimony being borne. Another is keenly sensitive to the taunts and reproaches of men, and the harvest of these is the only harvest that he seems to gather. Consider Jeremiah among the Jews, Brainerd among the Indians, and a thousand others.

Let it not be supposed, however, that the words of life come with most power from an afflicted heart. It is often well that the heart should have had experience of affliction. But the servant of Christ should not be content till the kingdom of heaven, which is righteousness, peace, and joy in the Holy Ghost, be fully come in his heart. God meeteth him that rejoiceth and worketh righteousness; and the command to rejoice in the Lord is a command that must be obeyed. Blessed is he that mourneth: why? because he shall be comforted. This mourning must pass away, and then the blessedness will appear in the consolation.

August 27.—"Thanks be to God which giveth us the victory through our Lord Jesus Christ."—1 Corinthians xv. 57.

"Fear not, little flock, it is your Father's good pleasure to give you the kingdom." There are two parties in this world; one consisting of the cross-bearers, the other consisting of the unconverted. In numbers the former are very few. If we sift the nations reputed Christian, correcting our own conceptions by the standard of Christ, the numbers will diminish faster than the army of Gideon. They are indeed a little flock. It may be that they do not exceed, even in this our day, one in a hundred of the population of the globe.

They were once fewer than they now are; and we have thus two wonders; one that they have succeeded in maintaining their footing upon the shore of this world; another that they should have an inviolable promise to the effect that they will actually obtain the victory and sit down upon the vacated thrones of the earth. For there is no special prowess to compensate for the paucity of their number; there are no advantages of rank; no superiority of discipline. The world thinks itself able to crumple them up as a piece of paper. There is no obvious reason why they should not be crushed at any moment. In fact the world has often trodden them under its heel, and exclaimed with a sense of relief, "There, they are gone;" but the next moment they were found springing up again in some quarter. The world has gained ever so many overwhelming victories over them; and is exceedingly provoked to find that it is none the better for all its victories. The Church unbrokenly lives on.

In fact what seem to the world to be its victories, are the victories of the Church. For Christ's people are fighting the fight of faith. They have no weapons of their own, but the stars in their courses fight for them. When persecuted most, they are most strong in faith; and when they are strong in faith, all things fight for them, even the heavens above and the earth beneath.

AUGUST 28.—"Thou, Lord, art good, and ready to forgive."—Psalm lxxxvi. 5.

God's commandment is good. The law of his will designates the only path in which it is good for men to walk. It cannot be that God's choice should be otherwise than best. But man has broken God's law, and discarded God's choice. He has left the path that infinite goodness appointed to him. The question now arises, How can it be good in God to forgive man for abandoning that path? Is it becoming to let man obtain such a stupendous victory, and proceeding by a forbidden path, possess himself of the very good that God placed at the terminus of the path of obedience? Is the arrogance of man gross enough to aspire to such a success as this, ,nd throw such contempt as this upon the law of God?

What then? must man suffer? Why not, rather than that man should enter heaven with a torn law of God for his banner? The welfare of the entire universe hangs by the adamantine chain of God's authority; let this be shattered, and chaos is come again.

What otherwise could never have been, has been brought about by the incarnation, obedience, and death of the Son of God. God is now good even when he forgives. All his perfections rejoice over the accepted sinner.

God is *ready to forgive.* Let us act upon this unimpeachable truth. Have we not too often approached God as though it would require an immense deal of persuasion to induce him to forgive us? If Christ be there, there is no reason why we should not expect to obtain it most promptly and profusely; for there is something more accomplished by our forgiveness than the mere mitigation of our inward torment; there is the honor bestowed upon Christ. This translates the matter to the very court of heaven, and invests it with more than archangelic dignity. God is ever ready to honor his Son; he is therefore ever ready to forgive those who have a true faith in Christ.

August 29.—"Whether therefore ye eat or drink, or whatsoever ye do, do all to the glory of God."—1 Corinthians x. 31.

We ought to be much affected by the condescension of God. He talks to us as to angels. What more could he say, in the way of commandment, to any being, than he here says to us? It is evident that he puts us in the first rank of his servants. He is willing to overlook the fact that we are moral cripples, spiritual lepers. He does not thrust us down into an inferior chamber and assign to us some base work, but he bids us do the work of Raphael; that is, to show forth the glory of God, in all our acts and movements, great and small.

He that assigns to us so comprehensive and exalted a function, gives grace according to the largeness of his command.

The will of God does not relate to the great movements of our life, passing over the lesser. He does not say, "Arise, go to Joppa," and then leave us to go there in any way we please. His will is to be the staple of our existence, and to go with us from breath to breath along the entire journey of life. Christ would not let go of the will of God to take up a piece of bread, after his forty days' fast. The Christian cannot partake of an abundant meal, if his "neighbor" stand hungering there; or if some pressing duty be to be discharged. No more in little matters than in great does he presume to live unto himself.

This command requires us to be ever looking unto God; and is designed to establish a perpetual commerce between our soul and him who loves us. People think this will hamper them; whereas it is just the being invested with a divine life. As well might they complain of being compelled to wear an emblem of royalty on the brow.

August 30.—"Though I walk in the midst of trouble, thou wilt revive me."—Psalm cxxxviii. 7.

Some obtain their experience early, others later, but it seems that all who live long in this world must learn by experience the bitter truth that the elements of trouble are very numerous in this stage of man's existence. The youthful heart, taught of God to desire happiness, takes counsel of its imagination how to seek it, and delights itself with dreams of earthly bliss which must soon be dispelled. Very often it gets angry with God for not equaling the creations of its own imagination, for allowing his divine power to be surpassed by the poor conception of a mortal; not considering that this is a world of rouble, because it is a world of sin. These disappointments in too many cases deaden the heart; destroy its poetry, its enthusiasm, its sensibility. But they that go with all their hopes and aspirations to God, and seek in him what the world cannot give, their hearts shall live. Wonderful it is to see in the Christian of threescore years, all the sensibility and enthusiasm, the freshness, and glow of youth. And yet it is no wonder, for the paradise he looks at, is in the skies, and is every day drawing nearer and becoming more glorious to the sight. His feelings partake of the nature of the immortal realms which he contemplates and seeks.

AUGUST 31.—"The Spirit and the bride say, Come. And let him that heareth say, Come."—Revelation xxii. 7.

To whom is the invocation addressed? To Jesus or to the sinner? If we connect the words with those that go before, it appears to be the Saviour that is invoked: if with what comes after, the invitation is to the sinner; "Let him that is athirst, come." But we need not adopt either view to the exclusion of the other. For he who with all cordiality says, "Come, Lord Jesus, come quickly," cannot be otherwise than greatly concerned to see his kingdom extended in the world. He will best show his solicitude for the coming of Christ, by laboring to induce men to come and take of the water of life.

"Let him that heareth say, Come." Thou hearest, thou hast long heard the Gospel. Thou art ever found in thy place in the congregation of the people of God, hearkening diligently unto the words of life. In this and in that gathering we meet thee, and thou art ever attentive to the exposition of God's word. Thou art interested in the various religious topics that are brought under discussion; and everything that promises to render thee more spiritual, more believing, more joyful in Christ is welcome to thee. But pardon me if I suggest that there is such a thing as being religiously luxurious. Remember what world thou art placed in. The question is not, what kind of piety might be appropriate to some Elysian plain, where all is odoriferous of heaven, and significant of triumph; but it is this, what kind of piety is most suited to thee in thy present condition? Thou art in this world to utter the invitations of God to fallen man. Thou hast a ministry, and it is to say the word "Come," in such tones as may be best adapted to draw the attention of men to the proffered mercy of God. Rejoice that in the benignant providence of God you are in these latter days furnished with so many facilities for extending the invitations of the Gospel to your fellow-men. He that gives to Tract and Bible and Missionary Societies, that gives in faith and simplicity and at some personal cost, he in his measure is saying to his fellow-men, "Come." But surely these agencies were not raised up by God in order that the main body of Christians might get easily off from the ministry of invitation assigned them.

Let every one who saith "Come, Lord Jesus, come quickly," see to it that his whole life be an enunciation of the Gospel, his whole being transfused with the spirit of invitation; and that there be in his looks, words, acts, manners, way of life, nothing but that which shall tend to make Christ attractive to his fellow-men.

The Spirit and the bride say, Come. We are the bride of Christ, and with us is the Spirit, if we earnestly and lovingly desire the coming of Christ, wrestle with Christ to set up his kingdom in the hearts of men, and with men to come to Christ. Let the bride in this way make herself ready.

SEPTEMBER 1.—"Yet a little while, and he that shall come will come, and will not tarry."—Hebrews x. 37.

Among many that profess to be the people of God, we find one (scarcely one in a thousand) whose manner of life seems to express his conviction that the time is short, very short. He is like one who waking from slumber finds that his barque has drifted within the influence of currents that are hurrying her fast towards the rapids, fast to destruction, and perceives in a glance that whatever is to be done is to be done at once, and done with all might. The accumulated business of life, so long lost sight of, is to be despatched with all possible expedition. The talents so long buried are to be dug up and got into circulation at once, that there may be a respectable return to exhibit when the Master comes,—who knows how soon? Energy, circumspection, perseverance, in fine the consecration of all the powers, must compensate so far as may be for the immense treasures of time that have been squandered. "He cometh, he cometh," is the motto of such a one. Other men, other Christians even, look on with astonishment, and fancy that the man must be beside himself to labor so vehemently. They bid him check his great zeal and mingle moderation with his earnestness. But he replies, "One thing I do. The past time of my life must suffice for apathy and self-indulgence. The Master whose service I have too long neglected, cometh quickly. He hath ordained me that I should bring forth fruit, and I must make the most of the brief season that remains."

A little while! A great work! The views of many Christians are very defective with respect to both of these facts. "Our Lord delayeth his coming," seems to be the impression on their minds. Their energies, their earnestness, their self-denial, their consecration, are exhibited in efforts that have no reference to the deliverance of their souls from baneful influences. The work of religion is one which is easily disposed of, they imagine, in an occasional hour, in the leisure moments which the greater business of life is generous enough to grant.

Is there not coming an hour when the sign of the Son of Man having appeared in heaven, all mankind will become aware that the sun of their probation is just about to sink forever, the Sun of Righteousness just about to rise in glory unconceived; and when the possessors of the Gospel who have left undone their Master's bidding, will be filled with terror and confusion at the thought of the immense work committed to them, and to which they had hardly put their finger; while they that knew he would not tarry, shall lift up their head, knowing that their redemption draweth nigh. Which of us shall be able to stand?

SEPTEMBER 2.—"Lead us not into temptation."—Matthew vi. 13.

If you ask me to show you a wise man, I will ask you to find for me a man who, morning, noon, and night, offereth to God this prayer. You find him, and you say to me, "Why, this is a poor man, a mean man, an ignorant man, an obscure man; I asked him some ordinary questions, and he could not answer them. In his hand was a book, and he told me frankly that having no wisdom of his own, he was obliged to make use of that book. And yet you tell me he is the wisest of men. His wisdom multiplied ten thousand times would not equal the wisdom of some that are known to me." To this I rejoin: Your wise man and mine are alike in one respect. They are exposed to a common danger. They have an enemy whose power enables him to laugh at all the wisdom of man, and whose malignity will bring everlasting ruin upon those whom he subjugates. Woe then to him who is foolish enough to trust in any wisdom of his own. He is daily led into temptation without knowing it, and daily succumbs; and day by day the fetters of the enemy are more strongly riveted upon him.

No man was ever so far advanced in the divine life, as not to need to utter these words. In fact the holiest breathe this petition with the most frequency. And if an angel should be sent from heaven into the midst of us, it would be ever upon his lips.

"This is a world of temptation, and it would be difficult so to dispose of ourselves as never to encounter temptation." True: and many advantages flow to the Christian from the fact that he is exposed to temptation. His graces are thus strengthened. His self-knowledge is increased. He relies more implicitly upon the word of God. But the tempter knows how to combine circumstances, and so to adapt his wiles to the spiritual state of a man, as at times to bring an unexpected and powerful temptation to bear upon him. With reference to such temptations as these the Christian offers up this prayer. God gives a man the shield of faith and the sword of the Spirit with regard to ordinary temptations, those that he is already familiar with; and gives him a spirit of prayer with regard to others, from which in answer to this prayer, he delivers him. There is one way of dealing with present temptations, and another way of dealing with those that are future. If, relying on our strength of faith, we cease to be apprehensive of new and subtle arrangements by which our affections may become entangled, we are almost certain to sustain damage.

If after all it pleases God to bring the petitioner into temptation, he is not brought into it as other men are. God will indicate, in the trying hour, the way of escape.

SEPTEMBER 3.—"If any man draw back, my soul shall have no pleasure in him."—Hebrews x. 38.

God taketh pleasure in them that fear him, and who manifest their fear to displease him by constantly and carefully pressing forward in that good path which he has opened up to them. When a man is pressing forward in the path of God, all heaven and earth rejoice, reflecting the joy of God. The sun shines not in vain for him; it lights him along the pathway of holiness. The earth is encouraged to run cheerfully her race of a thousand miles a minute

The Bible lives with reference to such a soul. Its commands, its promises, its invitations, all its words are clothed with their proper majesty, and bring to bear the influences of omnipotence upon this soul. But it is sad when such a soul in some evil day begins to slacken its energies; sadder still when it quite ceases to press forward; but oh how melancholy the spectacle when it actually begins to go back. The sun has his mission, and he continues to shine; and the earth too sweeps on in her orbit; the time has not come for the displeasure of God to enunciate itself; but it is none the less stern and terrible for its present silence.

You have come and looked upon the suffering Son of God. You have taken note of his dignity; of his humiliation; of his purity; of his death; of his perfect ability and fitness to save. You have looked into the lake which burneth with fire and brimstone; you have beheld the tree of life in the midst of the paradise of God; you have seen a Lamb in the midst of the throne as it had been slain; you have tasted of the manifold banquet of the word of God, and have had experience of the powers of the world to come; and after all, you conclude to go back. It appears now, that while you suffered yourself to be drawn to Christ, to be drawn by the cords of the gospel far on your way to him, there was all the time a forgotten cord attaching you to the world. Your chains seemed to be all severed by the mighty love of Christ; but your former master spun one of these chains to an invisible cord of immense extent, and you were not allowed to feel that there was any such cord until you had accomplished a large part of your journey to the kingdom of heaven. Your master watched his time;

and at length availed himself of the hold he still had upon you, and drew you backward. Many were astonished; for they had never perceived that very minute and long-drawn bond.

SEPTEMBER 4.—"Call unto me and I will answer thee, and show thee great and mighty things which thou knowest not."—Jeremiah xxxiii. 3.

Great and mighty things had been shown unto Jeremiah. Great discoveries of the glory of God had been permitted him. He had walked with God on most intimate terms. He had experience of the power of God to render him as a brazen column in the midst of hostile Jerusalem, and to sustain him in his most trying ministry. God also had shown him the great and mighty things of his wrath that he intended to bring to pass upon Judea, and upon the nations round about. Yet Jeremiah was not to rest satisfied. His business was to obtain the utmost measure of divine communication. He was now in the court of the prison. He is told to pray for great things. Another would have thought first of his own deliverance. But the great and mighty things which it pleased the Lord to bestow and Jeremiah to receive, related to the deliverance of the people of God from their future captivity, and the restoration of God's goodness to them.

We may learn from this, not to rest satisfied with any communications of God's grace that we have received, but to cherish a spirit of expectation and desire. The best evidence that we value what we have received, is when it has enkindled our aspirations for what is yet beyond. For you observe that God requires to be asked for the great and mighty things of his grace, before he bestows them. And if the path of duty take you to the court of the prison, you may, like Jeremiah, find communications such as were not made in the temple even.

SEPTEMBER 5.—"The Lord will not cast off forever."—Lam. iii. 31.

From the context, the meaning is evident. He casts off his people from certain experiences of his love of which they have shown themselves unworthy, until they are humbled and penitent, fervent and believing. God does not arbitrarily resume his benefits. There is ever an adequate reason, and if we search the records of our experience, we shall find it. We should very carefully note what it was in our conduct, what remissness or sluggishness or waywardness or worldliness, that caused the Spirit of God to cease from shedding abroad the love of God in our heart; and when we have been restored, we should be careful not again to grieve him. Happy are they to whom it is given to know that they are not finally cast off. Their contrition, their humiliation, their ardent longing of soul, are the best evidences that they are not.

SEPTEMBER 6.—"And I will put my Spirit within you, and cause you to walk in my statutes."—Ezekiel xxxvi. 27.

A sublime expression of sovereignty; but let none therefore say, "We must remain as we are until he puts his Spirit within us." For God observes a process in this as in his other works; and in every step of this process he requires the co-operation of man. He shows an individual that he is without the Spirit of God; that he is spiritually dead; excites in him desires after life and blessedness; shows him what he is not to trust in; what he is to trust in; teaches him to pray; answers his prayer; and excites in him faith in the Lord Jesus. Then only perhaps does an individual discover that he has been influenced throughout by the Holy Spirit. But he who refuses to do anything until he is sensible of the Spirit's influences, will never do anything in the way of working out his salvation.

SEPTEMBER 7.—"Thou, O Lord, remainest forever; thy throne from generation to generation."—Lamentations v. 19.

The instability of many of the things with which we have to do in this world, only tends to make the believer appreciate the more, by contrast, the immutability of his God. The Lord of all sits upon his throne, and before him the universe passes like a panorama. He is unchangeable in character as well as in sovereignty. As we follow the indications of geology into the dim chambers of what seems to be a past eternity, it is a comfort to think there was then the same God that we now know; presiding over the strange processes of those times with the same wisdom and power that now dwell in him; have the same boundless love that has been so marvellously exhibited in our dispensation; the very same Being in fact who became incarnate in the person of Jesus Christ, spoke graciously to man and made an atonement for the sins of men. Too often the idea of immutability is connected in the minds of men with that of insensibility. But this is an error. There is but one immutable Being in the universe, and his name is LOVE.

Clouds and darkness are around about the throne of God, so that men see not that throne, and remain voluntarily ignorant of its existence. The thrones of this world are alone visible to them. To know what monarchies they stand in awe of, we have only to ascertain from their conduct whose commands they obey, whose will they execute. We find that they are influenced by mandates that come not from the throne of God. But all these inferior thrones and dominions vanish away. How many have come and gone since the prophet wrote these words. And as the others have passed away, so those that now exist must disappear from earth. That government that has in it the elements of perfect stability, man has not succeeded nor will succeed in devising.

Thou, O Lord, remainest forever: to whom then shall we

go, but to thee? Our immortal souls awakened by thy Spirit, find themselves in the midst of a creation that crumbles at the touch, and are filled with consternation as they behold themselves cast upon the billows of a world that has no one element of immortality to which they can ally themselves, nothing akin to themselves to afford them a hope of companionship in the day when all beside shall have dissolved. We flee to thee, O Lord, and find in thee a thousand times more than even the permanency of present things would have yielded us.

What gives the unchangeableness of God such a value in our eyes is that we may take refuge in him and be made like unto him. When we shall have been made perfect in love, we shall be able to look from the calm heights of an inviolate safety, upon the elements of change and destruction.

SEPTEMBER 8.—"I will take away the stony heart out of your flesh, and I will give you a heart of flesh."—Ezekiel xxxvi. 26.

This stony heart is not what is commonly understood by a hard heart, an unfeeling heart. A person of a gentle tender yielding disposition may yet have what God regards as a stony heart. A heart insensible to the word of God is what is here spoken of. The commands, the promises, the invitations all fail to make an impression upon one with such a heart; he refuses to see his sin, his helplessness, his danger, his need, the holiness, the grace, the love of God. The mighty and countless motives of the Bible are lost upon him. He perhaps flatters himself that he has a great deal of sensibility. He weeps at a tale of distress; and the more fictitious it is, the more he weeps. He perhaps is religious, in his own and others' estimation. Israel, of whose stony heart the text primarily speaks, was exceedingly devout and imagined itself blameless in all the ordinances of the Lord.

In the physical system of man the heart sometimes ossifies.

The most fearful and also the most shameful condition into which a moral being can fall, the lowest depth that he can reach, is that in which his heart becomes unable to distinguish the voice of God. Around him are ten thousand utterances; an angel would be ravished with the harmony: all the day long in one way or in another, God speaks; but he hears not.

What an expanse of promise there is in this one word *I will give you a heart of flesh.* You will sail over it long and find no limits. All the fruit of the Spirit, all Christian graces with all their manifestations, all triumphs of faith, are comprehended in it. When this promise is verified, immediately the entire word of God puts on its appropriate power. From Genesis to Revelation, everything starts into life. In giving us the heart of flesh, God gives us everything that he has made. The heavens begin to tell us his glory, and the firmament to show us his handiwork; the lily addresses our faith and the wind whispers of the Spirit; and we look upon all things as made by Him and for him and for us who believe in him.

SEPTEMBER 9.—"In a little wrath I hid my face from thee for a moment; but with everlasting kindness will I have mercy on thee."—Isaiah liv. 8.

If God withholds from us the tokens of his love, an explanation may almost always be found in the fact that we had made light of them in some way or another. God gives his love unto us that he may draw us by its sweet influences to renounce evil and to embrace good. If we receive the expressions of his loving-kindness and manifest no corresponding readiness to forsake sin, then it becomes needful that we should take lessons in the value and virtue of his love, through the privation of it.

There is amazing condescension in this language. The Lord as it were apologizes to his people. It is but a little wrath; I hid my face for a moment only; I will make it up to you a millionfold with everlasting kindness.

We can imagine a certain believer replying; "Thou doest all things well; and after what thou hast already shown of thy wisdom and love, thou canst well be trusted with the government of thy people. Still blame me not, if I urge that thy wrath is something so fearful, so unendurable, that a little of it, even a grain of mustard seed of it, is to our feelings something altogether tremendous and mountainous. If thou pour out thy wrath upon those that know thee not, they may indeed pine for the loss of this and that temporal blessing, but the thought of thy anger gives them not a moment's unhappiness. But thy love is our life, nay, a thousand times more than life; it is that which raises life to an infinite value; and the loss of it reduces life to an infinite evil. Far be it ever from thee, Lord, to give us to taste of thy unmixed wrath. If it be needful that we should experience a little wrath, let there be much love mixed with it. Let us not be bereft of the promises. Let us see the light shining at the extremity of the dark passage that we have to thread. Treat us not as though we were so insensible to thy love that a large privation of it could be easily borne.

The language of the text will have a different meaning to different believers. Some have been permitted to experience such marvellous discoveries of the grace of God, they have been brought into such secrets of the divine favor, that the privation which seems to them utterly insupportable, would not affect another in the least.

SEPTEMBER 10.—"**Hear, and your soul shall live.**"—**Isaiah lv. 3.**

The true life of the soul is in union with God. The souls of men are dead, because they are separated from God. Each man walketh apart, liveth unto himself, cleaveth to the earth;

he calls it solitude when his fellow-men are not there. The word of God is life-giving. We have not to go to a distant planet for the bread of life. Without any movement of ours, it has already been introduced into this world. We have not to pay for the liberty to appropriate it. All the price required has been already paid. We have only to hear. If we hear, our souls shall live. If we hear not, then life and immortality shall never be their portion.

Hear the word of life. All the days of your life, you have heard it with your outward ear, but it has never made its way to your inmost soul. The adversary that has such dominion over you has lined the passage betwixt your outward ear and your inmost soul with gins and traps, so that the word may not travel in safety. We see hundreds of chariot loads of precious truth go in at the portal of your ear; but it is too manifest that none of it reaches the place of power in your mind.

Hear! Enter into conflict with your adversary for the possession of this truth. It is your life, therefore embrace it with the instinct of self-preservation. Let everything else go, in laying hold of this. There was a man who, after many years of labor, was returning from California with a number of bags of most fine gold. The steamer was wrecked, and finding himself in the water with his bags, he let them all go that he might seize an old plank that came floating along. He escaped with his life and without his bags. I am afraid that he never was quite reconciled to the loss of his bags. Suppose, however, that what seemed an old rotten plank, should turn out to have an inscription on it, guiding him to a treasure a thousand times greater than what he had cast away. In that case he never would give another thought to what he had relinquished, unless it were a thought of self-congratulation that he had made such a wonderful exchange.

SEPTEMBER 11.—"Wherefore the rather, brethren, give diligence to make your calling and election sure."—2 Peter i. 10.

The context sheds all the light that we need upon this passage, explaining both the nature of the diligence that we are to use, and the object to be obtained by it. "If ye do these things, ye shall never fall." The things are mentioned before: "Giving all diligence, add to your faith, virtue; and to virtue, knowledge; and to knowledge, temperance;" &c. The words "shall never fall" have an immediate reference to the words "to make sure." Let no one bring in here his theory of election to destroy the force of this passage. God has his elect ones; and he accomplishes his purposes with regard to them by teaching them to take heed lest they fall, and to use all diligence in making their calling and election sure. They that despise these admonitions make it certain that they are not elected.

It is not to be supposed that after an individual believes on the Lord Jesus Christ he must wait a good while and make great progress in holiness, before he can make his calling and election sure. There is no reason why he should not have assurance of faith at the moment when he first looks to Christ for salvation. He that thirsting comes to Christ and drinks, may with absolute confidence conclude that his name is written in the Lamb's book of life. But that which makes his calling and election sure then, will not suffice to make it sure in days that follow. There must be growth in grace; and there must be expanding evidence. The soul must keep adding to its spiritual stores; must show that it has commerce with the skies. It can no more derive assurance from past experience than it can derive life from it.

In an important sense, salvation is neither a past thing nor a future thing; but strictly a present thing. If Christ is my Saviour, then he is saving me to-day. If he is my Shepherd, then he is leading me to-day. If he is my Lord, then he is ruling me to-day. To-day he teaches me, warns me, encourages me, blesses me, intercedes for me, brings me to God, destroys the works of the devil.

SEPTEMBER 12.—"The Lord hath comforted his people, and will have mercy upon his afflicted."—Isaiah xlix. 13.

Perhaps throughout the wide domains of God, there is hardly any sight more remarkable than that presented by the little flock of believers who, in this world of iniquity and of misery where Satan's seat is, regard the Lord as their King and are kept by him through faith unto salvation Their existence is a marvel; their peace and joy another; their triumphs another. They are without a visible Leader, and have no visible Comforter; yet they pursue their wav and have an invincible hope.

The Lord comforts his people, ordinarily, not by changing the course of his providence, not by crowning them with an outward prosperity, but by opening their heart to attend unto the precious declarations of his word. The Spirit is the Comforter, and he is the Spirit of truth. Christ prayed that the cup might be taken away from him; but afterward we hear him saying, "The cup which my Father hath given me, shall I not drink it?" The Father answered his prayer by some inward memorial of his goodness, and the cup just now so dreadful is taken cheerfully and with unfaltering hand by the Saviour. When the soul is in some deep distress it imagines that nothing less than the removal of the very cause of the distress will ever comfort it; but God prefers to show his power to sustain and bless the soul in the midst of the trying providence. He is glorified when the believer is delivered from his gloom without being delivered from that which caused the gloom. This finds itself vanquished when it seems to be most triumphant; and is utterly at a loss to understand how its instruments of torture should produce no longer any pain.

SEPTEMBER 13.—"Make thy way straight before my face."—Psalm v. 8.

It is especially when a feeling has taken possession of the mind that the Lord calls us to enter some new sphere, to engage in some new labor for his glory, that we long for an explicit revelation of his will. It is to be feared that too many grieve the Spirit of God by dismissing this conviction of duty from their mind, when there cometh not some plain providential notice of what the Lord would have them to do. The Lord still teaches by his word, and the way is this. He shows us the greatness of the love of Christ, and constrains us by this to desire to be more engaged for the glory of God. He teaches us to observe our position, our aptitude and various circumstances. He takes away from our mind all bias, the great impediment to right judgment. And he gives us a quick understanding to perceive the suggestions and monitions of the Spirit. He gives us faith, and a willingness to go forward without a preliminary sense of strength.

SEPTEMBER 14.—"The Lord God will help me, therefore shall I not be confounded."—Isaiah l. 7.

Help is needed to discharge duties that are too great for us, to encounter dangers that are too severe for us, to face enemies that are too powerful for us, to bear up under sore disappointments, under the loss of friends, of health, of fortune, to sustain the consciousness of our deep demerit, and in fact it is difficult to exhaust the catalogue of the ends for which we need help. Yet there are very few who are visited with a sense of any such need as this. The reason is that men generally take no cognizance of their real duties, are not aware of their real enemies, avoid as far as they can the path of present danger, and stultify themselves with ideas of their own goodness. The man that does not attempt to climb the Alps has no need of a guide; the mariner who mystifies himself as to the condition of his ship and denies his danger, rejects the offer of help.

We need help from God to know our helplessness. The greatest of all our enemies is in the royal chamber of our inmost being and rules us with a rod of iron, though it be bound about with ivy leaves. We need help from God himself to become aware of the true character of this enthroned enemy, and to see the desolations he has wrought in our heritage. Alas for them who know not their need of help. The triumph of their foe is complete. They are led captive at his will, even though we see them occupying the high places of the earth, admired and followed by vast crowds.

It requires but little faith, comparatively, to use the language of this text when there is a very inadequate idea of the difficulties, dangers, impediments, humiliations that may be found in one's path. If a believer entertains the idea that the covenant relation in which he stands to the Lord, secures him against any very severe stroke, he may then use this language without knowing what he says. But he has a wrong idea. The Lord sometimes appoints unto his people tasks of a most formidable character, trials that seem studiously calculated to grind them to powder. If there be some contingency that the believer deprecates with all the might of his soul, the mere imagination of which is utterly dreadful to him, so that he is ready to say, "I will cheerfully meet all other conceivable forms of trial rather than this," it is not impossible that the Lord may see fit to single out this very trial for him.

The Lord wishes his people to feel that being allied to him, they are allied to all strength and need fear no evil. But he proceeds with unspeakable gentleness. He gives experience of his power to sustain, in various ways. He gives a sense of his own love, wisdom, and faithfulness that prepares the heart to encounter the desolation which it speedily dreads. And by the time that we come into the presence of the dreaded thing, faith has so far got the victory, that we wonder at ourselves for ever having felt such a shrinking from a trial so easily borne. Then is the Lord glorified.

SEPTEMBER 15.—"Let all those that put their trust in thee, rejoice."—Psalm v. 11.

"That put their trust in thee." Among all the people on the face of the earth, these are the only ones that properly speaking have anything to do with joy.

In thee—in the God of the Bible—the God of whom Moses wrote, whom David feared, whom Elijah served, whom Isaiah saw in the temple, whose angel succored Daniel, who was manifest in Christ, and who for Christ's sake gave the Spirit to the apostles and giveth it unto us. Some believe that they can improve npon the character of God in the Bible. They discover here a blemish, there another. They pity those who insist upon looking to God just as he is revealed in his word. Yet they call themselves Christians, and imagine that they are trusting in God. But they who do not implicitly trust his word cannot be said to trust in Him.

That put their trust in thee. They trust not in uncertain riches, for happiness and security against the possible ills of time, but in God. They show the trust they put in God, by daring to be singular, to be unconformed to the ways of the world, and boldly setting aside the decretals of society where these tend to hinder the fullest exhibition of pure religion. They trust in the Lord Jesus Christ for righteousness, sanctification, and complete redemption. They believe that every divine commandment is good, is the expression of wisdom and love, and they view disobedience as a fall from faith. They evince their faith in God, by surrendering themselves to the direction of the Spirit of God, to be guided by him in all things and in all times. A life of perfect faith would be a life of perfect obedience. There is faith, however, before there is perfect faith. The first lispings of faith are agreeable to God. There is the promise of eventual perfection in them.

Let these *rejoice.* For by faith they have access to a domain that is altogether enchanting and soul-satisfying. The romises of God are theirs, and winged by these they escape from the dark and frowning things of earth, to scenes that are radiant with all that is beautiful and heavenly. Other men are chained to earth; these sit in heavenly places. Other men are chained to the present; these expatiate in a veritable future, not illusory. Other men are chained to men; these walk with God.

SEPTEMBER 16.—"I the Lord am thy Saviour and thy Redeemer."—Isaiah xlix. 26.

What an inconceivable length and breadth, depth and height has every such declaration as this! The whole life-journey of the Christian is a journey into the treasures that lie heaped up in this sentence. In it, in fact, are all the treasures of wisdom and knowledge. After a month of some peculiar experience, let the believer come and look into this verse, and he will find what he never found before. In the avenue commanded by this verse, no two Christians are at exactly the same place; no two have gathered from it exactly the same amount of blessing.

When the repentant sinner looks upon the cross of Jesus Christ, he takes hold of the great, surprising truth, that the Lord of the universe has entered into a specific covenant for his redemption. He has found a friend, one pledged to go all lengths in the matter of his deliverance from danger, sin and sorrow, and looking upon the face of this friend sees it resplendent with an uncreated glory. His Saviour is seen by him to be no less a being than God. But his conceptions of God are yet exceedingly imperfect. Daily he meditates in the word; follows the Lord Jesus through all the scenes of his earthly ministry; avails himself of all the apostolic expositions; familiarizes himself with the visions of Isaiah, Ezekiel, Daniel and John. The character of God unfolds itself wonderfully tc his view; and as it does so, the words "I the Lord am thy Saviour and thy Redeemer" undergo many transfigurations, pass from one glory to another. The whole universe waits upon this little text, for all the hosts of heaven exist to make known Him whose relation to the sinner is set forth in this passage.

There are innumerable sorrows of life that cannot but take to flight when faith waves this sentence over them. Why art thou cast down, my brother? Hast thou found reason to believe that this Saviour and Redeemer is not so great a person as was once supposed; and that you have committed your destinies to a person who is very little more capable than yourself of bringing you to bliss and purity and glory? Your look seems to intimate that you have made such a discovery. If you really believe that He who has taken upon him to conduct you to paradise is a being of absolute power, infinite authority, matchless wisdom, unfailing faithfulness, and inexhaustible mercy, why art thou cast down? In the presence of his infinite perfection, lift up your petty ills and see what they look like.

SEPTEMBER 17.—"I, even I, am he that comforteth you."—Isaiah li. 12.

Your affliction is very great; but there is a corresponding greatness in your comforter. I that died on Calvary, that have all power in heaven and in earth, who am from everlasting to everlasting, I am he that comforteth you. I looked upon your sorrow long before you came into existence, and on every page of my word that I caused to be written, I introduced some word of comfort with reference to you. Turn over the leaves of Scripture and see how much I have been occupied about you in days of yore. With all wisdom and kindness I sought out such expressions as were calculated to dissipate your grief. In due time I became incarnate, and every loving thing that I did, I commanded that the news of it should be conveyed to you. I showed my pierced hands and feet to my disciples and instructed them to tell the gospel of my grace to you. I have comforted thousands and tens of thousands whose misery was quite as invincible perhaps as thine. Shall I at last fail with thee? Must I experience a new humiliation? Must it be at length proclaimed that thou hast lost something of superior value to what I can bestow, of greater worth than myself?

There is one disadvantage, as it seems to men, connected with these offices of mine. I can only comfort by means of the *truth*. I have no illusions to offer. The world with its illusions finds no difficulty in banishing this and that sorrow. But it banishes them to an isle whither the individual himself must soon come and find them stronger a thousand-fold than when they left him. My solace is for to-day, to-morrow and forever. This thou hast, that thou art not willing to take refuge from thy sorrow in the world's illusions. Thou hast summoned me and I am come. My name is Love. If there be excellence anywhere in the universe, it has been bestowed by me. All the glory and beauty and joy of the universe are mine; and a thousand times more.

SEPTEMBER 18.—"Is Ephraim my dear son? Is he a pleasant child? For since I spake against him, I do earnestly remember him still."—Jeremiah xxxi. 20.

Written according to the analogy of the English language, this would be, "Is not Ephraim my dear son? Is he not a pleasant child?" The sins of the ten tribes, represented by Ephraim, had required of the Lord to withhold from them the expressions of his kindness, and to give them into the hands of their enemies that they might have a taste of the great difference between the service of an earthly master and that of their heavenly master. But as a king whose son has transgressed the laws of the land, and whom it has been found necessary to send into exile, is still remembered as a son, and will be recalled as soon as justice allows, to his father's presence, so God yearned over those whom he had been constrained to banish for a season from his presence.

Believers are the sons of God in the midst of a perverse generation. When they forget their high descent and live as men that are yet in their sins, they bring a cloud over their conscience through which the rays of the divine love faintly penetrate. But when some sense of the bitterness of their situation has taken hold upon them, and longings for communion with God are intermingled with fears lest they have forfeited all hope of restoration, then they may hear the marvellous expressions of our text. Paternity is a bond not easily broken. What God hath wrought in you in former days, though it be much of it fallen into unsightliness and ruin, is yet a memorial of his grace that may be viewed as having an attraction for Him. Yes, if you will give God an opportunity of glorifying his Son by means of you, if Christ may yet be honored through you, there is no reason why you should doubt that God will take pleasure in you, and regard you as a pleasant son.

SEPTEMBER 19.—"All the ends of the earth shall see the salvation of our God."—Isaiah li. 10.

These words are remarkable as being the utterance of a Hebrew prophet, in days when Gentiles were viewed as castaways. What Christ long afterwards commanded is here prophesied. We now behold the beginning of the fulfilment. The ends of the earth are becoming in some sense acquainted with the wonderful ransom paid for sinners by the Lord Jesus Christ.

The universal preaching of the Gospel brings out first and foremost the great truth of the universality of man's apostasy and of his inherent opposition to the divine plan of salvation. The Gospel triumphs nowhere without a struggle, without a conflict. It has to endure the contradiction of sinners. But the salvation of God is seen in every country when men and women of that country embrace the truth as it is in Jesus. But it seems to the benighted people perdition, not salvation; and its proclaimers are counted destroyers, not benefactors. But there is power—and it is, in alliance with the Gospel, to be revealed from heaven in due time,—to convince all these ungodly men of their ungodly deeds, and make them sensible of their absolute need of just such a salvation as that which Christ offers.

Christ shall see of the travail of his soul and shall be satisfied. He shall see that for which his soul travailed in such indescribable anguish in the garden of Gethsemane; the joy that was set before him he shall experience, when his people shall be one in him, even as he is one with the Father; when the New Jerusalem shall come down from God out of heaven, and kings shall bring their honor and their glory into it; when his bride shall have been presented before the throne of his Father's glory, without spot or wrinkle or any such thing. He shall see of the travail of his soul and be satisfied, when all his people have seen of the travail of their souls and are satisfied.

SEPTEMBER 20.—"Because thou sayest, I am rich, and increased with goods, and have need of nothing; and knowest not that thou art wretched and miserable and poor and blind and naked."—Revelation iii. 17.

Take away the sense of need, and blessings are bestowed in vain. They are no longer blessings. Food is of no avail to a man whose appetite is satisfied. Blessed are they that hunger and thirst after righteousness; they shall be filled, but not in any sense that shall leave them unacquainted with need. They shall never hunger, as those who have not the means of satisfying their hunger; but only as those who have much goods laid up for everlasting days in Christ. The spring of our happiness is not in ourselves, but in Christ, and so it shall ever be; and the spiritual life that flows to us from him, meets and must ever meet, a desire in us. Desire is not banished from heaven; it walks hand in hand with satisfaction. The branch receives from the vine what the branch needs. Desire brings us to the throne of grace and desire keeps us there.

A Christian without a sense of need; what an unhappy spectacle! The Laodicean church had need of nothing. Was it that their cup was running over through the unmeasured outpouring of the Holy Spirit? Was the love of God so shed abroad in their hearts that they had no room for more? Not so. Could you satisfy the personal need of the true follower of Christ, he would immediately annex the need of his neighbor; and while there remained a single discoverable need in all the world, he would refuse to know himself unneeding.

The abundance of grace bestowed upon the Christian, has not the tendency to destroy his sense of need. Unto him that hath shall be given, and he shall have more abundance, more and more; for the Spirit of God so gives as to make us value his gifts and desire what he has yet to bestow. The sense of fulness accompanies very low degrees of attainment. If desire goes to sleep, it is because we loiter so much in the path of life, or turn aside to bypaths.

Worldly prosperity has ever been a great snare to the Church. Account for it as we may, desire for spiritual blessings is very much overborne by the acquisition of worldly wealth. A Christian community has some advantages over others, in the pursuit of wealth. Their personal expenditure is limited, in some degree at least, by their professed principles. They are the followers of one who made himself poor. They are industrious, provident, economical, self-subduing, guarded and thoughtful. They gradually become wealthy. Their wealth they look upon as the expression of God's favor. Pride, self-confidence, worldliness, are pretty sure to follow. Where your treasure is there will your heart be also. The place in their regard occupied by their earthly riches, interferes decidedly with the absorbing attractions that should belong to the things which pertain to life and godliness. Were there grace enough to maintain unbroken the consecration of our all to Christ, then the flowing in of worldly substance would not be harmful; it would be understood that Christ is just availing himself of our stewardship to pour abroad upon a needy world, not merely spiritual but temporal goods. But too commonly, this consecration fails, when the amount of what is to be consecrated, increases. As there never was a time, probably, when Christians had so large a share of the gold and silver of this world, as they now have, we may well believe that the admonitions contained in this epistle to the Laodiceans, deserve to be seriously pondered at this day, and zealously acted upon.

SEPTEMBER 21.—"He will not always chide, neither will he keep his anger forever."—Psalm ciii. 9.

The believer walks as seeing him who is invisible, and receives everything from the hand of his heavenly Father. He does not overlook the part that he himself may have had in bringing about a calamity; nor the part that his fellow-men may have had in it; nor the agency of evil spirits; nor the laws of nature, if so you choose to call them; but after noticing these causes his soul looks away to the Great Cause, to Him who sitteth upon the throne of the universe and is not unmindful of a fluttering sparrow.

God has not given a constitution to the universe that limits in the least his power to deal, at any and every moment, with each individual soul in the way that his blessed impulses may suggest. How lamentably defective, how strangely erring are those philosophies that imagine that the Almighty has tied up his own hands, and only loosens them at some great intervals to give the machinery of creation a new activity. Men in general conceive of God as without present liberty to do anything in the universe; with far less faculty of spontaneous action than they themselves possess. They may like or dislike, give or withhold, but God must let the course of nature flow unbrokenly on. But the Christian is not thus without God in the world. Not only are all things of him, but all things are through him and to him. He is not only at the beginning and end of time, but present with all his works throughout the entire course of time.

The Christian knows that there is a relation connecting him and God, and he sees and knows all things in this relation. You might suppose, perhaps, that in the day of his affliction it would be an aggravation of his grief to recognize God as the author of it; but I assure you that he is not at all willing to exchange this conviction for the notion that his affliction came undesigned. "Let me rather," he says, "feel that God is chiding me, than that God is without care for me. Woe is me, if I am cast adrift upon the ocean of circumstances. I would not desire a heaven that circumstances could give me. The light and glory of this universe is gone, the dignity of existence is destroyed, the attraction of the future is no more, when it becomes doubtful that God is in immediate relation with every one of his creatures. I know that He is mine and that I am His; and when He chides, I accept it as a gracious token of his interest in me, and rejoice to think that it will soon be succeeded by tokens of a heavenlier kind. If he chide, it is but for a small moment, the smallest possible moment that the necessities of my nature will admit of."

SEPTEMBER 22.—"Ye were as sheep going astray, but are now returned unto the Shepherd and Bishop of your souls."—1 Peter ii. 25.

Drawing nigh to Peter, many years after the ascension of his Lord, we find him reading; and looking over his shoulder, see that he is occupied with our own good Isaiah, and that his attention is directed to what we designate as the fifty-third chapter and sixth verse: "All we like sheep have gone astray." And when he takes up his pen to write to the churches, how readily and naturally do the words glide from him: "Ye were as sheep going astray." We need not suppose that Peter, writing this, was unmindful of the sad facts of his own early history, when he went astray denying the Lord that was about to lay down his life for him.

The knowledge that the Christian has of the natures of men is not so much insight as experience. Men resent the description he gives of the heart of man; but they should consider that he is relating what he has seen in his own heart, being taught of God that heart answereth to heart. He is no misanthropist, expressing his disgust at the treatment he has received from man, but a philanthropist, telling the result of certain experiments to which his own heart has been subjected.

Men desire independence. They wish to be let alone. They prefer to choose their own paths. They scorn the suggestion that a shepherd is necessary to them. Yet there is something occurring every passing hour to show them their need of a superior being to guide them; one who can see the end from the beginning; who knows the qualities and tendencies of all things; who looks upon dangers and losses before they arise and makes provision for them; who can tear in pieces the lion and the bear; can furnish a shelter from the storm, a shadow from the heat. At every moment evil in some form starts up, saying, "You are my prey; you are wandering in this world without God; you have not this mark upon your forehead." Nevertheless, men insist upon running the gauntlet of all the ills that line the pathway of life, until, all hacked to pieces, they sink into their final place of unrest and misery. Happy are they, alas how few, who perceive the forlornness of a life without God, and allow themselves to be found of the good Shepherd and brought back to his little flock and to its glorious destinies!

SEPTEMBER 23.—"If any man thirst let him come unto me and drink." — John vii. 37.

Who is this that stands in the midst of an assemblage of mortals and makes proclamation in a loud and fearless voice, that if any man, not merely in that assembly but throughout the whole world, desire happiness, he should draw near and obtain what he desires? Who is this that offers to heal all human woes and accomplish in behalf of the entire human family, deliverance from the curse? That speaks of himself as a fountain of the water of life springing up in the centre of the earth, and sending forth abundant streams to bless all nations, tribes, and tongues? That not merely undertakes the highest functions of deity, but reveals the deity as present in the very midst of the family of man, bringing to the doors and hearts of men the most distinctive gifts of heaven? He that speaks must be either a madman or God manifest in the flesh.

Draw nigh to him and behold. He opens the eyes of the blind; but that is little. He heals all diseases; that too is little. He raises the dead; even that is little. It is one thing to recall men from the grave; another thing to fill their souls with imperishable joy. Behold him then on the cross. He cries out, "I thirst." All the billows of the wrath of God pass over him. You ask, "How can this sufferer heal the woes of men? This thirster quench the thirst of the world?" Understand that those billows are of the wrath of God not against him, but against you and your fellow-sinners; and that he emerges from this deep baptism of anguish with a charter of life for all that shall believe upon him.

In the vanity fair of this world you see over many a shop a scroll bearing the words, "If any man thirst let him come hither and drink." The servants of Satan exhibit a thousand blandishments. What Christ alone can do, a thousand illusions of life profess to do. All that they can do is really to destroy the souls that trust in them.

The question for you is: Do you thirst? Have you desires ungratified? Aspirations after a higher, nobler existence; after purity, heavenly wisdom, love, usefulness, communion with the blessed, immortality and glory? Come then to the meek and lovely one, to him whose hand and feet were pierced. His word is nigh thee. Embrace it with thy heart, then shalt thou find him in thy heart; and in finding him, thou findest happiness and a crown of life.

SEPTEMBER 24.—"All thy children shall be taught of the Lord, and great shall be the peace of thy children."—Isaiah liv. 13.

They that are Christ's are Abraham's seed, and we are among the posterity whose privileges are here foreshadowed. The people of God are those that are taught of God, and they that are taught of God, have great peace. The throne of God is the seat of a great teacher. The course of nature is a course of instruction. The universe is one vast school. God writes lessons for men on the firmament, on the sea, on the sands, on the mountains, on the forests; yea on every leaf. We tread on problems; tasks are set us in the air we breathe. If we shut up all our senses and bury ourselves in the recesses of our being, even there some question shall address us, some lesson shall meet us. But sin makes men insensible to all this. The firmament may declare the glory of God; but they will hear so much of the declaration as they list, and no more Their minds are drugged with sin so that the instructions of creation and of providence are lost upon them. They are without God in a world where everything proclaims his presence, his perfections and his glory.

But some are taught of the Lord. They are taught concerning their own ignorance, their sinfulness, their danger. They are shown their need of something that is not in nature, even an Almighty Saviour, an All-wise Sanctifier. They are taught to behold all excellence in Christ, and to repose all confidence in him. They bring all their knowledge to God—all that they have been collecting since childhood—that he may look it over and cast away what he will. They want no opinions but the opinions of God; no wisdom but that which is from above.

Wonderful is the mystery of life. Creatures of clay, we are as gods in our liberty of choice, in our conscious freedom, and as devils in the abuse of that freedom. All the experiments carried on for the last six thousand years show that there is something fearfully amiss. One man uses his freedom in one way, another in another way; a thousand men in a thousand different ways; but it is manifest with respect to all, that they none of them hit upon a right theory and practice of life. They are perpetually coming in conflict with the machinery of the universe, getting entangled and bruised in the wheels of God's providence, and passing merely from one phase of confusion to another. "Why are we endowed with this liberty," say they, "but that we may use it? Why are we made voluntary beings but that we may carry out our volitions? We are permitted to act as we like, why is it not good to do so?"

Here is their mistake, their great and fatal mistake. Their liberty is given them in order that they may freely do the will of God. It would be derogatory to the character of God to make his intelligent creatures serve him by compulsion, by irresistible force. He disdains to be served otherwise than by choice and love. But the universe is so constituted that it is impossible for men to find true peace or solid advantage while they follow their own capricious wills. Everything repulses man, lacerates him, torments him. The wonder is that he is so slow to discover what is the true use to be made of his liberty. When at length he delights himself in the Lord, then does the Lord grant him the desires of his heart. When he chooses to do God's will, then he becomes as God in several most surprising respects. Apart from God, a worm; united to God, he is a temple of God, a throne of God.

SEPTEMBER 25.—"To us belongeth confusion of face, because we have sinned against thee."—Daniel ix. 8.

A great many of our confessions of sin fall trippingly from the tongue, as though the commission and the acknowledgment were all a mere matter of course. How little of self-reproach there seems to be in it all! How little shame, how little confusion of face! A public exposure—the attention of men drawn to one of the least of these sins—would fill us with unspeakable shame. Is God then nobody in comparison with man? Because God has forgiven us so readily, are we to make light of the sins committed against him? But in order that God might forgive us the least of all these sins, it was necessary that Christ should endure the contradiction of sinners, pass through the agony of Gethsemane, and die upon the cross.

Christians sometimes say, "Of what avail is it to be studying our committed sins? Rather let us exercise faith." Faith is everything indeed · but faith will never attain its proper proportions where there is no just idea of what it is that God has forgiven us. How can we rightly know the goodness of God, if we do not know the greatness of sin? In fact this is one of the exercises of faith, one of her most distinctive and honorable triumphs; the perception, namely, of what sin really is. Some Christians imagine that they will lose their peace in this way. Let them lose it, and get a better one. Do they not know that the Holy Ghost is the Spirit of truth, and that he is given to guide us into all truth, that relating to ourselves and that relating to God? Contrition and faith are not enemies; contrition and love, contrition and joy; all these in fact belong together.

SEPTEMBER 26.—"Rejoice, inasmuch as ye are partakers of Christ's sufferings."—1 Peter iv. 13.

Had Peter done as he promised to do, and followed Christ from Gethsemane, content to be bound with him, mocked with him, scourged with him, condemned with him, and crucified with him, what an incomparably exalted place would he have had in our regard. Nothing but his own treacherous heart hindered him from occupying this worthiest and sublimest of places occupied by mere finite men. However, as his Lord generously foretold, he followed him afterwards. He met the same hostility, the same bitterness and cruelty; and we read in the Acts that he rejoiced in being counted worthy to suffer for the name of the Lord Jesus. Oh! that we might have faith in the day of reproach and injury encountered in Christ's service, to perceive him, even the Prince of the kings of the earth, at our side, dividing with us the indignities that are heaped upon us. Who would not call that a light affliction? Who would not rejoice?

SEPTEMBER 27.—"I shall be satisfied when I awake with thy likeness."—Psalm xvii. 15.

Christ prayed for his people that they might be with him where he was ("where I am") and behold his glory. Christ is formed in us, the hope of glory; glorious now as revealed by faith, so that we rejoice with joy unspeakable and full of glory; but immeasurably more glorious upon the throne of the heavenly majesty, entrancing the universe with the image of the invisible God.

I shall be satisfied: let a man look into his heart and see how much is comprehended in this. He imagines almost that his heart is a bottomless abyss, and that God might empty into it all his treasures and fail to fill it. But his cup shall run over. He shall be satisfied. And throughout a never-ending eternity he shall never more be cursed with unsatisfied desires.

SEPTEMBER 28.—"I have seen his ways, and will heal him."—Isaiah lvii. 18.

The greater part of mankind pass through the earthly stage of their existence without anything that can appropriately be termed the knowledge of God. To others, however, it is given in some most solemn moment to find themselves suddenly in the presence of God and to be overwhelmed with the perception of his holiness, power, sovereignty, and omniscience. The scales fall from their eyes, and they behold that sublime and offended Majesty in whose august presence they, in willing unconsciousness, have been for many a long year committing their abominable transgressions. Then they exclaim with amazement and profoundest humiliation: "Thou hast searched me and known me; thou art acquainted with all my ways." The relations of that hour are very partial, very imperfect; were they otherwise it would be impossible to sustain them. Man has become so naturalized in the domain of falsehood, that to strip him at once of all his falsehood would be to rend his body and soul asunder and consign the immortal part of him to everlasting despair. There is reason to believe that such a day will dawn for the world at large; a day when the Lord shall be revealed in his glory, and every eye shall see him; and multitudes shall call upon the mountains to fall upon them and hide them from the face of him that sitteth upon the throne. But now we have as it were only adumbrations of the judgment that is to come.

Is there not something very humiliating and condemning in the thought that you are so bound up in falsehood, it has become such a part of your life, that it is necessary to proceed with great caution in removing from you the many folds of it?—Yet even the partial revelations of that hour when God enabled you to perceive him present in his holiness and majesty, filled your soul with terror, and you could not at all comprehend how peace and joy could ever consist with the discoveries then made. But perhaps this reflection then arose in your mind: that if God had intended you to have experience of his wrath alone, he would probably have still deferred the hour of manifestation, until you had passed the bourne of hope, the bourne of life.

"I have seen his ways, saith the Lord," and what terrible sentence may we not look for, as a sequence to this announcement? But lo, the most gracious of all words issue from his lips: "I will heal him." The knowledge which God has of our corruption and deep depravity, soon becomes to us a ground of confidence; he knows what we need; perfectly aware of what we are, he has undertaken to restore us, and he will certainly accomplish what he has taken in hand.

SEPTEMBER 29.—"For the iniquity of his covetousness was I wroth and smote him; I hid me and was wroth; and he went on frowardly in the way of his heart."—Isaiah lvii. 17.

God is love; and we were called into being that in our measure we might manifest forth this truth, by loving one another. But we are an apostate race; and each one, so far from seeking to be the servant of all, is bent upon serving himself of all. Men are consecrated first and foremost to the augmentation of their own gains. Ordinarily they understand by *covetousness* some extraordinary development of the passion for gain. But the question is not, what definition of it is given in man's code, but what in God's code? Now, God stigmatizes as covetousness all desire for gain that checks the exercise of faith in God and love to man; that is selfish in origin and in tendency; that is hostile to a spirit of humble contentment; that is inconsistent with perfect peace.

This age is intensely selfish, and yet finds it very difficult to become sensible of its selfishness. There are so many noble enterprises afoot; so many asylums built; so many colleges and schools established; missions for the heathen, home missions, city missions; patriotic funds, famine funds; in fine, mention if you can an evil that has lifted up its head in any part of the world, for which we have not made some benevolent arrangement. I do not shut my eyes to these generous schemes. It certainly looks as though the law of love were written on the forehead of the times. I would do all honor to the age, or rather to the Father of ages, the giver of every good and perfect gift. But ascribe it not to malevolence or envy, if I suggest that the age is simply giving of its abundance. With the one hand it gives its thousand, but with the other it grasps its tens of thousands. There is a spirit of profound calculation that has too much to do with these gifts. Almost all these noble benefactions have had their origin with the Church; but how few members of the Church give even tithes of all that they possess. Men think themselves benevolent because they look at what they give; God thinks them covetous, because he sees what they withhold.

The question is: How does God deal with his people when they become covetous? You will say, He chastises them and makes them poor in spirit. Nay, this is not his way. Were it such, then would his people wait for his providential correction and believe themselves justified in pressing forward in that evil path, until he should meet them. With an infinitely profounder wisdom God deals with them. He chastises them indeed, but it is by withdrawing himself. And they perceive it not. And now does their position become most dangerous. For being freed from many remonstrances addressed them by the Holy Spirit, they precipitate themselves faster and still faster along their chosen career. They become more and more worldly, more and more hardened. What shall hinder them from crossing that path beyond which the Spirit of God will never seek them?

What we need then to learn is this: To be on our guard against the earliest developments of this passion, and to hearken diligently to the reproof of the Spirit of God while his voice is yet distinctly audible: for let the evil inclination get but a little more strength and we shall make shipwreck of our faith.

SEPTEMBER 30.—"There is no peace, saith my God, to the wicked."—Isaiah lvii. 21.

The wicked are sometimes seen flourishing as a green bay-tree. Their cup of worldly prosperity runneth over. To the spectator their days appear to flow by in pleasantness and peace. They conform to the world's code of morals, and their praises are on the tongues of all. They fare sumptuously every day and fancy that they are to sit down at the banquet of everlasting life. Peace and prosperity are within their gates, if we may believe appearances. But we prefer to believe God. He knoweth all hearts. He knows what is worthy to be called peace.

That certainly is not worthy to be called peace, which cannot endure to face all truth. You look down deep into the heart of thė splendid sinner with whom all seems to go serenely, and you see a stone sealed with many seals. You ask, what is underneath that stone? Hist! breathe no such unwelcome interrogations as this. There is a mystery about that stone and all inquiry is disallowed, all mention of it forbidden. You are waved disdainfully away from those mysterious penetralia. There is One however who knoweth well the secrets of all hearts, and who is willing to make known to you the mystery of that stone and the chamber underneath. Hearken! Beneath that stone are buried many things, implacably hostile to the peace of that man. The law of his being is such that it is not possible to extrude them from the mind, to bury them in the depths of the sea; wherefore, as the only alternative they are buried in the depths of his own mind. There are the suppressed memories of innumerable sins, the blotted records of many experiences, the disregarded warnings of conscience. There, in that chamber are many forgotten passages of Scripture, once heard, once for a moment or more revolved in the mind; many words of Christ and his apostles. Many fragments of sermons and counsels of pious friends are there. Vows, prayers even are there. Nay, there are thunders there thunders of God's providence. Truth in her most tremendou forms is there. There these all are buried, but not forever. There is to be a resurrection, a terrible retribution. The man has made for himself a hell within himself, and has covered it over with a stone and bound down the stone with a few frail bands, and he calls this peace.

OCTOBER 1.—"The Lord shall be thine everlasting light, and the days of thy mourning shall be ended."—Isaiah lx. 20.

Indicated in the last verse of the preceding chapter, these glorious prospects are displayed before God's spiritual Israel. They that reject Christ reject all the good forespoken by the prophets, and the wrath of God abideth upon them. All things belong to them who belong to Christ. Christians are taught to contemplate not merely their own individual blessedness and perfection; but the unspeakable blessedness and unconceived glory of that condition upon which the whole Church of the living God shall, as the bride of the Lord Jesus, as the New Jerusalem come down from heaven, one day enter. They are now the light of the world; the Lord shall be their everlasting light. There shall be no night there. And this marvellous condition of things is immediately to succeed just such a condition of things as that which now exists, when darkness covers the earth, and gross darkness the people.

The Lord shall be thine everlasting light. He who by faith embraces the Christ of the gospel, who kisses the Son in the day of his humiliation when his visage is marred more than any man's, shall then be enraptured by the sun-eclipsing glory that shall burst from the countenance of Christ the King of kings, Lord of lords, his Christ, forever his, with all his glory his.

OCTOBER 2.—"Let us draw near with a true heart."—Hebrews x. 22.

Seek to sound the depths of the meaning of this word, *draw near.* Examine the supplications of a thousand suppliants, and they will show these suppliants scattered at a thousand different distances from God, but almost all at a great distance, and out of the whole perhaps only one *close* to the throne of grace.

There is much to hinder this drawing near. There is the inherited habit of unbelieving prayer. The supineness of the soul. Worldly care. Worldly joy. Inappreciation of the possible blessing. Fear of discovering some unheeded responsibilities. Want of realization of God's personality. And a multitude of others.

There are to be combats all along the road. It is here we must fight the good fight of faith. It is a noble victory when we get near to God; for it is a pledge of all other victories.

OCTOBER 3.—"He only is my rock."—Psalm lxii. 2.

O, happy Psalmist, who canst use this language? Not only is God thy rock; he is thine only rock. On him dost thou build thy confidence. He is thy only refuge, thy only safeguard.

How grievously do they insult God who rely in part upon him, in part on something else; and who with the utmost emphasis of their souls deprecate being left alone with God, shut up to him alone. They would fain eke out the insufficiency of their wealth by his riches of mercy; the inadequacy of their wisdom, by his treasures of wisdom; the imperfections of their strength, by his power; their defective title to heaven, by his readiness to save. The grace of the gospel they accept as supplemental to their own goodness. Sometimes it happens to such to be stripped of all their wealth, their wisdom, their goodness; and lo! to the surprise of their Christian friends, they are found to be the prey of an intense despair. Then is it seen how very slight and contemptible a part they had assigned to God in the matter of their salvation. They are unutterably wretched, because God alone is left them.

Happy are they who begin by recognizing God as their only rock. This rock is soon found to be marvellous in its properties. Beneath the footsteps of faith, springs of joy, peace, wisdom, hope, love start up, creating first an oasis, then a paradise; walls of every precious stone rise and enclose it; angels encamp around about it.

OCTOBER 4.—"The Lord is nigh unto all that call upon him in truth."—Psalm cxlv. 18.

That call upon him not because they think it a decorous thing, not as an act of homage merely, but because they need what he alone can give, and believe that he will give it to them, if they ask wisely and in faith.

They call upon him in truth, who make nothing of themselves, everything of Christ. They call upon him in truth, who overlook none of his attributes, but view him as his word reveals him. "If ye abide in me and my words abide in you, ye shall ask what ye will, and it shall be done unto you."

We bring God nigh to us by banishing falsehood from us, by making room for the truth in our hearts. "If any man love me he will keep my words; and my Father will love him, and will come unto him and make his abode with him."

OCTOBER 5.—"Be content with such things as ye have; for he hath said, I will never leave thee nor forsake thee."—Hebrews xiii. 5.

This promise was addressed in the first instance to Joshua; not because he was Joshua, but because he was a believer; nd it is valid for every believer.

The believer is to be content with such things as he has. "Behold Lazarus at the gate of the rich man, his body full of sores, without food, shelter, friends. Is he to be content with such things as he has? He has nothing." Yes, he has something. Let us try to take an inventory of it. He has a Father in heaven, upon the throne of thrones, possessing all wealth and exercising all power; forgetting him never and making all the vicissitudes and severities of life conduce to his ultimate unspeakable good. He has a Saviour in heaven; one that died for him and washed him from his sins in his own blood; his righteous Advocate ever interceding for him. He has a Holy Spirit who has taken up his abode in that polluted heart to make it angelic, spotless and perfect. The angels of heaven are his friends; they celebrated the day of his conversion with songs of transport; they hold his crippled limbs so that he does not fall; and they are waiting to convey him to paradise. All the saints in the light of heaven wait for him that they may know him and love him. He has promises more in number than it is possible to count, and each so precious that all the money in the world could not buy it. He has an inheritance ten thousand times more magnificent than the boasted patrimonies of earth. Everlasting life is his. His diseased body shall be fashioned like unto Christ's glorious body. To all his other treasures, he may well add this treasure, *contentment.*

Why art thou cast down? Perhaps thine earthly wealth has taken to itself wings and flown. Perhaps some great man has looked disdainfully upon thee. Perhaps some cherished scheme has been frustrated. Thou hast met with ingratitude. Some dear friend has fallen from thee. Some loved one has died. Some disease has taken hold of thee. Well, these things dispirit the children of this world; for in losing these they lose their all. But why should the loss of such things affect thee? The wealth that is lost, is nothing to that which remains to thee. The great man who despises thee is a very insignificant being in the presence of certain friends of thine. If thou losest a friend of earth, thou hast thousands of glorious ones who will never fail thee. Thou hast a throne prepared for thee in a region where no sickness is, where death never comes. Thou hast Christ with all his unsearchable riches. Wilt thou yet mourn because of the crumbs that have fallen from thy table?

It is in vain we talk of the unsearchable riches of Christ, if we greatly bewail the disasters of time. How shall the world ever learn that Christ is to us precious, if we are not content with such things as we have in the world, be they no matter how few, how mean?

OCTOBER 6.—"If any of you lack wisdom let him ask of God, that giveth to all men liberally."—James i. 5.

Wisdom is the last thing of the need of which men become sensible. Worldly wisdom indeed they desire to have in larger measure; but it is the rarest thing in the world to see a man who is deeply sensible of his need of that wisdom which God gives in answer to prayer. This only shows how amazingly unwise men are. It is because they have not this wisdom at all, that they are conscious of no need. Yet, would they but know it, this wisdom would give them virtually all that they so impetuously seek in the world. They long for a power by which they may rise superior to the ills of life. They long to lift themselves on high above their enemies. They long to possess themselves of all the good things of life. But as the world is constituted, it is impossible for man by dint of getting to satisfy this desire; or by quaffing the cup of pleasure to attain unto happiness; or by clothing himself with authority to escape all human enmity. Let God however breathe upon his soul, let heavenly wisdom become the tenant of his heart, and lo! "the slings and arrows of outrageous fortune" fall harmless at his feet.

What causes most of the misery of men, is that their minds are chafed and vexed by something in their condition. With this repugnant something they enter into conflict thinking that if they can only banish it, all will be well. Perhaps they do not succeed. There it remains, frowning upon them; and in their souls abideth torment. Perhaps after many struggles, they get rid of this repugnant thing; but scarcely have they begun to congratulate themselves upon their victory, when lo, on the opposite side, a new circumstance wearing the same scowl, enters into the circle. Yes, this earth would get rid of almost all her burden, and spring forward like an unyoked Pegasus, if men would cease from battling with their external condition, and seek from God wisdom; even wisdom to outweigh in the balances of heaven, the offers, illusions, dignities, comforts, discomforts, losses, trials, troubles of every day.

OCTOBER 7.—"We may boldly say, The Lord is my helper, and I will not fear what man shall do unto me."—Hebrews xiii. 6.

Here we have an admirable expression of Christian confidence. It is pure confidence in God, viewed as the source not only of one's own strength, but of all strength, so that there emains nothing in the world worthy to excite alarm. "The Lord is my helper," saith the believer. "I am not counting upon some future alliance with him; but speak from a deep and satisfying experience of his presence and faithfulness. I have been shorn of all my former conceit of strength; and have hearkened to the proposal of the Infinite One, a proposal to be unto me strength, wisdom, righteousness. On the day that I became bankrupt, I entered into the possession of all riches."

If the Lord be thy helper, and if all the power of man is inferior to that which accompanies thee, then why dost thou not do some great, some world-surprising thing? Thou hast no occasion to fear aught that man may attempt. To all the waves of hostility thou art able to say, "Thus far shall ye come and no farther." Ride now victoriously through the earth and establish thy beneficent dominion throughout all lands, giving men relief from the oppressions under which they have languished for so many ages. A similar suggestion was once made to the Lord Jesus Christ. Had he been willing to set aside the will of God, and to put himself under the guidance of that evil spirit of expediency that rules in the counsels of the princes of this world, had he accommodated himself to the expectations of the Jews and presented himself as a temporal and political Messiah, all the kingdoms of the world might have been his, but he would have been simply the vicegerent of the God of this world. "God is my helper; and I may avail myself of his power without limit."

But why does He help me? Because I have yielded myself unto his guidance. He giveth his power to those only who first accept of his wisdom. He giveth strength to those who have renounced all ambitious and selfish views; who have committed themselves unto him to be taught, moulded and used by him.

Nevertheless, when we call to mind that God delighteth in mercy; that the Lamb of God hath taken away the sin of th world; that the Triune God has a sublime enterprise on foot, looking forward to the transference of all kingdoms unto his Son; when we consider certain of the promises, as, for instance, this, "Greater works than these shall ye do;" and this, "He that overcometh to him will I give power over the nations, and he shall rule them with a rod of iron;" when we remember the words of Daniel, "The people of the saints of the most High God shall take the kingdom and possess the greatness of the kingdom under the whole heaven;" when we allow these soul-enkindling declarations to come home to our consciousness; does it not seem as though he, who in genuine faith is able to speak of God as his helper, and to look disdainfully upon all that man can do against him, should go forth clothed in a transcendent power and obtain some world-wide display of the glory of his Lord?

"When the Son of Man cometh, shall he find faith on the earth?"

October 8.—"Hope maketh not ashamed, because the love of God is shed abroad in our hearts."—Romans v. 5.

Alps on Alps arise, as the believer presses forward in his course. He beholds a summit, and exclaims, "My God will meet me there, and there will gainsayers be confounded." But when he reaches it, he receives not the expected testimony, and unbelievers make a mock of his disappointed hopes. He would be troubled; but in the absence of the external testimony, he receives an inward sweet assurance of the love and faithfulness of God, and in the very hour of his disappointment, his face shines with a singular joy. Looking up he sees a higher mount. Oh, he exclaims, it is there, not here, that God should meet me. I must reach the higher summit. He reaches it, and it proves to be a new summit of sorrow for him. Again, a wave of heavenly bliss rolls over his heart, and he refuses to be confounded. A still higher peak catches his aspiring eye.

Observe now, all his disappointments are real conquests. Those inferior summits mark the way that he must necessarily tread, in his course to the hill of transfiguration. In his *great* hope he is not confounded, only in his lesser hopes that lay hold of time, place, and circumstance. From every hill of disappointment, he carries off a rich spoil.

OCTOBER 9.—"**In all their affliction he was afflicted.**"—Isaiah lxiii. 8.

We need not feel so bitterly towards affliction, since we are indebted to it for the knowledge of this most wonderful fact, that our divine Friend enters into our sorrow with all his heart, and perfectly identifies himself with us in our tribulation. Sympathy is really a more valuable proof of love, sometimes, than the hindrance of the calamity would have been. Every king can scatter handfuls of gold and save many from want; but where is the king whose eye melts, whose heart overflows, in sympathy with the sons and daughters of want? Ah, we have to seek in heaven for such a king as this. "Saul, Saul," he says, "why persecutest thou *me?* I have felt keenly the reproaches thou hast uttered against my disciples; the stripes inflicted on them were to me the same as those that I endured in the house of Pilate; the drops of their blood were precious to me as those that I myself let fall from my own thorn-wounded head."

OCTOBER 10.—"I, the Lord, speak righteousness. I declare things that are right."—Isaiah xlv. 19.

An incontestable truth, one would say. Who will dare to deny that God speaks things which are right? That were at once the height of folly and of guilt.

Is it so? Then do all men dwell upon the heights of folly and of guilt. They have built for themselves permanent habitations there. There are innumerable things that men declare to be right; they do them and repent not at the remembrance of them; they commend them in others; yet these things are diametrically opposite to the things that God sanctions. You speak of a becoming pride; God says, "Blessed are the poor in spirit." You say that men should not submit to injuries and insults. He says, "Blessed are the meek." You think it a light thing when men neglect religion; God says, "One thing is needful." When men pray much, you talk of cant and hypocrisy; God says, "Pray without ceasing." In a word go through the Bible; compare its declarations with your own expressed views; and if you still insist that God declares things that are right, you must admit that you have hitherto been in thought, word and practice, wrong, wrong, wrong!

OCTOBER 11.—"Who was delivered for our offences, and raised again for our justification."—Romans iv. 25.

That we might not fall into the hands of the living God, Christ was delivered into the hands of sinful men. He stood before an earthly tribunal where Injustice sat in state, in order that we might escape the dread tribunal where infinite Justice sits. He was delivered up by sinful men to sinful men. Yet he was delivered up by a righteous God, with his own glad consent, to all the sufferings that man could inflict. He that was delivered up, was the only sinless being that ever walked this earth; was divine as well as human; his sinlessness as a man made him a meet sacrifice for the sins of men; his divine nature gave infinite value to his sufferings, so that it became right in view of them to offer all men deliverance from all the woe that they are obnoxious to, by sin.

How amazing that there should be found in all the wide world a single being reluctant to avail himself of the expiation thus made for sin. The utmost eloquence of men, the most terrible warnings in providence, the profoundest experience of the misery springing out of their league with sin, all fail to obtain for this wondrous gospel of the grace of God, entrance into the hearts of men. They say unto God, day by day, hour by hour, "Thou holy God, impute unto us all our offences. Let it be with us as though Christ had not died. Let there be no Gethsemane or Calvary for us. We know that we are not sinless beings and must forever drink without draining the cup which threw him into an agony of unutterable suffering; that we are not invested with omnipotence, and cannot rise from the grave victorious; our Calvary conducts us to endless torment. Nevertheless we wish to appear before the tribunal of divine justice with all our sins upon our head. Had we any other wish, we would express it by believing on Christ."

As for thee, O semi-believer, convinced of thy sins, sensible of their enormity, longing for deliverance, assured that Christ alone can give it, yet stopping there, spending thy days in lamentation, imploring grace and yet neglecting to appropriate it, why dost thou live as though Christ were still in the tomb? The unbeliever lives as though Christ had not died; thou livest as though he had not risen. Repent of this thy folly, and hasten to bear before the world thine own special testimony to the truth of Christ's resurrection, by a joyful trust in him that ever liveth to make intercession.

OCTOBER 12.—"Thou, O Lord, art a shield for me."—Psalm iii. 3.

In the battle of this world, the Christian is seen without a shield. And just where he is, is the thickest of the fight. The adversary hurls his best forces against that spot, evidently supposing that there is only this impediment between him and victory. It is wonderful then that the Christian should pass scathless through this shower of fiery darts. Those that are in the secret know that—while apparently unprotected—he is in reality defended by an invisible shield. While he abides in faith, God encompasses him round about and nothing can by any means harm him.

The Lord is a shield to him who has been taught what are the true dangers, what the true enemies, that beset the path of a man through this world—who knows and is not ashamed to confess that the god of this world is a being of tremendous power, with his servants in all high places, with the wisest and greatest of men among his captives, with a plenitude of resources, a knowledge of the heart, that a mere unaided mortal can do nothing against. Formerly he was the subject of that prince. Then at length he became sensible of the wrath of God that cometh upon the ungodly. "Whither shall I flee, where shall I find a defence?" became his cry of agony. The sky was darkened with the arrows of the Almighty. Then was revealed to him the cross of Christ. He saw that the Son of God was himself his shield, receiving in his own person the storm of wrath that should have come upon him. He has now peace with God. But he becomes exposed to the fierce assaults of the adversary. In the world he has tribulation Sin seeks to regain dominion over him. But Christ doth not leave him nor forsake him. He is to him a sun and a shield; a sun to give him the light of life, and a shield to protect him in the path of life.

God is a shield to me, says the believer; *to me*, all to myself. The shield of my fellow-soldier will be of little avail to me. I need a shield that I can call my own. And God, with all his perfections, all his grace, is mine as truly as though he were mine alone. All his promises are mine as truly as though no one else had any interest in them. All his providence is mine. There is a blessed and indissoluble connexion established by faith, between my weakness and his strength, my danger and his protection, my ignorance and his guidance, my sin and his righteousness, my world-wide necessities and his world-wide sufficiency, my unlimited aspirations and his endless glory.

OCTOBER 13.—"He will fulfil the desire of them that fear him."—Psalm cxlv. 19.

Let us look at these persons whose desires are to be fulfilled. They are worthy to be looked at; for there is not their like upon the earth. The desires of other men are their torments, the keenest elements of their misery; taking them up to all high mountains only to cast them deeper down. Other men find their desires, however comely and angelic they may at first appear, however they may descend to them upon a rainbow as from heaven, at last to be demons, domiciliated in their soul to make it as much like a hell as may be. So that they are ready to say, "Blessed is the man that desireth nothing."

There are some whose bitter experiences make them to look with wrath upon the heavens and the earth that God has made. The language of their heart, sometimes that of their lips, is this: "All this is very beautiful; but in all this beauty there is a profound and hateful snare. The sun moving so majestically over our heads, and pouring such unceasing floods of marvellous light around us, says, 'God is love, and delighteth in mercy; he is not far away; he maketh your wants his care;' but the sun only lies as it thus speaks. Its rising and setting, its magnificent panoramas in the western skies at even tide, its exquisite arrangements of light and shade in valleys and in glens, its care for every insignificant seed, all say to me, 'hope on, hope ever,' but it is all a cruel beguilement. Every tree, every leaf of a tree, every pebble, shell, blade of grass, ripple of a stream, everything keeps telling some tale of the power and beneficence of God, but it is a lying tale. The whole universe is fitted up as it were for the purpose of stimulating to the utmost our desires and aspirations, and strengthening to the utmost our confidence that they will be gratified; but it is one vast imposture. We are seduced to open the door of the heart to a troop of hopes which soon go mad and lacerate our sensibilities in a way that no language can express. God should have placed us in a world of desolation and of gloom; then we should not have been maddened through the influence of lovely and delusive prospects. We would have calculated on a miserable existence, and should have found it."

Alas, my friend that you should speak thus. Do you really believe that God finds satisfaction in tormenting you; and that he has made a world where hope is the arch-tormentor? You have set out with one fatal error, and have persisted in cherishing it. All things declare the glory and the goodness of God, and say, "Hope on, hope ever:" but to whom do they say it? To those who fear God; who know him as their king; who take his word as a lamp to their feet; who repent of sin, believe on his Son and embrace his promises. All things shall work together for good to them; and after they are tried they shall receive the promise, shall enter upon the fruition of their highest hopes and wildest imaginings. To them the universe speaks, and there is no delusion in its speech. But to you its language is this: "Knowest thou not that the goodness of God leadeth thee to repentance?" It is all intended to lead thee, a contrite and repentant sinner, to the feet of God. All true, all heaven-descended hope begins at the cross of Christ.

Seek ye first the kingdom of God and his righteousness, and all these things shall be added unto you."

October 14.—"I will hear what God the Lord will speak."—Psalm lxxxv. 8.

Wilt thou indeed? Art thou really purposed to ascertain what revelation there is of thy Creator's will concerning thee? After many a long year of fatal independence and destructive self-government, has it at length dawned upon thy perception that the Being who made thee, and who made all worlds, is, after all, the Being most competent to decide what life thou shouldst lead, most worthy to be trusted with the determination of thy lot and the accomplishment of thy happiness? After having hearkened to every other speaker and followed the suggestions of every benighted sinner, wilt thou at last hear what God the Lord has to say? Then let us rejoice over the auspicious hour that has at length come to thee. There is no greater moment in the whole of existence than that in which a wayward sinner pauses in his career to hear what God the Lord will say.

But note, that all this magnanimous determination of thine will amount to nothing, just nothing, if there be not in thee a willingness to hear *all* that the Lord will speak. If out of a hundred words of God, thou fix upon one and resolve to honor it, while the rest lie all dishonored, that word which thou hearest will turn against thee, and in the last day bring on thee additional condemnation. How many fancy that they are hearkening to God's word, while all the time they are only hearkening to their own hearts' lusts. Half a dozen pages would contain all their Bible—theirs truly, not God's.

It is impossible to hear what God the Lord will speak, while a thousand vain voices are allowed to have thy attention. There is too much noise in thine own heart for thee to hear. Thou art too much busied about thine own will, to become acquainted with the will of God. The Lord will not lead thee by the right hand, while another leads thee by the left.

OCTOBER 15.—"He healeth the broken in heart and bindeth up their wounds."—Psalm clxvii. 3.

Yet there are many that die of a broken heart. Some beautiful dream vanishes after having lured them to embark all their hopes and affections upon it; the phantom vessel disappears and they are left a prey to the angry billows; but even then, would they but know it, there is deliverance for them. Admit that all their hopes are blasted; God, whose matchless title is this, "The God of hope," remains. All the good you have dreamed of, and infinitely more, resides in him. God is not dead; why then should you die? The Physician of souls rejoices when some very shattered and woe-worn heart of man is brought to him to be healed: he has then a peculiar opportunity of showing what he can do. This Physician was himself made perfect through sufferings; made perfect to deliver others from suffering. His heart was once melted within him; he was wounded for our transgressions. He knoweth how to succor them that are tempted; to heal the broken-hearted.

Have you lost some very precious object? He teaches you that all truly precious things are precious to God, and are to be counted as altogether safe with him when they disappear from your sight. He then reveals to you something of his own excellence, his own preciousness, so that you are soon found rejoicing with joy unspeakable and full of glory. He does not make light of your affections, though they may have been erring; he makes no mock of your broken heart; your sorrow is sacred with him; but he brings you into a path that leads to a city where all the good are gathered together, and death and pain have no admission.

OCTOBER 16.—"Let us hold fast the profession of our faith without wavering."—Hebrews x. 23.

We have professed to believe that God gave his Son to bear our sins in his own body on the tree; that God has accepted us in his Son; that he is our heavenly Father, and Christ our perpetual intercessor; that not having spared his only begotten Son, he will with him also freely give us all things; that whatever we ask according to his will, we have the petitions that we desired of him; that not one jot or tittle of his word can pass away. Now the things we have thus professed to receive let us hold fast. Immense efforts are made to get them from our grasp. Sometimes we are left alone for a season that we may be lulled asleep; but the design never sleeps in the purpose of the adversary. Should a man walk through a crowded city with rubies, diamonds and precious pearls sprinkled over his garments, and expect that no attempt will be made to snatch from him these treasures, his security will not be so much misplaced as that of the man who, walking through this world with the promises of God conspicuous about him, fancies that no endeavor will be made to lessen his store. It is not that the promises are wanted; but it is wanted that men should not believe upon them. When, therefore, you hear a whisper to the effect that you have done well in giving evidence of your zeal and self-denial and independence of the world, and that now you may without any danger relax a little in the rigidness of your principles, remember that God abhors all wavering and instability: hold fast the profession of your faith. Know no change but that involved in progress. Hold fast what you have, while you add to it what you lack.

OCTOBER 17.—"The chastisement of our peace was upon him."—Isaiah liii. 5.

He rendered satisfaction to divine justice for the offences

committed by us, and exhausted the chastisement appointed to us, so that we have reconciliation with God. His spotless purity and the infinite dignity of his person immensely enhanced the value of his sufferings, so that without being the same in kind and in duration as divine justice would have demanded, had we, the offenders, been the sufferers, they were nevertheless abundantly ample as an atonement for the sins of men. In fact the justice and holiness of God and the honor of his law, are just as gloriously illustrated by the death of Christ, as is the kindness of God to a fallen world.

Peace having been purchased for us at so tremendous a price, the question remains, Have we peace? We see how it is to be obtained. Let us see in the death of Christ, the chastisement due to us, in the cup which his Father gave him all the wrath due to our iniquities; and let us put on the robe of Christ's immaculate righteousness given us at the cross. There are some that make the cross of Christ an excuse for sinning; but they really know not that cross; they contemplate not the real Christ, nor have any knowledge of his real sufferings. Forgiveness received there, actually there, not at an imaginary Calvary, forgiveness received in company with a sense of what was undergone by Christ, dissolves the power of sin in the soul and renovates the heart.

OCTOBER 18.—"It is good for me that I have been afflicted, that I might learn thy statutes."—Psalm cxix. 71.

What would this world be without calamity! Men talk about the mystery of present things. The mystery would be infinitely greater, if there was no affliction. We should be utterly at a loss to know what to make of the character of God, if unmingled prosperity were the lot of man. This world would then resemble a Hindoo heaven; and it would be necessary to suppose Hindoo gods presiding over it, in order to get rid of the monstrous anomaly of impenitent sinners occupying the seats of the blessed.

The Christian has reason to thank God that things have not been accommodated to his wishes. When the mist of tears was in his eyes, he looked into the word of God and saw magnificent things. When Jonah came up from the depths of ocean, he showed that he had learned the statutes of God. One could not go too deep to get such knowledge as he obtained. Nothing now could hinder him from going to Nineveh. It is just the same as though he had brought up from the deep an army of twelve legions of the most formidable troops. The word of God, grasped by faith, was all this to him and more. He still, however, needed further affliction; for there were some statutes not yet learned. Some gourds were to wither. He was to descend into a further vale of humiliation. Even the profoundest affliction does not, perhaps, teach us everything; a mistake we sometimes make. But why should we compel God to use harsh measures with us? Why not sit at the feet of Jesus and learn quietly what we need to learn?

October 19.—"Blessed is the man that endureth temptation."—James i. 12.

Blessed is the man that endureth whatever ordeal the Lord may see fit that he should be subjected to, for the discovery of his heart. These temptations are simply processes of examination; they are opportunities which the Lord giveth us of verifying our professions.

To men that boast of their inward goodness and strength, Providence often seems to say, "You have thought yourself obliged to speak of your own good qualities, because the vicissitudes of your life were not such as to bring out the evidence of these qualities; but I will now so order events that your goodness shall have a perfect opportunity of revealing itself."

Men that praise themselves ought never to find any fault when disappointments and disasters befal them; for if they indeed possess that strength of mind and superiority of character of which they boast, they will feel these trials little and their inward excellence will be enabled to speak for itself. In their case we too often see that pride cometh before a fall. Men are continually clamoring—without being aware of it—for some severer condition of life; they are continually challenging circumstances to assume a more forbidding and hostile attitude; they find themselves in an inadequate sphere; they are conscious of virtues that have never yet found expression; they urge God (by self-laudation) to put them into the fire and see if they will not come forth as gold.

Now the Christian does not boast, but he makes a profession. He professes to have renounced the idea of his own goodness, and to be as dependent on God for moral goodness as for physical. God says, "It is well; but men will not believe thee; I will put thee in a situation calculated to elicit the full evidence of this." The Lord perhaps raises him then to considerable distinction; all men praise him; and it is interesting to see the Christian preserving his humility and prayerfulness in the midst of this fiery trial. He professes to fear God rather than man. Then men bring great rocks and say, "Fear God, by all means; all that we ask is that you should give up an infinitesimal part of what you call the fear of God, and do our will in one most insignificant particular; otherwise we will grind you to powder beneath these rocks." "Grind," is his reply; and we see that his profession was not in vain. He professes to have a spirit of submission to all the appointments of the Lord. Then the Lord proceeds to deal with him in a way that seems to him altogether strange and unaccountable and uncalled for; the things that befall him seem to him not to have been in the bond; it strikes him that submission is hardly the thing called for and that he does well to be angry. But happily he considers that the providence of God has taken this provocative aspect for the very purpose of enabling the spirit of submission in him to manifest itself more unimpeachably; and so he endures.

I wish to remember always, and especially at the time when my will is suffering opposition, when a stone seems to be given in reply to my request for bread, that the stone so given is much better than bread; the opportunity of glorifying God by yielding my will to his, is much more valuable than the good then withheld. Blessed is not the man that is exempt from trial; but blessed is the man that endures it, maintaining to the end his patience, zeal, hope, love and joy.

OCTOBER 20.—"When he is tried, he shall receive the crown of life, which the Lord hath promised to them that love him."—James i. 12.

This is a very evil world. It lieth in wickedness. The Prince of evil reigns over it. No wonder the Christian longs to take the wings of a dove and flee away and be at rest. But it is well for him to bear in mind that in this very world, where the enemies of God appear to have everything their own way, there is wonderful scope given for the exhibition of love to God. In some respects heaven cannot equal it. In heaven it is not given unto love to declare itself by suffering. There are no reproaches to be borne there; no humiliations to be encountered; no injuries to be sustained. We see from the example of the Lord Jesus Christ how that even divine love itself is able to clothe itself with honor by means of suffering. Our only chance of signalizing our love to Christ by long-suffering, meekness and self-renunciation, is that which we now enjoy.

We see here that they who endure temptation are they who love God. We profess to love God more than self and all its possessions. If the Lord lays upon us a tax of one per cent., he gives us to that extent an opportunity of showing our sincerity. If the tax amount to ten per cent., then the opportunity is so much greater; if to fifty per cent., then it looks as though the Lord had confidence in us. He takes us at our word. He believes in our whole-hearted love. And if the tax swallow up everything we have, and leave us utterly bankrupt of all worldly good, then let us consider that God has only taken what we long ago recognized as his; and let us call to mind that there is a precious relation between the trial endured and the crown of life. "*When he is tried, he shall receive the crown of life.*"

There are some whose piety is of so utterly defective a character that it is well understood beforehand that they cannot endure trial. They can only maintain their position in the church by the most tender and delicate treatment. How then will they pass in safety through the terrors of the day of the Lord? He cometh with a rod of iron; and everything that can be broken in pieces by that rod must be broken. The bruised reed indeed he will not break; he heals it and gives it strength, and it becomes a rod in his hand. He bestows the most tender and delicate treatment; but it is by way of preparation for the trial. And after the trial, *the crown of life.*

OCTOBER 21.—"He is long-suffering to us-ward, not willing that any should perish, but that all should come to repentance."—2 Peter iii. 9.

We read elsewhere of "God our Saviour, who will have all men to be saved." The Gospel, promulgated for every creature, is the expression of this divine willingness that men should come to repentance. "Knowest thou not," says Paul to the hardened sinner, "that the goodness of God leadeth thee to repentance?" Thus we see that all the goodness so profusely exhibited in the providence of God to men generally, is an expression of God's will that they should turn away from their sins and seek his grace. Day by day, during many, many years, he supplies the table of the impenitent man with palatable and suitable food; clothes him and his with raiment; fills his granaries and his coffers; and does it all not simply that he may meet the temporal wants of this sinner, but that he may touch his heart and lead him to turn penitently to his God. The sun returns to the east day after day, not because a law of nature requires it, but because the God of nature is the God of grace, and would have all men come to repentance.

Many there are who reckon confidently upon a future display of the mercy of God, who yet are utterly unobservant of the mercy now shown. They seek the mercy of God in the wrong place, that is to say at the judgment seat; while they spend their days in treasuring up wrath against the day of wrath. They utterly object to the doctrine of a hell, which they repudiate as involving the sacrifice of God's perfections. Well, if they like, there shall be no hell. God wishes not that there should be any. He is ready to cancel, with respect to them, every denunciation of future punishment contained in the Bible. He is ready to exceed, a thousand fold, all their conceptions of divine goodness. He will not only destroy, for them, the hell of unquenchable fire, but the inward hell whose materials are heaped up within their own heart, the hell of sin, which, if undestroyed, will nullify for them all the heavens of creation. He will purify them from all unhallowed affections and unlawful desires; give them the tastes and aptitudes of heaven, the love of Christ, the hatred of sin; and will then give them to dwell in the place for which he has fitted them. God is not willing that any should perish; his unwillingness is written upon the face of universal things; but they who come not to repentance, cannot but perish. In the day of the flood, the door of the ark shall not be open; if you insist upon making God a liar, if you regard his prophesied wrath as a fiction, you can surely reproach no one but yourself when you find that he hath spoken truth. If you flatter yourself with the idea that God will accommodate himself to your impious unbelief, and falsify his own word to show that you were right in viewing him as a liar, you do but evince the amazing and persistent blindness of your nature.

OCTOBER 22.—"I abhor myself, and repent in dust and ashes."—Job xlii. 6.

It is difficult to conceive of higher testimony than that which was borne to the character of Job. To be distinguished among a few, is as much honor as men generally dare to aspire to. But the mere thought of being distinguished above all men dwelling on the face of the earth, is enough to intoxicate the soul of man. Now of Job, it was deliberately stated, that there was not his like upon the earth, a perfect and upright man, fearing God and eschewing evil. And by whom was this testimony borne? By God himself, by the Being that knew infallibly all men. And who can look upon the character of Job without admiration? His keen sensibility to reproach, the agony caused by his dim intelligence of what those providences signified, only served to bring out more conspicuously his noble trust in God, his inextinguishable hopefulness. In the presence of his calumniators he held fast his integrity; without at all meaning to deny that he was a fallible being dependent for all on the mercy of God, he yet refused to admit their insinuations and allow that he had been living the life of a hypocrite. But when God was revealed in his glory, such a flood of light was poured upon his character, that the least sin seemed too odious to contemplate, a burden greater than his memory could bear.

As for thee, O reader, tell me, hast thou ever been brought to abhor thyself? A flush of indignation is thy response. The very suggestion fills thee with disgust. O pardon me, dear reader! It is evident that thou art a much better man than Job. He was—above all men that lived in his day—a man after God's own heart. But thou art greatly his superior. If God looked down from heaven with so much satisfaction, when Job inhabited this earth, if the divine words of commendation were passed from angel to angel through all the celestial ranks; how must heaven be affected as it looks down upon thee! If the miseries of Job were appointed to thee, thou wouldst endure them all with a patience and a piety surpassing those of Job! Else why dost thou declare that thou hast never known, will never know, self-abhorrence?

OCTOBER 23.—"Let him that glorieth, glory in this, that he understandeth and knoweth me."—Jeremiah ix. 24.

This is an intellectual age. Of nothing do men boast more than of their stupendous knowledge and sublime wisdom. They play with worlds, the worlds of geology and astronomy. But there are a great many competitors for fame; and out of thousands that seek to be glorified of men, scarce two or three succeed in attaining an eminent place in the world's regard. It is surprising that among the vast numbers doomed to disappointment there should be so few led to inquire whether there may not be honor to be obtained in some other quarter. What think you—we would say to such a one—what think you of gaining honor in the presence of the angels of heaven, of clothing yourself with distinction among the sinless ones, of obtaining an understanding that will qualify you to stand close to the very throne of God?

Imagine a temple of fame; upon lofty seats are seen Plato, Cicero, Goethe, Kant, Arago, Lamartine, Byron, Dante and many others of the world's immortal ones; an angel descends from heaven with a chaplet of unfading glory; goes from one to another of these applauded ones and finally leaves the temple, chaplet in hand; at the foot of the steps he sees a poor despised creature eating a crust of bread and softly murmuring, with a heart full of joy, the name of the Crucified Friend of man; he greets him with the utmost respect and bestows on him the chaplet.

OCTOBER 24.—"The Lord gave and the Lord hath taken away."—Job i. 21.

But if he gave, why should he take away? Why does he resume what he has transferred to another? But he has transferred nothing to another in such a sense that it has ceased to be his own. The most exalted of created beings has nothing whatever in this sense. The kingdom of God is a kingdom where every inch of the soil belongs to the sovereign, where all the property belongs to him, and where he is ever at perfect liberty to dispose of everything as he will. And this arrangement is not arbitrary, but gracious. He disposes of all things with reference to the happiness of all.

Men insist upon being the sovereigns of what has been committed to them. They hold it for themselves and not for him. Then when they lose it they gnash their teeth; they are without consolation. What is worse than their loss, they see a tyrant upon the throne of the universe. As far as their own misery is concerned, this tyranny is a real one. Viewing God as a tyrant, and being ever in bitter conflict with his government, it is the same to them, in respect to their wretchedness, as though God were a tyrant. Therefore Christ says in the parable: "Thou knewest that I was an austere man, gathering where I had not strewed." Oh, what torment, what an antepast of future woe do men give unto themselves, when they malign God in their thoughts!

On the other hand, they who look upon all their possessions as strictly speaking the possessions of God, and who cherish a perpetual readiness to yield everything at his command, sustain no losses. They do not perhaps get broken into the habit of parting company with loved and familiar things without a pang; but with the pang there is the consolation of knowing that God has taken his own for some sufficient reason, and that a God of boundless goodness still sits upon the throne of the universe.

OCTOBER 25.—"Behold what manner of love the Father hath bestowed upon us, that we should be called the sons of God."—1 John iii. 1.

When by a divine rescript we are designated the sons of God, a pledge is given that the following petition of Christ shall be fulfilled in our behalf: "That the love wherewith thou hast loved me may be in them." Christ is the Son of God; but we are to be exalted to his own height of glory and majesty; we are to sit with him upon his throne; and it is to be manifest to all the universe that we too are sons of God. He has this pre-eminence over all, that he is what he is by virtue of his own incomparable merit; and we shall be what we shall be by virtue of the same merit, not ours but his. When Christ shall appear we shall be like him, for we shall see him as he is.

There are so many mere honorary titles in this world, that men are led to look upon the titles given in the word of God, as also honorary. But this is a serious error. When God gives titles, he bears testimony to the character of a man, makes known the man's relation to Him, and gives an earnest of what he intends to make of him. Christ gave Peter, in the days of his instability, when he was like a wave, driven with the wind and tossed, gave him even then the title of Peter, or rock, foreshadowing what he intended to make of him.

Beloved, we are now the sons of God,—called so and constituted so. We have consequently unlimited life, unlimited wealth, unlimited privilege. Much has been bestowed, much is yet to be bestowed. When God says to me, "Thou art my son," he opens to me the door of an ascending stairway leading up to his throne. By the grace of God the steps are there before me and the liberty to ascend; but every several step is to be gained by an expanding faith, is to be conquered by the grace of God in me. If I have feeble conceptions of what God means by calling me his son, I shall linger in the lower steps; if I have higher and more correct views I will run boldly up the pathway of light. Let me believe that God has gone as far as it is possible for God himself to go in the enunciation of my privileges; that he has told me to look upon the seraphim and cherubim as no nearer to him than I myself am or am to be; that I have part and lot the most intimate in all the glory, majesty, affluence, power and blessedness of God; that my name is written along with his own over everything; that every being in the universe is commanded to love me under pain of being accounted guilty of treason against the Sovereign of the skies. I am a son of God, and therefore the representative of the invisible God. The world indeed knoweth us not, because it knew him not. But there is to be, in an hour known to God, the manifestation of the sons of God.

OCTOBER 26.—"The Lord is good to all."—PSALM cxlv. 9.

The Lord is good;—this is an independent proposition. He is good to the good, to all the heavenly companies that do his bidding, and rejoice in his government. That he should be good to sinners of earth, habitually violating his precepts, is a statement that goes far beyond the other. To a few of them? To thousands of them? To all of them? He has so made mankind that it is impossible for the least of them to exist without countless specific acts of kindness shown by God. Even corporeal life, what does it involve? Processes of infinite number and variety. Was it an act of surprising kindness on the part of Christ to give sight to the blind, and is it nothing that God should this day continue to you this wonderful faculty? Is there any less wisdom, power or goodness displayed in the preservation of an organ than in the bestowing of it? Physiology will tell you there is not. Look then at your various faculties and members and susceptibilities and tastes; at your physical and mental endowments; and understand that the multitude of God's thoughts towards you in a single hour are so many that they could not be expressed in the largest volume ever written. If you are affected by this consideration, then extend your gaze beyond yourself and see the lines of relationship by which God has brought all things to your door. In some far off field you see grain growing, so that in some future day that appetite of yours may be regaled. And that grain is waited upon by universal nature. The very stars have a commission to care for it.

God is thus good to all. Were it not that he opened his hand, the desire of no living creature would be satisfied. Well, therefore, may the Psalmist say, "Let everything that hath breath praise the Lord." Mankind, however, are far from doing thus. Judging from the murmurs, loud complaints, deep curses, reproaches, expressions of surprise, repinings, sighs, groans, tears, looks of vexation and disappointment, from all the tokens of dissatisfaction that meet us on every side, we can only conclude that men look upon God as the very opposite of good to them. They have no mind for the eulogy of God. "Let everything that hath breath praise the Lord," says the Psalmist; but his exhortation is in vain. The hearts of men may glow with admiration sometimes; but God is not the object. And nothing is gained by the augmentation of benefits. Generally indeed the more marked the goodness of God to them, the less they are disposed to praise him. What then is to be done? Could the difficulty in their heart be removed, could they be recovered from the dominion of sin, then would they rejoice in him, and even the least mercy would fill them with rapture. This is what God in his goodness has done. He hath provided a Saviour, through whom men may escape from that horrid heart of theirs which swallows up the goodness of God like a mighty Maelstrom; he has commanded his gospel to be preached to every creature.

OCTOBER 27.—"That where I am, there ye may be also."—John xiv. 3.

Lord, is this thy desire? Didst thou take such a desire as this to heaven with thee? When thou wert parted from thy disciples and a cloud was about to receive thee out of their sight, were these sweet and love-expressing words still hovering on thy lips? When thou didst ascend up far above all principality and power, and might and dominion, when the hosts of heaven clustered gladly and adoringly around thee, were thine eyes still fixed on us, and did the desire still predominate in thy heart, that where thou art, there we might be also? Did this desire still follow thee to the throne where thou rulest heaven and earth? Has it kept possession of thy breast during all these ages? And now that thou art surrounded by thy Daniels and Pauls, Elijahs and Johns, Abrahams and Peters, Luthers and Wesleys, Whitefields and Brainerds, is there this still wanting in the cup of thy blessedness, namely, that we thy saints on earth should be with thee, where thou art? Then, O, our loving Lord, help us to reciprocate this desire, to set our affections on high, to lay aside every weight and run the race before us. Make us rapidly meet for the inheritance of the saints in light. Walk with us in our wilderness, that we may walk with thee in the place of thy glory.

OCTOBER 28.—"I will run the way of thy commandments, when thou shalt enlarge my heart."—Psalm cxix. 32.

God enlarges our heart by taking away from it the idea of our own righteousness and of our own strength; by taking away from us hardness of heart and insensibility; by delivering us from the oppressive fear of an offended God; by casting out a great deal of selfishness; by breathing into us the new life of faith in Christ, and making us buoyant with the delightful assurance of God's undeclining favor; by the love of God shed abroad in our hearts.

Then no wonder that we run the way of his commandments. These are no longer grievous, for they are paired with promises; and with every indication of duty there is an indication of help. We run; we have not now to be dragged. It is no longer the place of task; it is the place of pleasant communion and co-operation with him who has said, "Without me ye can do nothing." The way of his commandments, is simply a way where love finds beautiful opportunities of expressing itself.

But alas! are there not many among us that need greatly to have their hearts enlarged? Their pace in the divine course is not even a fast walk. What is it that chokes their hearts? Here is a brother, whose heart is choked, we have too much reason to fear, by an all-absorbing and exclusive attachment to "The Church;" and who is not aware how unkind a part he is acting toward that very branch of Christ's Church which he thus ignorantly and injuriously idolizes. Here is a brother whose heart is choked by a false charity which inclines him to regard all men as pretty nearly safe, and not in need of his self-denying efforts. How many have their hearts so occupied by mercantile matters or political questions, that it is impossible for them to make haste in the doing of Christ's commandments.

OCTOBER 29.—"And rejoice in hope of the glory of God."—Romans v. 2.

Happy the soul that is able to find its joy in the indulgence of such a hope as this. Fallen man rejoices in hope of his own glory; not of his own true glory, but of a false and worldly glory, utterly disconnected with the glory of God. That soul is already largely redeemed that has learned to identify its own interests with the glory of God. And this hope shall be fulfilled; nothing is more certain. The glory of God must go forth triumphant one of these days, and conquer all the detestable glory that men and devils have been bringing like a pall of bedizened sackcloth over the face of universal things.

The Christian is even now greatly conversant with the glory of God; but the more that he knows of it the more passionately does he long for that moment when it shall be manifested with all its appropriate sublimity; when every eye shall see it; when the idolized ones of earth shall hide their heads in caves and dens; when Christ shall be admired in his believers; when they shall be filled with the Holy Ghost, and their bodies made like unto Christ's glorious body; when the New Jerusalem shall come down from God out of heaven, having "the glory of God."

OCTOBER 30.—"I will strengthen thee, yea, I will help thee, yea, I will uphold thee with the right hand of my righteousness."—Isaiah xli. 10.

Even in the giving of promises, God has made manifest that he giveth liberally and upbraideth not. The necessity of reiterating promises, is sometimes irksome to us; we want people to take us at our word. But God knows the stupendous strength of unbelief in the heart of man. If a mountain of granite is to be reduced to powder by successive strokes of an instrument, there must be a vast number of strokes. If we wish to form some conception of the nature of unbelief let us look at the mighty stores of promise accumulated with a view to its overthrow. The guilt of it, who can tell? God says, "I will strengthen thee;" yet we dare not go forward without a weapon. He says, "I will help thee;" yet we lie down miserable if there be no provision in the house for the morrow's wants. He says, "I will uphold thee;" yet we shrink from taking up some responsibility pointed out to us by him. "I will uphold thee," he says, "by the right hand of my righteousness; I pledge my own infinite ability that thou shalt prevail; I pledge my righteousness; so that if I uphold thee not, my righteousness remains to me no more: my justice is forfeited; I am become like the gods of the heathen, unholy, not to be relied on. Wilt thou make me such a one?"

Oh, that Christians would consider how grossly they asperse the character of God and misrepresent him to the world, by failing to embrace and act upon these exceeding great and precious promises.

OCTOBER 31.—"**I am not ashamed of the gospel of Christ.**"—**Rom. i. 16.**

This seems a very moderate declaration of attachment; but very few can go so far as this. The gospel of Christ is the word that sets forth Christ. It is nothing apart from Christ. As He is honorable, so is it; as He is excellent, so is it. To be ashamed of it, is to be ashamed of Him.

Are you ashamed to speak, look, and act in such a way as to show your conviction that you and all men are lost sinners until recovered by the grace of God; and that you are dependent upon this grace for all power to conquer sin, resist temptation, know the truth? You flatter yourself that you are not ashamed of the gospel of Christ, because when you are with Christians, you laud Christ; but on other occasions you keep back the "one thing needful," and give unscriptural prominence to the many things not vitally needful. Are you willing to speak as Christ spoke; to express the opinions expressed by the Son of God; to talk in promiscuous companies of the necessity of cutting off a right hand, plucking out a right eye; to make mention of unquenchable fires, and a never-dying worm; to tell men that except they repent, they shall all likewise perish; and to discourse of the mansions in the skies, and the return of Christ to judge mankind? If our conversation is quite of another character, if reference to these things is never or seldom made by us, is there not the strongest reason to believe that we are ashamed of the gospel of Christ? In fact, the presence of gospel truth in very many societies where Christians are frequently found, would be as startling as the presence of Christ himself. We are not even conscious of the humiliating defeats that we, professors of the gospel, have sustained.

NOVEMBER 1.—"Thou, Lord, wilt bless the righteous."—Psalm v. 12.

Having bestowed righteousness, thou wilt express thy pleasure in that righteousness. We should not need a revelation from heaven to tell us this. It ought to be an unquestionable, self-evident axiom, that God who has all gifts at his disposal, will bestow his best gifts upon those who please him most.

But there is none righteous, no, not one. Well, in the absolute sense of the word, Christ is the only righteous one that ever sojourned on this earth. He knew no sin. But they that believe on him, their faith is counted to them for righteousness. They receive of his fullness. Through him the unjust are justified. Amd having been brought nigh to God, what is to hinder that they should obtain deliverance from sin? They ask and receive. They are changed into the image of Christ. God blesses them by bringing their wills into coincidence with his own; and then their ulterior blessedness becomes a thing as inevitable as the eventual triumph of the will of God.

It is because a man has no goodness of his own on which to

build any hope, that he is enabled so assuredly to anticipate the very highest measure of blessedness of which it is possible to conceive. For consider, the righteousness on which his hopes are founded, is an infinite righteousness; the merit of all heavenly beings added together would make nothing approaching it. While a man clings to the idea of his own merit, he shrivels up his destiny into nothing; when he loses that idea and knows nothing but the merit of Christ, crucified for sinners, the Lord of all, his destiny expands into a roll like that of the illimitable heavens, all written over with words of beauty and of wealth.

"*Thou, Lord, wilt bless the righteous.*" It does not become a sovereign to bestow little favors. As God has shown forth his eternal power and Godhead in creation, so in what he will do for the righteous, he will take care that there be a magnificent and all-eclipsing display of his regard for righteousness.

What we need is, ever to believe that God ever remembers this purpose of his; and to say, in every situation of life, God is blessing me, by preparing me for future blessing. While Christ is preparing for me a place in heaven, he is preparing me on earth for that place in heaven. There is, therefore, a connection of the most intimate and necessary kind between the disappointments, humiliations, losses, sorrows, afflictions of the believer on earth, and the dignity, felicity, purity, splendor, power, to be found by him at the right hand of Christ.

NOVEMBER 2.—"Unto you therefore which believe, he is precious." — 1 Peter ii. 7.

Before you, seated in the cavern of this world, the wizard of this world causes to appear, one after another, scenes of beauty, dissolving scenes that scarce have presented themselves to your vision before they have gone, leaving you in darkness. The wizard shows them to you that he may bind you to him.

self forever. "All these things will I bestow upon you," he says, "if you fall down and worship me." "The realities are in my chambers," he says; "I give them to whomsoever I will." Infatuated man, madly pursuing these vanished visions, descends deeper and deeper into the region of death and despair. Happy he, unutterably happy, if, ere it be too late, his eyes be anointed with a celestial eye-salve and he discover that all the glorious visions that ever darted across his path or illumined his conceptions, when they dissolved as visions became reconstituted as realities in Christ. Yes, this is the wondrous knowledge that the believer obtains by faith. All exquisite music died out in Christ, to live in him forever; all beautiful sunsets vanished not into night, but into the blessed reality of Christ; all lovely flowers faded to bloom perennially in him; the smile of youth, the look of love, the scintillation of genius, the burst of eloquence, everything that lent a momentary radiance to life, has its apotheosis in Christ, is found in him by the believer.

Christ is precious to me, because I believe that the beauty and attractiveness of all admirable things owe their charm to him, and yield their charm to him. They crossed my path that they might speak to me of him. My enthusiasm staggered like a drunken man in the pathway of this world, and only knew its vocation when it discovered him.

When he cometh, the new Jerusalem cometh; the paradise of God cometh; the river of the water of life; saints; angels; the new heaven; the new earth; all beauty, all splendor, all sanctity; the fruition of all right desires, the realization of all lovely dreams; love; in a word all that is precious cometh; nor will it ever after be possible for me to conceive of a good not found in the region irradiated by his smile.

NOVEMBER 3.—"Comfort ye, comfort ye my people, saith your God."—Isaiah xl. 1.

And how were the servants of God to comfort the people of God? By telling them of Christ. This became the burden of Isaiah's prophecies, as recorded in the fortieth chapter and onwards; and all the prophets his successors continued this strain. This was the banquet that God saw fit to provide for his ancient people. They demanded other comfort, and demanded in vain. When Jesus himself appeared, they refused to accept the comfort; they saw no beauty in him that they should desire him. They asked for one that should deliver them from the Roman yoke; make them honorable and powerful above all nations; and spread a favoring mantle over all their sins. They would none of God's comfort. But the banquet which they scorned to honor with their presence, was not left without guests; the broken and contrite of all nations, the poverty-stricken, the sick, the blind, these came and partook; and lo! they were comforted, they were made whole and crowns of everlasting joy were seen upon their heads; while the rejecters soon found themselves the poorest and unhappiest in creation, deprived of the very shadows which they had preferred to the substance.

We are to comfort God's people by presenting Christ to them, and showing them their need of this very Messiah and no other. And if they are unwilling to be comforted in this way, we are not at liberty to give them comfort in any other way. Any other way is a way of delusion.

NOVEMBER 4.—"Surely goodness and mercy shall follow me all the days of my life."—Psalm xxiii. 6.

When Love divine was about to follow Christ back to heaven, he said, "Not so; I am no more in the world, but these are in the world." So this Love has ever since tarried with the people of God

The Christian knows that goodness and mercy shall go with him all the days of his life, as two attendant angels. He knows that they have followed him hitherto. But it is sometimes difficult for him to perceive that they *are* with him. When Jeremiah was in that deep, dark dungeon, where there was no water, but mire, it seemed as though goodness and mercy had left him and gone to walk on the battlements of Jerusalem. Men came to the border of that pestilential pit and asked him mockingly where those companions of his now were. But Jeremiah's eyes getting accustomed to the darkness soon discovered them there. They gave him some bread of heaven to eat. Then when Jerusalem was taken, and the proud enemies of the prophet were carried into captivity, Jeremiah remained in the land; goodness and mercy followed him all his days. Persecution is not so persevering as they are. When Elijah was under the juniper-tree, goodness and mercy awoke him and ministered unto him. "Why do you flee for your life?" they said; "have we fled from thee?" "I do well to be angry," said Jonah, insulting these heavenly attendants to their face. He said to goodness, "Thou art an imposter, not goodness, but unkindness:" and to mercy, "Thou art severity, thou hast no beauty, get thee gone." Did they follow him still? They sat down and said to him, "We will not go." They might have spoken of the depths of the sea whither and whence they had accompanied him; but they spoke to him of the much cattle that was in Nineveh, and of an immense number of innocent little children.

How often have I been ready to use the language of Jonah; how often frowned on these celestial ones, and motioned them angrily away, because they would not take the form my fancy painted yet have they still followed me. Be astonished, O earth!

NOVEMBER 5.—"As the heaven is high above the earth, so great is his mercy toward them that fear him."—Psalm ciii. 11.

Perfect love casteth out fear; but not the fear here spoken of. There is no torment in this fear. It is at home in company with the most unlimited confidence. The man that trusts in God is the same as the man that fears God; the two expressions are convertible, and are over and over interchanged in the word of God. Let the man that thinks he fears God, see to it that he trusts in God: and let the man that thinks he trusts in God, see to it that he fears God.

He fears God who has a high sense of the value of his favor, and cannot bear that any cloud should come in for a moment between his conscience and the smile of God. He that is most assiduous in the endeavor to please God; who is most distressed at the thought of his displeasure; he to whom his commandments are not grievous; who beholds with satisfaction all the attributes of God; he it is that fears God. You observe that this fearer of God is in the enjoyment of God's infinite mercy; so that the spring of his devotion is not the apprehension of wrath. The love of God shed abroad in his heart leads him to fear God.

How much David knew of the height of the heavens, what estimate he formed of the distance of the heavenly bodies, we know not. Doubtless he viewed them as at distances more vast than any that separate the different points of the earth's surface. He would have heard with much surprise a statement to the effect that a journey of four hours performed at the rate of the velocity of light, 200,000 miles a second, would take us only to the outskirts of our system; a journey of three or four years would take us to the first fixed stars; a journey of 60,000 years would take us to the stars of a certain distant nebula; and that we should even then be probably in the lower parts of creation. What would have been the effect of such a revelation as this, upon his mind? His conceptions of the power, wisdom, majesty, immensity of God, would have been vastly augmented; but think you that his conceptions of the mercy of God would have not been elevated? They would have been elevated; for the mercy of God is in the nature of God; grows as that grows upon us, expands as that expands before us; and when through Christ we have entered into relation to it, every star becomes an exponent of it, every insterstellar space a link in the endless chain that measures it.

NOVEMBER 6.—"As far as the east is from the west, so far hath he removed our transgressions from us."—Psalm ciii. 12.

Among those who read the Bible, how small a proportion, what an insignificant minority are the broken and contrite in heart! How rare a thing it is to see a man who is bowed down beneath a sense of his sinfulness, and who finds it difficult to conceive that there should ever be pardon for him! How small the number of such!

Now see what honor God has put upon these few. A great deal of his word seems to be intended just for them. God, so to speak, passes by the crowds of those who are comfortable in spirit and have an easy faith in the mercy of God, to come to some poor faltering sinner and convince him of the freeness and unmeasured fulness of divine mercy. You and I must often see that the word of God is not troubling itself about us, but about some deeply-convicted, hesitating, trembling soul.

NOVEMBER 7.—"Keep thy heart with all diligence."—Proverbs iv. 23.

Keep that which is good, *in* it; that which is evil, *out:* thoughts, feelings, purposes, imaginations, desires. Especially, keep God's word in it. Quench not the Spirit. Cherish a memory for what is good. Be as a gardener; be as a banker.

For the mind is God's wonderful gift.

As our thoughts, so our words and acts.
As our thoughts, so our future life.
Be as the pilot.
Thermopylæ.
Our peace easily destroyed by unwatchfulness.
God looks at the heart.
Has given us suitable objects to think about,—to love.

NOVEMBER 8.—"The water that I shall give him, shall be in him a well of water springing up into everlasting life."—John iv. 14.

"Art thou able, O Christ, to slake the thirst of my soul? Dost thou know what strength of desire there is in me? Consider what seas of goodness have, in the providence of God, been poured upon me without in the least diminishing the force of aspiration within me. Whatever is given, seems only to stimulate my imagination and send it soaring a higher flight. Thus it would appear that in the very nature of things I never can know satisfaction. Give me everything that I can now conceive of, and scarcely will I have looked upon it before my conception has found its wings again; and where my conception goes there also goes my desire. How then canst thou give me water to quench the thirst of my soul? Knowest thou my soul and her thirst? Where hast thou that water?"

He that formed thee knoweth thee. Thy conception cannot exceed the conception of God; must indeed, even in its wildest flight, fall infinitely short of it. Thine is a conception of desire; his is a conception relating to the satisfaction of that desire. Wonderful therefore as thou art in thy mental constitution, gigantic as is the power of aspiration in thee, He that made thee is infinitely more wonderful. It would indeed have been the greatest mistake on his part, to make a creature with a power of conception which he himself could not overtake. He has made no such mistake as this. All his perfections testify that he is able to satisfy thee. Let it be therefore firmly settled in your mind that there is no absolute and invincible difficulty in the way of your blessedness.

There is a disordered thirst that nothing can assuage. The torment remains, however often or abundantly you answer the call of the patient for water. Oh, if you could give him some water that would reach the seat of his disease, subdue his fever, and recover him from that mad disordered thirst, you would approve yourself the very physician that he needs. Now this is what Christ does. He knows well that if he gave thee all wealth, all luxury, all art, all renown, all success, all power, all beautiful sights and sounds, yet would not these unbounded largesses tend in the least to slake the thirst of thy soul for happiness. But the water that he giveth thee, goes to thy soul and cures the terrible disease that has made havoc of thy life; changes the character of thy desire; causes to spring up in thee emotions and affections corresponding to the wise and loving thoughts of God; and then satisfies these desires.

Has the water that Christ has given thee become, O Christian, a well in thee? Hast thou within thyself a well of perennial purity and bliss, of beautiful thoughts, delight in God, willingness to do his will, peace, strength to resist temptation, love to your fellow-men, anticipation of glory? If there be in thee this inexhaustible well of all that is desirable, then hast thou enough not only for thyself, but for thy neighbors, for all mankind in fact. Yes, if thou alone of all the family of man, were in possession of such a well, from thee there might go forth streams to make glad the entire face of earth, to satisfy the entire wants of men. For this well in thee, is Christ in thee.

NOVEMBER 9.—"A rewarder of them that diligently seek him."—Hebrews xi. 6.

It is a great moment in a man's life when he ascertains that he does not know God. The next step is to ascertain that one ought to know God. After this a man may still go knocking at many wrong doors; but let us hope that he will at length reach the right door, even the Bible, and conclusively set himself to seek God therein.

If we want to know what it is to seek diligently, we need no dictionary; we need only look around us; in every community there are men who seem to have assigned themselves this articular task of exhibiting in their own persons, what diligence is. It is true they are not seeking God; but having seen with what consecration they seek *their* object, we shall be at no loss to know what it is diligently to seek God.

Is it that the Lord conceals himself from us? That he has shut himself in from our gaze, like an oriental king, within many enclosures; and stationed cherubim with fiery swords at every gate, to make it impossible for us to approach him? Nay, not so. Whatever difficulties there are have not been interposed by him, but by us. So far as God is concerned there is a clear course before us. No man that ever lived in the world enjoyed better opportunities of finding God than I that write, or you that read this meditation.

He must be sought with an undivided heart. He must be the supreme object of search. To many he is but one object of search out of many. They go out into the world seeking various things, and bring home in their bag a hundred spoils of earth, with one or two words of God at the bottom; what wonder if these words are stifled by the company they are found in. In fact the words themselves flee away at the first opportunity; they will not stay to breathe that fetid atmosphere. A man that diligently seeks God, has renounced the search of other things; to this one port he hies him crowding all canvass, watching all that favors, all that opposes; knowing that the provision on board will suffice only so far as to that port. To neglect the least gale that blows, to lose the least current, to be overburdened with cargo in the least degree, may involve the destruction of all. The commander of such a vessel thinks of the port and of the means of reaching it, while he eats, while he drinks, while he talks, while he sleeps even; his eye continually wanders from his chart to his compass, thence to his sails, thence to the sky, thence to the sea, thence to his men, thence to his chart again.

NOVEMBER 10.—"I will not let thee go, except thou bless me."—Genesis xxxii. 26.

There is an erroneous idea of submission abroad in the world. Quite likely, the error obtains in the Church to some extent. There are many things in our condition here to which we are simply called to submit. God has placed them, and woe to him who would seek to displace them. But there are other things which have been placed in our way expressly that we might enter into conflict with them and overcome them. There are difficulties placed in our path, to give us opportunities of evincing what faith, courage, perseverance, wisdom, energy, prayerfulness, devotedness are in us. God withholds some things from us, with a prohibition; it is treason to go on seeking them; and he withholds other things, by way of incitation; that we may be stirred up to engage with all faith and assiduity in the search for them; and that the conquest of them may be the reward of valiant and all-conquering endeavor.

If we understand the Christian doctrine of submission, as implying that we are to drag ourselves feebly, faintly along the pathway of life; that there is to be no great forth-putting of power in connection with us; we understand it wrongly. Because we are the servants of God, are we therefore to be without energy, choice, decision, determination, perseverance? Is the voluntary part of our nature to be plucked up by the roots? Is there nothing in the way of enterprise to challenge the highest exercise of all our powers? Surely there is. Behold David, the Shepherd's boy. When he saw the bear and afterwards the lion come near the flock, he did not say, "God hath sent these, and it would be fool-hardy or sinful in me to resist them." Perhaps he said, "God has sent these to prove me, that I may show what courage and fidelity and faith are in me." At all events he engaged them in the name of his God and slew them.

When we ask and do not obtain, we are not always to suppose that our suit is dismissed: sometimes we are simply challenged by the silence of God to be more urgent, more believing. The Syro-Phenician woman would have done wrong had she gone away submissive, when Christ gave signs that her prayer was not to be granted. By faith Jacob had power with God and prevailed. Faith creates a new condition of things, so that it becomes expedient for God to grant what otherwise would have been withheld. He will say "No" to less faith and "Yes" to more faith. All things are possible to him that believeth. When we get nigh to God, let us make the most of our advantage. Let us obtain great blessings not only for ourselves, but for others. Let us view God as he is revealed at the cross, and not care much for the apparent frown of his providence, but contend with it and get the better of it, by faith.

NOVEMBER 11.—"Godliness is profitable unto all things, having promise of the life that now is, and of that which is to come."—1 Timothy iv. 8.

The life that now is. Covetousness reading this begins to glow with delight; it exclaims, "This is the very thing I seek; 'the life that now is;' and of course 'that which is to come.' Religion is a good thing after all; I will give myself to it at once." But the promise is not to thee, O covetousness; it is to godliness. It is to the soul in which covetousness is dead;

to the godly soul, which says, "One thing is needful;" whose affections are set on things above; which looks upon the favor of God as life, and upon worldliness as death. This promise is to the follower of Christ who has taken up his cross and covenanted to abandon the paths of worldly pleasure. Yes; the promise of the life that now is can only be made to him who has learned to look upon life as a means of serving God, glorifying Christ, revealing the truth and working out salvation. He that is absorbed in the life that now is, loses both this life and that which is to come; he that is godly, that lives unto God, gains this life and that which is to come. Gains this life, because his sorrow is worth, a hundred times over, the joy of the ungodly; his life is not a prey to vanity; his days are so many steps toward a blissful condition; and God approves. Gains it, because all things work together for his good;—gains it, because all the promises are his; he has peace; he has joy, love, humility, purity, and a hope that will not fail him.

NOVEMBER 12.—"The angel of the Lord encampeth round about them that fear him, and delivereth them."—Psalm xxxiv. 7.

Many are the afflictions of the righteous, but out of them all the Lord delivereth them. If wordly men are competent to effect the deliverance, the Lord accomplishes it by them. If saints are needed, saints are employed. If the impediments cannot be removed in this way, if supernatural aid is necessary, then the angels receive their commission. If an army of these invincible ones are needed, they are sent, and under the guidance of their leader they encamp around about the imperilled believer. If the work to be performed is beyond the prowess of any created beings, the Omnipotent Spirit hastens to put forth his irresistible energies in behalf of his servant.

All our biographies are necessarily very imperfect. We

have not in this world the materials for writing them. The most remarkable incidents have to be omitted, or just shadowed forth, as the documents relating to the operations of one's invisible attendants are not with us, but in the other world. If only our eyes were opened, like those of the servant of Elisha, to behold these celestial auxiliaries with their fiery chariots!

NOVEMBER 13.—"I have loved thee with an everlasting love."—Jeremiah xxxi. 3.

God considered that this life of ours is very short, very fugitive, and that crowd it as he might with expressions of his kindness, he never would be able to give anything like a sufficient revelation of his love. So he resolved to take time beforehand, a great deal of it, and fill all heaven and earth, from the very beginning on continuously, with the manifestations of his love to the creature that was to live in this our day, was to hover for a little about the middle of this century, and then be gone. When by the recovering grace of Christ we have been brought to take delight in the knowledge of the love of God, we find that God was mindful of us, in the far off days of a by-gone eternity; and myriads of years ago placed in the depths of space suns, whose rays swift-travelling, should reach our locality in our day, and assure us that he thought of us when the morning stars first sang together. He thought of us; and scarce had the transgression of Adam brought a curse upon the world in which we were to have existence, when God hastened to announce that in the fulness of time, his own Son should come into the world, and absorb in his own person the manifold curse. If we labor in vain to find the beginning of this love, much more shall we labor in vain to learn the future duration of it.

November 14.—"I will put my law in their inward parts and write it in their hearts."—Jeremiah xxxi. 33.

The law of God is written in our hearts, when it is the best expression of our desires, the best description of our tastes and affections, the best enunciation of our resolutions, the true exponent of our faith, the most conspicuous thing in our memories. It is written in our hearts, when our words give utterance to it in thousand fold modulation; when our acts embody it; when our influence is its influence. When Christ abides in our heart by faith, then is the law written in our hearts. When we are led by the Spirit of God. When we call ourselves unprofitable servants and repudiate our own righteousness. When the love of God is shed abroad in our hearts by the Holy Ghost given unto us.

November 15.—"The secret of the Lord is with them that fear him."—Psalm xxv. 14.

Of the fear here so honorably spoken of, suffice it now to say that it is not by any means a sentiment that repels from God, but on the contrary one that draws to God. They that fear the Lord, in the honorable and Scriptural sense, are they who are powerfully affected by the promise here given. To the great majority of men, alas, to many who assume the name of Christians, the promise here recorded possesses no charm. Their spirits are no way stirred within them by the prospect of being made the confidants of God. They shall not be his confidants. This singularly exalted condition is, for them to whom is the promise, like a day-star arising in the heart,—like a cynosure drawing them patiently, perseveringly, earnestly on in the pathway of obedience, faith and love. Abraham was the friend of God; and God approved himself a friend indeed; he would not hide from him the thing which was hidden from all the rest of the world. Moses too was the friend of God, and brought into surprising intimacy; the secret of the Lord was with him. "Henceforth," said Christ to the apostles, "I call you not servants but friends; for all things whatsoever I have heard of my Father, I have made known unto you."

And doubtless there are those now upon the earth who recline as it were upon the bosom of their Lord and drink in his most secret communications, unintelligible to others. They partake of hidden manna. "To him that overcometh, Christ giveth a white stone, and in the stone a new name written which no man knoweth, saving he that receiveth it."

But, in Christ is not the veil done away, so that we all with open face behold the glory of the Lord? Yes, but we do not all behold all glory. The degrees of glory are in number infinite. Great is the mystery of godliness; and veil after veil must be removed before we shall see him as he is. Perhaps there is nothing we all so much need to learn as this, that there is something beyond, of which our past experience is not able to give us any conception. The mystery that lies before us we are not conscious of: we are conscious of what we know, not of what we do not know. It is a great thing to be brought to see the veiled glory before us in our path; to get the conception of an attainable intimacy that is much beyond anything we have known.

Men may pervert; Satan may counterfeit; but the word of God remains in its integrity for the children of God. The secret of the Lord is with them that fear him. Not in the way of some new revelation, extra-scriptural; but by opening their eyes to behold wonderful things in the word of God; things that ordinary eye hath not seen, ear not heard, heart not conceived.

NOVEMBER 16.—"Thou wast slain and hast redeemed us to God by thy blood."—Revelation v. 9.

Men of this world look with ineffable scorn upon the customs, sentiments and language of those whose chief pleasure is in celebrating the dying love of Christ, crucified for sinners. They detest, they loathe the language of many of our hymns; for example, such lines as these:

> "Dear dying Lamb, thy precious blood
> Shall never lose its power,
> Till all the ransomed church of God
> Be saved, to sin no more."

Religion in some sober and decorous form, (they say) we revere; but this canting Methodism with its absurd vocabulary, ringing the changes on such expressions as—Lamb, bleeding Lamb, wounded side, dying love, fountain filled with blood, lover of my soul, precious Redeemer,—this insane and driveling piety we cannot away with. They would flee away from a prayer meeting, where these and similar expressions were uttered in hymns or prayers. Suppose, as they fled from such a place, the apostle John should meet them, seize them by the hand and hurry them into a chamber of such stupendous dimensions that it was impossible for any finite eye to discover either the walls or the ceiling; bathed in an unearthly radiancy; redolent with odors issuing from golden vials; interpenetrated with the seraphic melody of countless golden harps, and the harmonious chants of myriads of voices; and should bring to their notice that these beatified myriads were engaged in adoring the same being whom those Christians were praising, and addressing him, the King of kings, and Lord of lords, in the very same—the identical language that they had found so offensive in that first assembly. Would this suffice to convince them that the wrong taste, the fallacious judgment, the insanity are on their part rather than on that of the psalm-singing

NOVEMBER 17.—"Your adversary the devil, as a roaring lion walketh about, seeking whom he may devour."—1 Peter v. 8.

The reference here would seem to be to the efforts made to intimidate the followers of Christ, by penal enactments, sanguinary edicts, or by popular violence. The early Christians were summoned before magistrates and commanded to renounce the faith they had embraced or had shown themselves ready to embrace, by some unequivocal act of homage to a heathen divinity or to the image of the emperor. Satan made himself as terrible as possible, saying, "Cast away your confidence, or I will tear you limb from limb." But it was not by resisting him that men were devoured; it was by succumbing to him. They that were terrified by his roar, and driven from the obnoxious path, became his prey. Though we have no Roman Emperors to launch against us withering edicts, yet the adversary has not by any means ceased to go about as a roaring lion; he still deals in intimidation. Thousands are hindered from coming out of the world by his monitory roar, which threatens them with the wrath of the world if they have anything to do with the life of faith. Sometimes the consciousness of sin is made the means of producing alarm. The convinced sinner is made to see his sins standing like so many genii of tremendous stature and intolerable wrath along the pathway of redemption. The aim of the adversary, in these loud heart-melting roars, is to drown the still small voice of the Spirit of God, so that we may not hear the assurance of divine help and infallible deliverance. The adversary roars now like a lion; but if we meet him, he becomes less and less a lion, and eventually takes to ignominious flight; but the Spirit of God, speaking like a dove, if we refuse to hearken to him, shall finally be heard in a voice louder than ten thousand thunders, shall come to us clothed in all the wrath of the Lamb; and who shall then be able to stand, what heart shall then endure?

NOVEMBER 18.—"Mark the perfect man and behold the upright; for the end of that man is peace."—Psalm xxxvii. 37.

We are here called upon to observe the providential wisdom and faithfulness of God, shown in his care of the good. We are not merely to glance at these good ones, but to keep our eye upon them; for though God's providence may, for a season, appear to be adverse to them, yet at the end it will be found that he has led them carefully by his all-righteous hand. Not that they will die in affluence, in splendor, or in great worldly honor; but they shall exhibit their sure trust in God by a tranquil and serene deportment, by a heavenly peace, by a prayer breathed for their enemies in the very hour when they are stoned to death.

But there are many who say, "Show us the perfect man; let us see the upright man; we look for such in vain." We answer, The Judge of all the earth sees some whom he is willing thus to designate; it is a reproach to you, if you know them not. He says not, the perfect angel, but the perfect man; in other words, the sinner, who has turned from the error of his ways, and become, in most important respects, what God would have him to be. The eye of God, wandering over the outspread ranks of humanity, reposes at length upon one who having recognized his deep-dyed guilt, his imminent danger, and fled for refuge to the Redeemer, has consecrated himself to God, identified himself with the cause and with the people of God, and given himself to the study and pursuit of perfection. Such are living epistles, known and read of all men; by their lives religiously condemning, convincing, inviting, persuading others. Their testimony, like that of the word of God, is disliked and spoken against.

If indeed you have sincerely looked and looked in vain, then be alarmed at the thought of the evil days upon which you have fallen. For such men are the salt of the earth; and when they are withdrawn, swift destruction cometh. If there are none such, how much reason is there that you and I should seek by the grace of God, to be such.

NOVEMBER 19.—"He that overcometh shall inherit all things."—Revelation xxi. 7.

Sell all that thou hast and give to the poor, says Christ. Except a man forsake all that he hath, he cannot be my disciple. Having food and raiment, let us be therewith content. Give us this day our daily bread. We are crucified unto the world and the world unto us.

Naturally, we grasp at all. We embrace with our hands all that we possibly can, and embrace the rest with our desires. What we are not able to inscribe with our name as possessor, we inscribe with our name as candidate. Now, when we go over to Christ, we have to detach ourselves from all this. We renounce all. We bring the little of the world that we possess, and the remainder of the world that we longed after, and lay all down at the feet of Christ. By faith we learn to behold all excellence in him, and to find our world in him. When perfected in this we inherit all things.

It is a dishonorable thing for the sons of God to be co-partners with ungodly men; and the ungodly possess this earth and the things that are therein; the degradation of sin has passed like a tremendous wave over the whole globe, and rendered all unfit for the people of God. But a day cometh when the wicked shall be driven hence; when a new heaven and a new earth shall appear; then the saints shall inherit all things. The idea of possession current in this base world, involves the idea of privation for others. We only possess when others do not possess. But in the world to come of which we speak, it is very different. Nothing is so much deprecated there as exclusive possession. A thing is there only possessed when all possess it. It is the world of love, and nothing else is called gain that involves privation for others. What makes this inheritance of all things so entrancing, is that many others inherit with us. Their joy, their glory, their wealth, are the most important elements in our joy, glory and wealth.

NOVEMBER 20.—"The God of all comfort."—2 Corinthians i. 3.

God is represented to us as the God of all patience and consolation, the God of peace, the God of hope, the God of grace, the God of comfort, all expressions denoting his relations to his people, and designed to reveal him to them as the all-sufficient and inexhaustible fountain of peace, patience, and comfort. As often as the word comfort is mentioned, and how often it is! our thoughts should be spontaneously turned from the petty, the misnamed comfort of earth, to the infinite Comforter. Do we know him as the God of all comfort?

He brought his people out of Egypt; removed them from the land of Goshen to the wilderness; from their homes, their hearths, their associations, their accustomed board, to a waste and howling wilderness, where no fields waved with plenty, where no fertilizing and gladdening streams were seen, where the sun smote them by day, and wild beasts prowled by night. Was he in this a God of comfort? Many of them thought not, they murmured against him. Yet their descendants through all generations, regarded this act of God as an amazing proof of his love: as indeed it was. In the absence of earthly comforts, the sufficiency of God came out gloriously. No people were ever more tenderly cared for than they were. He led them with the gentleness of a good shepherd. He would very soon have brought them into a land flowing with milk and honey, had they suffered him

NOVEMBER 21.—"The Lord taketh pleasure in his people." Psalm cxlix. 4.

If this world should resolve to send an embassy to the most high God, whom would it choose? Well, the princes of this world would be represented; the brother of some Czar, or the nephew of some Emperor would go for them. The bishops and high clergy would be represented by some legate of ample wealth. The literary world would send some Gœthe, or Confucius, or Plato. The merchants would send a Rothschild. The artists would find a Raphael. There would be an ermined judge and a decorated physician. The military would send a Hannibal, the transcendentalists a Kant. All orders would be represented. But if, as the servant of some one of this company, a meek and lowly Christian might obtain permission to go, this one alone of all the company would be permitted to enter the audience-chamber of God. He taketh pleasure in such, not in the wise, the noble, the wealthy, the mitred. Like him may we learn to take pleasure in such.

NOVEMBER 22. "This is the promise that he hath promised us, even eternal life." 1 John ii. 25.

Not that we shall be exempt from loss, disappointment, sickness, human unkindness, embarrassment, vexation, insult, defamation, humiliation; not that we shall have in this world all the displays of providential favor on which we may have calculated; these are not the things promised; the promise that he hath promised us is eternal life. God may have dealt strangely with thee, O my soul; but say frankly, has he at all dealt with thee in a way to hinder the fulfilment of the promise made thee?

We are saved by hope. He that believeth hath eternal life; he hath entered upon it; he is living a new life, one that stretches out into eternity; but what he has experienced is only the beginning of it. We know not yet what we shall be; as the infant little knows what is the life it possesses, what its endowments, its susceptibilities, its privileges.

This promise of eternal life is the door opening out from the gloom of this world into the ever-blooming paradise of God. To the common ear of man it is an empty sound. Men care nothing for eternal life, because they know nothing of life. A man must have experience of life before he can hail with rapture the promise that that life shall be eternally his. What is life? Life in God is life. A vital conscious union of the soul with God through Christ; so that the individual is transferred to God; his body, his soul, his understanding, his affections, his desires, his purposes, all under the direction of God; not in such a way as to diminish in the least his individuality, his voluntariness; but to enhance it, refine it, perfect it; this is life. Now with regard to the mere life of the body, hardly any one has it in perfection; death and decay have set their marks on all. Of even the merely corporeal life of paradise, we have but a faint shadow. Similarly, with regard to those who have entered upon eternal life, spiritual life is with them a matter of degree; one has it in one degree, one in another; but who has it in perfection? According to the degree in which we possess it, does the simple promise of eternal life seem to us a sufficient dowry; a talisman under the influence of which deserts are no longer deserts to us, privations no longer privations.

Eternal life and all things essentially conducive to it; such is our portion. Sometimes Satan may creep into our imagination and persuade us that some bright and beautiful phantom, some lovely creation wrought out of the stuff that rainbows are made of, is absolutely necessary to the web of our eternal life, and then we cling to it with something of the tenacity of our love to Christ; Satan laughs, but we awake in spite of him, and notwithstanding the scar at heart, soon satiate ourselves with that better portion, now better understood. God builds the bridge by which we pass into the unclouded region of eternal life, stone by stone, as we step by step advance; every day he lays down the stone on which we are that day to put our foot. Some beholding the far-stretching morass before them and discerning no bridge, refuse to advance; they wait for God; but God has put down a stone for them, and will add no other until they have begun to walk.

NOVEMBER 23.—" Thy people shall be willing in the day of thy power." Psalm cx. 3.

Voluntarily, heartily following thy banners; volunteering to yield their substance, to forsake their hearths, to fight the good fight of faith. In that day there will be no constraint or distraint; no legal enactments to maintain a ministry; no political alliance, no dependance on the state. The willingness of Christ's people will afford all the scope that is requisite for the manifestation of Christ's power. Then shall be heard a loud voice exclaiming, " Now is come salvation, and strength, and the kingdom of our God, and the power of his Christ." The great dragon, that old serpent, is cast out, when there is no longer aught intermediate between Christ and his people: when his servants are willing to recognize him as their own Master.

Oh, reader! Brother or sister, hast thou anything of the spirit that animated Isaiah in the hour when he said, " Here am I, send me?" How few there are that have wills like the will of Christ. How difficult it is to find a workman for Christ when the work is at all difficult. How long must we advertise for a missionary to go out into the highways and hedges, that he may constrain men to come in. But when the work is of a less trying character, the emoluments greater, how many candidates we have. Oh, what an unwilling age it is, with all its boasted piety. All the world's promises must be mingled with the promises of Christ, in order to induce Christians, what we call Christians, to do some special work for Christ. Christ and the king must go into partnership, then men will enlist under the banners that are called by kingly courtesy the banners of Christ. Oh, the dread blindness that has fallen upon us all. When, oh, when shall there be found a willing people for Christ? Men that shall say with Paul, "I do this thing willingly," and give proof of what they say? A Church voluntarily contributing, laboring, preaching, abstaining, and in a word, accomplishing all the functions of a Church, unconstrained, and purely because Christ wills it?

NOVEMBER 24.—**"His truth shall be thy shield and buckler."—Psalm xci. 4.**

When the adversary heard, by the waters of Jordan, a voice from heaven exclaiming, "This is my beloved Son in whom I am well pleased," he started like one who suddenly discovers a hostile army in the heart of his dominions. Fast he followed him on whom the Lord had lain help, followed him to the wilderness, and rained upon him those missiles by which he had conquered in ten thousand battles. He said to himself no doubt, "Adam was the Son of God and bore the image of God; was I not victorious over him? Who is this that cometh down from God out of heaven? and what is his armor?" His armor was simply the word of God. This was his shield and buckler; and all the fiery darts of the adversary were hurled in vain. The shield by which Christ came victorious out of his combats with the prince of the power of the air, he took not away with him to heaven, but left for his people. Satan gnashes his teeth when he sees it in the hand of some puny stripling, a candidate for heaven; for it tells him of maddening defeats sustained by him of old. Yes, thou little one, thou hast a buckler of amazing virtue! If the shield of Achilles was sung by Homer, who shall sing the praises of thy shield?

This shield has strange properties. It is only against the adversaries of the Lord that it is of any avail. It is only a follower of Christ that can lift it. It is only while one walks in the appointed path that he can lift it; let him turn to the right hand or the left, and immediately it becomes heavy as iron. What a sad spectacle to see a poor deluded being dragging it after him with all his might. Instead of a shield it is to him a fearful incumbrance. Not there, not there, my friend! Come to the king's highway; then will it be to you a shield indeed!

NOVEMBER 25.—"O grave, where is thy victory?"—1 Corinthians xv. 55.

In great cities we find monumental arches, columns, obelisks and tablets, telling of victories won by man over man; but death writes his name loftily on all these, saying, "Man's victories are my victories." But the monumental trophies of death are found in all cities great and small, in all places, in fact. Death lords it everywhere and over all. Scarcely has humanity begun to put on nobility or virtue in any quarter, before death appears and sweeps away the excellent object, terrifying the stricken admirers with the display of its prodigious power.

Yet we make bold to say, "Where is thy victory, O grave? Where, O death, thy sting?" We tell death to the face that the captives whom he has apparently taken are not to be found in his chambers. In fact we can point to them in mansions where death has no admission. We can show the Son of God, once dead on Calvary, standing at the right hand of the Majesty on high. And with him the saints redeemed from the earth, the noble, the beautiful, the virtuous, dwelling in habitations not made with hands, clothed in purity, exempt from pain and sorrow, and not at all despondent because of their mortal remains sleeping in dust. How art thou become a picture of confusion, O death, standing there with a crumbling bone in thy hand and looking at a celestial being walking amid the groves of the New Jerusalem, once connected with earthly life by that bone, now wearing many crowns of perfection bestowed by him who died and rose again! After having conquered all, behold, thou art thyself conquered, and a new inviolable life given to those who once succumbed to thee. Behold the keys of death and hades are in the hands of our Lord; and what wonder if hereafter thou shouldst be compelled to restore even the dust of the once dead. Sweep as thou wilt with thy scythe from pole to pole; there is a sword impending over thee. Thou thyself shalt die. What canst thou do to him whose life is hid with Christ in God? He will sit upon a throne in the day when thou shalt be driven to darkness.

NOVEMBER 26.—"Them also who sleep in Jesus, will God bring with him."—1 Thessalonians iv. 14.

The Jews who gnashed with their teeth on Stephen, hurried him forth without the walls of Jerusalem, and stoned him to death with a fury like that with which they had crucified his master and forerunner, would have been confounded to learn that the stoned Stephen was after all not dead, but sleeping a heavenly and exquisite sleep. They will see him when he awakes; when he comes forth again, his spirit from the chambers of the skies, his dust from the chambers of earth; when Stephen, with his face shining indeed like that of an angel, cometh with the thousands of saints and with the king of saints. This sleep of the righteous is simply with reference to this world; they are disrobed for a season from this visible scene; they are in a slumber so that we cannot hold converse with them. Their awakening has also reference to this earth; they are to come again with powers sublimely recruited. But while asleep with reference to us, they are awake with reference to heaven. They are with the spirits of just men made perfect.

The advent we look for is the advent of all the good. We look back to them in history; we look forward to them in prophecy. Their advent will be a baptism of fire for this earth. Heaven will come with them. The throne of God with them; Christ with them. Shall we be there? When the Lamb's book of life is opened, shall our names be read off? If we now live in Jesus, we shall sleep in Jesus, and afterwards appear with him in glory.

NOVEMBER 27.—"I am he that liveth and was dead."—Revelation i. 18.

Yes Lord, the fact of thy death is an inextinguishable fact. Nothing is more impossible, more inconceivable, than that the prints of the nails should be effaced from thy hand, the memory of thy agony from thy heart or from thy Father's heart, the chants of angels and redeemed ones die out and leave no echo in heaven. The story of the cross has indeed inwoven itself with all existences; the whole universe has bathed in it and got a richer life. Thy death is the expression of divine love to me; and I have consequently a most profound interest in the memorials of that death. Thy cross does not merely tell of God, but of me; of God's love to me; and when thou sayest, "I am alive for evermore," that is the same as saying, God's love for me liveth for evermore. God and I live together in thee. The story of the cross is the story of me; it is my name and my magnificent destinies that are inwoven with all existences, mentioned in all chants of heaven. There is not an angel of heaven that would venture to remain ignorant of me. For, Christ tasted death for me.

November 28.—"My mercy will I keep for him for evermore."—Psalm lxxxix. 28.

Ever bestowed, never exhausted. The vessel that contains it is one that can never be emptied. God himself is a vessel of mercy to communicate mercy to me; and I am a vessel of mercy to receive that mercy. To say that God will keep mercy is to say that God will keep himself. There is mercy in him; and I am its object. Mercy first makes me an appropriate object for itself, and ever after keeps me so. I can say to my soul, "Soul, thou hast much goods laid up for many years: laid up too in a granary safer than any granary of earth; enough for thy wants in time and in eternity; eat, drink, and take thine ease. Eat the food of angels; drink the water of life; experience the true rest of the soul in Christ."

November 29.—"The Lord hath set apart him that is godly for himself."—Psalm iv. 3.

Set him apart by making him godly; teaching him to set his affections upon things above; to hunger and thirst after righteousness; to count all things worthless in comparison with the excellency of the knowledge of Christ; to meditate day and night in God's word; to cultivate a prayerful habit of mind; to delight in the society of the people of God; and to hold all personal interests of trivial moment in comparison with the interests of the Gospel, the extension of Christ's kingdom, the salvation of souls. Take a worldly man in the midst of worldly companions; with them seeking now pleasure, now wealth, now renown; with them despising the Bible and the men that reverence it. Let now an arrow from the quiver of the Almighty, an arrow dipped in the blood of the Lamb, wing its way to his heart. Suddenly a mighty revolution is wrought in that heart. Repentance creates a perfect anarchy, and faith erects the throne of God; he is now a new man, a godly man.

He begins with joy to relate his new experiences to his companions; they listen with amazement; draw off to a little distance to see if the fit will pass; and when they find him a veritable believer, an enthusiastic and incurable servant of Christ, they flee far from him as though he were a leper. It is not that he is alienated from them, that he takes no longer an interest in them; he takes, it is likely, a deeper interest in them than ever he did before; but his new feelings, aims, tastes are such as they cannot at all sympathize with. Thus he is set apart.

But he is set apart *for the Lord*. For the Lord to bless. To receive the manifestations of God. To understand the designs of God. To be comforted by the promises of God. To be the servant of God, his witness, his steward, his son. To declare the Gospel. To be the depository of the Holy Spirit. To suffer. To be poor in spirit. To search the word. To run the race of glory. To come off conqueror. To inherit all things.

Perhaps, O reader, you are not thus set apart. You are at home in the world, and the world is at home with you. You are of it. There is nothing that jars in your intercourse with it. And perhaps you know of some one that is set apart from you and your world. You feel that there is a wall betwixt him and you, a high impracticable wall. What he loves, you cannot love; what he beholds, you care not to behold; what he disdains, you value; and what he flees from, you allow. You know that he was not always thus; and there is something deep within you testifying that nothing less than a divine power has wrought this change. Now if God hath set him apart for himself, what is your condition? He has been taken and you have been left. He has been taken for God; you have been left for Satan. He has been taken for mercy, you have been left for wrath. The ark has received him, the deluge awaits you. He has been sealed with the seal of God; the destroying angel will pass by him and speed to you on whose forehead is not seen the name of God.

NOVEMBER 30.—"The peace of God which passeth all understanding." —Philippians iv. 7.

It is possible that by the peace of God is here meant the friendship, the amity of God. To get anything like a conception of the peace of God, it is needful to know the barrier of enmity once existing between you and God. We may view the barrier which you erected around yourself to hinder God from approaching you, to exclude his messengers, his word, the voice of his providence, his law, his summons to judgment, every remembrancer of him. Or, we may contemplate the tremendous rampart, higher than the highest heaven, deeper than the lowest hell, built by the perfections of God around his inviolable majesty, forbidding every transgressor even to look upon him; of which not the combined force of all angels within, or of all devils without, would ever have removed one stone. But this mighty middle wall of partition, Christ, designated the Breaker, hath pierced with gateways, adorned with gates of pearl; and every several stone, once breathing defiance, is now made transparent for the smile of God to come through to you, and for the vision of your everlasting inheritance to stream upon you. Truly such a peace as this absolute peace between the most Holy One and you, a once rebellious worm, passeth understanding. This amity is not a merely negative thing, not merely the removal of wrath. This peace of God is like music. Harmony is the perfection of sound, not the absence of sound. The return to the soul of God, in peace, leads at once to an ineffable discourse, a melodious commerce of the two spirits finite and infinite. And not only so; but this peace begets another peace (if it be another) between the various souls thus reconciled to God. They are so brought together in harmony that a marvellous correspondence of love spontaneously commences. Separated formerly by a multitude of individual interests, they now love one another in fervor and purity. There is a harmony in the different powers and appetites of the individual soul. There is peace within; peace with God, peace with the people of God. This spiritual music beginning at the throne of God and flowing through all godly souls in heaven and in earth, and returning to the great source again, is by the unreconciled unheard, unsuspected; it passeth understanding.

DECEMBER 1.—"The eyes of the Lord are over the righteous, and his ears are open unto their prayers."—1 Peter iii. 12.

This is a truth quite distinct from that of the omniscience of God. That God should be omniscient is one thing; that his omniscience should be for me, is another thing. Yes, it is a sublime proposition that omniscience and omnipotence should enter into everlasting alliance with the weakness and blindness of a creature. The righteous ones here spoken of are they that fling away their own righteousness as dross, and make themselves very insignificant. It is not because they are wise that heavenly wisdom wings its way to them; not because they are good and strong that divine goodness and power are their perpetual auxiliaries. You need not envy them the attention they receive from the King of kings; they would never have been noticed by him if they had had any such righteousness as you boast of.

How hard it is for you to see what is the true life divinely appointed for man and hastily relinquished by him. Man's perfection is something utterly different from what man considers it to be. Man goes on building himself up in goodness. He expects or aims to carry his edifice to the skies. A little more and I shall be there, he says as often as he puts down one new stone. He does not take note that the heavens are rising above him. Though a thousand giants should undertake to help with his tower, and should carry it to the height of a mile, would he be any nearer the heavens? Mount Blanc would look down in pity and tell him of the moon a quarter of a million of miles high. The moon would look down in pity and tell him of the sun a hundred millions of miles high. The sun would look down in pity and tell him of Saturn a thousand millions away. And Saturn would say, "We are in the lowest depths of the heavens. Ascend to us and your elevation will be, in comparison with the starry heavens, as the tiniest ant-hill in comparison with Chimborazo." For six thousand years humanity has been possessed by this mad dream of a perfection starting from earth and growing up into the heavens. It is a forlorn error. No, the perfection of humanity is in giving way to God. Cast down, cast down that paltry edifice; give up the notion of your own independent goodness; and make room for the goodness of God in you. Let God work in you to will and to do of his good pleasure. And think not that this self-renunciation is death; it is the true life; the life of God in the soul is life indeed; the energy of God is energy indeed; and the moral beauty of God is moral beauty indeed.

DECEMBER 2.—"Heaven and earth shall pass away, but my words shall not pass away."—Matthew xxiv. 35.

On the day when these words were spoken, had it been announced in Rome that there was one then speaking whose words would never pass away, some would have said, "It must be the Emperor, his words will outlive all." Others would have fixed upon a certain historian; others upon an orator; others upon a poet. But no one would have conceived that a despised Galilean seated upon a hill opposite Jerusalem, and conversing with his disciples, was speaking words that would outlive all others. The speaker died by the hands of men; he passed away from earth; but his words have been living in the world with a most tremendous life from that day to this. They smote Judaism; they went forth and assailed all religions of the earth; they returned and overthrew Jerusalem; they wrestled with Rome in her pride and overcame her; the mightiest systems fled from before them; they made the wilderness to blossom as the rose. After the lapse of eighteen centuries our report is this, that every day eight thousand copies of the Scriptures, the testimony of Jesus, are added to the many millions already existing in hundreds of languages.

Especially, had the philosophers of Athens and of Rome heard the words of which this immortality and universal victory were predicted, would they have deemed their fulfilment incredible. That he should be crucified and his doctrine be none the less promulgated; that his disciples should be hated of all men, yet should none the less spend their time and strength in preaching his gospel; that the Jews should be carried captive into all lands; and a multitude of other things of equally improbable realization, were distinctly foretold by him.

What a wonderful thing that we should be in the world along with these all-conquering words. A legion of angels would not effect such changes in the successive generations of men, as these words of the Lord Jesus. We have something that will outlive the heavens and the earth, and will judge us, you and me, in the last day.

DECEMBER 3.—"He that believeth not is condemned already."—John iii. 18.

He has pronounced his own condemnation. Christ is the test of all men and of all things. Every man that hears of Christ, discovers the outline of his character, gets a vision of his voluntary suffering, and death, and glorious resurrection, and unchanging love, and yet believes not on him, every such man declares himself to be unworthy of everlasting life. There is no affinity between him and Christ, and it is easily calculated, therefore, what are his true affinities. There is no need for him to perpetrate any signal act of infamy in order to bring down condemnation on himself. God has drawn nigh to him in the person of the Son; and, before the essential perfections of deity, this man has not bowed the knee. When Christ appears in glory, of course every knee shall bow; but in the case of many this tardy homage will be no homage. It is not because of his dazzling glory and irresistible sovereignty that God claims to be honored and adored; but because of his moral excellencies, because of the attributes that were revealed upon the cross.

DECEMBER 4.—"Unto the upright there ariseth light in the darkness." —Psalm cxii. 4.

There was thick darkness no doubt in the den where Daniel lay; in the dungeon where Paul and Silas sat; and in the living prison where Jonah was confined. There is no light s beautiful, so precious as that which ariseth to make glad the countenance of the righteous as he gropes in darkness. He says, "It is well for me that I have had experience of the darkness that I might be enraptured with the light." Before the light ariseth, there must be a victory of faith in his soul. He must acquiesce in the darkness for the sake of him that sent it. He must say, "This is the proper place, the proper condition for me." He must wrap his calamity about him like a cloak, because of him who hath sent it. Thus a day-star arises in his heart; after that the day breaks for him. If the light that is in you be darkness how great is that darkness. The Holy Ghost lighteth up a light within you, whose mild radiance will go far to dissipate your surrounding darkness.

If you muffle up this inner lantern, in vain will you wait for light to arise externally upon your path.

DECEMBER 5.—"They that be wise shall shine as the brightness of the firmament, and they that turn many to righteousness, as the stars forever and ever."—Daniel xii. 3.

If we could look into the books of immortality, and turn over its pages of the future, and trace the paths of light belonging to the names that are now ascendant in our skies, we should see them to be of length unequal: one brilliant luminary of our day soon vanishing into night, and another passing on, but sooner or later, like all the rest disappearing from the heaven of fame. But when the lights of this world shall have gone out, then will be seen coming up in indescribable splendor and overwhelming glory, the names that have nothing now connected with them but ignominy and obscurity. Then will it be known who are the wise; and men will marvel that they should have ever remained ignorant a single moment of this unquestionable truth, that they who turn many to righteousness are wise above all others.

DECEMBER 6.—"The Lord loveth judgment and forsaketh not his saints." Psalm xxxvii. 28.

The faithfulness of the Lord to his people is secured not more by the fact that he delighteth in mercy than by the fact that he loveth judgment. The propitiation made for sin is so effectual that by it all the perfections of God become pledged to promote the everlasting interests of those who believe. It is God in the unlimited fulness of his nature, not a part of God, that is made favorable to the sinner by the blood of Jesus The believer should understand that he is not taking refuge in one perfection of God against another; but that it is God himself, with all his attributes, that is reconciled to him. Before he was clothed with the righteousness of Christ, every divine attribute was against him; love as well as justice. And after he is brought nigh through the blood of the Lamb, the justice as well as love of God guarantees his safety and blessedness.

Consider and confess: dost thou not feel, speak and act, in thy intercourse with God, as though there were but a partial reconciliation, as though in Christ there had accrued to thee but a small measure of the divine benignity? Does it not seem to thee when thou wouldst appropriate largely of the grace of God, as though his justice interposed and said, "Enough?" Does not the holiness of God, in thy conception, take out from every promise its largest benison and give thee a husk? If so, then there is a grievous wrong continually done by thee to the Lamb that was slain, and to every perfection of God. Is God divided? Did Christ die to obtain for thee the crumbs that fall from his Father's table, and is it necessary that another Christ should die to obtain for thee permission to sit down as a guest, as a child?

If there be in us a genuine faith in Christ, then is God wholly ours. Christ himself has not a more infinite love to expatiate in than the meanest believer hath. God is reconciled to us, or he is not. If reconciled, then every promise is ours in its utmost conceivable amplitude. We are as free to take of the water of life as Paul was, or as John was. One disciple is designated "the beloved" because he has a singular faith. We must believe the love that God hath towards us, and then we have the love.

There are many who wonder that they experience in such feeble measure the power of divine truth to animate and elevate and bless their souls. They marvel that they should daily be in communion with him at whose right hand are pleasures for evermore, with whom is the fountain of life, yet that they should be so unacquainted with the joy unspeakable that many saints have experienced. But how could it be otherwise? Unbelief nullifies God. Faith finds a living God. God gives himself as faith gives itself. Where there is but a little faith, the tide of divine love is constrained to narrow itself down accordingly. But God is there, even the same God whose smile enraptures the seraphim. Christ has brought you to him and to the infinite fulness of his nature. God is not in your future; he is in your present. Listen no longer to the lie of unbelief, but understand that there is even now for you, this day, this hour, the love wherewith the Father loved Christ. You have not a half Christ; you have not a portion of God.

DECEMBER 7.—"The steps of a good man are ordered by the Lord, and he delighteth in his way."—Psalm xxxvii. 23.

A good man is one whose steps are ordered by the Lord. Having come to the conclusion that there is none good but God, he has sought such an alliance with God as secures to him the benefit of the divine goodness. A good man is one in whom you can behold the goodness of the Lord. To the world's apprehension a good man is one who is able to order his steps aright, able of himself to know and to pursue the best path. This is a fundamental error; and religion can only begin with its overthrow.

God has a book in which is written the ideal history of every man; the biography as it would have been had the man's steps been ordered by the Lord; and another in which is written the actual history of every man. The books are open side by side, and what a contrast do they present. "Oh that they had hearkened to my commandments!" saith the Lord; nor is it possible for any one to look upon these two records without taking up the lamentation. What a hallowed and beautiful path is traced in the one; what honorable conflicts and glorious victories; what nobleness of enterprise, what steadfastness under difficulties, what beneficence, what usefulness! What a sublime romance! What genuine heroism! What a utilization of the man's faculties! What wealth of influence poured around! In comparison with this divine romance, behold the actual life portrayed in the other book. How mean! how contemptible! how disordered! What fearful confusion! What awful plunges into vanity! What wild pursuit of phantoms! What Herculean strife with windmills! What a waste of faculties! What blundering even in the matter of doing good! What shipwreck of unpiloted affections! What torment of unintelligible aspirations!

Suppose the book of your ideal biography should drop from heaven upon your path. You, with your worldly and gross heart, take it up and look into it; at first seeing a good deal about tribulation, privation, persecution, bonds, defamation, poverty, and tears, you are ready to throw it away. But stay, my friend; it is from heaven; see if there be not something precious coupled with these expressions. At one end of a sentence you find, "they that mourn," "poor in spirit," "they that are persecuted," "through much tribulation;" but what at the other end? "Joy," "blessedness," "kingdom of heaven." Remember the disordered steps of your past life. See how much misery you have experienced, even in the path of your own gratification. How unsatisfactory is the retrospect. Are you not willing to live the life that God has sketched for you? Take this book and live this life; and your biography will be a valuable contribution to the libraries of heaven. Angels will read it and find in it all the elements of beauty, nobleness, sublimity.

This your ideal life is written in the Gospel May God help you to see it there and to give it actuality in what remains of your mortal term.

DECEMBER 8.—"In the fear of the Lord is strong confidence, and his children shall have a place of refuge."—Proverbs xiv. 26.

The best thing that a man can do for his children, is to fear the Lord. Piety is not hereditary; but there is a strong probability that the children of a truly God-fearing man, will be converted and brought to make the Lord their refuge. Yet how many there are who make the alleged interests of their children a pretext for not giving themselves and all they have unreservedly to the Lord. They would lay up treasure in heaven, were it not that they must lay up for their children. Their faith is sadly defective. The very efforts they are making to secure a portion for their children in this life, tend to hinder the transmission of an everlasting portion to them.

A parent cannot possibly do anything better for his child than leave to him an example of simple and unworldly faith. Like Noah, build for your children an ark of safety of gopher wood, rather than a palace of brick and stone; haply the Lord may incline them to enter it. You cannot do better for your children than to show them that there is something in your heart more sacred than even the love of children; and that is the fear of the Lord. The example of faith is the best of legacies. See to it that as far as your labors are concerned, your children may have a place of refuge and the way to it be unimpeded.

DECEMBER 9.—"My people shall be satisfied with my goodness, saith the Lord."—Jeremiah xxxi. 14.

The Lord's people are satisfied with his goodness, even in this life, in such a sense that they willingly forsake all and follow him. In the privation of all other things they are still so satisfied with the love of their divine Saviour, that they cast no regretful looks behind. Ah, but there are some, esteemed the people of God, who seem not to be satisfied with the simple goodness of their heavenly Father: there is too manifest a grasping after the riches and dignities of the earth. Would that they and all might understand that if they only sought to know more of the love of God, they would see it to be satisfying.

We see how much wisdom was given to Paul when he was led to pray that he and others might know more of the length and breadth of the love of God, when he was enabled to count all but loss for the excellency of the knowledge of Christ. Of course it is impossible to be satisfied with the goodness of the Lord if we do not know that goodness. We must know and believe the love that God hath towards us. When a certain man had found a treasure in a field, he went with joy and sold all that he had and bought that field. The perception of Christ's love to them individually, is vague and dim on the part of many; and no wonder therefore that they are tormented with so many vain desires and imaginations. But this word "satisfied" points to something that eye hath not seen, nor ear heard, nor heart conceived. To be contented is a blessed and beautiful condition of the soul; but do not suppose that it implies the extinction of desire. Paul was a person of singular contentment, and of singular power of aspiration. But he that has provided for our contentment will in due time crown our highest aspirations. He has shown his power by overcoming the mighty craving of our soul for worldly good; and he will show his power hereafter by transcending our highest conception of happiness. But let contentment have her perfect work.

DECEMBER 10.—"Our Saviour Jesus Christ, who hath abolished death."—2 Timothy i. 10.

When Adam sinned then was there the abolition of life. The empire of death began. Death advanced by steps. There was a process observed in the establishment of his kingdom.

He needed subjects, and therefore he did not cause the bodies of Adam and Eve to crumble to dust at once. He showed what he could do when Abel fell by the hand of his brother. He made havoc of everything heavenly in the spiritual nature of man; brought out his instruments of torture to assail and overthrow his physical glory; and went forth conquering and to conquer. But Christ, who is the Life, in due time sets up his kingdom of life, abolishing death. What a glorious word for the confusion of the great abolisher!—he himself must be abolished.

Death was once between me and God. The king of terrors had pitched his throne in the very path, the only one, that led to God. There was an eclipse of God unto my soul. But Christ abolished death. The eclipse passed. The favor of God, which is life, reached me through him who had died that death might be crucified in him. Then contrition, hope, faith, love, obedience, and other tokens of the new creation appeared in me. The fear of death is abolished by him who hath prepared a place for me. And even this body will not die, no, not a hair of my head perish, if Christ refuse consent. The world to which we aspire is not an undiscovered country from whose bourne no tidings have been wafted back to us. We are conversant with it. There are continents on this globe about which we do not know so much as we do about that world. We are acquainted with many of its inhabitants and with the life they lead. We know their manners and customs, their laws and principles, their employments, their government; their tastes and distastes; their desires, and their songs.

DECEMBER 11.—"The cup which my Father hath given me, shall I not drink it?"—John xviii. 11.

Art thou unwilling, O believer, to drink the cup which thy Father giveth thee? It is a very different cup from that which the Saviour consented to drink for thee. It is wreathed around with the declaration, "All things shall work together for good to them that love God." It comes to thee by the hand of Jesus, the hand that was pierced for thee. In it you behold as in a transparency a crown of glory that fadeth not away, purchased for you by the Saviour's righteousness. He tha spared not his own Son for you, who was so tender of you as to suffer his Son to hang in your place, can you suspect him of offering you a cup of poison? What an unpardonable insult were this to offer to your heavenly Father! Yet just such insults are daily offered by those who reject the cup which their Father presents them, and steal away to some other path that they may not have to drink this cup.

To look upon an affliction as indicative of alienated feelings on the part of God, is base indeed for those who profess to believe the testimony of the cross. May not the Father and the Saviour be trusted to govern us, to guide us, correct us, bless us? Shall we teach them what our interests demand? Teach him who is Love, what is the way of love? Does the mother not know what the child can bear? You have been asking for precious things; for fruits of the Spirit; for love, joy, and peace; for knowledge, strength, and patience; for victory and glory; and the Lord presents you with a cup of humiliation and sorrow. Instead of enriching you with new hopes and joys he seems to come to you for the purpose of crushing and annihilating the few that you have. Nevertheless, for the Father's sake, in Christ's name, take the cup. Have you not agreed to surrender life's joys and treasures when he that gave them demands them again? What is the meaning of the faith you profess, but just this, that as you have let God choose for you a Saviour and a way of life, so you are to let him choose for you all your circumstances, all your experiences. Take the cup and drink it. Lo! one by one, the precious things you were demanding, are found to have been in the cup, and to have been communicated by means of it. So that the great and unendurable affliction from which you shrank, is ascertained at last to be the greatest of all your blessings, and to stand in the retrospect of your life a monument to the riches of divine grace, towering high above all the other monuments of your path.

May we have wisdom to choose the very cup which the Father chooseth for us. Balaam had not this; and entreated God to choose rather for him the cup which he, Balaam, desired for himself. Seeing that Balaam had more confidence in his own wisdom and discrimination than in God's, God at length suffered Balaam to have the cup of his own choice; and all know the melancholy results. And may there not be around us Christians whose cup is of their own choice rather than God's, who have taken the cup out of the left hand of God, and are living lives of worldly ease and dignity and affluence, felicitating themselves that they are exempt from so many bitternesses that once fell to the lot of Christians; and all because they had not wisdom to see a cup, preferred of God, in his right hand? The words "much tribulation" written over the gate of an avenue, almost of themselves carry conviction to the minds of many Christians that such an avenue is not the one that they are called to pursue. Are we of their number? Or of the number of those who have it profoundly engraved in their conviction that the will of the Lord, whatever its aspect, is the one path of life, and that the greatest of all calamities is when we get God to deal with us after our own wisdom, and to lead us in the pathway of our own crude desires?

December 12.—"The Lord is thy keeper."—Psalm cxxi. 5.

Thou art willing to be kept by him. Thou knowest thine own helplessness and ignorance; the power and malignity of the adversary; the sufficiency, love and faithfulness of the Lord Jesus Christ; the reality of the Spirit; thou distinguishest his still, small voice; the word of God is a lamp to thy feet; thou meditatest therein day and night; thou hast the shield of faith. Thou knowest the voice of thy keeper, and knowest not the voice of strangers. In prosperity, in adversity, and in the intervening lulls, thou dost equally seek the guidance and help of the good Shepherd. He is now thy keeper; and therefore it is certain that in that day of unutterable wrath which is so fast hastening to break upon the earth, he will keep thee in all serenity and security.

DECEMBER 13.—"For the same Lord over all is rich unto all that call upon him."—Romans x. 12.

There is a beautiful conception of the character of God involved in the use of the word "rich" in this connection. For he is said to be rich not in respect of what he has, but of what he bestows. Used of men the word indicates one to whom much has accrued; but it is used here of God to designate one from whom infinite wealth of blessing accrues to the sons of men. It is for us he is rich; his wealth is ours; we have a marvellous and inexhaustible treasury in him. God, in fact, proposes to take sinful men and make each of them a treasury full of the wealth of God.

He is rich unto all that call upon him. They call, and he answers by communications of his wealth. There is of course an agreement between God and them, as to what constitutes wealth. They have been taken into the divine laboratory, and have seen the various things called wealth in earth and in heaven, seen them subjected to powerful tests and their true nature revealed. What is called wealth among men has lost its value; for they have seen it tested by an infallible chemistry; and especially has the knowledge of heaven's wealth made them look disparagingly upon it. They have seen and appropriated the jasper of faith; the sapphire of love; the chalcedony of joy; the emerald of hope; the sardonyx of humility; the sardius of self-knowledge; the chrysolite of sincerity; the beryl of holiness; the topaz of contentment; the chrysoprasus of long-suffering; the jacinth of patience; the amethyst of self-denial. To the eye of an angel they have a breast-plate radiant with surpassing riches; though to man they may seem clothed in a wretched garb.

The same God is rich unto all. Oh, let us entertain no contracted view of the fulness of blessing that dwelleth in our reconciled God! Let us neither exclude ourselves, nor others. The God of Daniel, Paul, and John, that same God that was found so rich by them is ours, is yours, is mine. And that same God whom you approach, that same Saviour in whom you delight, is your neighbor's. Oh, what a bond should this create between you and him! The same love that fills you with such rapture is shed abroad in his heart; the same visions of a beatific hour to come are yours and his; the same sacred pierced hand that fills your cup each morning with the wine and milk of divine grace, fills his cup. Consider this; and beware how you look coldly on him on whose eye of faith the smile of Christ is ever breaking.

December 14.—"Blessed is he that considereth the poor."—Psalm xli. 1.

In other words, blessed is he that blesseth. Happy is he who makes it his chief concern to bestow happiness on others. Rich is he who seeks to enrich. "Consider thyself," says the world; "study the advancement of thy interests; for there is none to do thee good if thou neglect thy own good. Will men sell and buy for thee whilst thou art busied about the poor? Will they supply thy wardrobe if thou empty it for the poor?

Will they send medicines to thee and a physician, when thou forgettest thy health in solacing the miseries of others? Consider the poor, of course; but take good care that consideration for them do not swallow up or even encroach upon a due consideration of thyself, thy children, thy near of kin."

In opposition to all this, our text, like many others in the word of God, teaches us—if we suffer ourselves to be taught so strange a truth, so hard a lesson,—that he best considers himself who considers the poor rather than himself, and makes it his chief business in the world to communicate good unto his fellow-men. For the poor have a friend; even God the source of all good; and there is no more direct way to the heart of God than to alleviate the sufferings of our fellow-men, to deny ourselves for the good of others.

Consider the poor; give attention to them; study their necessities; wisely consult as to the best mode of alleviating them. Think not that attention is wasted when given to the poor, even if some important commercial speculation has to wait. What the word of God says in general, the providence of God says in particular. "Consider the poor," says the former; "consider this poor man," says the latter. Indiscriminate charity is not the thing here commended. The vocation of a Christian is to be a benefactor; and this being his vocation he is not to grudge any pains that may be required in order to ascertain who are the really needy, and what the most effectual way of relieving them.

There are some necessities which men do not mention because they do not feel. They know not their spiritual destitution; and they know not the bread of life which is profitable for this world and for that which is to come. The Christian is to consider the soul-penury of men, and tell them of the banquet of life which Christ has spread for them. In this view even the richest of our fellow-men are poor enough and need that we should consider them. Blessed is he that takes knowledge of the necessities of his fellow-men, and devotes himself to their alleviation. God will take knowledge of his necessities, and will see to it that he want no good thing.

DECEMBER 15.—"The Lord shall preserve thee from all evil."—Psalm cxxi. 7.

This is an invitation to thee to give over the keeping of thyself entirely into the Lord's hands. Let him be thy keeper and he will keep thee from all evil. That no harm ever befals the Christian, cannot be said. But while he follows that which is good, no harm befals him. While he suffers the Lord to guide him, he is preserved infallibly.

It is only by faith that we can appreciate the guidance of the Lord as being everything that an enlightened love could desire for us. When we have made ourselves over to the Lord and to his guidance, often the very things are suffered to come upon us which we would most certainly have characterized as evil. We are prepared for trials; but they come in a form that we should have thought to be impossible. We had formed some particular conception of the goodness of God; settled it in our minds that this goodness would prompt him to act in a certain way towards us; when lo, we find him acting in a quite contrary way; and it will go hard if the thought do not incontinently arise, that God is without the goodness we had imputed to him, and that our faith has overshot the limits of the reality. Oh, what a dishonoring thought! As though we, imbecile and infatuated worms, could invent a God superior to the God that really exists. But God in due time, if we pursue the way of faith, vindicates himself to us. Our minds are disabused of their vain fancies. We get a loftier conception of the goodness of God. A foundation is laid for experiences of a far more blessed kind than those of which we were disappointed.

DECEMBER 16.—"Ye shall seek me, and find me, when ye shall search for me with all your heart."—*Jeremiah* xxix. 13.

A reference to the context will show that this declaration is intended for those who are smarting under the chastisements of God; for those of his professing people who have brought upon themselves by disobedience and worldliness, the rebuke of the Most High. Out of the cloud there comes a voice telling of the blue sky beyond and of the way in which it may become visible. The blessings connected with the uplifted light of God's countenance are not to be recovered by those who have once enjoyed them, save by a whole-hearted, intense, persevering, all-sacrificing search for them.

It has pleased God at various times in the history of his Church, to bestow upon her some distinguishing tokens of his regard. Legitimately these should have had no other effect than to make her more humble, more self-mistrusting, more zealous, more earnest in the pursuit of perfection. But often a different result has been witnessed. She has plumed herself upon these as constituting a glory of her own; or she has rested satisfied with these, so as not to long for something better and more essential; or she made light of them as though there were nothing special about them. Then God has revoked the blessings, and left the Church to her denuded and inglorious state. Thenceforward, God is in no haste to bestow anew what has been so deliberately forfeited.

He is wonderful in the inflexibility with which he has carried out this principle. The distinct understanding of it would be of immense benefit to the Church and to each member of the Church. Search the annals of the Church. Bring the Church as she now is into contrast with the Church as she once was, and see how much she is without. Impute it not to the sovereignty of God, to an arbitrary and unexplained exercise of his royal will, that we languish now under many disabilities The privileges that have been withdrawn were lost through the gross and culpable negligence of the Church They are recoverable; for the promises relating to them have not been torn out of the Bible; but they are only to be recovered by a whole-hearted, fervent, and indomitable travail at the throne of grace, accompanied with a thorough consecration to his will. "If the salt have lost its savor, wherewith shall it be salted?" is a text that might utterly discourage us but let us lay hold of this kind and loving assurance: "Ye shall seek me, and find me, when ye shall search for me with all your heart."

DECEMBER 17.—"As the earth bringeth forth her bud, and as the garden causeth the things that are sown in it to spring forth; so the Lord God will cause righteousness and praise to spring forth before all the nations." —Isaiah lxi. 11.

Isaiah had a vision of the Lord upon his throne surrounded by the seraphim; and the seraphim seem to have had a vision of the renewed earth, of what it shall be in the day when the glory of Christ shall be everywhere perceived, and when there shall be the manifestation of the sons of God. We are yet but in the seed-time; but it is interesting to observe that the seed is carried to all shores and scattered among all nations, and that everything is fast hastening to the hour when, at the new creating voice of God, the kingdoms of the world shall become the kingdoms of our Lord and of his Christ, and when righteousness and praise shall fill the face of the whole earth. A nation shall be born in a day; the whole earth shall bring forth at once.

Were it not that men are accustomed to behold just such a transformation, nothing would seem more idle or preposterous than the expectation that beautiful and odoriferous and fruitful trees and shrubs, should spring from the earth as a result of the scattering of sundry seeds therein. How utterly unlikely to the eye of sense, or to the imperfect vision of infantile faith, does it appear that the preaching of the Gospel, the poor and checkered attempts to make known God's despised word of life, should ever eventuate in the imparadising of earth. Of itself it will not. God gives it an opportunity to show what it can itself do; and the hours of this protracted opportunity, how heavy, how almost insupportable to him who longs to behold the glory of God in the land of the living! But the coming of the Son of Man to inherit all nations, and extinguish all rule that is not of him, hath an absolute connection with the attempts of his people to preach the Gospel to every creature.

DECEMBER 18.—"Whither the forerunner is for us entered, even Jesus." Hebrews vi. 20.

We have an anchor of the soul, even hope; and that hope is within the veil, where Jesus is. With Jesus the hope of the believer hath soared from earth and made its home in the heaven of heavens; and the presence of our hope there is the pledge of our own future presence there. How flattering, delusive, treacherous, is earthly hope. What horrid wounds it inflicts upon the heart that it pretends to bless. How it spreads its imitation heavens around, even where deadly miasmas exhale. But when we escape the wiles of this enemy, and become acquainted with the hope that beams upon us from the loving eyes of him who is extended on the cross, then may we be glad with exceeding joy. Here is a hope that nothing can injure. It died in Christ only to live forever in a region where there is no death. Our hope ascended up with him and met with him a welcome from the angels. We are already anchored at the throne of God.

DECEMBER 19.—"The Lord shall be unto thee an everlasting light, and thy God thy glory."—Isaiah lx. 19.

There cometh a time when the hidden relations now existing

between the Church and her God, shall be altogether manifest; when the tabernacle of God shall be with men; when the Church shall be clear as the sun, fair as the moon, and terrible as an army with banners. She will possess not solely an inward glory in her purity and moral resemblance to her Redeemer, but the glory of God, even the heavenly glory that dazzles the seraphim, shall invest her with an inconceivable splendor. No longer in his humiliation and in discredited divinity will Christ dwell in the midst of his little flock, as when on the earth in his flesh. No longer discernible as now only by the power of the Spirit and by the eye of faith, he will then dwell among them in the glory which he had before the world was; nay, with an enhanced glory. They shall see his face and his name shall be in their foreheads. The sun himself shall have no glory by reason of the glory that excelleth, when mortality shall have been swallowed up in life, when Christ shall be glorified in his saints and admired in every one that believeth, when the righteous shall shine forth as the sun in the kingdom of their Father.

DECEMBER 20.—"I have set the Lord always before me."—Psalm xvi. 8.

The habit of mind that is here indicated is very important, very rare, and very hard to be attained. Every Christian no doubt perceives, though more distinctly at certain times than at others, how exceedingly desirable it is that he should have a continual consciousness of the presence of the Lord, and what a grievous loss he is sustaining all the time that his Spirit forgets to realize that presence. And if he could attain unto this sublime habit of the soul by any single impulse and concentrated effort, he would put forth the needed violence and take possession of this blessed kingdom. But habits are not acquired in this way even when the Spirit of God is the teacher. He is indeed a wondrous teacher, and is able to give a rapid acceleration to all the movements of the soul; and to accomplish in weeks what would be wonderful in threescore years or a thousand years. Therefore there need be no despair: but let us distinctly understand the way in which he works, in order that there may be co-operation on our part and not hindrance.

Let us have it fully impressed upon our minds that the life to which the Lord is calling us, is not a life of occasional communion, of interspersed prayer, of pious seasons, but a life of unbroken communication with God, of never-interrupted co-operation with Christ. "Without me ye can do nothing." "Whatsoever ye do in word or deed, do all to the glory of God." "Abide in me." "Lo, I am with you always." Besides so many declarations of the word, there is the continual testimony of our experience, the testimony of our many mistakes, and follies and embarrassments, assuring us that we can of our own selves do nothing. For what we do without the Lord we do disobediently; and this single fact stamps it with a certain measure of opprobrium, no matter how commendable it might seem from other points of view. On the other hand whatever we do with the Lord, has an everlasting value; it may be but the tying of a shoe-string, yet if it be done in faith and in an enlightened dependence, as in the very presence of the Lord, it has a value that no vicissitudes of time can ever destroy. The will of the Lord abideth forever; and whatever is done with a right reference to that will, is celestial in character, immortal in destiny.

Let us enthrone in our minds this great truth, that nothing whatever is insignificant when a relation between it and God is perceived. Life is profane because men choose that it shall be so, by disconnecting it from God; not because God has chosen that it be so. Christ lived a human life, and there were every day thousands of trifling secularities in that life, as you perhaps may designate them; but all was exalted, all was sacred, according to the judgment of heaven. And he that is filled with the fulness of God, he in whose heart Christ abideth by faith, is careful all the day long lest any little thing divorce him from his Lord. He sets the Lord always before him; he seeks to see ever the vision that Isaiah saw in the temple.

DECEMBER 21.—"I will pour my Spirit upon thy seed, and my blessing upon thine offspring."—Isaiah xliv. 3.

"Let little children come unto me," said Christ, and says it still. God delighteth in mercy; and delights in the hearts of little children because there is a greater readiness in them to receive his mercy than in adults. There are fewer hindrances; less to repel the Spirit of God; less of the world. The world is indeed there, and it develops itself with an astonishing rapidity; oh, then, how great the responsibility of those who have the direction of the young. How knowest thou, O parent, but that the Lord has called thee to the knowledge of the truth very specially for this end, that thou mightest lend thyself to the Spirit of God in the matter of educating that child for the courts of the New Jerusalem.

There is no need that any truth should be deposited in the mind of the child before religious truth. In fact, truth is mutilated when it is taken away from religion. The truths of religion are difficult and mysterious to the man, because he started in life and passed through infancy and childhood without them. It is easier for a child to learn the momentous truth that "of Him, through him, and to him are all things," than it is for a person of mature years. How much unfaithfulness must there be in parents and guardians, even in those whom we esteem believers, when their children exhibit so little of the Spirit's influences. The blessing of the Lord, as we learn from other passages of Scripture, allies itself with the teachings and efforts and prayers of parents

With the influences of the parent there are soon commingled a multitude of other influences; wherefore it is of the more urgency, that the tenderest years should be improved. The enemy will quickly sow tares, if you do not pre-occupy the soil with the seed of life.

DECEMBER 22.—"Let all flesh bless his holy name forever."—Psalm cxlv. 21.

There is such a revelation of the holiness of God in all places of his dominion, that it is the manifest duty of all men to look to him alone and to give thanks at the remembrance of his holiness. For he is righteous in all his ways and holy in all his works, and not merely in the work of man's redemption. There is no idolater who is not compassed about by the tokens of the unity and holiness of God. God does not lay aside any of his perfections when he works his wondrous will in heathen lands. He is what he is, in every act that he does. And every one is responsible for failing to discern his true nature.

But it was especially perhaps in view of the Gospel of God's infinite grace, to be proclaimed by every creature, that the Psalmist calls upon the whole human family to bless the holy name of God. Let all flesh bless the holy name of him who so loved the world as to give his only begotten Son, that whosoever believeth might live. But even this sufficeth not. Men hear of this love unmoved. The Gospel is proclaimed, yet the empire of the God of this world continues. There is more in God's scheme of mercy to mankind. The Spirit shall be poured upon all flesh; then shall all bless his holy name forever.

"Hallowed be thy name, thy kingdom come, thy will be done on earth as it is in heaven;" these are the petitions that break instinctively from the lips of the believer. We see that the men of God, the prophets that lived so long before the days of Christ, had already a missionary spirit, and offered up prayers in behalf of missions while yet the middle wall of partition stood strong and consolidated.

DECEMBER 23.—"Let the wicked forsake his way and the unrighteous man his thoughts, and let him return unto the Lord."—*Isaiah* lv. 7.

The following reason is assigned, why he should forsake his ways and thoughts:—"For my thoughts are not your thoughts, neither are your ways my ways. For as the heavens are higher than the earth, so are my ways higher than your ways, and my thoughts than your thoughts." Man will have it that his way, his designs, his plans, his theory of life, are better than those of God. God's scheme of human life is published everywhere and brought before the notice of all; but all disdain it; they do not consider it any improvement upon their own. The way of righteousness, of self-denial, of faith, has no attraction for them.

But really the way that God has marked out for man is in every respect sublime and worthy of its author; and if man had walked therein he would have been angelic in dignity, wisdom, power and happiness. The intention of God regarding man includes his investiture with every grace and perfection. The thought of God is that man should set his affection on things above; take up his cross and follow Christ with all love and loyalty; and be, each one in his particular province, a benefactor to mankind. Alongside of this most elevated yet most suitable standard, how mean and grovelling appear the actual ways of men, how base and earthly their thoughts. For so many thousands of years they have gone floundering on in the mad quest of happiness, obstinately seeking it where God has told them they shall find nothing but misery. The wonder is that God should invite them to return; that instead of leaving them to the fruits of their own choice he should provide for them a way whereby they may regain the highway of holiness

---

DECEMBER 24.—"Lord Jesus, receive my spirit."—Acts vii. 59.

Christ, on the cross, out of the deep gulf of woe into which, by the sins of the world, he found himself sinking, cried out in anguish, "My God, my God, why hast thou forsaken me?" and, receiving strength in his soul, he soon exclaimed with expiring breath, "Father, into thy hands I commend my spirit." He tasted death; tasted far more of it than the believer is called to do; and knew the blessedness of having one to look to in his expiring hour. Well knows he therefore how precious it is to have an almighty friend in the darkness of such an hour. The believer may look with unwavering confidence, as always, so in his last earthly moments, to him who knows so well what death is.

Imagine a company of men pursuing another, reviling him, stoning him, and driving him towards a frightful cavern. Amidst their imprecations he enters it; and as a stone is rolled upon the mouth of the cave, his enemies rejoice greatly in their victory. You shudder as you think of the wretched lot of that castaway. But know that in the very moment when that stone was rolled upon the cavern's mouth, a marvellous transformation took place. The cavern became a palace; a multitude of happy and radiant beings flocked around your persecuted friend, and leading him up flights of noble stairways conducted him to a throne and crowned him with a diadem. The crowd without are congratulating themselves upon having driven the object of their hatred into everlasting night and solitude; how surprised will they be hereafter, should the stone and the rock flee away and the hated one be seen upon a throne surrounded by a troop of exalted friends.

God is constructing paradise out of the rejected elements of this world. Christ first; then they that believe in him and suffer with him. They are in the estimation of men, the refuse of humanity. Not only when Stephen died, but on a thousand occasions since, the rejoicings of men in the death of the saints have been heard on the one side, and on the other side the glad acclamations of the angelic host welcoming them to glory, honor, and immortality.

DECEMBER 25.—"Unto us a child is born, unto us a son is given: and his name shall be called Wonderful."—Isaiah ix. 6.

At the very outset, the mother of mankind was informed that she was also to be the mother of some wondrous being who would snatch the race from the condition incurred by sin. Prophet after prophet arose, spoke of this future personage, sighed for his advent and passed away. How astonished must the Hebrew readers of Isaiah have been at the description given by him of the coming man. A child, a son of man; given to us and of us; yet so wonderful in his nature that you may ascribe to him all the perfections of the godhead. We know that God will not give his glory to another; this child of humanity is then no other than God himself, the mighty God, the Father of Ages.

Here is something that never would have entered into the conception of any man, even the wisest or the boldest. But supposing that men, having been led to look for such an incredible event as the birth of God in the line of fallen man, had undertaken to surmise what would be his manner of life on the earth, how different would all their fantasies have been from the reality. They would have made the deity overshadow the humanity, so that there would be no proper manifestation of this. But the humanity of Christ remains in its integrity, and there is a perfect revelation of the two natures without the least encroachment of the one upon the other. And in him we see how this humanity of ours may become wedded to divinity so that the latter may be exhibited through the medium of the former, and in ten thousand acts and words there be an uncommingled operation both of God and of the creature. "That they also may be one in us, as thou Father art in me, and I in thee."

DECEMBER 26.—"He hath sent me to bind up the broken-hearted."—Isaiah lxi. 1.

Happy is he whose heart is broken in such a sense that he will no longer expect from earth what earth cannot give, and who is in despair of all below the sky. Yes; though he may esteem himself the most wretched of beings, and though he indeed have sorrows far more poignant than those of other men. Other men do not discover their true misery, their true bankruptcy, and do not so intensely feel their need of a special provision sent from the throne of God. They are reconciled to the sterilities of the world. But this one is broken-hearted because he found as he imagined some heaven, in contrast with which the wilderness condition of the world came out very distinctly; and when his oasis vanished he found himself un utterably and hopelessly ruined. So he thought: until he heard a voice saying, "If any man thirst let him come unto me and drink. Come unto me all ye that labor and are heavy-laden, and I will give you rest." Why will ye die? Is there no balm in Gilead? No physician of the soul? No fountain opened? Christ's heart was broken, that yours might he bound up.

DECEMBER 27.—"He was numbered with the transgressors."—Isaiah liii. 12.

That glorious being whom Isaiah saw upon a throne, high and lifted up, surrounded by the enraptured seraphim, left his throne at a time appointed and taking the form of man came into this every-day world of ours and dwelt among us. What was his reception? Did not every knee bow and every tongue confess that he was Lord? If he had come in power and in majesty, with undeniable and irresistible glory, such a reception perhaps would have awaited him. Men would have fallen before him and given him at least external homage. But this was not what he sought. His moral attributes are his true glory. It is in his truth, wisdom, goodness, purity, and condescension that he is distinguished from the gods of the heathen, rather than in omnipotence and omniscience. These are not so much attributes of his character as of his position. He would be served not because he is all-mighty, but because he is good, holy, and condescending. Therefore he came into the world in a manner that permitted the fullest manifestation of his character; and if his power and majesty were in some measure veiled, it was in order that there might be a more perfect revelation of his moral perfections. There was then seen in the family of man one being in whom dwelt all the fulness of the Godhead.

Tell us now, what was his reception? He was numbered among the transgressors. Instead of saying, "Here is a being of wondrous excellence, angelic in purity, heavenly in nature;" instead of saying even, "Here is a good man;" men said unhesitatingly and unblushingly, "This is a bad man; one with whom we cannot associate; an impious being, violating the most sacred laws; blaspheming the most holy things; profaning the Sabbath; consorting with the vile; overthrowing the faith of many; a dangerous man, a transgressor of the deepest dye, one that must be hunted from the bosom of society, one that must be as soon as possible sent out of this world." Yes, they decided that any other man, though he were a Barabbas, might live; on any other man the sun might shine, the wind might blow, the ordinary bounties of heaven descend; but upon this one, never; the earth cannot bear the burden of him. However contemptible an opinion a man may have had of himself, yet could he loudly and passionately cry, "Away with this Jesus, crucify him, it is not fit that he should live where I live!"

Thus the world was tried; thus its bitter and inveterate hostility to God was detected, thus did it become manifest that Satar was the god of this world. And are things altered? No! Those who rejected Christ had no special venom in their hearts. They were average specimens of humanity. In whatever generation Christ's lowly advent might have taken place, he would have been numbered among the transgressors. Those that make the nearest approach to him in character, those that live godly in Christ Jesus, they suffer persecution, they are reckoned as flagrant transgressors. In fact every generation has had the opportunity given, and has had it not in vain, to show what it thought of Christ. Oh, what a fearful exhibition of the corruption and blindness of man is given in the statement that God came into the world, and was numbered with the transgressors and put to a shameful death!

DECEMBER 28.—"So shall my word be that goeth forth out of my mouth; it shall not return unto me void."—Isaiah lv. 11.

A vast deal of rain falls upon the sea; a great deal upon the desert; upon immense tracts of earth where there is no cultivation; it is in fact but a comparatively small part of the snow and rain that yearly descend from the skies, that is made instrumental in the fertilization of the earth. Yet who will say that the rain and snow descend in vain? In many regions yet unvisited, the rain that periodically falls is an invitation to man to go forth and fulfil his mission, to subdue the earth, to co-operate with the providential processes of God in making the wilderness to blossom as the rose, and to plant groves of myrtle trees where briars and thorns now abound. If men choose to congregate in immense numbers in the narrow con fines of cities, leaving the earth unsubdued and unreplenished, at least God will show that he is not wanting to the earth. The responsibility of most of the desolations of earth, is with man.

It is not to be denied that God's word is abundantly proclaimed without saving results. Out of a thousand hearers one is affected; and he that hears it once with the heart's response, hears it with insensibility a thousand times. But imagine an army sent forth with an assurance of victory; it may be that thousands of javelins are hurled without result; that there are many repulses from this and that fortification; many unsuccessful skirmishes; but the expedition is at length crowned with success, and when it returns, returns victorious. The multitude of unsuccessful endeavors preceding the final triumph only served to display the prowess of the enemy and the severity of the strife; and thus to enhance the value of the victory.

God's word shall not return to him void. It shall accomplish that whereto he has sent it. For it is to be borne in mind that there are mighty resources in the word of God, and that it can at any time summon to its aid twelve legions of angels. For instance among the words of God are these:— Ask of me and I will show thee great and mighty things which thou hast not known. Omnipotence is with it. Let the faith of those who have the word be only adequate, and it will clothe itself with all the strength of God. Christ, who has all power in heaven and earth, holds that power in behalf of his word militant. The works that I do, shall the believer do; and greater works: whatever he shall ask, I will do it.

In the mean time, we see how terrible is the power of the adversary; how strongly fortified in its sin is the world; how absolute the need of omnipotence to bring the kingdoms of this world into subjection to Christ. We know not the word we fight with; we are ignorant of the resources placed at our command; and our battling is languid and lifeless, like that of soldiers who are waiting for their lord.

DECEMBER 29.—"The redeemed of the Lord shall return and come with singing unto Zion, and everlasting joy shall be upon their head."—Isaiah li. 11.

Time and again the Lord brought back his ancient people from captivity, even those that valued the liberty of returning; and each time perhaps they thought it was the final redemption of which the prophets had spoken such glorious things, and were looking for crowns of everlasting joy. But in the times preceding the first advent of the Messiah they discovered by bitter experience that it was possible for them to be enslaved even in their own land, in the midst of Jerusalem, in the courts of the temple; to be enslaved by Jews, by high-priests; and to be as wretched in Zion as ever they had been in Babylon. In the days of Christ how sadly were they oppressed. Not by the Romans; Christ scarcely made any allusion to them, knowing that the Jews were suffering from a far severer bondage. He made known to them the true Zion of refuge and the true redemption, when he said "Come unto me all ye that labor and are heavy-laden, and I will give you rest."

The redeemed of the Lord shall return, effectually redeemed from all iniquity, triumphant over sin and misery, crowned with glory, honor, and immortality. If you ask, when? I reply that it shall be in the day when the New Jerusalem cometh down from God out of heaven, and in the day when the manifestation of the sons of God taketh place. "Ye are not in darkness that that day should overtake you as a thief."

DECEMBER 30.—"Prepare to meet thy God."—Amos iv. 12.

For thou must meet him. The only uncertainty relates to

the time; and even that uncertainty does not exist in the mind of God. It is not more true that God is, than that thou shalt stand before him. Thou art flurried and agitated at the thought of going into the presence of some fellow-man clothed with authority; and wilt thou make no preparation to meet thy God? The companion with whom thou wert feasting yesterday, received his summons in the night. Inquiring for another this morning thou wert informed of his recent departure. Almost every hour some one is called from thy neighborhood into the presence of God, and thy turn will surely come.

Life is given that thou mayest prepare to meet thy God. Thy path is crowded with monitors that seek to arouse thee to a sense of the awful future so fast hastening. The winds whisper it; the skies proclaim it; the earth mutters it; the mountains repeat it; all life, all change, all beauty, all joy, and all sorrow breathe this admonition, "Prepare to meet thy God."

He is *thy God.* He made thee, gave thee all thy powers, all thine opportunities, gave thee a work to do, and the means of doing it. He will have a multitude of questions to ask thee; alas! that I should say it, he will have a multitude of charges to bring against thee. Thou hast heard his thunder in the skies; thinkest thou he is not able to clothe himself with unendurable terrors, or thinkest thou he will forbear to do it? Thinkest thou that God will never make so much of thee, an insignificant, ephemeral, helpless being, as to set thee up on high before him, and deal with thee as an object for his wrath, his vengeance, his fiery indignation? The thought is utterly delusive. Since God has made so much of thee as to fashion and endow thee wonderfully, to create a world of beauty and splendor for thy habitation, a sun to light thee by day, and stars to shine for thee by night; since he has treated thee as a being of great consequence by giving his word to be thy guide, and above all by giving his Son to die for thee, think not that thou shalt escape his notice in the great day of account. Thou hast made war upon the universe of God, thou hast sought to make him contemptible in the eyes of his creatures by despising his commands and discarding his authority. The interests of the entire universe demand that there be a meeting between thee and God, and that it be distinctly settled, who is in the right, God thy Creator and Governor, or thou his rebellious creature.

DECEMBER 31.—"Even so, come, Lord Jesus."—Revelation xxii. 20.

This prayer of the beloved disciple is his legacy to the church. Being permitted to write the closing words of Scripture, he finds three little words which seem to him expressive of more love to man, and to comprehend more of blessing and advantage to the world than any number of other words. The prayer, "Come, Lord Jesus," is the epitome of all the prayers that the believer is called upon to offer. It is a prayer for the overthrow of Satan's kingdom; for the extinction of sorrows, the cessation of pain, the wiping away of tears; for the descent of the New Jerusalem; for the sanctification and perfection of saints; for the creating anew of all things; in a word, for the new heaven and the new earth wherein dwelleth righteousness.

To be indifferent about the coming of Christ, is to be indifferent about the most sacred interests of humanity. If the apostles looked upon the advent of Christ as the hope of the world, and knew of no greater benefit that they could bestow upon mankind than to offer up this prayer in faith, we may well adopt their sentiment and follow their example. Let this prayer never die on our lips while we have breath: "Even so, come, Lord Jesus, come quickly!"

INDEX TO TEXTS.

GENESIS.

DEUTERONOMY.

1 SAMUEL.

1 CHRONICLES.

JOB.

PSALMS.

2 TIMOTHY.

HEBREWS.

JAMES.

1 PETER.

2 PETER.

1 JOHN.

REVELATION.

www.ingramcontent.com/pod-product-compliance
Lightning Source LLC
LaVergne TN
LVHW020554110826
845149LV00002B/264